THE ETERNAL CRIMINAL RECORD

THE ETERNAL CRIMINAL RECORD

James B. Jacobs

Cambridge, Massachusetts
London, England 2015

Printed in the United States of America

First printing

Library of Congress Cataloging-in-Publication Data

Jacobs, James B., author.
The eternal criminal record / James B. Jacobs.
pages cm
Includes bibliographical references and index.
ISBN 978-0-674-36826-2
1. Criminal records—United States. 2. Criminal records—Access control—United States. 3. Criminal records—Expungement—United States. I. Title.
KF9751.J33 2015
345.73'0123—dc23 2014015343

Lovingly dedicated to my wife, Jan,

our children, Tom and Sophi,

their spouses, Caroline and Jon,

and our grandchildren, Rowan and Anna

CONTENTS

PREFACE

MOST ACADEMICS come to criminal record issues via their commitment to offender rehabilitation and reentry. While I share that concern, I was drawn to criminal records via research on gun control. The 1968 Gun Control Act established the foundational principle of U.S. firearms policy. "Law-abiding" people should have easy access to firearms, while "criminals" (and a few other unreliable categories) should be prohibited from purchasing or possessing firearms. A felony conviction distinguished a law-abiding person from a criminal; years later, Congress disqualified persons convicted of domestic violence misdemeanor convictions. The 1968 act required a person purchasing a firearm from a federally licensed firearms dealer (FFL) to fill out a document swearing he or she had never been convicted of a felony. However, there was no way for the dealer to verify the truth of these statements. In response, gun control proponents lobbied for a law mandating that prospective purchasers be subjected to a criminal record check by a designated state or county "chief law enforcement officer." The NRA and other gun owners' rights groups opposed the idea on the ground that criminal record checking would require a substantial waiting period.

The logjam-breaking compromise that allowed passage of the 1993 Brady Handgun Violence Prevention Act added a provision to the bill requiring that, by 1998, the U.S. Department of Justice (DOJ) create a computerized National Instant Criminal Background Check System (NICS) that would inform an FFL within three business days whether a pending firearms sale could be completed. However, at that time, most states' police and court records could not support such a sophisticated information system. Consequently, Congress authorized hundreds of millions of dollars to upgrade criminal records. The result, perhaps the most important legacy of the Brady law, was massive federal assistance to improve police and court records. By 1998, NICS was operational.

The nationally integrated rap sheet system (Interstate Identification Index, or "Triple I") made it possible for a police officer with access to a computer to find out practically instantly whether a suspect or arrestee had ever been arrested federally or in any state. This upgrade of the nation's criminal record infrastructure, both police records and court records, also made criminal background checking for non–law enforcement purposes much easier, faster, and cheaper. Numerous private information vendors emerged to meet the growing demand for criminal background reports. The availability of inexpensive background checking plus the vendors' aggressive marketing stoked the demand.

When I later turned my full-time attention to criminal records jurisprudence and policy, I assumed that there was little research and writing on criminal records issues. I was wrong. There is an impressive corpus of studies and reports produced by SEARCH, the National Consortium for Justice Information and Statistics, an organization created in 1969 by the Law Enforcement Assistance Administration (LEAA) "to improve the quality of justice and public safety through the use, management, and exchange of information; application of new technologies; and responsible law and policy, while safeguarding security and privacy." SEARCH (not an acronym) has produced more than a dozen book-length reports on such topics as standards for security and privacy of criminal record history information, public attitudes toward uses of criminal history information, appropriate criminal justice and non–criminal justice uses of juvenile records, commercial sale of individual criminal history information, proliferation of criminal background checking, and consequences of identity theft for operation of state criminal record repositories.

The NYU Law seminar on criminal records policy and jurisprudence (which I taught three times in five years) unearthed dozens of interesting and important legal, policy, and jurisprudential criminal record issues—for example, whether the exclusionary rule applies to searches predicated on mistaken records; whether a "three strikes and you're out" recidivist sentencing premium is unconstitutional; whether a witness or testifying defendant can be impeached with prior conviction(s); whether any constitutional right is violated by a police chief distributing to local merchants an "Active Shoplifters" bulletin that includes the names and photos of persons previously arrested but not charged; whether an alien defendant's guilty plea is valid if his defense lawyer mistakenly told him that a drug trafficking conviction would not affect his immigration status; whether an employer who discriminates on the basis of criminal record violates Title VII of the Civil Rights Act; whether the Freedom of Information Act can be used to obtain individual criminal history information from the FBI; whether a state criminal record expungement prevents prosecution of the expungement beneficiary for violating the federal felon-in-possession-of-a-firearm law. The more I focused on criminal records issues, the more I saw their centrality for law enforcement, adjudication, and correction and to the criminal justice system's impact on society. (My mentor and friend Frank Zimring called criminal records the "800-pound gorilla in the room.") Just by itself, the annotated appendix of Supreme Court cases at the end of this book makes a strong case for the importance of criminal records for criminal law, procedure, and justice policy.

Except for the juvenile justice area, criminal justice scholars have treated criminal record policies as unproblematic and inevitable. The whole range of criminal records—including criminal intelligence databases, police blotters, rap sheets, court records, presentence reports, prosecutors' files, probation files, jail and prison databases—warrants scrutiny, but to date these diverse and overlapping records have never even been catalogued. It is past time to ask (1) how criminal justice agencies and courts are using individual criminal history information and (2) whether these criminal records are suitable for non–criminal justice users. Although this is the first book to focus directly on the creation, dissemination, use, and consequences of criminal records in the United States, I am not writing on a blank slate. There is a long sociological tradition illuminating the consequences of criminal labeling. Indeed, the juvenile court movement was sparked by the insight that a criminal record inflicts a stigma that has enormous negative consequences for the convicted person. The juvenile court founders sought to protect delinquent youth from the stigmatizing effects of a lifelong criminal record. In the mid-twentieth century, a number of "labeling theorists," including Howard Becker, Edwin Lemert, and Ed Schur, argued that people stigmatized as criminals are treated like criminals and often come to define themselves as criminals. Erving Goffman's classic, *Stigma: Notes on the Management of Spoiled Identity* (1963), is full of insights about how stigmatized persons cope with their spoiled identity, that is, by trying to hide it, embracing it, or apologizing for it.

Many criminologists have confirmed that legitimate employment is the most important predictor of rehabilitation and that an indelible criminal record is a barrier to legitimate employment. Economist-criminologist Shawn Bushway and others have produced scholarly studies estimating a criminal record's negative impact on future earnings.

Sociologist Devah Pager's 2007 book *Marked* reported the results of a field study that found that a drug conviction diminished a white job seeker's chance of getting an employer callback by 50 percent and an African American job seeker's chances by roughly 64 percent. Macro-sociologists Robert Samson and John Laub showed an empirical link between legitimate employment and desistance from crime. Shadd Maruna's qualitative studies confirmed their quantitative research. Criminologist Al Blumstein and his colleagues found that, depending on the crime, if a first-time arrestee goes five to eight years without a second arrest, his chance of a future arrest is no different than that of a never-arrested person; however, only 30 percent of those in Blumstein's first-time arrestee sample reached that five-to-eight-year threshold.

The "reentry movement" itself has produced an impressive corpus of scholarship on criminal records. Books like Jeremy Travis's *But They All Come Back* (2005), Joan Petersilia's *When Prisoners Come*

Home (2003), and Michelle Alexander's *The New Jim Crow* (2010) have given academic saliency to the legal (de jure) and discretionary (de facto) obstacles encountered by released prisoners and offer many recommendations for ameliorating these obstacles. The American Bar Association's National Inventory of the Collateral Consequences of Conviction and Margaret Love, Jenny Roberts, and Cecilia Klingele's treatise, *The Collateral Consequences of Conviction* (2013), have documented for lawyers, scholars, and policy makers the extensive collateral consequences of a criminal record.

Our subject is also illuminated by scholarship on information technology and privacy. Much of this book is, in essence, an exploration of how computers and information technology have changed the status of criminal records in U.S. society. James Q. Whitman's article "The Two Western Cultures of Privacy: Dignity versus Liberty" (2004) explains how European countries conceptualize a criminal conviction as personal information, while the United States treats criminal records as public information. I greatly benefited from my NYU colleague Helen Nissenbaum's *Privacy in Context* (2010) and from discussions with her.

This book culminates, extends, and synthesizes my own research and writing on criminal records policy and jurisprudence issues. My first foray was a 2006 article for a law school symposium on mass incarceration. I argued that mass incarceration was just the deep end of a much larger pool of arrests and convictions, with only a small fraction resulting in a prison sentence. For those convicted felons who are not incarcerated (more than half), the stigmatizing criminal record is the most serious consequence of being convicted. A subsequent article (with Tamara Crepet) explained how the expansion of criminal law and the intensification of law enforcement since the 1970s have resulted in the proliferation of criminal intelligence and investigative databases and police, prosecution, court, and corrections records. At the same time, the information technology revolution has led to a vastly greater dissemination of criminal record information. For a large segment of the U.S. population, a criminal record has become the most important marker of public identity.

Comparative research with two European collaborators deepened my appreciation of how exceptional American criminal records policy is. Over several years, I coauthored four articles with

Dimitra Blitsa, a Greek lawyer, who earned her LLM at NYU. Two of these articles compared interjurisdictional criminal record sharing in the United States with interjurisdictional criminal record sharing among EU member states. The other two articles compared the availability of sex offenders' identities in the United States, the United Kingdom, and continental Europe. Although anxiety about "sexual predators" is present in Europe, there are no online sex offender registries like those in the United States.

Elena Larrauri (Pompeu Fabra, Barcelona) and I compared employer access to criminal records in Europe and the United States. In the United States, a public or private employer can obtain any job applicant's or employee's criminal record by ordering a criminal background check from a commercial information vendor. In continental European countries, an individual's criminal history is regarded as personal information. There are no commercial information vendors. We found ourselves stymied by a lack of both legal and empirical studies on whether employers had other means of finding out about prior convictions. Consequently, we conducted our own study in Spain. Our first article contrasted the Spanish commitment to keeping criminal records confidential (in order to further individual privacy and rehabilitation) with U.S. policy and practice. Our second article sought to determine to what (if any) extent Spanish employers engaged in criminal record–based employment discrimination. (Some of the material in Chapter 9 is adapted from James B. Jacobs and Elena Larrauri, *Are Criminal Convictions a Public Matter? The USA and Spain*, 14 Punishment & Society, 3–28 [2012].)

A number of colleagues have encouraged and assisted me all along the way. I particularly want to thank Frank Zimring and David Garland, dear friends and generous advisors. Lauryn Gouldin worked with me during the 2011–2012 academic year on the chapters on criminal intelligence databases and commercial information vendors. I am grateful to Frank Anechiarico, Sharon Dolovich, David Garland, Elena Larrauri, Jeff Manza, and Erin Murphy for participating in a daylong workshop in February 2013 on an early draft of the book. Big thanks to Sally Hines, Jessica Henry, Jim Levine, Judy Greene, and Issa Kohler-Hausmann for extremely helpful comments and suggestions at a half-day workshop in October 2013. From June 2013 until February 2014, Alessandro Corda (Italy) and Lili Dao (Canada), 2013 NYU LLM graduates, worked with me on polishing the manuscript. I could not have finished without them.

Sections of Chapter 13 draw on ideas presented in previously published work. The subsection about disqualification from public contracting is informed by Frank Anechiarico and James B. Jacobs, *Purging Corruption from Public Contracting: The "Solutions" Are Now Part of the Problem*, 40 N.Y.L. Sch. L. Rev. 143 (1995), and Ronald Goldstock and James B. Jacobs, *Monitors and IPSIGS: Emergence of a New Criminal Justice Role*, 43 Crim. L. Bulletin 217 (2007). Some of the material in the subsection devoted to Ban the Box is also discussed in Jessica S. Henry and James B. Jacobs, *Ban the Box to Promote Ex-Offender Employment*, 6 Criminology & Public Policy 755 (2007).

Judge Martin Marcus, Assistant Manhattan District Attorney Sally Hines, Assistant U.S. Attorney Gerard Ramker, and criminal records specialist Madeline Neighly patiently responded to my many questions. John Baldwin provided helpful editorial suggestions on the near-final manuscript. Dan Goldberg, Greg Arutiunov, Claire Tan, and Tara Singh provided timely and effective research assistance at various points. I received valuable comments from Lisa Kerr on a draft of the introduction and from Larry Crocker, Antony Duff, Doug Husak, John Kleinig, and Danny Markel on Chapter 11. Harvard University Press editor Elizabeth Knoll provided encouragement and sage advice from beginning to end. All along the way, I was encouraged by Dean Ricky Revesz and supported by the Law School's Filomen D'Agostino Research Fund. In 2012–2013, this project was supported by a John Simon Guggenheim Memorial Foundation Fellowship.[1]

1 INTRODUCTION

> To be labeled a criminal one need only commit a single criminal offense, and this is all the term formally refers to. Yet the word carries a number of connotations specifying auxiliary traits characteristic of anyone bearing the label. A man who has been convicted of housebreaking and thereby labeled criminal is presumed to be a person likely to break into other houses; the police, in rounding up known offenders for investigation after a crime has been committed, operate on this premise. Further, he is considered likely to commit other kinds of crimes as well, because he has shown himself to be a person without "respect for the law." Thus, apprehension for one deviant act exposes a person to the likelihood that he will be regarded as deviant or undesirable in other respects.
>
> —Howard S. Becker, *Outsiders: Studies in the Sociology of Deviance* (1963)[1]

> Today, background checking—for employment purposes, for eligibility to serve as a volunteer, for tenant screening, and for so many other purposes—has become a necessary, even if not always a welcome, rite of passage for almost every adult American. Like a medical record, a bank record, or a credit record, a background check record is increasingly a part of every American's information footprint.
>
> —SEARCH, *Report of the National Task Force on the Commercial Sale of Criminal Justice Record Information* (2005)[2]

AN ESTIMATED twenty million Americans, about 8.6 percent of the total adult U.S. population, have recorded *felony convictions.*[3] The number of individuals with recorded misdemeanor convictions is several times greater.[4] Indeed, a conviction is not a criminal record prerequisite; a criminal record is created for every arrest, regardless of the ultimate disposition. All told, federal and state criminal record repositories contain criminal records for approximately 25 percent of the U.S. adult population.[5] In addition, criminal investigative and intelligence databases probably hold information on hundreds of thousands more people (e.g., suspected gang members, organized crime members, suspected terrorists).[6] These numbers have increased significantly over the last several decades on account of aggressive policing in the name of the war on drugs, zero tolerance, and broken windows.[7] This criminal labeling creates a social divide between "law-abiding citizens" and "criminals." It also reinforces the divide between African Americans and whites because of the disproportionate number of African Americans who have criminal records—in some cities, as much as 80 percent of young African American men.[8]

The police-created rap sheet, based on arrest and booking, is the best-known criminal record. However, it is best not to think of a criminal record as a single document. Information about arrestees, defendants, detainees, probationers, inmates, and parolees is recorded in numerous and overlapping files, records, and databases. Court dockets and case files constitute a massive reservoir of information about defendants.

The criminal record is a kind of negative curriculum vitae or résumé. Most readers are familiar with the self-created résumé that is prepared for college admissions and employment; it contains only positive, even embellished, information. By contrast, the criminal record contains only disreputable information.[9] The longer the record, the more likely the offender will be defined, formally or informally, as a career criminal.

Comprehensive records on suspects, arrestees, pretrial detainees, defendants, probationers, inmates, and parolees make possible the processing of more than twelve million arrests per year. However, criminal records perform more than a bookkeeping function. They drive decision making at every step of the criminal justice process. Other things being equal, law enforcement agencies, courts, and corrections treat people with criminal record histories more severely; the more serious and extensive the record, the harsher the treatment. The practice is so deeply entrenched that it is rarely defended or even explained. Sometimes this criminal biography–based determinism reflects a belief that repeat offenders deserve greater punishment, but more often it reflects a belief that repeat offenders require more intense monitoring or incapacitation to prevent future offending.

The police give greater attention to an individual listed in an organized crime, gang, or other criminal intelligence database. In deciding whether there is probable cause to arrest, the police will be more likely to detain, search, and arrest the person who has a criminal record. Prosecutors give weight to the prior record in deciding whether to request bail and, if so, how much. Pretrial service agencies use formal risk assessment instruments to predict whether an arrestee presents a low, medium, or high risk of flight and danger to the community. These instruments assign significant weight to the arrestee's prior criminal record, including arrests that did not result in convictions. Judges have prior record information in front of them in deciding on pretrial release or detention. Prosecutors base their charging and plea-bargaining decisions on the suspect's prior record.

Sometimes the most important issue in plea-bargaining is what, if any, permanent criminal record will result. For many, perhaps the majority of, defendants the most serious consequence of an arrest is the resulting criminal record. It triggers negative formal (de jure) and informal (de facto) collateral consequences—for example, forfeiture of voting and firearms rights, ineligibility for occupational licenses, employment discrimination, and, for noncitizens, removal and deportation. If there is a trial, the defendant's decision whether to testify often turns on the existence of a prior record that the jury would learn about on cross-examination. If convicted at trial or by guilty plea, the defendant's prior record has a significant impact on the sentence. Recidivists are subject to heavy sentence enhancements. Probation, jail, and prison officials base their classification decisions (e.g., maximum vs. minimum security) and programmatic assignments on the probationer or inmate's prior criminal record. Certain criminal records render prison inmates ineligible for some prison and early release programs. Parole boards consider criminal records in making early release decisions.

The criminal justice system's harsher treatment of those with prior records is not inevitable but a deliberate and mostly unexamined policy choice. Is it fair to treat persons with criminal records more severely? Having served their sentence, haven't they paid their debt? Are they perpetually to be treated as the "usual suspects"? Should police keep fingerprints, DNA profiles, and arrest information on defendants who ultimately were not convicted of anything or of a minor crime? Is it reasonable for police, prosecutors, courts, and corrections to treat prior arrests as a "black mark" because they predict future criminality? Is it proper for prosecutors to bring more severe charges against persons with prior convictions and arrests? Is it proper for judges to enhance the sentences of recidivists? Are restrictions on prison assignment and early release justifiable?

Created for criminal justice purposes, criminal records today are widely used to assess, sort, and categorize people in such diverse contexts as immigration, employment, housing, university admissions, voting, possessing firearms, serving on a jury, and qualifying for social welfare benefits.[10] In an anonymous society where only a minuscule number of people are known personally to one another, an individual's criminal record is considered one of the most important markers of character.

A criminal record is for life; there is no statute of limitations. Under the drumbeat of law and order politics since the 1970s, negative criminal record consequences have proliferated. A steady accretion of federal and state laws bars ex-offenders, or at least certain ex-offenders, from a range of citizenship rights, social welfare benefits, and public and private employments. The more transparent and efficient the criminal records system, the less chance an ex-offender has to blend successfully into society. The greater the discrimination against those with prior records, the more likely the ex-offender will recidivate. What sociologist Devah Pager says about convicted persons sentenced to prison applies to all those with felony (and even misdemeanor) records:

> [Ex-offenders] are institutionally branded as a particular class of individuals. . . . The "negative credential" associated with a criminal record represents a unique mechanism of stratification, in that it is the state that certifies particular individuals in ways that qualify them for discrimination or social exclusion. It is this official status of the negative credential that differentiates it from other sources of social stigma, offering greater legitimacy to its use as the basis for differentiation.[11]

This book shines a bright light on criminal records policies and practices in order to render them problematic rather than inevitable.

Rarely asked is how much influence the criminal justice system should have in defining and categorizing people. The accessibility of an individual's criminal history, due to publicly accessible court records, legislatively authorized access to rap sheets, and agencies' information-sharing policies is a striking example of American exceptionalism.[12]* In continental Europe, convicted persons have a privacy interest in their arrest and conviction records.[13] The records are not publicly accessible.

Today, in the United States, court records are more publicly accessible than ever before. Until computerization and the revolution in information technology, court records existed in practical obscurity. It took serious effort and expertise to find out whether someone had a criminal record and, if so, for what crimes. Today, court records are better organized and indexed. Many can be searched electronically. Private companies sell criminal background information to employers, landlords, volunteer organizations, and anyone else interested in finding out about someone's criminal history. Hundreds of companies advertise criminal background checks to ensure reliable and honest business associates, employees, tenants, and volunteers.[14] They warn employers that they will be held civilly liable if, having failed to obtain a criminal background check, an employee with a criminal record injures a customer, client, or fellow employee. Easily accessible and cheap criminal record information stimulates demand, and demand stimulates supply.

Criminal background checking has become a routine feature of American life.[15] Many federal and state laws require certain public and private employers to obtain criminal background reports on job applicants. Even when not required by law, the majority of large employers conduct or commission criminal background checks for job applicants. In 1996, 51 percent of employers surveyed by the Society for Human Resource Management conducted or commissioned criminal history checks on at least some prospective

---

* "American exceptionalism" refers to U.S. policies that diverge sharply from those of other developed Western countries. The expression was coined by the French writer Alexis de Tocqueville in the 1830s. In *Democracy in America* he observed that "[t]he position of the Americans is . . . quite exceptional, and it may be believed that no democratic people will ever be placed in a similar one." *Democracy in America*, vol. 2 (1835), chap. 9, 36.

employees. By 2003, that number had increased to 80 percent; 68 percent of employer respondents reported conducting criminal background checks for all hires. Ninety-two percent of employers responding to a 2009 survey reported obtaining criminal background information for at least some hires; 73 percent required criminal background checks for all hires.[16]

After the September 11, 2001, terrorist attacks on the World Trade Center and the Pentagon, Congress mandated criminal background checks for perhaps a million workers, including airport baggage screeners, port and chemical plant workers, workers in the transportation industry, private security personnel, and individuals handling certain biological agents. This response to 9/11 demonstrates the widely held belief that a criminal record is a valuable predictor of future unreliable and dangerous conduct.

Easy access to individual criminal history information arguably enables government employers and regulators to better protect the public as well as the government's own interests and functions. It allows adoption agencies, immigration officials, and federally licensed firearms dealers to make better-informed decisions. Businesses and volunteer organizations screen prospective and incumbent employees and volunteers for honesty, reliability, and self-discipline.[17] A 2002 survey of California employers found that although most employers would consider hiring a convicted misdemeanant, less than one-fourth would consider hiring someone convicted of a drug offense, 7 percent a property-related offense, and less than 1 percent a violent felony.[18] Some landlords require criminal record checks for prospective tenants. Political campaigns (and media) sometimes check to see whether opposing candidates and their top staffers have criminal records.[19] Attorneys obtain criminal background information on opposing parties, prospective witnesses, and potential jurors.[20] Information vendors urge private individuals to use criminal background reports to make informed decisions in selecting babysitters, roommates, friends, and lovers.[21]

The federal government and each state make their own criminal records policies. For example, states differ with respect to whether rap sheets include juvenile arrests and adjudications; whether they contain arrests and convictions for minor offenses; whether summonses are recorded; whether arrests that do not result in convictions are reported to non–criminal justice requesters; and which, if any, arrests and convictions can be sealed or expunged. Indeed, each criminal justice system agency in each state has considerable discretion over what information to record and to whom access should be granted. Each state has laws authorizing access to rap sheets for certain (not necessarily the same) categories of private sector companies and volunteer organizations. Local police departments and prosecutors' offices have policies on, or just respond on an ad hoc basis to, requests for criminal record information from private sector agencies, organizations, private detectives, lawyers, and others who lack statutory designation. Court records are open to the public and increasingly accessible online. Some corrections departments (e.g., New Jersey) post to a website the names, photos, and conviction offenses of their inmates. In a few states, prisoners' disciplinary records are publicly accessible.

A great deal of discrimination against persons with criminal records is mandated by law (e.g., disenfranchisement, jury service, firearms possession, and occupational licenses).[22] Discretionary discrimination in employment and housing is pervasive. Although criminal record–based employment discrimination is proscribed by the Civil Rights Act of 1964 if it disproportionately excludes protected minorities from the hiring pool, it can be justified by proving business necessity.[23] Perhaps more important, such discrimination can be hidden by other explanations for hiring choices.

This book illuminates the criminal record policy choices that have been made or ignored and identifies choices still open to us. It underscores the serious consequences that individual criminal history records have for our criminal justice system and for our society. Part I describes the U.S. criminal record infrastructure, consisting of police records, court records, and criminal record information held by commercial information vendors. We will encounter important policy choices. For example, (1) What controls should there be on creating and populating criminal intelligence databases? (2) Who should have fingerprint-supported access to the national (Triple I) rap sheet system? (3) Can rap sheets be made more user-friendly? (4) Should courts sell copies of their criminal case docket? (5) Can/

should commercial information vendors be regulated more effectively?

Part II takes up three crucial criminal record policy issues. (1) When should suspected criminal law violations trigger creation of a criminal record? (2) To what extent should criminal records, once created, be subject to revision, either by addition (e.g., certificates of rehabilitation) or subtraction (e.g., expungement)? (3) What can be done to reduce the number of erroneous criminal records and to remedy mistakes due to erroneous records?

Part III deals with why U.S. criminal records are publicly accessible. (1) Are open criminal records an inevitable feature of our commitment to transparent court proceedings? (2) To what extent must/should an open-records policy apply to nonconviction records, that is, arrests, dismissals, and acquittals? (3) Do the dominant theories of punishment require or justify publicly accessible criminal records?

Part IV examines the criminal justice system and non–criminal justice system consequences of criminal record policies. (1) Is it justifiable for law enforcement agencies, courts, and correction agencies to base decisions on prior criminal record? (2) Can long-term and lifetime forfeitures, disqualifications, and ineligibilities imposed on persons with criminal records be justified? (3) Should public and private employment discrimination based on criminal record be prohibited?

The use and proliferation of criminal records, and their consequences for criminal justice and society, range over dozens of contexts, laws, policies, and issues. I don't expect the reader to agree with all my observations, conclusions, and recommendations. I do hope to persuade you that criminal record policies and jurisprudence deserve serious attention.

PART I

THE PRODUCTION AND DISSEMINATION OF CRIMINAL RECORDS

PART I IS DEVOTED to the production of criminal records. It consists of four chapters necessary for understanding the policy challenges and choices raised in Parts II, III, and IV. These chapters explain the criminal record sources that we now have and raise questions about what criminal records should be produced, for what purposes, and with what controls on dissemination. Chapter 2 examines police intelligence and investigative records created at the local, state, and federal levels. These records are important because, although vital to good police work, especially in an age of terrorism, they effectively label, without any due process, someone as a possible perpetrator of past crimes (investigative databases) or as a possible perpetrator of future crimes (intelligence databases). Computerization and information technology have made it easy to create, populate, and link such databases. Sound policy analysis and regulation lag far behind.

Chapter 3 deals with rap sheets, the most venerable and widely used criminal record. We will see that the rap sheet is the nation's criminal justice informational infrastructure's most used criminal record. It took tremendous effort and expense over many years to achieve today's nationally integrated rap sheet system, which allows a police officer anywhere in the United States to rapidly find out whether a suspect or arrestee is wanted or has been arrested or convicted at any time anywhere in the United States. This nationally integrated rap sheet system links together thousands of decentralized police agencies. However, shining a light on rap sheets also exposes a number of mostly overlooked but important policy issues: Which summonses and arrests should trigger the creation of a rap sheet? Should juvenile arrests be recorded and remain on an individual's permanent rap sheet? Is a rap sheet system built on arrests suitable for use by employers and other non–law enforcement entities? And should arrests that do not result in convictions be purged from the rap sheet?

Chapter 4 explains that court records are an independent source of individual criminal history information. The courts need to create and maintain comprehensive indexes and files to facilitate and document the adjudication of criminal cases. Although these records were not designed for public consumption, unlike in other countries, they have always been open to members of the public and the media. Here, too, advances in computers and information technology have made court records far more accessible than could have been imagined a few decades ago. Their enhanced accessibility has put into the public domain information that heretofore had existed in practical obscurity. Strikingly, in the face of the new information technologies, courts have not sought to limit access and dissemination of court records but, to the contrary, have decided to make many records available online and to sell whole criminal record databases to commercial information vendors.

Chapter 5 discusses commercial information vendors who market and sell criminal background checks to private and volunteer sector organizations and to anyone else who is interested. Some of the largest information vendors download court and other publicly accessible criminal record information to their own proprietary databases. This, in effect, has created a privatized source of criminal record information so that criminal record policy is no longer solely in government hands. The extent to which the private information vendors should and can be effectively regulated is a pressing issue.

While Chapters 2–5 cover a lot of ground, a complete description of the nation's criminal record infrastructure would have to take into account records that are produced, held, used, and disseminated by criminal justice agencies other than police and courts, that is, pretrial services agencies, prosecutors' offices, probation agencies, jails, prisons, and parole agencies. All these agencies create files and databases, which they populate with information about criminal suspects and defendants. Some of this information is highly personal. However, what information exists, what forms it takes, who has authorized access to it, who uses it for what purposes, and how secure the information is against leakers and hackers are questions beyond the scope of this already substantial volume.

2 INTELLIGENCE AND INVESTIGATIVE DATABASES

> The U.S. government has access to a vast amount of information. When databases not usually thought of as "intelligence," such as customs or immigration information, are included, the storehouse is immense.
>
> —National Commission on Terrorist Attacks upon the United States, *The 9/11 Commission Report* (2004)[1]

> Anti-gang policies have led to gang databases filled with the names and pictures of students of color who have not been convicted of any crimes, but have been victimized by police or school racial profiling. The result in Salt Lake City, Minneapolis, Minnesota, Orange County and Los Angeles, CA and a number of other cities, is that children are stuck in these criminal databases indefinitely.
>
> —Courtney Bowie, Senior Staff Attorney, ACLU Racial Justice Program (2012)[2]

POLICE DEPARTMENTS are the most prolific criminal record creators. The rap sheet, the best-known police-created criminal record, is examined in Chapter 3. The daily log of arrestees ("stationhouse blotter") is discussed in Chapter 10. This chapter deals with criminal intelligence and investigative databases that collect information about persons who may never have been arrested. These databases record information about people suspected of past crimes or considered to be at risk of committing future crimes. The police may specially monitor people so designated. If police suspicion about such "suspects" became known, the suspects would likely suffer reputational injury.

In practice, the line between investigative and intelligence databases is blurry. Investigative databases are usually backward looking (i.e., to crimes already committed or being committed), while intelligence databases are forward looking (i.e., to the risk of future crimes).[3] Names might be added to an investigative database because of suspected involvement in a crime or conspiracy. Names of persons reportedly interacting or communicating with suspected gang members, organized crime figures, or possible terrorists might be added to an intelligence database. Although police intelligence and investigative databases are not publicly accessible, access is afforded to police with a need to know and sometimes to personnel in other government agencies. There is always a risk of intentional or inadvertent leaks.

Investigative Databases

Police create investigative files in order to solve serious crimes and build cases that will persuade a jury or judge to convict. They add information obtained from physical and electronic surveillance, witness statements, informants' reports, forensic tests, and hunches.* Numerous investigators, from one or more agencies, contribute to the investigative file or database. Because the purpose of a criminal investigation is to determine whether there is probable cause to make an arrest, information can be added to an investigative file without probable cause or reasonable suspicion.

The more people who have access to an investigative file, the more reason for concern about criteria and procedures for adding names and information. The police rarely disclose to the investigative target that she is under investigation because it might alert the suspected individual that she has been betrayed by an informer or is being monitored by physical or electronic surveillance. The dilemma is that if too many law enforcement personnel and others have access to the investigative file or database, a person who may never be charged with a crime may be erroneously stigmatized as a criminal. If too few police and others have access, officers with different bits of relevant information may not connect the dots. In its 2004 report, the 9/11 Commission wrote:

> The biggest impediment to . . . connecting the dots . . . is the human or systemic resistance to sharing information. . . . [The

* The NYPD, for example, uses the Omniform information system to store information about arrests, arrestees, victims, witnesses, and criminal incidents in a centralized database. Internal police files and databases, which are used to support investigations and prosecutions, contain more detail than rap sheets.

YBP Library Services

JACOBS, JAMES B.

ETERNAL CRIMINAL RECORD.

Cloth 396 P.
CAMBRIDGE: HARVARD UNIV PRESS, 2015

AUTH: NYU LAW. LEGAL-POL. ANALYSIS OF DATABASE & SCREENING SYSTEM. APPENDED W/SUPREME COURT CASES.
LCCN 2014015343
ISBN 0674368266 **Library PO#** SLIP ORDERS

				List	39.95 USD
6207 UNIV OF TEXAS/SAN ANTONIO				**Disc**	17.0%
App. Date	5/06/15	CRJ.APR	6108-09	**Net**	33.16 USD

SUBJ: 1. CRIMINAL RECORDS--U.S. 2. CRIMINAL RECORDS--EXPUNGEMENT--U.S.

CLASS KF9751 DEWEY# 345.730123 LEVEL ADV-AC

YBP Library Services

JACOBS, JAMES B.

ETERNAL CRIMINAL RECORD.

Cloth 396 P.
CAMBRIDGE: HARVARD UNIV PRESS, 2015

AUTH: NYU LAW. LEGAL-POL. ANALYSIS OF DATABASE & SCREENING SYSTEM. APPENDED W/SUPREME COURT CASES.
LCCN 2014015343
ISBN 0674368266 **Library PO#** SLIP ORDERS

				List	39.95 USD
6207 UNIV OF TEXAS/SAN ANTONIO				**Disc**	17.0%
App. Date	5/06/15	CRJ.APR	6108-09	**Net**	33.16 USD

SUBJ: 1. CRIMINAL RECORDS--U.S. 2. CRIMINAL RECORDS--EXPUNGEMENT--U.S.

CLASS KF9751 DEWEY# 345.730123 LEVEL ADV-AC

> requirement of a "need to know" before sharing] assumes it is possible to know, in advance, who will need to use the information. Such a system implicitly assumes that the risk of inadvertent disclosure outweighs the benefits of wider sharing. Those Cold War assumptions are no longer appropriate. The culture of agencies feeling they own the information they gathered at taxpayer expense must be replaced by a culture in which the agencies instead feel they have a duty . . . to repay the taxpayers' investment by making that information available.[4]

Expanding access to investigative and intelligence databases increases the risk that information will be leaked or hacked. For example, a 2004 New York City Comptroller audit found that more than 2,000 former New York Police Department (NYPD) employees still had active user IDs allowing them access to the NYPD's Omniform system.[5]* When investigative information is purposefully or inadvertently made public, an individual who may never be prosecuted is stigmatized as a criminal.

Criminal Intelligence Databases

CRIMINAL RECORDS AND POLITICAL DISSENTERS

Criminal intelligence databases are populated with information about people who should be watched or monitored because they might have committed a past crime or might commit a future crime. At various points in American history, such information gathering has violated civil liberties and generated political controversy.† For

* Not surprisingly, the same problem occurs in other countries. *The Independent*, a British newspaper, reported that British police officers and staff working in police departments who abuse their access to police databases, by, for example, sharing the information they are privy to with friends and family, are not likely to get fired. Ben Chu, "Just How Secure Are Police Databases?" *The Independent*, July 13, 2011, http://blogs.independent.co.uk/2011/07/13/just-how-secure-are-police-databases/.

† As this book goes to press, the National Security Administration's program of collecting information about persons who make phone calls to certain places or people has ignited just such a furor. See, e.g., *New York Times*, The Opinion Pages, Room for Debate, June 9, 2013, http://www.nytimes.com/roomfordebate/2013/06/09/is-the-nsa-surveillance-threat-real-or-imagined; Ewen Macaskill, Gabriel Dance, Feilding Cage, and Greg Chen, "NSA Files: Decoded, What the Revelations Mean for You, Part Two,

example, during the 1960s, the NYPD's information gathering on anti–Vietnam War protestors and organizations touched off a political and legal firestorm. Several political action groups filed a class action suit under the Civil Rights Act against the mayor, police commissioner, and other officials who were part of the NYPD's Security and Investigation Section (dubbed "the red squad").[6] The class action suit eventually was resolved by a consent decree (known as the Handschu decree, after Barbara Handschu, the civil rights lawyer who brought the case). Enforcement of that decree generated litigation for the next quarter century.[7]

According to the Handschu decree, the NYPD's Intelligence Division's Security and Investigation Section (PSS) would have sole authority to investigate political activity and only when criminal activity was reasonably suspected. When the PSS suspected that a political group was engaging in criminal activity, it first had to submit an "investigative statement with a factual predicate" to a three-person Handschu Authority (two deputy NYPD commissioners and a civilian). In addition, the consent decree prohibited the NYPD from sharing information about political activity with other law enforcement agencies unless those agencies agreed to abide by the consent agreement.

The NYPD sought to terminate the consent decree after 9/11 because critics faulted federal, state, and local law enforcement agencies for not connecting the dots that might have illuminated the Al Qaeda conspiracy and prevented the attack.[8] The federal district court agreed to modify the Handschu guidelines[9] so that, in the future, an investigation could be authorized by the commanding officer of the intelligence division or the deputy commissioner of intelligence.

Whether a record should be created is a question that also arises in ordinary policing. Some police departments require officers to fill out "contact cards" with information about persons who are stopped

---

All the Data about Your Data," *The Guardian*, http://www.theguardian.com/world/interactive/2013/nov/01/snowden-nsa-files-surveillance-revelations-decoded#section/1; Dianne Feinstein, "Continue NSA Call-Records Program," Editorial and Debates, *USA Today*, October 20, 2013, http://www.usatoday.com/story/opinion/2013/10/20/nsa-call-records-program-sen-dianne-feinstein-editorials-debates/3112715/.

and searched, regardless of whether there is an arrest. This information can be assigned to intelligence databases (e.g., of suspected gang members) that may prove useful in solving past or preventing future crimes, deploying police resources, and monitoring individual police officers' conduct. In Los Angeles, police officers file Suspicious Activity Reports (SARs) documenting conduct, both criminal and noncriminal, believed to be "reasonably indicative" of terrorist or criminal activity. According to the *Los Angeles Times*, even reports deemed unfounded by the LAPD are kept for a year and shared with a Joint Regional Information Center, which retains the information for five years.[10]

A recent controversy in New York City over creating and keeping records of police contacts that did not result in arrests further illuminates the policy issue. In order to assess the claim that the NYPD was stopping and frisking African Americans without probable cause or reasonable suspicion,[11] the NYPD agreed to require officers to record information about every person stopped and frisked.[12] This triggered complaints that those whose names were recorded in the stop-and-frisk database were, in effect, being labeled as criminals or potential criminals. *New York Times* columnist Bob Herbert wrote:

> What [those who've been stopped have] left behind, however, if they've shown their identification to the cops or answered any questions, is a permanent record of the encounter, which is promptly entered into the department's staggeringly huge computerized files. Why the Police Department should be keeping files on innocent people is a question with no legitimate answer. This is Big Brother in Blue, with Commissioner Kelly collecting more information than J. Edgar Hoover could ever have imagined compiling.[13]

In 2010, the New York state legislature prohibited the NYPD from populating a database with the names of persons stopped and frisked but not arrested.[14] The NYPD complied but did not erase names of those who had been stopped and frisked *in the past.* The New York Civil Liberties Union challenged this policy as "a gross violation of the privacy interests of millions of New Yorkers."[15] In late 2012, a state appellate court ordered the NYPD to discontinue use of the database in order "to *protect people from the stigma flowing from public access to records of unsupported criminal charges.*"[16] Subsequently, the city agreed to delete the information.[17]

THE NATIONAL CRIME INFORMATION CENTER

The proliferation of criminal intelligence databases is nicely illuminated by the history of the FBI's National Crime Information Center (NCIC), a collection of FBI intelligence databases that provide support to federal, state, and local law enforcement agencies.[18] There are twenty-one NCIC databases, called "files."[19] Seven files contain information on different categories of stolen property. Fourteen contain information about persons: the Supervised Release File, the National Sex Offender Registry File, the Foreign Fugitive File, the Immigration Violator File, the Missing Person File, the Protection Order File, the Unidentified Person File, the U.S. Secret Service Protective File, the Gang File, the Known or Appropriately Suspected Terrorist File, the Wanted Person File, the Identity Theft File, the Violent Person File, and the National Instant Criminal Background Check System (NICS) Denied Transaction File.

After the 9/11 terrorist attacks on the World Trade Center and Pentagon, the United States Department of Justice (DOJ) and the Central Intelligence Agency (CIA) were roundly criticized for failing to share intelligence information that, when seen as a whole, might have revealed the Al Qaeda conspiracy. The DOJ and the new Department of Homeland Security (DHS) added suspected terrorists to the NCIC's Violent Gang File and renamed it the Violent Gang and Terrorist Organizations File (VGTOF).[20] The proponents of this initiative aimed to enlist the assistance of local and state police in identifying terrorist suspects who might be encountered in the course of unrelated criminal investigations.[21] (In 2009, the list of Known or Appropriately Suspected Terrorists was again separated from the Gang File.)

In 2003, President George W. Bush announced the creation of the Terrorist Screening Center (TSC), housed in the FBI but staffed with designees from the Departments of State, Justice, and Homeland Security.[22] The TSC consolidated several terrorist watch lists into the Terrorist Screening Database (TSDB), commonly called the "TSC Watchlist."[23] In 2008, the Watchlist contained 400,000 names,[24] and the vast majority were not U.S. citizens or legal residents.[25] Those names also are submitted to the Transportation Security Administration's "No Fly" and "Selectee" lists, the FBI's NCIC Known or Appropriately Suspected Terrorist (KST) file, the Department of State's Consular Lookout and Support System (CLASS) for passport and visa screening, and the DHS's Treasury Enforcement Communication System (TECS) database for screening persons entering the country. The war on terror is being fought with information technology that seeks to "connect the dots."[26]

"Nominations" to the TSC Watchlist, which may be made by the TSC director, the FBI, the CIA, DHS, and other federal agencies,[27] must meet two requirements. First, the nominee's biographical information must be sufficient to match or disassociate the nominee from other persons on the Watchlist.[28] Second, the nomination must be supported by "reasonable suspicion," that is, "articulable facts which, taken together with rational inferences, reasonably warrant the determination that the nominee is known or suspected to be or has been engaged in conduct constituting, in preparation for, in aid of or related to terrorism and terrorist activities."[29] According to the TSC, although some individuals on the Watchlist have criminal records, "None of the information pertaining to a nominee's criminal history is contained or referenced in the TSDB."[30]

Audits cast doubt on how reliably the TSC's standards are applied. In 2009, the DOJ's Office of the Inspector General reported that some nominations were being approved with "little or no derogatory information."[31] The inspector general criticized the FBI (which administers the TSC) for failing to expeditiously remove from the database the names of individuals cleared of terrorist involvement.[32] In 2010, the *New York Times* reported that, during the preceding three years, 81,793 people had requested to be removed from the TSC Watchlist; 25,000 petitions were pending.[33] Misidentifications (misspellings, multiple people with the same name) are a persistent problem, especially considering the diversity of individuals that may be nominated.[34] This is a good example of the difficulties of properly managing criminal and quasi-criminal databases.

The Protection Order File (POF), added to the NCIC in 1997,[35] is a *quasi-criminal intelligence database* that is populated with names of individuals ordered by a family court or criminal court judge not to have contact with an assault or harassment victim. These individuals, in effect, are considered at risk of committing a future crime. For example, a family court judge may order a husband or boyfriend not to visit a complainant's home or workplace. A criminal court judge may order the defendant in a domestic violence case to refrain from contacting the victim.[36] Violation of a protection order is punishable by criminal contempt.

Suppose a police officer stops a motorist for speeding and carries out a routine check of the motorist's identification. The NCIC informs him that the motorist is subject to an order of protection,[37] adding the caveat "WARNING—THE FOLLOWING IS AN NCIC PROTECTION ORDER RECORD. DO NOT SEARCH, DETAIN, OR ARREST BASED SOLELY ON THIS RECORD. CONTACT ENTERING AGENCY TO CONFIRM STATUS AND TERMS OF PROTECTION ORDER."[38] Based on this warning, the officer may question the driver and passenger. Perhaps the information will, consciously or unconsciously, persuade the officer to arrest the driver for the traffic violation rather than to issue a summons. Not surprisingly, the POF has been put to other uses. In 1996, Congress added individuals subject to protection orders to the categories of people ineligible to purchase or possess a firearm.[39] Thus, with respect to forfeiture of Second Amendment rights, a domestic violence protection order is equivalent to a felony conviction.

The Immigration Violator File (IVF), created in August of 2003 in the wake of the 9/11 attacks, is another example of a quasi-criminal database.[40] It supplanted the Deported Felon File, which contained the names of aliens deported on account of a conviction for drug or firearm trafficking or "other serious crime."[41] Subsequently, the IVF expanded to include names of persons subject to an outstanding Immigration and Naturalization Service (INS) order of removal from the country and names of persons violating certain registration requirements. Civil liberties groups opposed the creation of this NCIC file, arguing that, in effect, it labeled suspected visa violators as criminals. In *National Council of La Raza v. Gonzales* (2007), several nonprofit organizations and a labor union argued that entering civil immigration information into the NCIC database violated the NCIC's authorizing statute.[42] According to the plaintiffs:

> [T]he NCIC statute limits the FBI's power to collect and exchange criminal justice information to narrowly delineated categories. The *civil* immigration records and administrative warrants at issue in this case are not "crime records" under the statute. In addition, the individuals who are the subjects of those records have not been charged or convicted criminally, and are not subject to criminal warrants.[43]

The district court dismissed the case because the plaintiffs lacked standing to sue. The United States Court of Appeals affirmed.[44]

GANG DATABASES

Gang databases are the best example of the proliferation of criminal intelligence databases. Although gang membership is not a crime, the police consider gang members to be possible perpetrators of past crimes and at risk of committing future crimes. Police officers, with access to local and regional gang databases,[45] use the information to deploy resources, determine the effectiveness of antigang initiatives, investigate unsolved cases, monitor gang members, and, in marginal cases, guide discretion on whether to make an arrest.[46]

Suppose a police officer stops a suspect ("S.") for a traffic violation, initiates a background check, and learns that S. is a member of a street gang. The officer may decide to arrest S. and conduct a thorough vehicle search rather than let S. off with a warning or summons. From the police standpoint, that is good police work. From the civil libertarian's standpoint, it is discrimination based on a label that might have no grounding in fact.

Prosecutors and judges consider an arrestee's gang status in making charging, bail, plea-bargaining, and sentencing decisions. Task forces target gang members for aggressive prosecution.[47] It is easier to prosecute D2 as an accomplice if there is evidence that D2 and perpetrator D1 belong to the same gang. The prosecutor is likely to be less inclined to offer a diversion program or a favorable plea bargain to a suspected gang member.[48] In the event of a trial, gang membership may be admitted into evidence to establish motive; if so, the jury may consciously or unconsciously be more inclined to convict. Some states provide sentence enhancements for gang membership. In exercising sentencing discretion, judges likely consider gang membership an aggravating factor. Recently, Congress debated whether gang membership should constitute grounds to remove a permanent resident from the country or to deny an undocumented alien legal status.[49]

"School resource officers," stationed in some schools, inform school personnel about suspected gang members. Likewise, school personnel may tell the police about students they believe to be gang members or at risk of joining a gang.[50] To prevent youth crime, some localities have created multiagency collaborations involving the prosecutor's office, court, police, and schools. In Los Angeles County, a youth deemed to be at risk of joining a gang can be referred to a diversion program, where he or she may be monitored, searched, and required to submit to drug testing. Private employers do not have direct access to the gang database but may employ an (off-duty) police officer who is willing to find out whether a prospective employee is a suspected gang member.[51] As more and more people have access to the gang database, the more likely the information in the database will migrate to other files, records, and databases. Once information becomes publicly accessible, it cannot be made confidential again.*

Because being listed in a gang database can have significant negative consequences, establishing criteria for adding names to the database is crucial. In some cities, a significant percentage of minority male youth are listed in the gang database.[52] Gang labeling often depends on information provided by informants whose identities

---

* Jails and prisons also maintain intelligence databases on inmates' gang affiliations. Correctional agencies track prison and suspected gang members by taking photos of tattoos, scars, or other identifying marks. This allows for an "effective communication between a correctional agency and a state police agency and improves data accuracy because data can be entered as soon as they are gathered." Mark S. Fleisher and Scott H. Decker, *An Overview of the Challenge of Prison Gangs*, 5(1) Management Quarterly 1, 7 (2001).

cannot be disclosed and on information from a police officer who reports having seen an individual associating with a known gang member or flashing a known gang hand signal or wearing gang colors. A police department is unlikely to have procedures for vigorously cross-examining such reports.

The FBI* instructs state and local law enforcement agencies that before entering a name into the federal Violent Gang File, the agency must determine that, at the time of arrest or incarceration, the subject either admits gang membership or meets any two of the following criteria:

1. Has been identified by an individual of proven reliability as a group member;
2. Has been identified by an individual of unknown reliability as a group member and that information has been corroborated in significant respects;
3. Has been observed by members of the entering agency to frequent a known group's area, associate with known group members, and/or affect the group's style of dress, tattoos, hand signals, or symbols;
4. Has been arrested on more than one occasion with known group members for offenses consistent with group activity; or
5. Has admitted membership in the identified group at any time other than arrest or incarceration.[53]

---

* In 2005, the federal government established the National Gang Intelligence Center (NGIC) to facilitate information sharing and integrate intelligence about gangs among federal, state, and local law enforcement agencies. The NGIC has access to each participating agency's gang database. It is composed of representatives from several different organizations, including the FBI, the U.S. Drug Enforcement Administration, the U.S. Bureau of Prisons, the United States Marshals Service, the U.S. Department of Defense, U.S. Immigration and Customs Enforcement, and the U.S. Customs and Border Protection. (The NGIC does not maintain the National Crime Information Center, where the Gang File and other FBI files are held.) See Federal Bureau of Investigation, National Gang Intelligence Center, http://www.fbi.gov/about-us/investigate/vc_majorthefts/gangs/ngic; Federal Bureau of Investigation, National Gang Intelligence Center, *2011 National Gang Threat Assessment: Emerging Trends*, at 6, http://www.fbi.gov/stats-services/publications/2011-national-gang-threat-assessment.

The criteria for entering a name into California's statewide Cal-Gang database are even more expansive. A name can be entered into the database if law enforcement officers find that at least two out of the following ten criteria are met. The person

1. Admits gang membership or association
2. Is observed to associate on a regular basis with known gang members
3. Has tattoos indicating gang membership
4. Wears gang clothing, symbols, etc., to identify with a specific gang
5. Is in a photograph with known gang members and/or using gang-related hand signs
6. Is named on a gang document, hit list, or gang-related graffiti
7. Is identified as a gang member by a reliable source
8. Is arrested in the company of identified gang members or associates
9. Corresponds with known gang members or writes and/or receives correspondence about gang activities
10. Writes about gangs (graffiti) on walls, books, paper, etc.

In other words, for example, one can be added to the database for appearing in a photograph with known gang members or writing about gang activities.[54]

The guidelines give police enormous discretion. Who counts as a "person of proven reliability"? How often must a person be observed "frequenting" a "known gang area" or "associating with known gang members?" Who is actually a gang member? Compliance depends entirely on the good faith and competence of local police officials who are more likely to fear the negative consequences of failing to identify a gang member who later engages in a violent crime than the consequences (of which there are none) of erroneously labeling someone a gang member. An individual who believes that he has been wrongly included in the database has no way to challenge the decision.*

---

* California has, however, recently adopted a bill providing that a local law enforcement agency must give a minor under eighteen a written notice before including her in

A name will probably remain in a gang database for years, perhaps indefinitely. The CalGang guidelines provide that a name should be purged if there has been no gang activity for five years and the individual is more than twenty-five years old.[55] However, there is no guarantee that the purging procedure will be followed. Even if it is, the local police department or individual police officers might retain purged gang members' names in their own files.

Gang and organized crime databases have not attracted as much legal and political attention as terrorist databases (probably because they do not have a "political" aura), but there have been numerous lawsuits. For example, in 1994, the American Civil Liberties Union (ACLU) sued the Garden Grove (California) Police Department for photographing and questioning three female Vietnamese American high school students in a mall. The police said that the students were wearing baggy pants and tight shirts, but they were not known to be affiliated with a gang.[56] The police department settled the case by agreeing that, before adding an individual's name and photograph to the database, it would document its "reasonable suspicion" of gang involvement. Moreover, the department agreed to purge from its database photographs and records of suspected gang members for whom it lacked reasonable suspicion. Again, compliance depends on the good faith and competence of the police.

The Dangerous Mentally Ill as a Quasi-Criminal Database

According to federal law, a person who has "been adjudicated as a mental defective or committed to a mental institution" cannot possess firearms.[57] States are responsible for transmitting the names of such individuals to the NICS, which enters them into a database. (This is a good example of a law enforcement–created and –maintained noncriminal database.) On account of insufficient resources and

a "shared gang database." The notice would also be sent to her parents or guardian. The minor or her parents can then provide written documentation to contest the gang member designation. Senate Bill 458, 2013–2014 Legislative Session, adding section 186.34 to the California Penal Code.

information and concern for the privacy of mentally ill persons, the majority of states have been unable or unwilling to send NICS information about persons adjudicated mentally defective or involuntarily committed to a mental hospital. The NICS Improvement Amendments Act of 2007 authorized grants to state agencies to increase reporting. There was pressure for more action after the 2013 massacre of schoolchildren in Newtown, Connecticut. However, many mental health professionals oppose assigning mentally ill persons to a database that implicitly defines those listed as potential criminals.[58]

A Remedy for Reputational Injury?

Should there be compensation or another remedy for a person who is stigmatized by an erroneous criminal label? The issue is poignantly illuminated by the case of Dr. Stephen Hatfill, whom FBI and DOJ officials wrongly labeled as responsible for mailing anthrax-laced letters in September 2001, one week after the 9/11 terrorist attacks. Exposure killed five persons and injured seventeen.[59] The FBI mounted a massive investigation called "Amerithrax."[60]

In a May 24, 2002, *New York Times* article, columnist Nicholas Kristof wrote that bioterrorism experts had shown him a list of possible suspects, including a "middle-aged American who has worked for the United States military bio-defense program and who had access to [infectious disease] labs at Fort Detrick, Md."[61] As time passed, Kristof divulged more information. It became clear to some readers that he was referring to Dr. Steven Hatfill. Hatfill's anonymity was totally shattered on June 26, 2002, when the Associated Press reported that the FBI had searched his home. On the August 6, 2002, CBS *Early Show*, U.S. Attorney General John Ashcroft called Hatfill a "person of interest" in the anthrax investigation.[62]

In early August 2002, DOJ officials succeeded in having Hatfill fired from his job at Louisiana State University, where he was working on a federally funded training grant for first responders to a bioterrorism attack.[63] An ABC News article on January 9, 2003, stated that federal investigators considered Hatfill "the man most likely responsible for the bio-terror attacks."[64] The story quoted "an unnamed government official, speaking on condition of confidentiality," as saying that there was probably enough evidence for an indictment but not a conviction.[65]

On November 18, 2005, Hatfill filed suit in federal district court in the District of Columbia against U.S. Attorney General John Ashcroft, the DOJ, the FBI, and various other FBI and DOJ officials. He also sued several media companies that had identified him as the anthrax terrorist.[66] Hatfill's lawsuit against the government, as later amended, alleged three causes of action: (1) violation of Fifth Amendment due process; (2) violation of First Amendment rights to free speech and to petition the government for redress of grievances; and (3) violation of the federal Privacy Act. (Hatfill did not sue the government under a defamation theory because the Federal Tort Claims Act does not waive sovereign immunity for defamation suits.)[67] The judge dismissed claims against the individual defendants but permitted the Privacy Act claims against the DOJ and the FBI to proceed.[68]

Congress passed the Privacy Act of 1974 to protect individual privacy against federal officials' misuse of information stored in federal databases. To prevail under the Privacy Act, Hatfill had to prove that government personnel had disclosed information contained in one or more Privacy Act–protected records located in *"a [federal agency's] system of records."*[69] The government sought to have the lawsuit dismissed on grounds of "law enforcement privilege,"[70] because to confirm or deny that certain investigative techniques had been employed would reveal and jeopardize the effectiveness of law enforcement techniques and sources.[71] If Hatfill overcame that obstacle, he would then have had to prove that defendants had disclosed to journalists information obtained from a government database.

In a pretrial deposition, an FBI special agent admitted that the FBI's Amerithrax investigative database labeled Hatfill a person of interest[72] and that information about Hatfill could be retrieved from the Automated Case Support System (ACS),[73] the FBI's electronic database for pending investigations. What's more, ACS files were not password protected and could be accessed by thousands of federal, state, and local law enforcement officers.[74] On June 27, 2008, DOJ announced a settlement[75] whereby it agreed to pay Hatfill

$2.825 million plus an annuity of $150,000 per year for twenty years.[76]

The Hatfill saga raises important questions about the propriety of law enforcement officials' direct and indirect labeling of criminal suspects and of leaking information to the media. Admittedly, the police sometimes have legitimate reasons for providing investigative information to some members of the public in order to apprehend a suspect or to allay public anxiety. For example, in the anthrax investigation, FBI agents showed Hatfill's photo to people in a Princeton, New Jersey, neighborhood from which the anthrax letters were mailed in order to find out whether someone might remember having seen him mail a letter. That was a reasonable disclosure. Likewise, it would be appropriate for police investigators to solicit the public's assistance in apprehending a fugitive suspect by putting that suspect's name and photo on a "Ten Most Wanted" list. By contrast, it would not be reasonable for the police, without a bona fide investigative justification, to announce to the public or to some favored reporters that they consider a named individual guilty of crimes. Being publicly pronounced guilty by the police or prosecutor could be just as injurious to reputation as being convicted.*

While determining what should qualify as an investigative purpose that justifies disclosing various types of information is not an easy task, anonymously leaking incriminating information should be presumptively wrong and actionable. Law enforcement agencies' disclosure of investigative information to the public should be direct, open, and transparent, that is, through public statements, press conferences, and press releases. Adopting that policy would be a significant step toward ensuring that the flow of information to the public is the result of a policy decision, not an individual officer's whim, personal bias, suspicion, speculation, or desire to please a particular journalist.

---

* Until 1996, an "exemption from prosecution" procedure allowed Chinese prosecutors to publicly declare a defendant guilty without formal adjudication. See James B. Jacobs and Daniel Curtin, *Remedying Defamation by Law Enforcement: Fallout from the Wen Ho Lee, Steven Hatfill and Brandon Mayfield Settlements*, 46 Criminal Law Bulletin 223–248 (2010), note 98.

The FBI and some other law enforcement agencies have rules and regulations about communicating investigative information to the media and the public. State legislatures could adopt or adapt them as a safe harbor justification for divulging investigatory information. Violations would constitute a prima facie defamation case that the defendant official or agency would need to rebut by proving a bona fide investigative purpose. The defendant would also escape liability by proving the incriminating information to be true (that is, the plaintiff was convicted). Calling someone guilty before she pleads guilty or is found guilty does not cause extra reputational injury.

The FBI's website states that information regarding ongoing investigations is "protected from public disclosure" in order to protect "the privacy of individuals involved in the investigation prior to any public charging."[77] The NYPD's "confidentiality policy" prohibits the disclosure of sensitive information whenever such a disclosure is not "required in the execution of lawful duty."[78] The law enforcement officials in the Hatfill case would have violated these policies by leaking investigative information to journalists.

The DOJ expressly prohibits leaking investigative information.[79] Section 1-7.530(A) of the United States Attorneys' Manual states that "components and personnel of the Department of Justice shall not respond to questions about the existence of an ongoing investigation or comment on its nature or progress."[80] Other DOJ policies regarding the release of information relating to criminal proceedings apply to "the release of information to news media from the time a person is the subject of a criminal investigation until any proceeding resulting from such an investigation has been terminated by trial or otherwise." Because unauthorized disclosures "[tend] to create dangers of prejudice without serving a significant law enforcement function," DOJ employees should "refrain from making available" information from polygraph examinations and information regarding a suspect's refusal to cooperate with certain aspects of an investigation.[81]

Conclusion

Computers and the information technology revolution are both a boon to law enforcement and a threat to civil liberties. To an extent not dreamed of in previous generations, today's police agencies have a vastly increased capacity to gather, store, classify, merge, and retrieve data about persons and events. Balancing the need to protect civil liberties while gathering information on possible terrorists is one of the greatest law enforcement challenges of our time. But "ordinary" criminal databases also pose civil liberties threats. Creating a new intelligence database for a particular crime problem—for example, domestic violence, hate crime, or pornography—should be considered a serious policy decision. Every criminal intelligence database has the potential to stigmatize those who are named. Thus, such databases should be created only when absolutely necessary and not for every category of crime. Access to these databases ought to be rigorously controlled; a one-size-fits-all formula should not apply. Few people need to know about a corruption investigation, but many agencies and investigators need access to information about suspected terrorists. Much attention needs to be paid to data security. Real harm can be done by leakers and hackers.

The most effective check on abusive investigative and intelligence databases is self-regulation by law enforcement officials. Toward that end, the FBI and DOJ have promulgated guidelines that attempt to balance the individual's interest in reputation with the society's interest in solving and preventing serious crimes. But we should not have to take on blind faith that police are adhering to their guidelines. There should be independent monitoring by an inspector general or a citizens advisory board.

New intelligence and investigative databases are easy to create. Plausible crime prevention or national security reasons for creating new "quasi-criminal" databases can almost always be easily constructed. Particularly disturbing is the move to aggressively expand state and national databases on individuals labeled as dangerously mentally ill and therefore at risk of perpetrating a massacre or engaging in other firearms violence. The desire to stop dangerously mentally ill people from committing such atrocities is obviously reasonable, but in so doing a huge number of innocent people could be stigmatized as "mad and bad."

Admittedly, much work would need to be done to flesh out the details of a remedy for both intentional and inadvertent disclosures of information from investigative and intelligence databases. A statutory solution would be preferable to a common law remedy, although both should be considered. Among the many issues that need to be considered are whether individuals or agencies should be held responsible (individual leakers are notoriously hard to identify) and whether liability should turn on intentionality, strict liability, or another standard. With respect to agencies, should a good faith and competent antileak policy provide a safe harbor? Should there be statutorily fixed damages or damages varying with the extent to which the victim can prove injury to his or her reputation?

However these issues are resolved, they should not be ignored. A factually innocent person whom government officials have branded as a criminal deserves some kind of redress. The revolution in information technology guarantees that once defamatory allegations have been made public, they are impossible to recall. The stigmatizing allegations will be subject to retrieval from the Internet and other sources. There is no assurance that even a retraction remedies reputational injury. Formulating an appropriate tort remedy is an enormous challenge, but we ought not to turn a blind eye to government officials who, without a bona fide investigative reason, wrongfully brand innocent individuals as criminals.

3 LINKING BODIES TO CRIMINAL HISTORIES

The business of the Bureau is to aid police departments throughout the country in capturing and identifying criminals . . . a million fingerprints now in the Department of Justice records at Fort Leavenworth, Kansas . . . will be transferred to Washington. There the fingerprints will form the nucleus for the greatest collection of criminal traces that this Continent has ever enjoyed.

—*Time Magazine*, "CABINET: A Million Fingerprints" (1924)[1]

[D]ata on offenders needed by prosecutors, courts and correctional authorities should be collected and made centrally available. . . . [T]he goal should be to develop an index drawn from the records of the criminal justice agencies across the country. With such an index a sentencing judge, for example, could learn where information might be found bearing on an offender's response to treatment in other jurisdictions. Disclosure of the information itself would remain, as at present, entirely within the discretion and control of the individual agency that held it. This would help avoid the dangers of developing national "dossiers," but would greatly speed collection of data for making decisions on disposition of cases—a major source of present delays and injustice.

—President's Commission on Law Enforcement and Administration of Justice, *The Challenge of Crime in a Free Society* (1967)[2]

ANYONE INTERESTED in criminal records policy or, for that matter, in the administration of criminal justice needs to understand what a rap sheet is, who has access to it, and what it is used for. Until the second half of the nineteenth century, individual criminal history records consisted of haphazard notes maintained by local police departments that were just being created in some big cities.[3] As police departments grew larger and more bureaucratic, they required a more systematic way to record and file information about arrests and arrestees. They also required an identification system that would enable police to link records with flesh-and-blood persons who might use aliases or otherwise try to hide their true identities.

The "rap sheet" developed in the first decade of the twentieth century. "Rap" is commonly thought to be an acronym for "Record of Arrest and Prosecution," although scholars have traced the etymology to a different root.* In some states (Massachusetts, for example), the rap sheet is called "criminal offender record information" (CORI) or simply an individual criminal history record. Whatever it is called, the rap sheet is a lifetime record of an individual's arrests and, ideally, charges, dispositions, and sentences resulting from those arrests. (As we will see, a substantial percentage of rap sheets lack dispositions for one or more arrests, requiring users to query the relevant police department, prosecutor's office or court to find out how the arrest was resolved.) While the rap sheet was created by police for police use, it immediately proved useful to prosecutors, judges, and correctional agencies and to all types of non–law enforcement agencies, organizations, associations, and individuals.

Identity Databases

Reliable identification of arrestees is essential for effective law enforcement in a society where people are not personally known to one another or to the police.[4] Before the invention and adoption of modern fingerprinting, the police could keep records on people who were arrested along with their names and physical descriptions, but if some time later they arrested an individual who gave a different name, it was difficult to determine whether it was the same person whom they had previously arrested. Even photographs were hard to match and laborious to search.[5] In the nineteenth century, some

---

* An early meaning of "rap" was a blow to a person or a sharp tap on an object. By the end of the eighteenth century, to "get or take the rap" for something was well-established slang for being blamed, rebuked, or held responsible. Criminal justice agencies adopted the term "rap sheet" as the name for the document on which criminal charges against an individual were recorded. The Louisiana Supreme Court is credited with first using "RAP sheet" as an acronym for "record of arrest and prosecution." A few states then adopted "Record of Arrests and Prosecutions" in statutes referring to an individual's criminal history. See Elizabeth G. Thornburg's chapter in James E. Clapp, Elizabeth G. Thornburg, Marc Galanter, and Fred R. Shapiro, *Lawtalk: The Unknown Stories behind Familiar Legal Expressions* 211–13 (New Haven, CT: Yale University Press, 2011).

police departments created so-called rogues' galleries—collections of sketches or photographs (daguerreotypes) of criminals and suspects.* In the 1880s, the Bertillon system of identification based on physical measurements, standardized photographs, physical measurements, skin color, scars, and thumb-line impressions marked a step forward.[6] Toward the end of the nineteenth century, Francis Galton invented fingerprinting as an identification technique. His 1892 book *Finger Prints*[7] was a landmark in forensic science.[8†]

Because every individual has unique fingerprints, a person's identity could be linked to a criminal record by matching his current ten fingerprints to a ten-fingers set of prints that were recorded after a previous arrest. It is hard to imagine that a modern society could be policed without fingerprints. As the Supreme Court recently observed:

> [In] every criminal case, it is known and must be known who has been arrested and who is being tried. . . . An individual's identity is more than just his name or Social Security number, and the government's interest in identification goes beyond ensuring that the proper name is typed on the indictment. Identity has never been considered limited to the name on the arrestee's birth certificate. In fact, a name is of little value compared to the real interest in identification at stake when an individual is brought into custody. "It is a well recognized aspect of criminal conduct that the perpetrator will take unusual steps to conceal not only his conduct, but also his identity. Disguises used while committing a crime may be supplemented or replaced by changed names, and even changed physical features." . . . An "arrestee may be carrying a false ID or lie about

---

* In the late nineteenth century, inspector Thomas F. Byrnes of the New York Police Department published some of his photos with criminal record biographies in *Professional Criminals of America* (New York: Cassel, 1886).

† Galton found that no two individuals' fingerprints have the same loops, whorls, and arches, not even those of identical twins. However, in order for fingerprints to be useful in forensic identification, police needed a classification method that would enable retrieval and matching. Most countries adopted Sir Edward Richard Henry's classification system based on Galton's three categories plus a division of loops into two classes.

his identity," and "criminal history records . . . can be inaccurate or incomplete."[9]*

For most of the twentieth century, taking fingerprints required the police to dip the arrestee's fingers in ink and then roll them onto fingerprint cards, of which copies were prepared for the criminal record repository, the FBI, and the local police department itself. Beginning in the mid-1990s, ink and paper fingerprinting began to be replaced by faster, cleaner, and more accurate digital fingerprinting using optical live-scan devices.† An electronic search seeks to match the scanned fingerprints with fingerprints that are stored in the FBI's nationwide Integrated Automated Fingerprint Identification System (IAFIS), containing the fingerprints of forty-seven million individuals. It is the largest biometric database in the world.

Today, DNA profiles are also used for identification purposes. Like fingerprinting, DNA enables the police to match bodies with criminal records. DNA is even more useful because it is easier to match the DNA from a known felon stored in a database (offender profile), to the DNA from a crime scene (forensic profile)—a situation referred to as a "cold hit"‡—than it is to match a fingerprint fragment with a set of stored fingerprints of known individuals. All fifty states and the federal government require the collection of a

* The quote is from *Maryland v. King*, 569 U.S. – (2013), where the court held that when officers make an arrest supported by probable cause, taking and analyzing a cheek swab from the arrestee is a reasonable booking procedure for Fourth Amendment purposes and thus not an unconstitutional search.

† Live Scan is an inkless fingerprinting technology that electronically records friction ridge skin by rolling the skin over a specially coated glass platform and recording the information on a charged coupled device. Fingerprints related to criminal cases are usually stored in the city's or state's Automated Fingerprint identification System (AFIS) or in the FBI's Integrated Automated Fingerprint Identification System (IAFIS). These technologies map fingerprints and create a spatial geometry of the minutiae of the print, which is changed into a binary code for the computer's searching algorithm. See, e.g., Kären M. Hess, Christine H. Orthmann, and Henry Lim Cho, *Police Operations: Theory and Practice* 371 (Independence, KY: Delmar Cengage Learning, 6th ed., 2013).

‡ "When CODIS recognizes a match between an offender and forensic profile, it is referred to as a 'cold hit.'" See http://www.dna.gov/glossary/#C.

biological sample from people convicted of felonies. Since 2012, New York is the only state to require collection of DNA from convicted misdemeanants. Twenty-eight states and the federal government currently authorize collection of DNA from arrestees. Of those states, fifteen limit DNA profiling to serious felony arrests; thirteen permit DNA to be collected from all felony arrestees, and seven permit collection from all felony and some misdemeanor arrestees. At least four states allow collection of DNA samples from some juvenile arrestees.[10] The National DNA Index (NDIS)—considered the highest level in the Combined DNA Index System (CODIS) hierarchy—contains DNA profiles contributed by federal, state, and local participating forensic laboratories;[11] in 2014, it stored over thirteen million DNA profiles, of which 11,015,147 are offender profiles, 1,922,415 are arrestee profiles, and 565,159 are forensic profiles (i.e., unnamed DNA traces from crime scene evidence).

Production of Rap Sheets

After an individual is arrested for a felony and for most misdemeanors, she is "booked," that is, photographed, fingerprinted, and, increasingly, DNA-swabbed.[12] The identification and arrest information is sent to the state's "criminal records repository" in order to determine whether the arrestee already has a criminal record or is a wanted suspect or fugitive in that or another jurisdiction. If the person has never been arrested before in that state, the arrestee's name and fingerprints are entered into the offender identity databases, and a rap sheet will be created. The criminal record repository also assigns each new arrestee a state identification number (SID), which allows a searcher to locate an individual's rap sheet by number as well as by name or fingerprints. There is only one rap sheet per individual in each state, but the same individual will have a separate rap sheet in every state (or federal jurisdiction) where he or she has ever been booked. (The FBI serves as the criminal records repository for federal arrests.)

A rap sheet includes some or all of the following information: names and addresses provided by arrestee; location of crimes; date of crimes; arrest precincts; arrest charges; docket numbers (the numbers the court assigns the record-subject's cases); courts where the record-subject has been arraigned; formal (prosecution or grand jury) charges; warrants issued; dispositions of the cases; sentences (incarceration, probation, fine, etc.); whether the case file is sealed; whether the arrestee has been adjudicated as a sex offender and dates of paroles.[13]

Criminal Record Repositories

Up until the second or third decade of the twentieth century, if an arrestee used an alias and was not personally known to the police who arrested him, there was no way to look up his prior criminal history in other states. Even in the same state, one police department's information was not routinely available to other police departments.[14] Without a centralized state-level arrestee index, a local police department was unlikely to identify a person who had a criminal record, or was a suspect or fugitive in another municipality in the same state, let alone in another state. The Pinkerton National Detective Company, retained by companies and public entities to carry out background investigations and track down fugitives, had the most comprehensive national information.[15] In 1924, Congress established the Bureau of Criminal Identification (BCI), which later became the Federal Bureau of Investigation (FBI).

California established the first state criminal records repository (the California Bureau of Criminal Identification) in 1918. It requested California's local police departments to submit copies of arrestees' names, fingerprints, and arrest information, thereby establishing an information system that provided law enforcement agencies throughout the state with identity and criminal history information. In 1930, only nine states had state-level criminal records repositories that coordinated the criminal records of that state's hundreds of police departments. Today, there is a criminal record repository in every state—for example, the Kansas Central Repository, the Nevada Criminal History Records Repository, and the New York State Division of Criminal Justice Services.[16] These state-level criminal record repositories serve as the backbone of the nation's criminal record infrastructure. By December 31,

2012, the combined state criminal history repositories held rap sheets for 100.5 million individuals.[17] (More than one state repository may hold a rap sheet for the same individual, but each state rap sheet will only contain information about the individual's in-state arrests.)

As a defendant's case proceeds through the criminal justice process, court personnel are supposed to send (these days electronically) information about the prosecution and adjudication of the case (e.g., plea, judgment, sentence) to the state's criminal record repository. However, in most states this is done manually. Because of personnel shortages, bureaucratic delays, and lack of incentives, it is often not done at all. Therefore, many rap sheets lack disposition information, that is, convictions, acquittals, and dismissals.

The rap sheet system was created by and for the police. The police don't need any special incentive to record arrestee and arrest information. They must take and check fingerprints in order to confirm the arrestee's identity and to record the identification and arrest information in order to keep track of the case and to enable them to recover information about the arrest should the same individual be suspected or arrested in the future. However, because the rap sheet system wasn't specifically designed for use by prosecutors and judges, they do not have a strong incentive to update case information in the rap sheet system. Instead, they usually input their actions and decisions into their own information systems. Routinely they do not inform the police about dispositions and fail to transmit charge and disposition information to the criminal records repositories. We will return to this problem in Chapter 8.

Evolution of an Integrated Nationwide Criminal Record Information System

In 1897, the National Bureau of Criminal Identification (NBCI), created by the International Association of Chiefs of Police (IACP) to share criminal record information, started encouraging IACP members to submit arrestee fingerprints.[18] In 1905, the Department of Justice created the BCI to collect copies of fingerprint cards prepared by local police departments. However, police department participation was spotty.

In 1924, the U.S. attorney general appointed twenty-six-year-old J. Edgar Hoover to be director of the BCI (renamed the FBI in 1935). Hoover recognized that the FBI could establish an indispensable role for itself by serving as the clearinghouse for individual criminal history records from all U.S. police departments.[19]* The federal penitentiary in Leavenworth, Kansas, transferred 800,000 criminal fingerprint records to BCI's Criminal Identification Division. BCI also took over the fingerprints collection of the International Association of Chiefs of Police (IACP) and Hoover, with the IACP's support, urged local police agencies to mail copies of arrestees' photos, fingerprints, and offense information to the BCI.[20] In return, the FBI would provide participating departments with information about the identity, fugitive status, and past arrests and convictions of an arrestee or other person of interest.[21] The FBI functioned as an information broker, directing a law enforcement agency looking for out-of-state information about a suspect's or arrestee's criminal record to the state repository likely to have that information. The Identification Division quickly became the FBI's largest division.[22] (In 1992, the Identification Division was reorganized and renamed the Criminal Justice Information Services [CJIS] division; it is located in a large complex in Clarksburg, West Virginia.)

Despite its growing clout, the Identification Division was hamstrung by the fact that the rap sheets that local state repositories sent to the FBI often did not include postarrest information,[23]† most

---

* In 1952, Hoover reflected that "the United States has no need for a national police agency. The present system of law enforcement, local, state and national, working together in voluntary and fraternal cooperation, can fulfill its responsibilities. What is needed is not a new structure of law enforcement, but strengthening, improving and making more efficient the present arrangement. That is what intelligent law enforcement officers are now attempting to do, and with the aid of America's citizenry, it can be done." J. Edgar Hoover, *Civil Liberties and Law Enforcement: The Role of the FBI*, 37 Iowa L. Rev. 175, 194 (1952).

† According to a 1982 report by the federal Office of Technology Assistance (OTA), improvements had been made since Congress first started paying attention to adding dispositions to rap sheets, but nationwide dispositions were recorded on only 66 percent of rap sheets. See Office of Technology Assessment, *An Assessment of Alternatives for a National Computerized Criminal History System* (Washington, DC: U.S. Government Printing Office, 1982).

importantly case dispositions. This meant that it could tell an inquiring law enforcement agency only what offenses the person of interest had been arrested for and where.[24] The FBI had no way of knowing whether the arrest had been resolved by pretrial diversion, dismissal, acquittal, or conviction. If the inquiring agency wanted to know the disposition of an arrest, it had to contact the police department, prosecutor, or court that processed the case. While the inquiring police department or prosecutor's office was usually able to use its connections to obtain this information from colleagues in other jurisdictions, employers, landlords, and other criminal record consumers rarely found chasing down the missing information worth the time and effort. It was easier and less costly to pass over the applicant.

The Triple I ("III"): A National Rap Sheet System

The FBI began computerizing criminal history records in 1963.[25] The 1965 Law Enforcement Assistance Act, passed in the aftermath of urban riots following the assassination of Martin Luther King Jr., expanded the federal role in law enforcement. Congress authorized the establishment of an FBI National Crime Information Center (NCIC) to facilitate the flow of information among federal, state, and local law enforcement agencies. In 1967, the President's Commission on Law Enforcement and Administration of Justice concluded that U.S. law enforcement urgently needed an efficient nationally integrated system for sharing individual criminal history information. In 1968, NCIC staff began work on creating an information system that would allow police departments throughout the country to find out almost immediately whether a suspect or arrestee had a criminal history or was wanted by any police department.

In 1969, the Law Enforcement Assistance Administration (LEAA)[26] funded the creation of SEARCH, the National Consortium for Criminal Justice Information and Statistics,[27] "to improve the quality of justice and public safety through the use, management, and exchange of information; application of new technologies; and responsible law and policy, while safeguarding security and privacy."

SEARCH is composed of one gubernatorial appointee from each state and eight at-large appointees selected by SEARCH's executive director. It provides state and federal criminal records repositories and law enforcement agencies with training, resources, and best practices on information technology (IT) initiatives and information sharing to improve the creation, storage, retrieval, and use of criminal record information.[28] SEARCH immediately started working on a criminal record information network that would (1) assign state criminal record repositories primary responsibility for collecting and maintaining individual criminal history information,[29] and (2) enable states to access each other's criminal record databases.[30]

The result was the Interstate Identification Index, called "the III" or "Triple I." The "Triple I" makes a significant contribution to coordinating the highly decentralized U.S. law enforcement. Triple I enables a police officer, anywhere in the country, almost instantly, to find out whether a suspect or arrestee has a criminal record or is wanted or is a fugitive in any jurisdiction. There are an estimated 14,000 law enforcement agencies in the United States.[31] Practically every county has its own elected prosecutor and, at least until recently, its own county courts. Until the 1930s, only a few states centralized their rap sheets. Consequently, it was unlikely that police would find out that the person they just stopped or arrested had a criminal record or was wanted by police in another county in that state, much less in another state. It took a major multiyear federal initiative to modernize and integrate criminal records to the point where they could support the modern-day Triple I.

The Brady Law and the National Instant Criminal Background Check System

The nationally integrated criminal records system serves a number of needs beyond routine policing. For examples, the 1993 Brady Handgun Violence Prevention Act called for the creation of a National Instant Criminal Background Check System (NICS) that could, within three business days, inform an inquiring federally licensed firearms dealer whether the prospective purchaser was disqualified from possessing a firearm. Because NICS depends heavily on the Triple I to determine whether a prospective firearms purchaser is disqualified from purchasing or possessing a firearm on account of a prior felony or misdemeanor domestic assault conviction,[32] Congress provided hundreds of millions of dollars in grants to upgrade and computerize police and court records. NICS, physically located at the FBI's CJIS headquarters in Clarksburg, West Virginia, became operational in 1998.

In 1998, the Crime Identification Technology Act (CITA)[33] authorized $1.25 billion over five years to upgrade state criminal history record systems, improve police identification capacity (e.g., DNA profiling), and promote integration of national, state, and local criminal records systems.[34] More grants followed.[35] However, despite all the money and effort, lack of recorded dispositions on rap sheets remains a problem. In 2012, only eighteen states had rap sheet databases that included dispositions for more than 80 percent of arrests.[36] In Kansas, it took over 600 days to record a disposition on a rap sheet. (By contrast, New York State has an interface between its court records system and its rap sheet system that permits disposition information to be posted within a day; however, many old rap sheet entries still lack dispositions.) Thus, if Triple I does not indicate whether a prospective firearms purchaser who was arrested for a disqualifying felony was subsequently convicted of a felony, NICS personnel must contact the county prosecutor or court to find out whether the case resulted in a felony conviction. They are usually able to make this determination within the three-business-day time limit. If they do not notify the firearms dealer that the sale must not be completed, the dealer may complete the sale.

Making Rap Sheets Available for Non–Criminal Justice Purposes

State and federal criminal record repositories are free to establish their own policies regarding access to their criminal records, unless there are state or federal laws requiring them to provide or deny access to certain categories of individuals, agencies, and organizations. For example, beginning in the early 1970s, Congress began chipping away at the FBI's policy of refusing to share criminal record information with non–law enforcement agencies.[37]

Congress directly authorized certain industries, businesses, and voluntary associations to obtain (upon payment of a modest fee) job applicants', employees', and volunteers' criminal histories from the FBI,[38] including federally chartered or insured banks and state and local licensing agencies (1972);[39] the securities industry's self-regulatory organizations (1975);[40] and the Nuclear Regulatory Commission (1986).[41] The 1993 National Child Protection Act (NCPA) authorized states to designate organizations that provide child care or child care placement services to obtain from the FBI a nationwide criminal background check to determine whether an employee, job applicant, or volunteer has a prior conviction that "bears upon an individual's fitness to have responsibility for the safety and well-being of children." Subsequently, Congress extended the same privilege to organizations providing services and/or care to elderly and disabled persons.[42] In 1996, the Housing Opportunity Program Extension Act authorized federally funded housing authorities to obtain criminal background checks on tenants and tenant applicants.[43] The 1998 Volunteers for Children Act provided that, in the absence of state law authorizing access to rap sheets, organizations and businesses dealing with children and vulnerable groups could obtain criminal background checks from the FBI.[44]

The September 11, 2001, Al Qaeda terrorist attacks on the Pentagon and World Trade Center caused Congress to increase the number of public agencies and private businesses that could obtain criminal records from the FBI. The 2001 Patriot Act mandated that employers involved in transporting hazardous materials conduct criminal background checks for an estimated 3.5 million employees.[45] Other laws require criminal background checks for persons who (1) have access to controlled areas of maritime facilities;[46] (2) have access to biological agents;[47] and (3) work as port security personnel, airport and airline employees, and air marshals and who work in certain other transportation positions.[48] Moreover, the 2002 Maritime Transportation Security Act mandated that any person who has unescorted access to secure areas of facilities and vessels have a Transportation Worker Identification Credential (TWIC). There must be a criminal background check and security threat assessment for each TWIC applicant. According to the regulation on Permanently Disqualifying Criminal Offenses and Interim Disqualifying Offenses, an applicant will be permanently disqualified from holding a TWIC or a Hazardous Materials Endorsement (HME) if he or she was convicted or found not guilty by reason of insanity for felonies including espionage, sedition, and treason; a federal crime of terrorism as defined in 18 U.S.C. 2332b(g) or comparable state law; or a crime involving a transportation security incident, murder, or unlawful possession, use, sale, distribution, manufacture, purchase, receipt, transfer, shipping, transporting, import, export, storage of, or dealing in an explosive or explosive device.[49]

A driver will not be issued a TWIC or an HME (in effect, an occupational license) if he or she was convicted or found not guilty by reason of insanity within the previous seven years, or was released from prison in the last five years, for felonies including unlawful possession, use, sale, manufacture, purchase, distribution, receipt, transfer, shipping, transporting, delivery, import, export of, or dealing in a firearm or other weapon; extortion, dishonesty, fraud, or misrepresentation, including identity fraud, bribery, smuggling, and immigration violations; distribution of, intent to distribute, or importation of a controlled substance; arson; or rape.[50]

In 2004, Congress authorized the FBI to provide private security companies with criminal history information on prospective employees.[51] The 2004 Intelligence Reform and Terrorism Prevention Act directed the attorney general to prepare a report "mak[ing] recommendations to Congress for improving, standardizing, and consolidating the existing statutory authorizations, programs, and procedures for the conduct of criminal history checks for non-criminal justice purposes."[52] The resulting 2006 Attorney General's Report on Criminal History Background Checks criticized providing access to criminal records by piecemeal lawmaking because it "has led to a great disparity in the level of access by specific industries and within specific states."[53] The report recommended increasing the number of organizations authorized to obtain rap sheet information from the FBI, to include, among others:

> (A) priority employers, and subsequently, if capacity allows, all employers, for use in decisions regarding an individual's employment suitability; (B) entities placing individuals in non-employment positions of trust, such as persons having access to vulnerable populations, client residences, significant organizational assets, or sensitive information; (C) any person or entity when the Attorney General determines such access promotes public safety or national security; and (D) consumer reporting agencies or other third parties that: (i) are acting on behalf of one of the above authorized users of FBI-maintained criminal history record information; (ii) meet data security standards established by the Attorney General, including being certified through a public or private program approved by the Attorney General as being trained in applicable federal and state consumer reporting laws and in Attorney General standards relating to the secure handling of criminal history record information; and (iii) are prohibited, with limited exceptions, from aggregating the criminal history information obtained through these fingerprint-based checks for resale.[54]

This recommendation, which Congress has not adopted, would have radically increased non–criminal justice agencies' access to rap sheet data, perhaps rendering court files a less important source of criminal record information.

State Authorization for Private Organizations to Access Rap Sheet Information

In 1972, Congress passed a crucial criminal records statute allowing private organizations to obtain rap sheet information (for a modest fee) from the FBI. It authorized the FBI to conduct nationwide criminal background checks on behalf of a non–law enforcement agency or organization designated by state statute if approved by the U.S. attorney general.[55] States eventually passed (and the attorney general approved) more than one thousand such statutes, which authorized various businesses and volunteer organizations to indirectly obtain FBI criminal background checks by submitting requests to their state repository. All such background checks require fingerprints that must be taken and submitted by a police agency or certified private company. The state and the FBI charge a processing fee that the requesting party usually passes on to the job applicant.

In 2005, the FBI processed approximately 9.8 million criminal background checks for non-criminal-justice-related public agencies and private organizations.[56] By 2013, the number had practically doubled to 17 million, accounting for slightly less than half of all FBI fingerprint-supported background checks.[57] Thus, the rap sheet system created by police for the police is now more often used to provide criminal biographies for non–criminal justice purposes.

National Crime Prevention and Privacy Inter-State Compact

The creators of the Triple I aimed to decentralize the national rap sheet system by eliminating the need for the FBI to hold a duplicate rap sheet for every state and local arrestee.[58] In Phase 1, states would continue sending the FBI copies of every arrestee's fingerprints and arrest information, and the FBI would continue to respond to requests for nationwide criminal history information by sending the requesting party all the rap sheet information it held. In Phase 2, states would send to the FBI fingerprints and arrest information only for an individual's (John Doe's) first arrest in that state. Once a state is Phase 2 compliant, there is no need for the FBI to hold copies of rap sheets from that state. When all states are Phase 2 compliant, the FBI, via Triple I, would direct requests to every state repository holding John Doe's fingerprints. However, as of 2014, only a minority of states were Phase 2–compliant.[59]

The main impediments to states becoming Phase 2 compliant are state laws preventing dissemination of rap sheets to non–criminal justice organizations. These laws make little sense since, under Phase 1, the FBI responds to police and criminal record requests for rap sheet information regardless of whether the request is made for a law enforcement or non–law enforcement purpose. Historically and presently, when a state transmits a duplicate rap sheet to the FBI, it has no control over the FBI's dissemination of the information. Even if a state's own laws prohibit its repository from transmitting rap sheet information to a private employer, once that information is sent to the FBI, the FBI can (and does) disseminate it to any state repository making a request, whether on behalf of a criminal justice or non–criminal justice organization. The state that created a rap sheet has never had a say in how the FBI disseminates it.

At the FBI's and SEARCH's urging, Congress passed the 1998 National Crime Prevention and Privacy Inter-State Compact to encourage Phase 2 compliance.[60]* The Compact is "privacy neutral" because it gives the requesting state the same access (i.e., complete access) to other states' rap sheets that the requesting state has in Phase 1. However, because an interstate compact supersedes state law, signing the Compact makes it possible for states to provide rap sheets that they could otherwise not provide, that is, rap sheets requested on behalf of private entities. Nevertheless, only thirty states have ratified the Compact; eleven additional states and territories have signed memoranda of understanding that commit them to follow the Compact Council's relevant directives and rules.[61]

Rap Sheet Inscrutability

The rap sheet was created by and for police use, not as an all-purpose negative résumé for use by employers, landlords, volunteer organizations, and others. While police are accustomed to reading and interpreting rap sheets, the same is not true of many non–law enforcement users. Despite efforts to make rap sheets more user-friendly, they are difficult to decipher because they use state criminal code numbers and abbreviations to indicate charges, and jargon to refer to procedures and decisions. The problem is compounded because different states had (and, to some degree, still have) different rap sheet formats and, of course, different penal code numbers for criminal offenses.[62] Moreover, when an individual's rap sheet contains overlapping arrests, it is particularly difficult for a layperson

* An interstate compact, as prescribed in the Constitution (Article I, Section 10, Clause III), is a contract between two or more states that must be ratified by Congress. See Council of State Governments—National Center for Interstate Compacts, "Understanding Interstate Compacts," http://www.cglg.org/projects/water/CompactEducation/Understanding_Interstate_Compacts—CSGNCIC.pdf.

to figure out which court hearing, ruling, or disposition corresponds to which arrest. Lay users are unlikely to be willing to invest the time and money to investigate missing information (dispositions), ambiguities, and possible errors. Thus, there is a real danger that non–law enforcement users will interpret the rap sheet as more serious than it really is.*

The rap sheet has evolved over time. In 1992, the National Task Force on Criminal History Record Disposition Reporting called for criminal history records that were easier to understand.[63] In 1995, SEARCH convened the National Task Force for Increasing the Utility of Criminal History Records to recommend a standard format for criminal history records.[64] Its report observed:

> To make informed decisions, the criminal justice system needs complete, accurate, timely, accessible, and easily understandable criminal history record information. The complexity of the criminal justice system and the large number of agencies that have roles in the processing of criminal cases and the custody and supervision of offenders add to the difficulty of establishing complete, accurate, and intelligible criminal history records. Increasing numbers of citizens are being affected by the quality and legibility of criminal history records because of the expanding uses of these records for noncriminal justice decisions, such as licensing and employment eligibility. The criminal history records now produced by the State repositories differ significantly in content and format. Implementation of the Interstate Identification Index (III) system has increased the need for uniform criminal history records. Information concerning record subjects that may be relevant for criminal justice purposes, as well as authorized noncriminal justice pur-

* NLETS, a Phoenix-based interstate justice and public safety network for the exchange of law enforcement–, criminal justice–, and public safety–related information, is currently working on a project named CHIEF (Criminal History Information Exchange Format) funded by the Bureau of Justice Statistics. The goal is to create a uniform criminal history record format, the NIEM (National Information Exchange Model) rap sheet.

> poses, may exist in databases other than the criminal history record system. State criminal history records increasingly contain "flags"—symbols or notations, such as "F" for felony conviction. Many flags are based on particular requirements under State law, raising a concern that their inclusion on interstate rap sheets may cause confusion if the basis for the flags is not generally understood throughout the country or defined on each record.[65]

The task force made four recommendations. First, states should develop procedures for including all arrest, dispositions, and correction data for records that it transmits for all felony and misdemeanor offenses except those that the FBI does not accept.[66] The second recommendation enumerated the information that rap sheets should include.[67] The third recommendation suggested a presentation format.[68] The fourth recommendation proposed a standardized transmission format.[69] Subsequently, the Joint Task Force for Rap Sheet Standardization proposed several updates. The most recent, Interstate Criminal History Transmission XML Version 4.1, was issued in 2011.[70] Although there is no legal compulsion for states to adopt these proposals, in the past they have proved influential. The trend is toward greater standardization.[71]

Community Notification Laws and Online Sex Offender Databases

The 1994 rape and murder of seven-year-old Megan Kanka in New Jersey by a paroled sex offender living anonymously in the Kankas' neighborhood ignited a political movement that led to passage of a New Jersey "Megan's Law," followed by a federal Megan's Law, and, ultimately, by a Megan's Law in every state.[72] Although Megan's Law details differ from state to state, they require convicted sex offenders to register (name, photograph, fingerprints, and place of residence[73]) with the police or other designated agency, and require the designated agency to make the relevant community aware of the presence of convicted sex offenders in their locale. In time, community notification for highest-risk registrants came to be implemented by posting identity and offense information on publicly accessible websites. It is possible for anyone with access to the Internet to look up the names and photos, addresses, car models, and license plate numbers of serious sex offenders who live in any county in the United States.[74]

In 2005, the Department of Justice launched the Dru Sjodin National Sex Offender Public Website (NSOPW), named in memory of a college student who was kidnapped, sexually assaulted, and murdered by a previously convicted sex offender. The NSOPW links state, territory, and tribal sex offender registries,[75] thereby enabling anyone, using first and last name, locality, zip code, or address, to search online for the identity of previously convicted sex offenders who live in their community (or, for that matter, in any U.S. community).[76] The searcher can query all state sex offender registries. If there is a match, the searcher is directed to the relevant state's sex offender website to find further information.

In 2006, Congress leveraged its control over federal grant money to "encourage" states to establish publicly accessible sex offender databases that comply with federal standards. The Adam Walsh Child Protection and Safety Act[77] provided that, in order to receive its maximum federal criminal justice grant, a state must comply with Sex Offender Registration and Notification Act (SORNA) minimum standards for sex offender registration and community notification.[78] SORNA requires states to assign convicted sex offenders to one of three risk-based categories according to their sex crime conviction and lifetime criminal record. Further, states must "make available on the Internet, in a manner that is readily accessible to all jurisdictions and to the public, all information about each sex offender in the registry." Posted sex offender information must include their name, photo, physical description, sex offense conviction history, place of work or schooling, vehicle description details, and license plate number. States may choose to post additional information. SORNA requires a convicted sex offender to register with the police or other designated agency in each jurisdiction where he resides, works, or attends school. For initial registration purposes only, a sex offender must also register in the jurisdiction where he or she was convicted. Individuals convicted of sex offenses in foreign countries must also register, unless the foreign conviction "*was not obtained with sufficient safeguards for fundamental fairness and due process for the accused under guidelines or regulations established* [by the Attorney General; emphasis added]."

Time will tell whether these initiatives will remain limited to sex offenders or lead to more controls over and disclosure of other convictions. Montana and Indiana have registries for individuals convicted of "violent crimes." Chicago has a registry for persons convicted of firearms offenses.[79] Registries have been proposed for persons convicted of methamphetamine trafficking, domestic violence, hate crimes, arson, and animal abuse.[80]

Posting Rap Sheets on the Internet

There is a trend toward more states making rap sheets accessible online. A 2001 SEARCH survey revealed that "some form of criminal history record or 'rap sheet' information is accessible online in 13 of 38 States responding to a recent e-mail survey on the availability of such information on the Internet."[81] In Kansas, the state Bureau of Investigation administers a Criminal History Record Check website that enables any individual, company, or organization to obtain criminal history record information on any individual for a $20 fee per request.[82]

Conclusion

The U.S. nationally integrated criminal record system links otherwise decentralized and autonomous police departments to one another. If it was used only for law enforcement purposes, it would not generate much controversy. However, concerns have been raised with respect to the suitability of the rap sheet system for non–criminal justice system users. Every state authorizes its criminal record repository to provide rap sheet information to government agencies for licensing and employment purposes. In addition, all states authorize their criminal records repositories to provide certain private sector employers and not-for-profit organizations with rap sheet information. While private security companies, schools, child services organizations, banks and financial institutions, and hospitals and medical facilities, are almost always authorized to obtain rap sheet information, states differ with respect to the access afforded to other categories of employers and voluntary organizations. Moreover, Congress directly authorizes access to the FBI criminal record database to various categories of organizations.

The problem is that rap sheets are not well suited to the needs and expertise of non–criminal justice system personnel, who have no easy way of chasing down missing rap sheet information. Suppose an employer sees an arrest without a corresponding disposition. Will the employer take the trouble to contact the arresting police agency or court? If so, how likely is it that the employer will get the missing information from busy police, prosecutors, or court clerks who may have no time and little inclination to search for the requested disposition information? It is much easier for the employer to move on to a job applicant who has no arrests on her record.

Even if an employer obtains the job applicant's full rap sheet, it is often difficult to read and interpret. For one thing, because criminal codes define general offenses—that is, assault, reckless endangerment, fraud, and theft—it is impossible to know with any specificity what the crime entailed. For another thing, pervasive plea-bargaining means that the conviction offense may be far different from the actual criminal conduct. It is unlikely that an employer will obtain the relevant police reports pertaining to the job applicant's prior arrests.

It is instructive to contrast the comprehensibility of criminal records and credit reports. The credit bureaus use risk models to translate credit history information into easily digestible credit reliability scores.[83] A user immediately knows that a credit score of 750 falls into the second quartile, while a score of 250 falls into the lowest quartile. There is no criminal record analogue, no way to compare the riskiness of two offenders: one who has two arrests for offenses A and B within the past five years, and a ten-year-old conviction for offense C; and the other who has one conviction for a more serious offense D just two years ago. Translating individual criminal histories into criminal history scores would be a daunting challenge given the huge number of different criminal offenses, extenuating circumstances, and participation in rehabilitation programs.

Moreover, the data from which credit scores are calculated are probably much more reliable than criminal history information. Outstanding credit card bills and bank loans are easily obtained; not so with prior criminality. Seeing the world as divided between "criminals" and "law-abiding citizens" is simplistic. A significant percentage of people who have never been convicted or even arrested have also committed crimes, sometimes serious and/or multiple crimes.[84] Consider the vast number of never-arrested people who have committed, but have never been arrested for, insurance or tax fraud; driving while intoxicated; possessing or selling illegal drugs; and engaging in domestic violence and other assaults. A good deal of chance (as well as prejudice) determines who gets arrested and, if arrested, charged.

The false positive rate is also high. Put aside the fact that some percentage of people arrested and not prosecuted were not guilty of any crime and that some who are convicted (at trial or upon plea) are not guilty. More important is the number of people who have been convicted but who do not recidivate. Even if the recidivism rate is as high as 40–50 percent, half of the people who are convicted do not recidivate, although some number of these have recidivated without being caught. Only a small percentage of people who are convicted of a crime will become "career" criminals. Most "street criminals" age out of crime by their thirties.* Although risk assessment tools have improved, it is impossible to predict accurately whether a particular individual will or will not recidivate. The best we can do is assign probabilities based on the previous conduct of individuals with similar characteristics—for example, age at first arrest, number and type of prior offenses, current age, marital status, and current employment.

---

* U.S. crime statistics show a consistent relationship between age and crime. Despite the declining crime-rate trend since 1990, the curve has maintained a similar shape across different types of crime, including robbery, burglary, and forcible rape. Adolescents and those in their early twenties are most likely to engage in violent and street crime.

4 COURT RECORDS

People in an open society do not demand infallibility from their institutions, but it is difficult for them to accept what they are prohibited from observing.

—U.S. Supreme Court (per Chief Justice Warren Burger), *Richmond Newspapers v. Virginia* (1980)[1]

Throughout the courts a sprawling amalgam of papers reflects action in connection with judicial proceedings. It is not misleading to think of courthouse papers as comprising a vast library of volumes for which docket sheets are the tables of contents. Without the card catalogue provided by alphabetical indices, a reader is left without a meaningful mechanism by which to find the documents necessary to learn what actually transpired in the courts. The indices thus are a key to effective public access to court activity.

—United States District Court for the District of Massachusetts, *Globe Newspaper Co. v. Fenton* (1993)[2]

UNLIKE RAP SHEETS, court records have always been available for public inspection. In *Nixon v. Warner Communications, Inc.* (1978), the Supreme Court observed:

> It is clear that the courts of this country recognize a general right to inspect and copy public records and documents, including judicial records and documents. In contrast to the English practice. . . . American decisions generally do not condition enforcement of this right on a proprietary interest in the document or upon a need for it as evidence in a lawsuit. The interest necessary to support the issuance of a writ compelling access has been found, for example, in the citizen's desire to keep a watchful eye on the workings of public agencies, . . . and in a newspaper publisher's intention to publish information concerning the operation of government. . . . It is uncontested, however, that the right to inspect and copy judicial records is

> not absolute. Every court has supervisory power over its own records and files, and access has been denied where court files might have become a vehicle for improper purposes.[3]

Accessible in theory was not the same as accessible in practice. Moreover, there has never been a national database of court records, that is, no court-records equivalent of Triple I. A searcher interested in finding an individual's "national criminal record" would have to search court records in every state where that individual might have lived, worked, or traveled. Indeed, in those states where there is no state-level index of criminal defendants or cases, the searcher would have to check court records in every county where the defendant might have gotten into trouble. Thus, while court records have always been publicly accessible,* they enjoyed "practical obscurity" before statewide court-record centralization and, more importantly, the advent of digitized records. Today, court records, criminal and civil, are far more accessible and searchable than they were a generation ago. And the trend is clearly in the direction of greater centralization and electronic access.

Centralization of Court Records

Searching court records used to be much more difficult because each county had its own court and each county court kept its own records. Without a statewide master index of all criminal defendants and cases in all of that state's courts, a searcher had to identify the specific courthouse(s) that held the information about the person of interest. The obvious courthouse(s) to visit were those in the counties where that person of interest had resided. However, many people have lived or worked in several counties, not all of which are

---

* To my knowledge, only the United States and Canada permit anyone to look at case files without having to persuade a judge or clerk that she has a good reason to see the file. For example, in the United Kingdom, criminal court records are not automatically available for public inspection. Court clerks exercise tremendous discretion in permitting or rejecting requests for access (e-mail communication with John Baldwin, emeritus professor and former dean of the University of Birmingham law faculty). See Chapter 9.

easily identified. In addition, the person of interest might have been prosecuted in counties in which he neither resided nor worked.

The searcher would have had to make a trip to the courthouses and, once there, ask the court clerk whether there is a court file in which the person of interest is listed as a party. If the searcher finds a promising lead, she had to ask the court clerk to retrieve the file. If the clerk was absent or busy, or if the file couldn't be found or was being used by a judge or someone else, the searcher would have to return on another day. Some files had to be retrieved from off-site archives. If the searcher wanted to copy all or part of the file, she had to stand in line to use the courthouse's coin-operated copy machine. This process was not impossible to navigate, but it was likely off-putting to an ordinary person and costly for a private investigator. Moreover, there was always the possibility that the identified person, though sharing the same name, was not actually the right person.

In the early twentieth century, law reformers began lobbying for unified state court systems,* that is, the state's courts "organized and managed in such a way as to provide, as nearly as possible, a uniform administration of justice throughout that state."[4] This required centralization, coordination, and uniform administration, which in turn promoted centralization of court records. Today, in the twenty-six states that have a unified court system, it is possible to search a statewide case file index.[5]

Computerization of Court Records

State courts began to computerize their records in the 1970s. By the mid-1980s, some courts had, for each pending case, an electronic docket sheet that judges, prosecutors, and defense lawyers could access. Over time (and with the assistance of federal grants), court personnel scanned old docket sheets into the database. In

---

* The movement to unify state courts dates back to Harvard Law School Dean Roscoe Pound's address to the 1906 American Bar Association's convention. Pound called the American court system archaic and wasteful of judicial resources. See R. Stanley Lowe, *Unified Courts in America: The Legacy of Roscoe Pound*, 56 Judicature 316 (1973).

unified court administration states, it became possible to retrieve an individual's statewide criminal cases going further and further back in time.[6]

Although some states formed judges' committees to consider what information, if any, to redact and whether the database should be available for sale to commercial information vendors, computerization did not cause fundamental rethinking of public access.[7] Some state court administrators created publicly accessible electronic databases that could be searched by defendant's name or case number to retrieve limited amounts of case file information from all or many of the state's courts. For example, the Washington State courts' online database allows a searcher with a defendant's name or case number to locate the court that holds the case file.[8] As the IT revolution progressed, some court systems' databases made more information from court files available online, including disposition information.[9] This made courthouse visiting less necessary or not necessary at all. Court records no longer existed in "practical obscurity."[10]

The federal courts' PACER (Public Access to Court Electronic Records) system is the United States' most advanced computerized court records system.[11] In the early 1990s, a searcher could dial into PACER with a modem to access and download information. In 1998, PACER became accessible via the Internet. Some federal districts adopted and encouraged electronic filing of motions and briefs. Older case files were gradually scanned into the database. Today, a searcher with a case number or the defendant's name can use PACER to search the federal cases database as far back as 1989 (and, in some districts, back to the 1960s or even the 1950s). For post-1999 criminal cases, PACER provides instant access to indictments, pretrial motions, attorneys' briefs, sentences, and written judicial rulings and opinions. (Downloading costs ten cents per viewed page.)[12] The docket sheets for pre-1999 cases are available online, but the searcher must visit the relevant courthouse or a Federal Records Center to see the case file itself.[13] Federal court documents are even more easily accessible via RECAP, a project of the Center for Information Technology at Princeton University. RECAP encourages PACER users to download to RECAP any legal document they obtain via PACER.[14] RECAP provides free access to documents that are available from PACER for a fee. (Because government documents are not copyrighted, a private organization can lawfully republish them.)

There is a great deal of variation in the extent and sophistication of court records computerization.[15] New York State, for example, has a unified court system and an electronically accessible IT system ("eCourts") with a dedicated "Webcrims" that makes it possible to retrieve docket sheets for pending criminal cases.[16] Users can search by ID number or defendant name. Although Webcrims makes only pending cases electronically accessible, the New York State Office of Court Administration (OCA) provides any requester, upon payment of a $65 fee, any individual's New York State criminal record, including arrests, charges, dispositions, and sentences, back to 1987 for New York City courts and to the early 1980s for other counties' courts. In other states (e.g., Maine), case file information cannot be accessed remotely.[17]

Active Dissemination of Criminal Record Information

About twenty state court systems sell copies (downloads) of their docket sheets to commercial information vendors.[18] Connecticut, for example, offers a year's subscription with monthly updates to its docket sheet database of criminal conviction cases for $1,100; a one-time download costs $300.[19] Ohio sells its most recent electronic compilation of county court records but requires purchasers to subscribe to regular updates.[20] In 2007, the New Jersey court system had twelve standing orders for its docket database; half included monthly update orders.[21] New Jersey also makes dockets electronically available.[22]

Some states, such as Idaho, only allow bulk electronic court records to be distributed "for scholarly, journalistic, political, governmental, research, evaluation, or statistical purposes."[23] Bulk distribution of electronic court data is generally not allowed, but the state supreme court can grant access to electronic bulk court data for one of these purposes. To use the records for other purposes technically constitutes contempt of court.

In Arkansas, commercial vendors succeeded in changing a policy that prohibited courts from providing them access to court record databases. Under the new policy, a commercial purchaser must sign an agreement to regularly update its database. Moreover, the purchaser must promise to verify convictions by visiting or contacting the county courthouse where the conviction was rendered. A commercial information vendor who violates the terms of the agreement may be required to forfeit a $5,000 bond.[24] As of early 2014, no vendor has had a bond forfeited.[25]

Types of Court Records Containing Individual Criminal History Information

Much more information about the charges against defendants can be gleaned from court records than from rap sheets. This could make a criminal record search based on court records more thorough and nuanced than a rap sheet search, but it also reveals more personal information about the defendant and the victim. In order to assess the comparative advantages and disadvantages of court records and rap sheets as information sources, it is necessary to know what information court records contain.

CALENDARS (SOMETIMES CALLED DOCKETS)

Courts routinely produce a publicly accessible daily (arraignment) calendar, or docket,* that lists which arrestees and defendants will appear in which courtroom for arraignments, pretrial hearings, guilty plea allocutions, trials, and sentencing. The calendar enables defendants and their friends and family members, victims and witnesses, and lawyers to get to the right courtroom at the right time. It also enables journalists and commercial information vendors to find out who has been charged with what crimes, thereby confirming that a particular individual has a criminal record. Many courts now make their calendars available online.[26]

---

* *Black's Law Dictionary* (9th ed., 2009) defines "docket" as a "schedule of pending cases" and notes that it is sometimes called a court calendar.

DOCKET SHEETS

A docket sheet provides a chronological history of the defendant's court appearances and lists the documents contained in the case file.[27] For example, the docket sheet available from the federal Public Access to Court Electronic Records (PACER) system in *U.S. v. Peters* lists orders, motions, and the defendant's appearances in the case.[28] It shows the date following a postponement of defendant Peters's arraignment. The U.S. Second Circuit Court of Appeals has held that because "the ability of the public and press to attend civil and criminal cases would be merely theoretical" otherwise, the public, including the media, has a qualified First Amendment right to inspect docket sheets.[29]

ONLINE CASE INDEXES

An online case index is a database of cases that can be searched by a defendant's name or identification number. It allows court personnel to determine where a case file is physically located[30] and the date, time, and location of the next court appearance.[31] Some indexes provide information about only pending cases,[32] while others contain entries for all cases filed since a certain date, whether pending or completed.[33] Prior years' indexes have to be searched at the courthouse.[34]

For example, an online name search for "James Jacobs" in the case index system for the Superior Court of California, County of Sacramento, shows that Gregory Duke Churchill used "James Jacobs" as one of a number of aliases. The case index reveals that Churchill (aka Jacobs) was charged with assault with a deadly weapon and provides a chronology of Churchill's court appearances. It shows that he ultimately pled guilty to one count of assault with a deadly weapon. The index includes information on Churchill's sentence: 150 days in custody plus five years' probation. It also shows that Churchill subsequently violated probation and was sentenced to thirty additional days' incarceration.

The information provided by this index search contains more details about the charges against Churchill than his rap sheet, although, importantly, it is information only about this case. Our search does not reveal whether, in the past, he faced other charges in this or other courts. Note also that this was a name, not a fingerprint, search. Name searches are susceptible to error and confusion because multiple people share or use the same name.

CASE FILES

Federal, state, and local courts create hard copy files on every civil and criminal case. The case file usually contains a defendant's rap sheet, indictment or information,* prosecutors' and defense counsel's pretrial motions (e.g., to suppress a confession), responses to motions, judge's rulings, and notations on plea, judgment, and sentence.[35] If there was a printed trial transcript, it will be available to the public although, in a few jurisdictions, not if there was an acquittal. In the event of an appeal, there will be an appeals court case file containing trial transcript and appellate briefs. (Increasingly, courts make appellate briefs available online.)[36] Published judicial decisions, often containing facts about the crime and the defendant, remain publicly accessible forever, even if the conviction is subsequently reversed or the defendant pardoned.†

Sealing and Redacting Court Records

In determining when and what criminal case file information should be sealed, a defendant's reputational privacy and rehabilitation must be balanced against the public's right to know. In New York State, when a case ends in a disposition "favorable to the defendant" (e.g., dismissal or acquittal), the case file must be sealed, that is, made inaccessible to the general public. Moreover, any document that permits identification of a sex crime *victim* must be sealed.[37] In Bronx County, the court clerk removes from the case file the New York State ID

---

* About half of U.S. states routinely use grand juries. In the non–grand jury states, formal charges are initiated by a sworn prosecutorial instrument, called an "information." When a case is initiated by an information, the defendant is entitled to an adversarial preliminary hearing at which the prosecution must prove to a judge that there is probable cause to hold the defendant to answer the charges.

† Spain and some other European countries anonymize a criminal defendant's name in published judicial opinions in order to protect reputational privacy. See Chapter 9.

sheet (the arrest record), the pretrial service agency's interview report (containing information about the defendant's current and prior residences, living arrangements, personal contacts, employment and income, and current schooling),[38] medical and psychiatric reports, probation or presentence report, grand jury witnesses' testimony, personal information about sex offense victims, and any document that the court specifically marks sealed or confidential.[39] In New Jersey, presentence reports, TASC (Treatment Assessment Services for the Courts) reports, bail reports, victims' letters, certain discovery documents, handwritten trial notes, jury lists, and competency/psychiatric reports are not publicly accessible.[40] In addition, when a sex crime victim's identity would be revealed by publishing the defendant's name (i.e., in cases of sex crimes within a family), the court's opinion will be published with the defendant's name anonymized.[41]

The federal courts do not permit public access to arrest and search warrant applications; presentence reports; juvenile records; documents containing identifying information about jurors or potential jurors; financial affidavits filed to obtain court-appointed counsel; ex parte requests for investigative, expert, and certain other services; cooperating witnesses' motions for downward sentencing departures; plea agreements indicating cooperation; and victims' statements.[42] Federal district court judges have discretion to seal other documents "if closure is essential to preserve higher values and is narrowly tailored to preserve that interest."[43]

Sealed documents and information can be unsealed for good cause.[44] For example, a California Coastal Commissioner pled guilty to soliciting bribes and racketeering.[45] In hopes of obtaining a sentence reduction, he filed two letters alleging that a high-ranking public official had approached him to obtain a favorable Commission decision. The district court sealed these letters to protect the high-ranking (uncharged) public official's reputation and the defendant commissioner's safety. The *Sacramento Bee* sought to have these letters unsealed. The district court judge refused, questioning the newsworthiness and truthfulness of the proffer letters and stated that he had not relied on these letters in reducing the defendant's sentence. The Ninth Circuit Court of Appeals disagreed, holding that the public official's reputational interest did not constitute a substantial government interest, unlike, for example, protecting the identity of jurors or sex offense victims. "Injury to official reputation is an insufficient reason for repressing speech that would otherwise be free" and to silence the press to protect a public official's reputation "is much more likely to 'engender resentment, suspicion, and contempt much more than it would enhance respect.'"[46]

PRESENTENCE REPORTS

In order to give the sentencing judge the fullest possible picture of the convicted defendant, the presentence report (PSR) typically includes a great deal of personal information (opinions, hearsay, even rumor and gossip) about the defendant.* For example, according to California law, "[a]t the time of the plea or verdict of guilty of any person over 18 years of age, the probation officer of the county of the jurisdiction of said criminal shall, when so directed by the court, *inquire into the antecedents, character, history, family environment, and offense* of such person, and must report the same to the court and file his report in writing in the records of such court."[47] Practically all jurisdictions treat the PSR as a confidential document to encourage people to volunteer information and to protect the defendant from disclosure of embarrassing information.[48]

Until 1975, a federal defendant did not have access to the PSR that the judge used to sentence him. That year, an amendment to Federal Rules of Criminal Procedure 32(c)(3) required that, before imposing sentence, the judge permit the defendant and his counsel to read the report, except portions containing diagnostic opinions, confidential sources of information, or information that, if disclosed, might cause harm to the defendant or others. (After sentencing, the PSR is transmitted to the Bureau of Prisons for use in classification decisions and to the Parole Commission.)†

---

* In *Blakely v. Washington* (2004), Justice Scalia commented that presentence reports result in sentences "based not on facts proved to [one's] peers beyond a reasonable doubt, but on facts extracted after trial from a report compiled by a probation officer who the judge thinks more likely got it right than got it wrong." 542 U.S. 296, 311–12 (2004).

† The Sentencing Reform Act of 1984 (SRA) eliminated parole for federal civilian defendants sentenced for crimes committed after November 1, 1987. However, federal defendants sentenced for offenses committed before passage of the SRA are still eligible

In 1988, the Supreme Court held in *U.S. Department of Justice v. Julian* that an individual could use the Freedom of Information Act to obtain his or her PSR from the correctional agency's files.[49] According to the court, Congress intended to exempt disclosure of PSRs to third parties in order to safeguard the record-subject's privacy interest, but that interest is not at stake when the record-subject himself or herself seeks the PSR prepared for sentencing. Thus, the defendant had the right to see the PSR, except portions containing diagnostic opinions, confidential sources of information, or information that, if disclosed, might cause harm to the defendant or others. The public has no constitutional or statutory right to see the PSR. (The government argued that prison inmates might be pressured by their fellow inmates to retrieve their PSRs for reasons of extortion.)

Despite persuasive reasons to maintain PSR confidentiality, a few states make PSRs publicly available.[50] They base that policy on the public's interest in knowing why a defendant received or did not receive a particular sentence. For example, California's policy, dating to the pre-computer era, makes PSRs publicly available for sixty days after judgment.[51] If, during that window, a commercial information vendor or any individual reads, takes notes on, and copies the PSR, its confidentiality is lost. In California, even after sixty days have passed, an "interested party" can petition the court to see a PSR. The defendant has the right to a hearing to challenge disclosure, but without a right to appointed counsel, it would be extremely difficult for a defendant to successfully litigate, especially against a media petitioner. Interestingly, neither California prosecutors nor probation officers have sought to change this rule,[52] perhaps casting doubt on the view that making PSRs publicly accessible would undermine their quality and usefulness.

COOPERATION AGREEMENTS

The need to protect information about witness cooperation has generated controversy.[53] Federal prosecutors rely heavily on coop-

---

for parole. See United States Courts, *Parole in the Federal Probation System*, http://www.uscourts.gov/news/TheThirdBranch/11-05-01/Parole_in_the_Federal_Probation_System.aspx.

erating witnesses, usually defendants who assist the government by providing information and testimony against their former criminal associates.[54] In exchange for a charge or sentence concession, the cooperating witness agrees to plead guilty and to assist the government in building cases against other individuals. If the cooperating witness is going to testify at trial, the cooperation agreement must be disclosed to the defense before that witness is called to testify. However, prosecutors argue that if the cooperating witness does not testify, it should not be necessary to place the cooperation agreement in the cooperating witness's case file or, if it is put in the case file, it should be sealed in order to protect the cooperator from retaliation. Prosecutors also argue that it will be more difficult to recruit cooperators if the fact of their cooperation can become public.[55] Journalists and some academics respond that the public has a right to know what kind of cooperation agreements prosecutors have negotiated with particular defendants and that cooperators know there is a risk of disclosure when they agree to testify if necessary.

Even when the prosecutor and judge agree that the cooperation agreement should be kept confidential, they disagree about how to do it. A notation on the docket sheet that the case file contains a sealed document would be a red flag indicating defendant cooperation with the prosecution. To prevent that tip-off, the federal district court in North Dakota requires that a sealed "plea supplement" be placed in every criminal case file. An observer will not know which sealed supplements are empty and which contain a cooperation agreement. Open government proponents argue that this solution fails to provide the public with important information about the concessions that prosecutors are making to obtain cooperation.

The Department of Justice has suggested two alternatives. The first is to remove all plea agreements (not just those involving cooperation) from PACER but permit courthouse access to the hard-copy plea agreement. This would make it somewhat, but not much, more difficult to find out who provided evidence against a particular defendant. The second proposal would make plea agreements unavailable from PACER and at the courthouse but would disclose them to defense lawyers who need them to represent their clients.[56] Critics argue that that proposal would put sensitive information in the hands of the very party most likely to retaliate against the cooperator, while keeping scholars, nongovernmental organizations (NGOs), and the media in the dark. Neither alternative is satisfactory.

In an insightful law review article, Professor Caren Myers Morrison proposes periodic release of cooperation agreements with the cooperating witnesses' names redacted, thereby permitting scrutiny of the federal prosecutors' concessions in exchange for assistance, but without disclosing the cooperator's identity. She argues that her proposal would protect the cooperator's physical safety, while satisfying the public's right to know about the "deals" prosecutors make with criminal defendants:[57]

> Unlike the more forgiving world of paper records and fallible human memory, in cyberspace, nothing is ever forgotten. Information remains eternally fresh, springing to the screen as quickly years later as it did on the day it was first generated. If all federal defendants run the risk of becoming a permanently stigmatized underclass, cut off from legitimate opportunities of mainstream society, cooperating defendants are further burdened with potential rejection by their former communities.[58]

Morrison is correct that what is of most public interest is the "deal," not the identity of the parties to the deal (although, arguably, there is a public interest in knowing what concessions were made to organized crime bosses and notorious white collar offenders). However, it might be difficult to judge the appropriateness of an information-for-leniency deal without knowing the background (i.e., the identity) of the defendant beneficiary. Furthermore, a knowledgeable person would likely be able to read between the lines and match deals with defendants; the more information included in the redacted cooperation agreement, the easier it will be to make the connection. Morrison's proposal, although perhaps the best compromise to date, is vulnerable to the criticism that it provides too much information to those who might want to retaliate against a cooperator and too little information to journalists and academic researchers who want to assess the fairness and wisdom of the deals prosecutors make. There may be no getting around the fact that publicly accessible court records present a certain risk to defendants and others whose actions and testimony are memorialized in court records.

DISMISSALS AND ACQUITTALS

Why should unproven charges against an individual be a permanent stain on character? Journalists, researchers, and some NGOs insist that to monitor police, prosecutors, and courts effectively, all cases, including dismissals and acquittals, must be available for public scrutiny. In any event, they say, even in cases that end in dismissal or acquittal, the charges will have been public for months, maybe longer, and the defendant will have appeared in court. In other words, the public will already have had access to the charges against the defendant.

State policies vary. In Massachusetts, for example, a case file can be sealed if the judge specifically finds that sealing is necessary to achieve a "compelling government interest that outweighs the First Amendment presumption of public access."[59] The defendant must demonstrate that he or she risks suffering specific harm (something more than general reputational injury) if the record is not sealed.[60] In *Commonwealth v. Doe*,* a Boston University freshman was arrested for rape. Finding the victim's allegations unsubstantiated, the prosecutor moved, and the court agreed, to dismiss the case in the interest of justice. The defendant moved to seal the record to protect his reputation. The Massachusetts Supreme Judicial Court affirmed the trial court's refusal, explaining that "a defendant must show that the interests of confidentiality and avoiding harm have specific application to him or her" and that "the value of sealing to the defendant clearly outweighs the constitutionally-based value of the record remaining open to society."[61] By contrast, New York State law requires that court records be sealed following termination of the case "in favor of the accused" (i.e., dismissal, acquittal), unless the judge finds that sealing the record would not be "in the interests of justice."[62] (Sealing and expunging records is the subject of Chapter 7.)

---

* Doe is a pseudonym. The court allowed a motion by the defendant to anonymize the case caption. *Commonwealth v. Doe*, 420 Mass. 142 (1995), at note 1.

Conclusion

Court records constitute the most available and most widely used source of information about the charges against criminal defendants. Criminal court records, including dockets and case files, have traditionally been publicly accessible. The Supreme Court has all but explicitly said that the public has a First Amendment right of access to court records. Because court records are open to the public and the media, it is important to focus on what information they contain. Court records include various dockets, indexes, and case files created to facilitate the processing of criminal cases from first court appearance through arraignment, pretrial motions, trial, and sentencing. The adjudication of a criminal case necessitates multiple court appearances and generates numerous recorded notations and documents. These are mostly recorded on docket sheets and assigned to case files. Both have been made increasingly available to the public by means of state court centralization, computerization, and online access.

The principle that court business should be transparent is firmly rooted in American tradition and constitutional law. Whether as a way of furthering judicial transparency or raising revenue, court administrators are increasingly required or authorized to sell their criminal cases databases to commercial vendors. This usually means indexes of case names, not the full case file. For the most part, consumers of criminal background reports are interested in whether a person of interest has been convicted or even charged with a crime. The details of the charges are likely to be of much less interest, although, arguably, more details would make for better decision making.

The most interesting policy questions involve which, if any, documents submitted to the court should and can be kept confidential. The best candidate is the presentence report, which often contains very personal information about the defendant. Most of this information about the defendant's childhood, adolescence, and current circumstances is a legacy of rehabilitation-oriented sentencing and is unrelated to the charges against the defendant. The state has not charged the defendant with being a bad son, husband, or father or with having a drug or sex addiction. Thus, the public's interest in having this information is weaker than its interest in having information about the crime itself. Therefore, there ought to be a presumption that the presentence report be sealed. By contrast, cooperation agreements are more closely related to the charges against the defendant and to the guilt of defendants against whom the cooperator has provided incriminating information. This is not personal information. In addition, there is a strong public interest in the deals that cooperators receive.

5 PRIVATIZING CRIMINAL RECORDS

> Consumer reporting agencies play a "vital role" in our economy by providing [creditors, insurers, and employers] the facts they need to make sound decisions. But by assembling and disseminating volumes of information about individuals, consumer reporting agencies have the power unduly to invade individuals' privacy and to cause unfair harm by disclosing inaccurate information.
>
> —Senate Committee on Banking and Currency, *Fair Credit Reporting: Report to Accompany S. 823* (1969)[1]

> No one should have to go to the courthouse to find out if their kid's baseball coach has been arrested, or if the person they're going on a date with tonight has been arrested. . . . Our goal is to make that information available online, without having to jump through any hoops.
>
> —Arthur D'Antonio III, founder of JustMugshots.com, quoted in the *New York Times* (2013)[2]

CRIMINAL BACKGROUND checking is a booming business. Hundreds of companies, for a modest fee, provide individual criminal history information to employers, landlords, volunteer organizations, and even governmental agencies. Some companies sell mobile apps that allow those with smartphones or tablets to conduct limited criminal background searches of databases. Some companies stream mug shots on a website, then offer to remove them for a fee.[3] Some not-for-profit organizations post specialized offender databases (e.g., domestic violence offenders) as a public service to inform potential victims about possibly dangerous individuals and, by naming and shaming, to deter criminal behavior. These developments vastly complicate criminal records terrain and policy options.

Commercial Information Vendors

Companies that sell criminal background checks range from large national firms that download bulk court data to their own proprietary criminal record databases to small companies that conduct criminal background checks by searching publicly available data. Barriers to entering the "industry"[4] are very low. In its 2005 report, the National Task Force on the Commercial Sale of Criminal Justice Record Information noted:

> In addition to a few large industry players, there are hundreds, perhaps even thousands, of regional and local companies. Given the number of vendors and the variety of business models they employ, the Task Force was unable to quantify the overall number of commercial vendors, the overall number of criminal background checks conducted for noncriminal justice purposes in the United States in a given year, or the overall revenues of this sector of the information industry.[5]

The National Association of Professional Background Screeners (NAPBS), the commercial information vendors' trade association, claims to have 700 members,[6] composed of "public record retrievers," "small and mid-size screening firms," "large screening firms," and "software and data providers."[7] It estimates the industry's annual revenue at $4 billion. A 2011 KPMG survey named the five "most significant national and regional competitors":[8]

1. Altegrity, formerly USIS, acquired HireRight in 2008 and Kroll in 2010. HireRight advertises that its Widescreen Plus database includes hundreds of millions of records from sources like county courts and sex offender registries, state Administrative Offices of Courts, Departments of Correction, Departments of Public Safety, and the federal Office of Foreign Asset Control (OFAC).[9] In 2008, USIS/HireRight claimed to have more than 27,000 clients, ranging from small businesses to global enterprises, including approximately 21 percent of U.S. Fortune 500 firms.[10]
2. LexisNexis's parent company, Reed Elsevier, acquired ChoicePoint in 2008 for $4.1 billion. In 2008, ChoicePoint, which Equifax (the credit bureau) spun off in 1997, was one of the largest data aggregation companies, holding more than 17 billion records (including 90 million criminal records) and serving 50,000 clients.[11] ChoicePoint built this database by

sending "runners" to copy courthouse records and by acquiring small local firms.[12] In 2002, ChoicePoint conducted approximately 3.3 million background checks; the "vast majority" were for criminal record searches.[13] In June 2004, ChoicePoint expanded significantly by acquiring RapSheets .com.

3. Sterling Infosystems acquired Tandem Select, AISS (from Acxiom), and BackCheck in 2011 and 2012. Sterling now calls itself the "the largest company in the world focusing entirely on background screening services." It claims that its 16,000 customers include 25 percent of the Fortune 100.[14] Sterling conducted 1.5 million criminal background checks in 2010.[15]
4. First Advantage boasts that its Our National Criminal File contains over 352 million criminal records (from all fifty states) and that it conducts more than 9 million background checks annually.[16]
5. ADP Screening and Selection Services, Inc., has a CrimLink database containing 120 million criminal records (from forty-three states).[17] The company claims to have conducted 1.7 million background checks in 2008, with 6 percent of the checks turning up a criminal record.

Three other very large information vendors are Accurate Background, Inc.; IntelliCorp Records, Inc.; and CoreLogic's National Background Data.[18] The information vendors obtain information from court records and other publicly available sources. Where electronic searching isn't possible, they send "runners" to courthouses.

Commercial information vendors solicit business by warning employers about the risks of failing to screen job applicants and incumbent employees properly. For example, "Violence, theft, and drug use are reasons alone to prescreen applicants. . . . [T]he consequences of shortcutting these simple steps can be devastating—ranging from massive financial settlements, bad publicity, and, in the worst case, loss of life."[19] According to the vendors, criminal background screening protects companies from civil liability resulting from injuries and damages caused by dishonest, unreliable, and dangerous employees.[20] Background checking may shield the employer from negligent hiring liability,[21] but not from *respondeat superior* liability that makes a principal responsible for tortious injuries caused by employees acting within the scope of their employment (see Chapter 14).

The digital revolution has driven down the cost of criminal background searches. For searching just its own databases, a commercial information vendor may charge $10–$20. US Search's "Instant State Criminal Search" costs as little as $9.85 for a one-state search. A nationwide court and other public records search costs $60–$80. Companies often pass the cost of the background check on to the job applicant.

An examination of criminal records policy options must recognize that there is now an entrenched private sector infrastructure of commercial information vendors that meets and stokes demand for criminal background checks. Like any business group, these companies and their trade association lobby for and against laws that affect them.

Customers

Private employers are the majority of criminal background check customers. Landlords, voluntary associations, banks, insurance companies, and other entities and individuals are also purchasers. Some government agencies find it more efficient and faster to obtain criminal background checks from private vendors than from government criminal record repositories.*

---

* The Privacy Act of 1974 protects personal information held in computer databases by federal agencies. It restricts unauthorized disclosure, grants individuals access to records about themselves and requires that record-subjects have an opportunity to challenge record inaccuracies. With minor exceptions, the act does not apply to federal law enforcement agencies. United States Department of Justice, Office of Privacy and Civil Liberties, *Overview of the Privacy Act of 1974, 2010 Edition* 4 (2010), http://www.justice.gov/opcl/1974privacyact-overview.htm; see also 5 U.S.C. § 552a. According to Chris Hoofnagle, director of Information Privacy Programs at the University of California, Berkeley Center for Law and Technology, federal agencies sometimes use private vendors as "private escrows for information that the government could not itself collect

Criminal Record Reports and Credit Scores Compared

The commercial criminal background checking companies report raw data to their customers, for example, that John Doe was convicted in 1998 for selling marijuana, convicted in 2003 for drunk driving (fine plus probation), convicted in 2007 for burglary (three-year suspended prison sentence), and arrested in 2010 for assault (no disposition). It is up to the customer to evaluate the record's seriousness and predictive value.

Compare a criminal record report with a consumer credit report. The credit bureaus translate credit history information into easily interpreted credit reliability scores. They furnish their customers with the record-subject's credit score (FICO),* ranging from 300 to 850 (the higher the score, the better the credit risk). Without examining raw data about the credit applicant's bill-paying history, customers can easily determine whether the credit applicant is an excellent, good, fair, or bad credit risk. Moreover, unlike a criminal record, a credit score can change over time as the person becomes more or less financially responsible.

Imagine a criminal record score analogous to a credit score. A high score would allay concern about a person's criminal propensities; a low number would indicate significant risk. An individual's score would improve as time from last conviction or arrest passed without a new crime. Employers could compare the criminal riskiness of persons with different criminal record scores.

Admittedly, constructing a criminal record score poses a formidable challenge. Criminal conduct is more complicated than defaulting

---

legally." Chris Jay Hoofnagle, *Big Brother's Little Helpers: How ChoicePoint and Other Commercial Data Brokers Collect and Package Your Data for Law Enforcement*, 29 N.C. J. Int'l L. & Com. Reg. 595, 598, 623 (2004). See also Daniel J. Solove and Chris Jay Hoofnagle, *A Model Regime of Privacy Protection*, 2006 U. Ill. L. Rev. 357 (2006). Jim Harper, director of Information Policy Studies at the Cato Institute, calls the Privacy Act a "paper tiger" because it does not apply to commercial information vendors. See http://www.politechbot.com/2005/03/18/catos-jim-harper/.

* The three major U.S. consumer reporting agencies or credit bureaus (Equifax, Experian, and Trans Union) rely on FICO credit-scoring software. Using financial information obtained from banks and other sources, the credit bureaus produce scores that may differ slightly for the same individual.

on a loan or filing for bankruptcy. Moreover, a statistical risk of recidivating does not tell us much unless we know what kind of recidivism. A risk of future drunk and disorderly conduct is different from a risk of domestic violence, which is different from a risk of embezzlement. Employers will be concerned about the risk of job-related criminality (although any criminal case might affect the employee's attendance, concentration, and performance). Different employers are concerned about different kinds of risk. Perhaps there would need to be more than one score, for example, a risk-of-dishonesty score and a risk-of-violence score. Recent advances in risk assessment instruments (mostly used to predict recidivism by pretrial releases, probationers, and parolees) have made headway in predicting future violence, but they are based on detailed information and clinical assessments that are not readily available to criminal background checking companies.[22]

Regulating Commercial Information Vendors

The Fair Credit Reporting Act (FCRA) of 1970 sought to regulate companies engaged in credit reporting.[23] The bill's chief sponsor, Senator William Proxmire (D-WI), observed that

> most Americans still do not realize the vast size and scope of today's credit reporting industry or the tremendous amount of information which these companies maintain and distribute. . . . While the growth of this information network is somewhat alarming, what is even more alarming is the fact that the system has been built up with virtually no public regulation or supervision.[24]

Proxmire was reacting to threats to informational privacy in 1970, well before widespread use of personal computers and even longer before the advent of the Internet.

The FCRA sought to balance banks', creditors', and employers' interests in making well-informed decisions with protecting record-subjects from dissemination of inaccurate, misleading, and outdated information.[25] It imposed obligations on "consumer reporting agencies" (CRAs), defined as "any person [including a business] which, for monetary fees, dues, or on a cooperative nonprofit basis, regularly engages, in whole or in part, in the practice of assembling or evaluating consumer credit information *or other information on consumers* for the purpose of furnishing consumer reports to third parties, and which uses any means or facility of interstate commerce for the purpose of preparing or furnishing consumer reports."[26] The FCRA defines a "consumer report" as

> any written, oral, or other communications of any information by a consumer reporting agency bearing on a consumer's credit worthiness, credit standing, credit capacity, *character*, *general reputation*, *personal characteristics*, or mode of living which is used or expected to be used or collected in whole or in part for the purpose of serving as a factor in establishing the consumer's eligibility for [credit, insurance, employment, or eligibility for government benefits or administrative purposes].[27]

This definition clearly applies to companies that provide employers with criminal history reports. However, the FCRA's primary focus was on preventing and correcting reporting errors, a topic we will return to in Chapter 7, and not on limiting disclosure of true criminal record information.

Notwithstanding its focus on consumer report accuracy, the FCRA originally prohibited CRAs from reporting arrests and convictions more than seven years old. However, in 1998, Congress eliminated the time restriction on reporting convictions.[28] Arrests more than seven years old that have not resulted in a conviction cannot be reported unless the record-subject is applying for a job that pays more than $75,000 per year.[29] The reason for linking reporting to salaries is not explained. Probably, the business community successfully argued that a higher salary indicates a position of greater trust and responsibility and that greater honesty, reliability, and self-discipline are more important for such positions.

Commercial Information Vendors' Resistance to FCRA Regulation

Seeking to avoid even the FCRA's very limited regulation, some commercial information vendors accompany their consumer reports with a seemingly disingenuous warning that the client may not use the report to make employment decisions.* Sometimes such disclaimers appear in fine print on a separate webpage.[30] Whether or not the client reads that warning, it gives the commercial information vendor, if sued, grounds to argue that its criminal background check was not meant for employment purposes.

PublicData.com denies being a CRA and directs potential customers to consult counsel before using individual criminal history information. Its website charges that the FCRA is unconstitutional: "We remain dedicated to the idea that all citizens of our free society should have access to all of the records that government collects (except information critical to national security and information involving ongoing criminal investigations). Likewise we will continue to lead the industry in 'low cost' real-time access to Public Records."[31]

Universal Background Screening offered background checks for both "personal" and "employment" purposes and explained that only the latter is governed by the FCRA.[32] Some companies refer employers who want criminal background checks to affiliated FCRA-compliant companies.[33] Others "caution" clients that their background reports cannot be used for employment purposes.

Some CRAs have tried to circumvent the prohibition on reporting more than seven-year- old arrests that did not resulted in convictions by informing clients that "[t]his applicant has an arrest/incident on his/her criminal history that is NOT a conviction, and is over 7 years old. In accordance with Federal guidelines, we need to verify that this applicant will make at least $75,000 per year in order to make this information available to you." A federal court in Pennsylvania

---

* See, e.g., http://www.criminalsearches.com/terms.aspx: "We are not a 'consumer reporting agency' and the information in our Site has not been collected for the purpose of furnishing 'consumer reports,' as such terms are defined in the Fair Credit Reporting Act (the 'FCRA'). You are prohibited from using this Site and any information in this Site (a) as a factor in establishing an individual's eligibility for personal credit or insurance, (b) as a factor in evaluating an individual for employment, (c) in connection with any personal business transaction with an individual, or (d) for any purpose for which one might use a 'consumer report,' as defined in the FCRA. You must certify that you will comply with these Limits on Your Use of Our Site prior to accessing information on this Site."

found in *Serrano v. Sterling* that this disclaimer violated the FCRA. Some courts have held that the appropriate test of whether a criminal record report is covered by the FCRA is how the information vendor reasonably expects its reports to be used.* It is difficult to see how commercial information vendors who market criminal background checks in the manner described in the previous paragraphs could persuasively claim that they do not expect their reports to be used to screen employees, renters, and insurance applicants.

State Regulation

About half the states have their own fair credit reporting laws.[34] A few impose tougher regulatory requirements on CRAs than federal law. For example, California, New Mexico, and New York prohibit CRAs from reporting arrests unless either (1) a conviction resulted or (2) charges emanating from the arrest are still pending.[35] A number of states, including California, Massachusetts, Montana, Nevada, New Mexico, New York, and Texas, prohibit reporting convictions whose sentence expired more than seven years earlier.[36] California, Minnesota, and Oklahoma require employers to provide employees and job applicants with copies of consumer reports (even if no adverse action is taken).[37] California requires CRAs to post privacy practices on their websites.[38]†

---

* See, e.g., *Ippolito v. WNS, Inc.*, 864 F.2d 440, 449–51, n. 10 (7th Cir. 1988): "[T]he plain language of the statute, 'used or expected to be used or collected in whole or in part' requires inquiry into the reasons why the report was requested and why the information contained in the report was collected or expected to be used by the consumer reporting agency." Also, *Heath v. Credit Bureau of Sheridan, Inc.*, 618 F.2d 693, 696 (10th Cir. 1980): "We believe a critical phrase in the definition of consumer report is the second requirement: the relevant information must be 'used or expected to be used or collected in whole or in part for the purpose of serving as a factor' with regard to enumerated transactions. This phrase clearly requires judicial inquiry into the motives of the credit-reporting agency, for only it 'collects' the information. Similarly, the term 'expected to be used' would seem to refer to what the reporting agency believed."

† Federal preemption of state law is based on the Constitution's supremacy clause. Preemption issues arise when Congress and the states both seek to regulate the same activities. State laws are preempted if they frustrate or are incompatible with the object of federal regulation. It is often difficult to determine when federal and state regulations are incompatible. See *Cisneros v. U.D. Registry, Inc.*, 39 Cal. App. 4th 548, 577 (1995).

There are real costs (ultimately borne by consumers) to making private information vendors comply with fifty-one different federal and state statutes. Moreover, job seekers living in states with looser regulation may be disadvantaged in competing for jobs with job seekers in states with stricter regulation. Thus, a federal regulatory approach is preferable to state regulation.

Noncommercial Criminal Record Providers

NGOS

Some advocacy groups post online individual criminal history information in furtherance of their sociopolitical agendas.[39] For example, the National Domestic Violence Registry (NDVR) posts the names of persons (women and men) convicted of domestic violence offenses or subject to domestic violence protections orders so that "individuals can make better informed choices about their private life":[40]

> NDVR is the first national database model for domestic violence convictions available to the public. We began this registry because we believe women need and would greatly benefit from knowing more about an individual before deciding to date them. The National Domestic Violence Registry is just that. It allows both women and men to have the opportunity of knowing if they are dating someone who has been abusive, predatory and violent in their past relationships.[41]

The NDVR database of domestic violence perpetrators can be searched by name or by state.

The FCRA explicitly preempted "inconsistent" state laws. However, to be preempted by federal law, the state law must conflict with the federal law's purpose. Courts have tended not to find more consumer-protective state laws to be inconsistent, despite the apparently clear congressional intent to allow CRAs to report all convictions. Thus, the CRAs lobbied Congress to pass a stronger preemption law. Compromise amendments in 1996 and 2003 prospectively preempted a few regulatory subjects but grandfathered many consumer-friendly state laws. See *Cisneros v. U.D. Registry, Inc.*, 39 Cal. App. 4th 548, 577 (1995).

Pet-Abuse.com, another advocacy organization, maintains an online database of convicted and charged animal abusers and a database of animal abuse cases.[42] Founded in 2001, it has documented over 19,000 cases of animal abuse from the United States, Canada, the United Kingdom, New Zealand, Australia, and Spain.[43] A visitor can search Pet-Abuse.com's database by zip code or county.[44] A "hit" provides information about the abuse incident, refers the visitor to news articles about the case, and sometimes provides the abuser's photograph.[45]

These NGOs are not covered by the FCRA because they do not provide consumer reports for a fee. They are analogous to newspapers or blogs that report on problems, expose wrongdoers, and advocate remedial action. As long as the information they post is true, they are protected by the First Amendment. Once such organizations obtain criminal record information from the courts or other publicly accessible sources, there is no way to prevent them from disclosing it in print or electronically.

EMPLOYER ASSOCIATIONS

Some employer associations maintain quasi-criminal databases for use by their members. For example, the National Retail Mutual Association (NRMA) hosts a Retail Theft Database populated with names of retail employees and shoplifters who either have been convicted of or have admitted to committing retail theft.[46] The NRMA website states:

> Less than five percent of theft incidents in the NRMA Retail Theft Database are prosecuted, so little criminal data exists for retail employers to screen applicants. Habitual offenders continue to move from one retailer to the next who are unaware of their history. [The database] is a unique product that was designed to stem the tide of inventory loss by creating a partnership of retailers through information sharing that goes beyond criminal background checks.[47]

The NRMA's website contains the following type of testimonial: "[Ninety-five percent] of the hits the Zale Corporation have gotten from NRMA Retail Theft Database in the last 3 years did not have a criminal record. The companies doing just criminal record background searches are simply missing a lot of dishonest people they don't need in their workforce."[48] NRMA emphasizes that its database is FCRA-compliant and therefore can be lawfully used to make hiring decisions. It also states that the database does not report incidents that occurred more than seven years ago, nor those that were committed by minors.[49] GIS, a major background screening company, maintains NRMA's database.

Several commercial background-screening companies, such as HireRight and FirstAdvantage, host similar databases. HireRight's National Theft Database includes half a million records about theft and shoplifting incidents submitted by 500 retailers.[50]

Blackmailers?

An emergent controversy that is generating considerable media and political attention involves companies that take advantage of publicly accessible criminal records to engage in a kind of blackmail.[51] They collect and post to their websites the names, photos (mug shots),* and other identifying information on arrestees and ex-offenders, then solicit from the people depicted a fee (as much as $1,000) to remove the information. The business apparently began in 2010 when an individual who just completed a three-year sentence for identity theft launched a website called Florida.arrests.org. The website posted mug shots publicly disclosed by police agencies. When people (or prospective employers) type a name into a search engine, they may be directed to the website where the mug shot appears, thus embarrassing the mug shot subject. Understanding the desire of the previously arrested person not to have her mug shot disclosed in this way, the company offers, for a fee, to remove the mug shot.[52] The record-subject is asked to submit an application for removal along with the fee, which will be refunded if the application

---

* The term derives from "mug," an English slang term for "face," dating back to the eighteenth century. The use of mug shot to mean "portrait or photograph in police records" appeared by 1887.

is rejected. One suspects that applications are rarely rejected. According to the Internet Crime Complaint Center:

> [H]undreds of complaints [were received] from individuals claiming they located their mugshots on 20 different websites, all of which allegedly use similar business practices. Some victims reported they were juveniles at the time of the arrests and that [they thought] their records were sealed. Therefore, their information should not be available to the public. Others stated that the information posted on the sites was either incorrect or blatantly false. Complainants who requested to have their mug shot removed, had to provide a copy of their driver's license, court record and other personal identifying information. However, providing such information puts them at risk for identify theft. Complainants were also subject to paying a fee to have their mug shot removed. Although they paid the fee, some of the mug shots were not removed. If they were removed, the mug shots appeared on similar websites.[53]

Blackmail has long been a puzzle for criminal law theorists.* A person has a right to disseminate or sell true information, but it is a crime to offer to sell it to a person likely to be humiliated by the information, even though the "victim" prefers to pay to control (suppress) its publication. Until late 2013, Mugshotsonline.com charged $98 to remove a mug shot from its website within twenty days; for

---

* Blackmail is legally defined as the criminal offense of attempting to extort money or property by threats of exposure of disreputable conduct. Blackmail is distinguished from the different crime of extortion. See Paul H. Robinson, Michael T. Cahill, and Daniel M. Bartels, *Competing Theories of Blackmail: An Empirical Research Critique of Criminal Law Theory*, 89 Texas L. Rev. 291, 293 (2010): "[B]lackmail has long been the favorite offense of clever criminal law theorists. It criminalizes the threat to do something that would not be criminal if one did it. If your acquaintance is having an affair, it is no crime to tell his wife of his infidelity. However, if you threaten to do so unless he pays you $100, that threat is criminal—even if he would consider it a bargain and quickly accept your offer. Unlike the similar but uncontroversial category of extortion—which involves conditional threats to engage in criminal acts, such as a threat to injure someone unless paid—this disparate legal treatment of the threat and the threatened activity makes blackmail seem like a puzzle or, in a well-known and often-repeated characterization, a 'paradox.'"

$178 it would remove it within two business days. It promised to waive the fee altogether if the applicant could prove that the charges connected to the mug shot were dismissed, expunged, or resulted in an acquittal.[54]

As criticism of these mug shot-posting-and-removing websites mounted, the schemes became more sophisticated. Some companies posted mug shots and arrest information, but did not solicit or accept removal application or fees. Instead, other companies offer mug shot removal services, that is, for a fee they offer to help mug shot subjects get their photos removed from one or more websites. Thus, Mugshots.com recommends that those who want their mug shot "unpublished" from its website hire Unpublisharrest.com, an "unpublishing company" that Mugshots.com works with.

> UnpublishArrest.com is comprised of experienced agents who are specialists in submitting licensing applications on behalf of it's [*sic*] clients to "The Mugshots.com Database" for permanent unpublishing, permanent publishing or editing of arrest records/mugshots contained within "The Mugshots.com Database." We have learned through experience what it takes to successfully submit applications to "The Mugshots.com Database." We are the billing and customer service agent for "The Mugshots.com Database." In most instances our submissions are successful for permanently unpublishing, permanently publishing or editing a public arrest record(s)/mugshot(s). The work is typically completed by the licensor within 24 hours.[55]

Unpublisharrest.com offers to have a posted record "permanently unpublished" according to the following fee schedule:

1 arrest including mugshot(s)—$399.00
2 arrests including mugshots—$798.00
3 arrests including mugshots—$1197.00
4 arrests including mugshots—$1479.00
5 arrests including mugshots—$1799.00[56]

If Unpublisharrest.com is unsuccessful in persuading Mugshots.com to remove the record, the record-subject's application fee is refunded.

Journalist David Kravets has written about the relationship between the companies that post arrest record information online and the companies that charge to remove the mug shots: "On the other side of the equation are firms like RemoveSlander, RemoveArrest .com and others that sometimes charge hundreds of dollars to get a mugshot removed. On the surface, the mug shot sites and the reputation firms are mortal enemies. But behind the scenes, they have a symbiotic relationship that wrings cash out of the people exposed."[57] Several state legislatures have adopted or are considering adopting laws to combat these mug shot posting and removing websites.[58] Utah and Colorado, for example, have taken a preventative approach by regulating how mug shots are disseminated by criminal justice agencies. A recently adopted Utah law prohibits county sheriffs from providing a copy of a mug shot to a person who intends to post it to a website that requires a fee for removal. In addition, a mug shot requester must sign a statement promising not to post it on a commercial website.[59] Colorado requires a similar signed promise from mug shot requesters.[60] Both states make it a misdemeanor for the requester to make a false statement about its intention.

Other states directly target the mug shot websites' practices. Georgia requires an Internet publisher of arrest information and mug shots to delete the information and photo without a fee upon request from individuals who were not formally charged or, if charged, had their case dismissed or resolved by an acquittal.[61] The website can continue to charge a mug shot removal fee to people who do not fall into those categories. Wyoming and Oregon have similar laws but extend the right to free removal to those whose arrest or conviction was expunged. Oregon also extends the right to those who have had their charges reduced to violations.[62] The Illinois legislature recently (effective January 1, 2014) passed a bill that prohibits collecting a fee for erasing, correcting, or modifying arrest or conviction information, including photographs.* JustMugshots,

---

* Public Act 098-0555 provides:

Sec. 2QQQ. Criminal record information.

(a) It is an unlawful practice for any person engaged in publishing or otherwise disseminating criminal record information through a print or electronic medium to

a Nevada-based mug shots website, unsuccessfully opposed the Illinois bill with the following argument:[63]

> Unfortunately the reality of the situation is that this bill will only serve to *create new hardships for those who have been arrested* and are seeking to minimize the visibility and impact of such an event. The unfortunate reality is that, if signed into law, this bill will make it nearly impossible for an Illinois citizen to have that information removed or corrected. Why?
>
> If SB0115 is signed into law the following things will inevitably happen, each putting an Illinois citizen at a severe disadvantage and likely causing further hardships than currently exist today.
>
> - Illinois arrests will become *PERMANENT* on the internet with *no way to remove the information*, regardless of circumstance;
> - Courtesy Removal Program requests will suffer a slower wait time due to decreased staff;
> - The citizens will have no recourse or ability to remove published arrest information—*EVER*.
>
> At JustMugshots we look to both our own proprietary Courtesy Removal Program and to the State of Georgia where legislators recently worked on and passed an outstanding bill, HB150. Both

---

solicit or accept the payment of a fee or other consideration to remove, correct, or modify said criminal record information.

(b) For the purposes of this Section, "criminal record information" includes any and all of the following:

(1) descriptions or notations of any arrests, any formal criminal charges, and the disposition of those criminal charges, including, but not limited to, any information made available under Section 4a of the State Records Act or Section 3b of the Local Records Act;

(2) photographs of the person taken pursuant to an arrest or other involvement in the criminal justice system; or

(3) personal identifying information, including a person's name, address, date of birth, photograph, and social security number or other government-issued identification number.

Available at http://www.ilga.gov/legislation/publicacts/fulltext.asp?Name=098-0555.

of these avenues for removal, via our internal program and via Georgia's fantastic new legislation, seem to strike the perfect balance in terms of providing the public with accessible and powerful information while protecting innocent citizens who were wrongly accused.

JustMugshots applauds Georgia, and strongly encourages other states to follow suit and take up laws similar to GA HB150 and to our own Courtesy Removal Program—the issues we're facing are very complicated and there are many different perspectives to view them from—but it is absolutely CRITICAL that laws intended to address these incredibly difficult issues do so while striking an [*sic*] crucial balance between the public's right to be informed and the citizen's right to be innocent until proven guilty.

The mug shot posting and removal business presents a good example of criminal law's blackmail puzzle. The First Amendment allows a person to disclose information about who has been arrested and for what. Many newspapers regularly publish such information. And it is no crime to sell information about arrestees and convicted persons to interested persons and entities; indeed, this is what commercial information vendors do. However, it is a crime to extract money from individuals by threatening to release true information that would expose them to humiliation and ridicule. Of course, the mug shot companies are not making such a threat. They have already posted the mug shot and are offering to remove it for a fee. To complicate matters more, they offer to consider removing the arrest information if the mug shot subject has a persuasive reason (in the eyes of the mug shot remover) for its removal. Technically, this is not blackmail and, to my knowledge, no one who engages in this business has so far been charged, much less convicted, with blackmail. According to Gene Policinski of the First Amendment Center:

At least one site, Mugshots.com, cloaks itself in constitutional robing, including the First Amendment value of insuring public-records transparency and the Sixth Amendment fair-trial guarantees. . . . But though the postings benefit the individual and the public, who gains from taking down the photo? The individual and his or her reputation, certainly—especially when prosecution was erroneous or failed to convict. But the benefit to society of a private company or person profiting from removing information from public view is, well, nonexistent.

There's the rub: Those public-spirited companies like Mugshots.com suddenly turn self-serving in demanding from $99 to $399 to take down a photo. Critics call the practice "unfair" or "extortion." But given that the postings are done by private companies, not public officials, legal cures proposed thus far seem as bad as the ailment.[64]

An Ohio lawsuit represents another line of attack on the mug shot websites.[65] The lawsuit, settled in December 2013 in federal district court, requires Citizens Information Associates, the company that runs BustedMugshots.com and Mugshotsonline.com, to pay $7,500 to the three plaintiffs.[66] It also calls for the company to stop charging for removing mug shots from their two websites. In the complaint, the plaintiffs claimed that the defendant companies engaged in "wrongful appropriation of their names, photographs, images, and likenesses for a commercial purpose that benefits only the defendants."[67] They based their lawsuit on Ohio's Right of Publicity statute. "A person shall not use any aspect of an individual's person for a commercial purpose."[68] Violation of this statute creates a private civil right of action, with potential damages of $2,500 to $10,000 per violation.[69] The idea behind Ohio's law and similar laws in other states is that a business should not profit from exploitation of someone's name or image.[70] A similar California lawsuit, filed as a class action, is pending against JustMugshots.com.[71] This strategy has a better, but by no means certain, chance of surviving a First Amendment challenge.*

* However, Jeff Hermes, the director of the Digital Media Law Project, is skeptical about the right of publicity lawsuits. He argues that the right of publicity is usually used to prevent unauthorized use of the value an individual has developed in his or her own identity. He states that a violation of the right of publicity occurs when a "name or

Yet another strategy to shut down the mug shot posting and removing companies is to persuade credit card companies not to do business with them. American Express and PayPal have ceased doing business with the mug shot companies. However, as long as other credit card companies will accept their customers' charges to the mug shot companies, business as usual will continue. Even if no credit card companies did business with the mug shot companies, those companies could operate by requiring checks, money orders, or cash. It is worth noting that after an October 2013 *New York Times* article on the controversy,[72] one of the major mug shot companies, mugshotsonline.com, announced that it would stop accepting payments for mug shot removals; instead, it would refer record-subjects to a mug shot removal company.

Google came up with another remedy. It has programmed its search algorithm so that when a person launches a name search that would direct the searcher to one of the mug shot companies websites, that suggested website will be far down the list, thereby making it less likely that the searcher will find the person-of-interest's mug shot. Time will tell whether any of these strategies will eliminate the mug shot companies.[73]

Conclusion

Individual criminal history information has become a commodity for which there is booming supply and demand. Hundreds of private firms that offer to conduct criminal background checks have a strong economic incentive to stoke demand by warning employers

---

likeness is used to suggest an endorsement or other association between a person and a product or service." He believes the right of publicity claim is helpful because it focuses the court away from the strong First Amendment protections to the coercive nature of the transactions encouraged by the mug shot removal industry. However, he concludes that the current formulation of the claim incorrectly conceives the right of publicity as relating to the transaction when it should relate to whether the website is taking advantage of a person to convey a message of endorsement. See Jeff Hermes, *Are Rights of Publicity the Fatal Flaw of the Mugshot Racket?* Digital Media L. Project Blog, January 3, 2013, http://www.dmlp.org/blog/2013/are-rights-publicity-fatal-flaw-mugshot-racket.

and others about the risks of hiring people with criminal records—dishonesty, unreliability, dangerousness, and civil liability for tortious injuries.

Some large national companies copy publicly accessible court and other criminal records into their own proprietary databases. They also scour the Internet for information posted by police and correctional agencies. Smaller companies conduct criminal background checks upon demand, mostly by searching the Internet.

Customers purchase criminal background checks to protect themselves from potential employees who might harm the company directly via theft and work disruptions or indirectly by making the employer liable for injuries inflicted on customers, clients, and other employees. Once background checking became readily available, many employers probably concluded that it would be negligent not to commission such checks. The costs of background checks can be passed along to job applicants themselves. Consequently, some surveys have found that as many as 90 percent of employers require criminal background checks for at least some employees. One SEARCH report is titled "The Criminal Backgrounding of America."[74]

A few private employer associations have created databases populated with names of individuals suspected of having committed crimes against member companies. Association members who have access to these databases likely regard the information provided as true whether or not it is based on convictions. If the information is true, its disclosure is protected by the First Amendment. If the information is untrue, it could be defamatory, depending upon how it is reported. In addition to the for-profit companies, a growing number of not-for-profits engage in disclosure of individual criminal background information. Some NGOs claim to be acting in the public interest by publicizing information about particular categories of offenses and offenders.

It would be constitutionally dubious, practically difficult, and politically inconceivable to outlaw commercial information vendors; they are too deeply entrenched legally, politically, socially, and financially. While more regulation is possible, the objects of such regulation are far from clear. Society clearly benefits from the free flow of information so that people and firms can make informed choices about their political representatives, investments, employees, and friends. There is something dangerous in leaving it to government to decide what information people should have and what information they should be denied.

PART II

KEY POLICY ISSUES

PART II CONSISTS of three chapters, each devoted to a different criminal record policy issue. Chapter 6 considers the rationale and desirability of recording arrests and other types of information on a rap sheet or other law enforcement database. Even now, not every police encounter with a suspected law violator results in a rap sheet entry. Police officers let some suspected violators go with a warning. Sometimes they issue summonses, which typically are not recorded on a rap sheet. By statute, some states do not record violations or low-level misdemeanors. Deferred prosecution is another, and increasingly popular, way for prosecutors to exercise control over a law violator without saddling the individual with a permanent record of conviction. When deferred prosecution is an option, the defendant's record becomes the focus of plea-bargaining. We will see in a later chapter the crucial importance of "record bargaining" when the suspect/defendant is a noncitizen.

Expunging an arrest or conviction is not much different than not creating the record in the first place. However, in practice, an arrest or conviction is unlikely to be completely erased once recorded; it probably will always exist in some file or database. Expunging and sealing administrative violations, deferred prosecutions, and adjournments in contemplation of dismissal are dealt with in Chapter 6 because they are closely related to not recording a conviction at all.

Chapter 7 considers the possibility of destroying (expunging) or sealing a criminal record years after the sentence has been served, thereby symbolically restoring the convicted person to citizenship in good standing. It also deals with the possibility of changing the record by adding positive information (certificate of rehabilitation). Chapter 8 examines the problem of erroneous criminal background checks due to incomplete or mistaken records. An injustice occurs, for example, when a person is arrested because of an apparently outstanding warrant that had actually been withdrawn, or when a person is arrested because of mistaken identity. Perhaps even more egregious, employers and other non–criminal justice system users may reject job applicants on account of an arrest that was never followed up with charges, much less a conviction. A commercial information vendor may mistakenly attribute a criminal record to the wrong person or report convictions subsequently reversed or expunged. We will canvass a number of proposals to address these problems.

6 WHETHER TO CREATE A CRIMINAL RECORD

We express a desire for rehabilitation of the individual, while simultaneously we do everything to prevent it. . . . We tell him to return to the norm of behavior, yet we brand him as virtually unemployable; he is required to live with his normal activities severely restricted and we react with sickened wonder and disgust when he returns to a life of crime.

—J. Lay, dissenting, *Morrissey v. Brewer* (8th Circuit Court of Appeals, 1971)[1]

Every year, additional crimes, increased punishments, and novel applications of the criminal justice system enter U.S. jurisprudence, sometimes coming in a predictable frenzy analogous to other recurring events in American society, such as the bacchanalia of New Year's Eve or the annual "madness" surrounding the months of March (for college basketball fans) and April (for procrastinating taxpayers).

—Erik Luna, "The Overcriminalization Phenomenon" (2005)[2]

ACADEMICS AND JOURNALISTS frequently remind us that the United States imprisons a greater proportion of its population than any other country. Less often noted is that the vast majority of convicted misdemeanants are not incarcerated; even the majority of convicted felons are not sentenced to prison. Thus, the basic punishment meted out in criminal cases is a conviction record that exposes the record-subject to discrimination, disabilities, and disqualifications. This chapter asks why so many people have criminal records and whether such labeling should and could be reduced.

The most obvious strategy for reducing the number of people with stigmatizing criminal records is decriminalization; if engaging in certain conduct were no longer criminal, it would not result in a criminal record. A second strategy for reducing the size of the criminally stigmatized populations is enforcing the criminal law less strictly, that is, making fewer arrests and pursuing fewer prosecutions. Police have always let off with a warning some law violators who could have been arrested. Prosecutors frequently dismiss prosecutable cases, sometimes contingent on the defendant successfully completing a pretrial diversion program; however, what record remains is an important policy issue.

Criminalization and Decriminalization

One reason that the United States has such an immense population of persons with criminal records is the overuse of criminal law.[3] Duke law professor Sara Sun Beale observes that

> [t]he term overcriminalization is broad enough to cover laws imposing penal sanctions on conduct that should be solely a matter of individual morality. It also includes legislation that criminalizes relatively trivial conduct, such as removing the tag on a mattress, which should be dealt with by civil provisions, or perhaps left to the good sense of the individual. Many argue that a good deal of so-called regulatory or "white collar crime" should fall outside the ambit of the criminal law, to be dealt with by other bodies of specialized civil law, such as corporate governance, environmental, or election finance law. Another facet of overcriminalization is the enormous expansion of federal criminal law to cover subjects that were previously the exclusive province of state law.[4]

It is estimated that there are around 4,500 federal crimes,[5] plus over 300,000 federal regulations that can be enforced criminally (so-called regulatory crimes).[6] On average, Congress creates sixty new crimes per year.[7] The number of state criminal laws is also constantly increasing;[8] hate crime, bullying, stalking, and sexting are examples of new criminal offenses.[9] If all or some of this currently criminal conduct were made legal or dealt with as administrative violations, far fewer persons would be labeled criminal.[10]

Nationwide, police made an estimated 12,196,959 arrests in 2012, including 1,552,432 arrests for drug offenses, 42.4 percent of the latter for marijuana possession.[11] In 2012, there were 543,995 disorderly conduct arrests, 511,271 drunkenness arrests, 70,190 arrests for curfew and loitering violations, 56,575 arrests for prostitution, 27,003 vagrancy arrests, and 7,868 gambling arrests.[12]

Over the past few decades, millions of people have been convicted of selling and possessing illicit mood and mind-altering drugs, especially marijuana. If possession of marijuana were not criminal, all those people (at least those who have not been convicted of other crimes as well) would not have a criminal record.[13] The current movement to decriminalize marijuana possession makes this point far from hypothetical.

Less Reliance on Criminal Enforcement

It is not always necessary or desirable to aggressively enforce criminal laws. Consider, for example, how tax evasion and tax fraud are dealt with. It is likely that millions of people could be criminally prosecuted for not filing tax returns, hiding income, lying about expenses, and fraudulently claiming deductions. Despite the massive pool of potential tax crime defendants, almost all violators are dealt with civilly. In 2013, the Internal Revenue Service assessed civil penalties in 37,942,652 cases. It initiated 5,314 criminal investigations and referred 4,364 cases for prosecution. There were, all told, 3,311 convictions.[14] That policy reflects a remarkable commitment to minimalist criminal law enforcement.

Another under-enforcement example is the law enforcement response to medical malpractice, which the American Association for Justice estimates to be the sixth biggest cause of death. Every instance of a nurse's or doctor's gross negligence causing death or injury to a patient could be a potential negligent homicide or assault prosecution. Nationwide, only thirty-seven doctors were criminally prosecuted for malpractice between 2001 and 2011,[15] fewer than four per year. Civil tort action and professional discipline, rather than criminal prosecution, are the usual responses to medical malpractice. Likewise, only a minuscule number of criminal charges are brought in response to millions of potentially prosecutable industrial "accidents" and environmental violations. Criminal prosecutions and criminal records are not inevitable; they are the result of policy choices.

Reclassifying Felonies as Misdemeanors

The very classification of criminal offenses has stigmatic effects. The stigma attached to "felony" is much greater than the stigma attached to "misdemeanor." There was a time when only the most serious crimes were classified as felonies. That is no longer the case; there has been significant inflation in criminal offense classification. Federal and state criminal codes classify a vast range of crimes as felonies, thereby triggering lifelong disqualifications, ineligibilities, and disabilities. (A prime objective of a plea-bargaining defendant is to plead guilty to a misdemeanor rather than a felony.) Downgrading some felonies to misdemeanors would not reduce the number of criminal records, but would ameliorate stigma. Unfortunately, the trend has been in the opposite direction.

Reclassifying Misdemeanors as Violations

The stigma of a misdemeanor conviction is not negligible. According to UCLA law professor Alexandra Natapoff:

> [T]he misdemeanor world is far larger, more pervasive, and more influential than it is given credit for. Misdemeanor dockets are approximately five times the size of felony dockets. Millions of petty offenders experience crushing fines and jail, and many misdemeanants will spend significant periods of time incarcerated whether their offenses warrant it or not. Once convicted, petty offenders suffer some of the same consequences as their felony counterparts.[16]

Some misdemeanors could be downgraded to an administrative infraction or violation. According to the influential Model Penal Code, a violation is not a criminal offense, is not punishable by incarceration, and does not carry moral censure.[17] When asked whether she has ever been convicted of a criminal offense, a person convicted of a violation can truthfully answer "no."

Routine traffic offenses are a good example of declassifying criminal offenses to violations. In the early twentieth century, driving offenses were classified as misdemeanors (a few, like reckless driving, still are). Nationwide, it is estimated that police issue 112,000 speeding summonses ("tickets") every day, or 41,000,000 annually.[18] If these offenses were graded as misdemeanors, tens of millions more people would be saddled with criminal records. How we label and classify matters.

New York State leads the nation in creating (administrative) violations. Examples include:

- Criminal solicitation in the fifth degree;
- Hazing in the second degree;
- Trespass;
- Unlawfully posting advertisements;
- Misconduct by a juror in the second degree;
- Failing to respond to an appearance ticket;
- Unlawful possession of marijuana;
- Disorderly conduct;
- Harassment in the second degree;
- Loitering;
- Appearance in public under the influence of narcotics or a drug other than alcohol;
- Loitering for the purpose of engaging in a prostitution offense;
- Unlawful prevention of public access to records;
- Exposure of a person;
- Promoting the exposure of a person;
- Offensive exhibition; and
- Unlawful possession of certain ammunition feeding devices (first offense).

Some people are arrested or issued a summons for committing a violation; others plead guilty to a violation after having been charged with a misdemeanor. The New York City Police Department (NYPD) reported 6,037 violations for 2013.[19] In the event of an arrest for a violation, the arrestee may be, but is usually not, fingerprinted. The district attorney's office prosecutes the violation and (except for traffic violations) the punishment is a fine and/or up to fifteen days in jail.[20] However, except for driving while ability impaired and loitering for the purpose of prostitution, the rap sheet record of the violation is sealed, and the defendant's fingerprints and photo destroyed or sent to the record-subject.[21] The law requires sealing of records held by the state records repository or by the police and the prosecutor's office, but not by a court.[22] (Thus, it is possible for an employer or landlord to find out about a prospective employee's or tenant's violation convictions by checking courthouse records.) In 2007, in response to a lawsuit, New York State's Office of Court Administration agreed that it would not include information about violations in Criminal History Record Search Reports that are available upon request to anyone interested in whether a particular person has a criminal record in New York State.[23]

Nonserious Crimes and Juvenile Offenses

It has never been the case that a criminal record is created for every person whom a police officer identifies as a criminal law violator. In many cases, the police just warn. It is an important policy question whether to record such warnings in a database, thereby creating a criminal or quasi-criminal record. The NYPD, in response to litigation over the legality of its stop-and-frisk policy, created a database with names and incident information about persons who were stopped and frisked, but not summoned or arrested. In 2010, the state legislature passed a law prohibiting the NYPD from adding information to this database. A few years later, a state appellate court ordered the NYPD to stop using the database altogether; eventually, the NYPD agreed to delete all the stop-and-frisk information (see Chapter 2).*

* A similar controversy in the United Kingdom demonstrates the fundamental importance of the decision of what police–citizen contacts to record and make accessible. In the United Kingdom, police warnings, called "cautions," have become a formal police

Many jurisdictions do not fingerprint and do not record on the rap sheet prosecutions that begin with a summons rather than an arrest. It remains to be seen whether mobile fingerprinting devices that can be carried in the squad car or on foot patrol will lead to more fingerprinting when summons are issued.) Some states do not record arrests for nonserious misdemeanors. A number of states do not record on the rap sheet juvenile arrests for offenses that would not be criminal if committed by an adult (so-called status offenses, such as curfew violation, running away, truancy, underage possession and consumption of alcohol and tobacco).

A 1974 FBI policy directive stated that rap sheet information transmitted to the FBI should be limited to "serious and/or significant offenses." Thus, police should not submit information about arrests for drunkenness, vagrancy, disturbing the peace, curfew violation, loitering, or false fire alarm.[24] Apparently, this policy was primarily motivated by the FBI's information-processing capacity. However, the FBI's position that "offenses committed by juveniles [were] also [to] be excluded unless a juvenile offender [was] tried in a court as an adult" was a response to the lobbying of juvenile justice reformers who wanted to protect a person from being stigmatized for life on account of a "youthful indiscretion."[25] While some states record all of a person's arrests, juvenile and adult, on a single rap sheet, others require juveniles' fingerprints and arrest information to be kept separately.

In 1992, the FBI's policy on accepting juvenile arrests for inclusion in the Triple I changed. Henceforth, the FBI would accept,

---

procedure meant to spare the arrestable person a criminal record. The individual can refuse a caution and opt to be prosecuted. A caution is recorded on the individual's police record. This practice was recently challenged before the European Court of Human Rights. M.M. (the applicant) abducted her grandson for three days in 2000 in order to prevent her son's girlfriend from taking the child to Australia. The U.K. director of public prosecutions issued a caution (to which M.M. agreed) rather than filing criminal charges. In 2006, M.M. was rejected for a job involving child care because of this recorded and reported caution. In 2012, the European Court of Human Rights ruled in *M.M. v. the United Kingdom* that the indefinite retention of police cautions and their disclosure in criminal record checks infringe individual privacy as guaranteed by Article 8 of the European Convention on Human Rights.

maintain, and disseminate juvenile criminal record information for juveniles adjudicated in juvenile proceedings as long as the offense was "serious and or significant." Moreover, information about an arrest for a "nonserious offense" would be accepted if it was connected to an arrest for a serious or significant offense.

In 2006, with computers having vastly increased information-processing capacity, the FBI announced that it would accept fingerprints and arrest information for nonserious offenses and all juvenile arrests.* The FBI explained that the new policy would (1) create a more uniform national policy so that law enforcement agencies and employers in a state requesting an FBI criminal history search would receive all information held by law enforcement agencies and employers in the state where the criminal record originated; and (2) provide public and private employers with valuable information on prospective employees:

> With the significant increase in requests for [criminal history record information] to conduct criminal background checks for noncriminal justice employment and licensing purposes, some NSOs [nonserious offenses] have acquired greater significance. For example, a state school bus driver applicant in one state with a history of certain traffic offenses in another jurisdiction may be disqualified from employment based upon those traffic offenses under the law of his or her state of residence. However, if those traffic offenses from another state are NSOs and are not included in the FBI's systems of records, a check of the FBI's records would result in a response to the inquiring agency that no prior record was located. As a result, individuals with potentially disqualifying criminal records may gain employment in positions from which they would otherwise be

---

* The proposed new "Includable Offense" policy states: "The Triple I System and the [Fingerprint Identification Records System] shall maintain fingerprints and criminal history record information relating to adult and juvenile offenses submitted by criminal justice agencies for retention, consistent with the FBI's capacity to collect and exchange such information, except where non-retention of such fingerprints is specified by the submitting agency." 28 CFR §20.32.

> prohibited. Therefore, permitting the FBI to retain and to exchange NSOs will assist in producing more complete and uniform background checks.[26]

This FBI policy change is a clear example of how the police-created and -maintained rap sheet system is shaped by the needs of public and private employers and other non–law enforcement entities. The FBI and, no doubt, state and local law enforcement agencies see it as part of their missions to assist employers in sorting people on the basis of criminal biographies.*

Not surprisingly, a number of liberal NGOs, including the National Employment Law Project, the American Civil Liberties Union, and the Brennan Center for Justice at New York University, opposed the FBI's proposal. Their joint comment submitted to the Department of Justice argued that including nonserious offenses, like disorderly conduct and public drunkenness (together accounting for 10 percent of all arrests in 2004) to an individual's criminal record would give prospective employers a distorted impression of the record-subject's criminality and character:

> [T]he FBI's proposed policy also has to be evaluated in the context of the limited standards that regulate employment screening decisions. For example, occupational screening laws typically do not specify reasonable age limits on disqualifying offenses, and they often do not identify the major disqualifying crimes that are directly related to the qualifications of the job. Instead, they rely on especially broad disqualifications, such as crimes of "moral turpitude," that can apply to even the most minor offenses, including drunkenness and disorderly conduct. Nor do most state and federal laws provide for "waiver" procedures that guard against such abuses. In the case of those

* In New York State, persons summoned or arrested for violations are not fingerprinted. Additionally, when an arrest results in a dismissal or conviction for a violation, the arrest information must be sealed. The Division of Criminal Justice Services (DCJS) will not disclose sealed information, even to state agencies that have authorized access to rap sheets. Most private employers do not have access to rap sheets.

> employers who can now also access the FBI's records, they routinely have no clear substantive standards regulating their screening decision. Thus, literally any offense can be considered disqualifying by most employers.[27]

The objecting organizations further argued that the proposed federal regulations would (1) harm African Americans and Hispanics, who are disproportionately subject to arrest for nonserious offenses; and (2) compromise the reliability of the Triple I by significantly increasing the amount of incomplete and inaccurate information. Nevertheless, the FBI implemented the policy.

Deferred Prosecutions

Some two dozen states have laws authorizing deferred prosecution agreements whereby criminal charges can be resolved without creating a conviction record.[28] Charges are put on hold for a specified period (e.g., six months or one year). If the defendant stays out of trouble and abides by certain conditions during a period of "prosecutorial probation," the charges will be dismissed. Sometimes deferred prosecution is called "prosecutorial probation," "adjournment in contemplation of dismissal," or "conditional dismissal." Sometimes it is authorized by statutes, which differ with respect to (1) which offenders are eligible; (2) the extent of the prosecutor's discretion; (3) the judge's role, if any; (4) the length of the prosecutorial probation period; and (5) whether records are automatically expunged or sealed upon successful completion.[29] The American Bar Association recommends that federal, state, and local governments develop, support, and fund "prosecutors and others seeking to develop, deferred adjudication/deferred sentencing/diversion options that avoid a permanent conviction record for offenders who are deemed appropriate for community supervision."[30] According to the ABA, an offender should generally be eligible for community supervision if she "i) poses no substantial threat to the community; ii) is not charged with a predatory crime, a crime involving substantial violence, a crime involving large scale drug trafficking, or a crime of equivalent gravity; iii) has no prior criminal history that makes community supervision an inappropriate sanction; and iv) is not currently on parole or probation, unless the supervising authority specifically consents."[31]

In the absence of a statute, prosecutors, judges, and defense lawyers can sometimes reach the same disposition through plea-bargaining.[32] Deferred prosecution is eagerly sought by defendants anxious to avoid a permanent record of conviction and by prosecutors desirous of resolving cases with a minimum expenditure of time and resources. Prosecutors can condition deferred prosecution on the defendant's participation in a rehabilitation program, threatening to reinstate charges and press for jail time if the defendant does not complete the program successfully.*

Federal Probation before Judgment

Some deferred prosecution schemes entail a guilty plea that is subsequently expunged if the defendant successfully completes prosecutorial probation. For example, federal law provides that a person with no prior federal or state drug conviction who pleads guilty to misdemeanor marijuana possession may agree to a year's probation before judgment.[33] If the defendant successfully completes the probationary period, charges are dismissed and the defendant is considered not to have been convicted.† If the defendant was less than twenty-one years old when the offense was committed, the criminal record may be expunged; in the future, the person can legally deny having been arrested and convicted for that offense.[34] A defendant

---

* In *Alabama v. Shelton*, 535 U.S. 654 (2002), the Supreme Court ruled that, if an indigent defendant was not assigned counsel, a suspended sentence could not later be activated. The state argued that it had an important interest in being able to threaten the recipient of a suspended sentence with incarceration if he violated the conditions of the suspended sentence. The court observed that this goal could be constitutionally achieved by means of "pretrial probation"; that is, the defendant is prosecuted only if he violates the conditions of the deferral. In that event, he would be assigned counsel if the charges carry a possible prison sentence.

† See 18 U.S.C. §3607(b): "A disposition under subsection (a), or a conviction that is the subjection of an expungement order under subsection (c), shall not be considered a conviction for the purpose of a disqualification or a disability imposed by law upon conviction of a crime, or for any other purpose."

who has a prior federal or state drug conviction or who has previously been the beneficiary of probation before judgment is not eligible for this disposition. To ensure compliance, prosecutors need access to a database of previous probation before judgment orders. (Such an unexpunged database is itself a type of criminal record.)

New York's Adjournment in Contemplation of Dismissal

New York State's version of deferred prosecution is called "adjournment in contemplation of dismissal" (ACD). There are two statutory provisions authorizing ACDs. One applies to first-time marijuana possession cases, and the other to all other offenses.[35] The former authorizes a six-month adjournment and the latter a one-year adjournment.* In accepting an ACD, the defendant must agree to "stay out of trouble" ("lead a law-abiding life") and, in some cases, to complete a treatment or community service program or pay restitution. The prosecutor has absolute discretion to reactivate the original charges if she determines that the defendant failed to comply with the conditions. While an ACD case is pending, it is accessible on New York State's online Webcrims database. The court's case management system shows the date on which the case will be permanently dismissed.[36] If the defendant successfully completes prosecutorial probation, charges are dismissed and records sealed, unless the district attorney persuades the judge that, in the

---

* The ACD's origin can be traced back to the common law writ of *nolle prosequi*, by which prosecutors could "dispose of technically imperfect proceedings instituted by the Crown; and to put a stop to oppressive, but technically impeccable, proceedings instated by private prosecutors." In nineteenth-century New York, the tradition of *nolle prosequi* gave birth to a unique New York disposition, the discharge on own recognizance (DOR). DORs were used by prosecutors to dispose of de minimis infractions. After deciding to grant a DOR, prosecutors would adjourn the case to a future (indefinite) date. If the defendant stayed out of trouble, the prosecutor would move that the charge be dismissed. John F. Wirenius, *A Model of Discretion: New York's "Interests of Justice" Dismissal Statute*, 58 Alb. L. Rev. 175, 178 (1994); see also Peter Preiser, McKinney's ACD Practice Commentaries, McKinney's Cons. Laws of NY (1999). The ACD statute codified a long-standing common law disposition intended to provide relief to first-time offenders who did not pose a future threat. "Adjournments in contemplation of dismissal are dismissals in the interest of justice." 640 PLI/Lit 539, 553 (October 2000).

interests of justice,[37] the record should remain publicly accessible. In reality, however, the record often is not promptly or ever sealed.

New York's ACD is a very popular criminal case disposition.[38]* In 2013, about 50 percent of defendants charged with a misdemeanor in New York City were convicted of a misdemeanor or violation. The other 50 percent's charges were resolved by dismissal; 29.1 percent of all misdemeanors were dismissed pursuant to an ACD).[39] ACD was most frequently used in low-level marijuana possession cases (21 percent of all misdemeanor marijuana possession arrests). In 45–59 percent of cases where marijuana possession was the top charge, the case was disposed of by ACD. Other charges frequently disposed of via ACD were misdemeanor (usually domestic violence) assault (15 percent), other minor drug possession (15 percent), theft of services (10 percent), and petit larceny (10 percent).

New York State's statute authorizing ACDs for marijuana possession provides that an individual may be afforded this disposition only once in his lifetime. To enforce this limitation, there must be a record of ACDs that allows prosecutors to determine whether a marijuana possession defendant is ineligible for an ACD.[40] However, there is no way for a prosecutor to know whether a defendant had a previous ACD for a non-marijuana offense. As Professor Issa Kohler-Hausmann observes:

> The sealing provisions in New York State Criminal Procedure Law provide for an interesting disjunction between factual and legal status of a defendant in the criminal justice system. The most glaring example of this is the fact that innumerable and

---

* Issa Kohler-Hausmann maintains that prosecutors use misdemeanors to "mark" law violators as criminals or quasi-criminals. Finding that the majority of NYC misdemeanor arrests are dismissed, usually after a six-month or one-year period of pretrial probation, she observes that "[t]he study of misdemeanor justice reveals that it shares some traits with the use of carceral power, but differs in important respects. The marking that occurs in cases that are eventually dismissed serves the kind of purpose that Foucault described, situating subjects in a network of power-knowledge by recording facts of their actions and status to be used by officials in other arenas of social life." See Issa Kohler-Hausmann, *Misdemeanor Justice: Control without Conviction*, 119 American Journal of Sociology, 351, 386 (2013).

> unknowable numbers of defendants come to an arraignment as a "first arrest" as stated on the official rap sheet, as known to their criminal defense attorneys, as perceived by the prosecutor and judge; but in actuality this encounter may not be their first arrest. In fact they may have had multiple prior arrests. That's because the CPL [Criminal Procedure Law] provides that fingerprints and photos must be destroyed upon sealing if the person has no prior criminal record.[41]

From the prosecutor's perspective, an ACD is often the best result in a misdemeanor domestic assault case because lack of victim cooperation makes the charges difficult to prosecute to conviction. The defendant avoids a criminal record and the prosecutor exercises some control over the defendant, while conserving office resources.

Perhaps because of high case volume and resource constraints, New York City prosecutors usually do not require ACD conditions beyond staying out of trouble, that is, avoiding rearrest. This contrasts with federal prosecutors, who have jurisdiction over crimes that occur on federal enclaves like veterans' hospitals, federal parks, post office facilities, and military bases. They can often rely on the federal agency (e.g., Veterans Administration, Park Service, Post Office, or Army) most interested in the case to take responsibility for verifying and confirming that the ACD defendant abides by the conditions of the deferred prosecution.

Other States' Prosecutorial Deferral Procedures

Other states have dispositions similar to New York State's ACD. Maryland has a "probation before judgment" (PBJ) disposition. Texas's version is called "deferred adjudication."[42] California's analogous procedure is "dismissal after conviction." Although there are differences, these dispositions all allow the defendant to settle the criminal charges without a permanent conviction record. They all recognize that the record is the most important consideration for a significant percentage of defendants and that the state itself frequently is best served by avoiding saddling the defendant with a permanent criminal label.

MARYLAND'S PROBATION BEFORE JUDGMENT

Under Maryland's PBJ,[43] with the defendant's consent, the judge may defer judgment and place a defendant on pre-plea probation (subject to reasonable conditions). All defendants, except those charged with sex offenses, are eligible for this disposition. Moreover, judges may, as a PBJ condition, impose a short jail term or home detention thereby making the PBJ an option for resolving more serious charges.

If probation is completed successfully and there are no other pending charges, the defendant may petition a court for expungement of police and court records relating to the PBJ.[44] Until expunged, the case remains on the Maryland Judiciary Case Search website. Maryland's PBJ is a versatile tool that may be used to impose a "shock" jail experience, while avoiding the negative consequences of a permanent criminal history record.[45]*

TEXAS'S DEFERRED ADJUDICATION

Texas's "deferred adjudication" disposition is available to defendants, except for those charged with driving under the influence, repeat drug trafficking near a school, felony sex crimes, and murder.[46] It requires a period of prosecutorial probation during which the accused must avoid arrest and comply with whatever conditions are agreed to. The period of supervision may not exceed two years for a misdemeanor and ten years for a felony. In Texas, unlike the other jurisdictions already discussed, the defendant's record is not automatically sealed or expunged after successful completion of deferred prosecution. Expungement requires a judicial order that prohibits criminal justice agencies from disclosing specific criminal history record information to the public and exempts a criminal history record from disclosure under the Public Information Act (Texas's equivalent of the federal Freedom of Information Act).[47] However,

---

* Serving a jail term without being convicted of an offense is perhaps not as strange as it might first appear. In New York, a defendant convicted of a "violation" (which is not a criminal offense) may be sentenced for up to fifteen days in jail. New York Penal Law § 10.00. In all jurisdictions, defendants who are remanded to pretrial detention, in effect, serve a jail term whether or not they are ultimately found guilty. If they do plead guilty, the time served in pretrial confinement counts against the jail or prison sentence.

even when the defendant's petition for an order of nondisclosure is granted, the court may still disclose the case file to law enforcement agencies, school districts, state licensing boards, and public hospitals. Texas's version of deferred prosecution diminishes the disposition's value to the defendant because so many agencies have access to the dismissed charges.

CALIFORNIA'S POSTCONVICTION DISMISSAL

California's "postconviction dismissal" (PCD) enables a defendant to resolve criminal charges without creation of a permanent criminal record. It is available to a convicted defendant who, on the current charge, has not been sentenced to state prison. A defendant who successfully completes probation or, if not on probation, stays out of trouble for a year can petition the court for a PCD. The district attorney's agreement is necessary, but not sufficient.[48] If the judge grants the PCD, the conviction on the defendant's rap sheet is replaced with a notation that the charge was dismissed. However, the defendant remains ineligible to possess a firearm and to hold certain public offices and is subject to other disabilities. The PCD defendant is instructed that

> 1) For questions by government employers or on government licensing applications, if you are asked if you have ever been convicted of a crime, you MUST respond with "YES—CONVICTION DISMISSED"; 2) You will not be allowed to own or possess a firearm until you would otherwise be able to do so; 3) Your dismissed convictions can still be used to increase your punishment in future criminal cases; 4) Your prior convictions can still affect your driving privileges; 5) If you have been required to register as a sex offender as a result of a conviction, you have to make a different motion to the court in order to be relieved of this requirement. A dismissal will not relieve you of your duty to register as a sex offender. Your status as a registered sex offender will continue to be available to the public on the Internet under Megan's Law; and 6) If your conviction prohibited you from holding public office, you still cannot hold public office after that conviction is dismissed.[49]

California's PCD is not really a deferred prosecution. Since it allows for retroactive dismissal of a recorded conviction, it is more like a conviction expungement or sealing. However, it is different from expungement because it does not remove all collateral consequences and it is different from sealing because the record is not just hidden, it is changed. From the defendants' standpoint, the main advantage of the PCD is that it applies to more charges. From the prosecutor's standpoint, it provides an incentive for a very large number of defendants to comply with the terms of their probation and it permits supervision of the defendant after the conviction has been dismissed.

How Is a Deferred Prosecution Recorded?

Deferred prosecution procedures differ with respect to who has access to information about a defendant's successfully completed deferred prosecution. New York seals the ACD record. Texas makes a deferred adjudication record available to courts and certain government agencies.

A successfully completed deferred prosecution should leave the defendant without a criminal record, but the state needs a database of deferred prosecution beneficiaries if it wishes to prevent a previous beneficiary from being afforded another deferred prosecution opportunity. Some jurisdictions limit this disposition to once in a lifetime, presumably because the once leniently treated individual who recidivates does not deserve a second lenient disposition. This policy assumes that the deferred prosecution is a benefit magnanimously extended by the prosecutor to the defendant. In fact, the prosecutor may have a strong preference for deferred prosecution because of uncertainty about proving guilt and/or desire to conserve resources. Thus, a once-in-a-lifetime deferred prosecution rule needlessly restricts prosecutorial discretion. Because the prosecutor's discretion extends to whether the defendant should be prosecuted at all and, if so, for what crimes, it should also extend to deciding whether to agree to a deferred prosecution disposition regardless of whether the defendant has had a previous case disposed of in the same way. However, in exercising that discretion, the prosecutor needs to know whether the defendant has previously been afforded a deferred prosecution.

Deferred Prosecution's Value to Defendant Undermined by Public Accessibility of Records during Probationary Period

Deferred prosecution leaves the defendant's arrest and charge information publicly available during the prosecutorial probationary period. For as long as a year, commercial information vendors can copy and download the pending charges to their proprietary databases and report them to interested clients. Even if the police and courts expunge or seal the arrest and charge information following successful completion of deferred prosecution, the information is likely to have been copied by commercial information vendors, thereby undermining the deferred prosecution's purpose.

New York State has partially addressed this problem by prohibiting commercial information vendors from providing clients information about matters that have been expunged or sealed. However, this does not prevent vendors from transmitting the information about the case before sealing or expunging takes place. It also assumes that the commercial vendors will know or be able to expeditiously determine that a particular arrest, charge, or conviction has been sealed or expunged. In addition (although enforcement has been weak), New York State Human Rights Law[50] prohibits employers from inquiring about or considering (1) arrests that did not lead to a conviction, (2) sealed violation-level offenses, or (3) youthful offender adjudications.

One strategy that would help to protect the confidentiality of sealed or expunged criminal record information would be for offices of court administration that sell criminal records to private vendors to require as a condition of sale that the purchaser keep its records current, including by erasing information about sealed and expunged charges.* The First Amendment probably makes it im-

* Such a policy might be vulnerable to a challenge based on the unconstitutional conditions doctrine. Constitutional law scholar and professor Kathleen Sullivan has called the doctrine "difficult to comprehend." Kathleen Sullivan, *Unconstitutional Conditions*, 102 Harv. L. Rev. 1415, 1416–17 (1989). Because it is lawful to condition welfare benefits on the waiver of certain rights and performance of certain conditions, it would arguably

possible to impose that obligation on information vendors who use publicly accessible court records for their background checks.

Conclusion

"Mass incarceration" is now on the radar screens of scholars, prisoners' rights advocates, media, politicians, and policy makers. Many commentators criticize the huge contribution of drug enforcement to state and federal prison populations and particularly to the disproportionate incarceration of African Americans.[51] The same critique should be leveled at criminal labeling that doesn't involve incarceration. From a societal point of view, criminalization may deter some drug users, but directly and indirectly, it increases the number of marginalized persons and deepens social stratification on the basis of criminal record. It also leads to incarceration if the individual is subsequently convicted. Decriminalizing some low-level crimes, like marijuana possession, would significantly reduce the number of people with criminal records.[52] This could be accomplished by legalizing drug possession or by downgrading possession to an administrative violation.

Reclassifying less serious misdemeanors as administrative violations is another delabeling strategy. However, the value of downgrading misdemeanors to violations requires that the public not consider violations to be criminal offenses. That seems to have worked in the case of traffic violations, but we do not know how various criminal record consumers interpret other violations. (Importantly, traffic violations are adjudicated in a separate traffic court.) Reclassifying some felonies as misdemeanors would also ameliorate stigma.

Deferred prosecution has become a popular criminal court disposition. It is not in the interest of the state or the citizenry to burden a feckless individual with a record that diminishes his or her chances of becoming a law-abiding citizen. Diverting defendants to treatment programs which, if completed successfully, result in

be lawful to make purchase of bulk court records contingent on the purchaser's agreement to report individual criminal record history accurately.

dismissal of the criminal charges is a good idea. However, like all diversion programs, deferred prosecution is vulnerable to "net widening." Undoubtedly, some arrestees who would otherwise not have been prosecuted accept deferred prosecution because they do not want to risk a permanent conviction record. Here there is a similarity with traffic "tickets." Because there is little if any stigma and collateral consequences, many people consider it not worth the time, effort, and expense to mount a defense.[53]

The record that will result from an arrest is one of the most important issues to be resolved in the processing of a criminal case. The increasing use of deferred prosecution is strong evidence that the criminal record itself is understood as punishment.

7 SEALING, PURGING, AND AMENDING CONVICTION RECORDS

Despite the good intentions and the evidently laudable goals of record concealment proponents, it is apparent that the system cannot and does not work. Record concealment is unworkable; it fails to lift other penalties attendant to the record; it sanctions deceit; its half-secrecy leads to speculative exaggerations; it frustrates constructive research; and it is not equally available to all.

—Bernard Kogon and Donald L. Loughery Jr., Los Angeles County Probation Department, "Sealing and Expungement of Criminal Records—The Big Lie" (1970)[1]

Procedures should be established that would allow some offenders to put their criminal offending entirely in the past and have the slate wiped clean. Nearly all other countries have recognized the value of doing this and have instituted laws to restore some convicts to full citizenship.

—Joan Petersilia, *When Prisoners Come Home* (2003)[2]

IN CHAPTER 6, we looked at how deferred prosecutions can result in expunged* or sealed† arrest and charge records after successful completion of prosecutorial probation. In this chapter, we turn our attention to expunging and sealing convictions after, usually long after, the sentence has been served. The purpose of this policy (available, to some extent, in every country)‡ is to encourage

---

* *Black's Law Dictionary* defines "expungement of record" as the "process by which a record of criminal conviction is destroyed or sealed by the state or federal repository." *Black's Law Dictionary* 603 (St. Paul, MN: West/Thomson Reuters, 7th ed., 1999). The verb "to expunge" comes from the Latin *expungere*, meaning "prick out, blot out, mark (a name on a list) for deletion." Medieval and Renaissance manuscripts used a series of dots known as *puncta delentia* to mark mistakes or material that should be deleted from a text.

† The etymology of "sealing," traceable to the fourteenth century, is "to place a seal on (a document)." From the 1660s it conveyed the sense of "to close up with wax, lead, cement, etc."

‡ Spain, for example, makes all convictions eligible for sealing after the sentence has been served and the defendant has been crime-free for a prescribed period of time,

rehabilitation and to recognize that a previously convicted offender has succeeded in turning his life around. The policy is predicated on the belief that a criminal conviction should not be a permanent stain on character but should come to an end, just as probation and imprisonment end. Criminologist Shadd Maruna speaks of a "right to re-biography": "Without this right, ex-offenders will always be ex-offenders, hence outsiders, or the Other."[3] After a certain period of crime-free behavior, the ex-offender has demonstrated that he has put his past offending behind him and deserves reinstatement as a citizen in good standing. Certificates of rehabilitation and pardons fulfill that same purpose, but without altering history.

Expunging or Sealing Juvenile Delinquency Records

The practice of sealing and expunging criminal records was pioneered in the juvenile justice system. Indeed, one of the two principal rationales for a separate juvenile court was to keep the juvenile defendant's (respondent's) identity and criminal conduct confidential. The juvenile court's proponents urged that the individual's juvenile court record be kept confidential during the respondent's minority and automatically sealed or expunged when the respondent turned twenty-one.[4] However, juvenile court statutes always included provisions authorizing a court to unseal the case file upon a showing of good cause. Some state statutes provided that an individual with a sealed or purged juvenile adjudication could, when asked, deny having been found guilty of a crime or of having been adjudicated delinquent.

For more than half a century, the desirability of juvenile court confidentiality went practically unquestioned. However, the Su-

---

which varies according to the seriousness of the conviction offense. In order to seal a conviction record, the penal code (Art. 136.2 Penal Code) states that the following requirements must be met: (1) A period of time after having served the sentence must have elapsed (six months, two years, three years, or five years depending on the sentence); (2) no further crime has been committed in the interim; (3) civil compensation has been paid or the person has been declared without money. See Elena Larrauri, *Conviction Records in Spain: Obstacles to Reintegration of Offenders?* 3 European Journal of Probation 50, 58 (2011).

preme Court's watershed 1967 decision, *in re Gault*, charged that juvenile court secrecy masked abuse of respondents' rights and interests. Conservatives attacked the confidentiality of juvenile criminal records as a threat to public safety.[5] As Professors T. Markus Funk and Daniel Polsby noted,

> A sentencing judge in a jurisdiction that aggressively expunges juvenile crime records by destroying them is in very much the same position as the prospective creditor or car buyer. A young adult is convicted of some crime and appears for sentencing. Now the judge must determine whether he is in fact a first (or second, etc.) offender, or whether he instead is so merely as a result of a statutorily imposed fiction. Assuming judges—and others in the employer class—might regularly observe the distinction between first offenders and chronic ones and make real-world consequences turn on it, the existence of uncertainty concerning whether one was dealing with an ingenue or a recidivist offender could be expected to produce two altogether unwelcome results. Just as one could expect information-impaired bidders to bid too little for good used cars and too much for bad ones, one could expect judges to sentence career criminals too leniently and genuine first offenders too harshly, but with a tendency, depending on the judge's degree of risk-aversion, toward being too harsh with actual first offenders.[6]

The trend has been to make juvenile court records increasingly available for both criminal justice and non–criminal justice purposes. As the Minnesota Council on Delinquency explains, "[A] lthough many people believe a juvenile record will not follow someone past 18, there are many ways juvenile records can be made public and ways private juvenile records can be accessed that can limit a young person's opportunities as an adult."[7] Today, in at least thirty states, the media can access juvenile offenders' identities for certain cases.[8] Some states make it even easier for lay people to gain access to juvenile records. Maine, for example, discloses any person's delinquency adjudications to any interested party for a $31 fee.[9] The Florida Department of Law Enforcement has made all rap sheet information, including juvenile arrests and adjudications, accessible to the general public.[10]

The United States, which invented a separate juvenile court committed to record confidentiality, now is exceptional for disclosing more juvenile offender information than most other countries or international standards allow. Nevertheless, while advocates for juvenile criminal record confidentiality are in retreat, they are not routed. Many old laws and regulations, and even some new ones, treat juvenile criminal records as confidential. A majority of states permit persons who have been adjudicated delinquent to request that their juvenile record be sealed.[11]

Sealing and Expunging Adult Convictions

Sealing and expunging records migrated from the juvenile justice system to the adult criminal justice system. The 1950 Federal Youth Corrections Act (1950) is a good example. It gave eighteen- to twenty-six-year-old federal offenders an opportunity to have their convictions "set aside," if a court released them early from probation.[12] Likewise, in the 1950s, 1960s, and 1970s, many states passed laws authorizing sealing or expunging some adult convictions.[13] As the Supreme Court observed in *Dickerson v. New Banner Institute* (1983), there is mind-boggling variation among the states:

> Over half the States have enacted one or more statutes that may be classified as expunction provisions that attempt to conceal prior convictions or to remove some of their collateral or residual effects. These statutes differ, however, in almost every particular. Some are applicable only to young offenders. . . . Some are discretionary, while others provide for automatic expunction under certain circumstances. The statutes vary in the language employed to describe what they do. Some speak of expunging the conviction, others of "sealing" the file or of causing the dismissal of the charge. The statutes also differ in their actual effect. Some are absolute; others are limited. Only

a minority address questions such as whether the expunged conviction may be considered in sentencing for a subsequent offense or in setting bail on a later charge, or whether the expunged conviction may be used for impeachment purposes, or whether the convict may deny the fact of his conviction. Some statutes, too, clearly were not meant to prevent use of the conviction in a subsequent prosecution.[14]

Which Convictions Are Eligible for Expungement and When?

Most states do not permit expungements for serious offense convictions, no matter how many crime-free years have passed since termination of the sentence. Beyond that, states' expungement eligibilities vary enormously. Mississippi permits the expungement of drug possession convictions if the person had not yet turned twenty-six at the time of the offense. In addition, any first-time misdemeanant, as well as anyone convicted of issuing a bad check, drug possession, false pretenses, felony larceny, malicious mischief, and shoplifting, can petition the court once for expungement. Presumably, despite the expungement, the state keeps a readily retrievable record of past expungements so that its one-to-a-customer rule will not be violated.[15]

In Illinois, a conviction resulting in a custodial (jail or prison) sentence is never eligible for expungement. However, three different policies are applicable to convictions punished by noncustodial sentences: (1) expungement for some minor crimes (e.g., shoplifting) two years after completion of a noncustodial sentence, whereupon charges are dismissed; (2) expungement for statutory rape where the perpetrator is less than five years older than the victim and for motor vehicle offenses (e.g., driving without insurance; reckless driving if the offender was under twenty-five) five years after termination of a noncustodial sentence; and (3) expungement of first-time drug possession offenses five years after termination of a probation sentence.[16] Any crime eligible for expungement is also eligible for sealing four years after termination of probation or other supervised community sanction; most misdemeanors and some drug and prostitution felonies can be sealed after four years. Only law enforcement agencies have access to a sealed record.[17]

Prior to 2010, Massachusetts rap sheets revealed nonconviction dispositions, such as continued-without-a-finding, dismissals, and not-guilty verdicts. The 2010 criminal records reform provided that the criminal record repository would not reveal dispositions favorable to the defendant to non–law enforcement inquirers. At the expiration of a first-time drug offender's probationary sentence, the court may seal all records, except for published decisions, court calendars, police blotters, and probation office files. Sealed convictions will not appear on Criminal Offender Record Information (CORI) reports, are not admissible as evidence, and cannot be used in a court proceeding. The Commissioner of Probation may seal adult criminal records five years after release from jail or final disposition for a misdemeanor and ten years after release from prison, other than felonies for firearms offenses, perjury, and escape.[18] Once a criminal record is sealed, the Commissioner of Probation must reply to inquirers that no record exists.[19] A person with a criminal record who is subsequently convicted of any offense anywhere in the United States is not eligible for sealing.

All state expungement provisions make a substantial period of crime-free time a prerequisite for eligibility. The length of the waiting period depends on the seriousness of the conviction offense. Utah has one of the nation's most liberal expungement laws. Offenses are expungement-eligible after varying periods of time have elapsed, for example, ten years for felony DUI, seven years for other felonies, five years for class A misdemeanors, four years for class B misdemeanors, and three years for all other misdemeanors and violations.[20] Convictions for sex offenses, homicides, felony DUIs, and violent felonies can never be expunged.

Rhode Island permits first offenders to apply for expungement ten years after completion of a sentence for a nonviolent felony and five years after completion of a sentence for a nonviolent misdemeanor.[21] Oregon permits first offenders to apply to a court to have a conviction set aside three years from the date of judgment for most misdemeanors and some felony convictions.[22] Colorado authorizes an ex-offender to petition a court to seal petty drug-related convictions and class 2 and 3 misdemeanor convictions three years after final disposition. Class 1 misdemeanors become expungement-eligible five crime-free years after final disposition. Class 5 and 6 drug felony convictions become sealing-eligible after seven years. There is a ten-year waiting period for all other drug-related convictions.[23]

Eligibility of Recidivists for Expungment

Should expungement or sealing be available only to first offenders? We should answer "no" if we believe that criminal conduct does not reflect a hardened antisocial character and has little, if any, value in predicting future criminal conduct. But such a presumption is not supported by common experience or by empirical data. We assume that others will, in the future, act "in character," that is, that a person we have always known to be honest will act honestly tomorrow and that a person we have long known to be dishonest will act dishonestly tomorrow. We know that a person's character can change, but it will take time for us to revise our view; the person in question will have to prove herself.

States differ as to whether recidivists are eligible to have more than one conviction expunged. For example, Indiana allows expungement of only one conviction in a person's lifetime.[24] Other states permit or are silent with respect to multiple expungements.

Expungement Procedures

Expungement in the United States is usually not automatic.* An individual with an expungement-eligible conviction must petition a

* In many countries (e.g., Netherlands; see Miranda Boone, *Judicial Rehabilitation in the Netherlands: Balancing between Safety and Privacy*, 3 European Journal of Probation, 63 [2011]), expungement policies tend (at least for the most part) to follow an "automatic" rather than "merit-based" model (e.g., France; see Martine Herzog-Evans, *Judicial Rehabilitation in France: Helping with the Desisting Process and Acknowledging Achieved Desistance*, 3 European Journal of Probation, 4 [2011]): the convicted person is deemed rehabilitated after the passage of a specified period of time without new criminal charges. However, under the "automatic model," an ex-offender cannot do anything to accelerate his eligibility. Shadd Maruna criticizes the automatic model because it promotes "passive"

court or agency (usually the state police or office of probations).[25] Usually, the prosecutor's office has a short time (e.g., ten to thirty days) to file an objection. A few states afford victims standing to object.[26] The standard for granting an expungement petition is vague. Some statutes require the judge to find that the person is "rehabilitated" or that the expungement is "consistent with the public interest."[27] What counts as proof of rehabilitation? Must there be apparently sincere contrition for past wrongs?[28] Does regular church attendance count? Paying child support? Doing chores to assist an elderly neighbor? Courts take into account evidence of rehabilitative effort, including diplomas and training certifications, work history, letters from employers, and successful completion of various training and treatment programs. The extreme subjectivity of decision making based on such evidence suggests that there may be no better criterion than absence of a new criminal charge for a specified period of time. That is an easy standard to administer and less susceptible to arbitrary decision making. Requiring proof of rehabilitation is likely to advantage white-collar and middle-class offenders.

Feasibility of Expungement

Developments in information technology and the emergence of scores of criminal background checking companies make it increasingly unlikely that conviction information that has been publicly

---

rather than "active redemption": " 'Virtue's Door Unsealed Is Never Sealed Again': Redeeming Redemption and the Seven-Year Itch," in Natasha A. Frost et al. (eds.), *Contemporary Issues in Criminal Justice Policy* 52 (Boston: Cengage/Wadsworth, 2009). See also Shadd Maruna, *Reentry as a Rite of Passage*, 13 *Punishment and Society*, 1 (2011). Some "hybrid" models also exist, requiring both proof of positive redemption and the passage of a certain amount of time (see, e.g., Article 179 of the Italian Penal Code). In Germany, expungement is essentially automatic, after a specified period without a new conviction or pending charges. However, there is also the possibility of early expungement upon the showing of rehabilitation (see Christine Morgenstern, *Judicial Rehabilitation in Germany—The Use of Criminal Records and the Removal of Recorded Convictions*, 3 European Journal of Probation, 20, 29–30 [2011]). In the United Kingdom, there is no discretionary judicial expungement. See Nicola Padfield, *Judicial Rehabilitation? A View from England*, 3 European Journal of Probation, 36 (2011).

available for years can be made confidential.[29] Convictions are increasingly recorded in commercial information vendors' proprietary databases and perhaps already reported to numerous clients. For an expungement or sealing order after expiration of sentence to be effective, it would be necessary to prohibit commercial information vendors from reporting expunged or sealed convictions. Unfortunately the First Amendment poses an insurmountable obstacle for such a proposal.[30] The government cannot constitutionally prohibit news media, bloggers, or anyone else from posting, printing, or discussing who has been convicted for what crimes,* nor could the government constitutionally order libraries to purge expunged conviction information from print or electronic publications or bar library users from looking at archived convictions, even if subsequently expunged. Similarly, the government could not prohibit private individuals from passing along to friends, neighbors, or to law enforcement official information obtained from court observations or word of mouth about a conviction that was subsequently expunged.

Some attempts to keep expunged record information confidential have not been successful. In *G.D. v. Bernard Kenny & The Hudson County Democratic Organization, Inc.* (2011), the beneficiary of an expunged drug conviction brought a libel suit against a political opponent who publicized his prior conviction. In dismissing the action, the New Jersey Supreme Court opined that

> [t]he expungement statute does not obliterate the record of a conviction. No one has argued that a newspaper that has

* Countries without U.S.-like protection of freedom of speech can enforce expungement laws by prohibiting communicating information about expunged convictions. For example, Australia makes it a crime to disclose an expunged conviction. Australian journalist Derryn Hinch was convicted, placed under home detention, and restrained from speaking to the media after revealing the names of two convicted sex offenders at a public rally and on his personal blog. Australia's High Court ruled that prohibiting disclosure of criminal record information was not unconstitutional. Dan Harrison, "I Don't Regret It," *The Age*, March 10, 2011, http://www.theage.com.au/national/i-dont-regret-it-hinch-unrepentant-in-face-of-jail-20110310-1bpc1.html. See also Australian Human Rights and Equal Opportunity Commission, *Discrimination in Employment on the Basis of a Criminal Record* (2004), http://www.hreoc.gov.au/Human_Rights/criminalrecord/discussion.html.

> reported on the arrest or conviction of a person whose record is later expunged must excise from its archives a past story or, similarly, that the New Jersey judiciary must razor from the bound volumes of its reporters a published case. Common sense tells us that an arrest or conviction may become general knowledge within a community and that people will not banish from their memories stored knowledge even if they become aware of an expungement order. The expungement statute—enacted at a time when law enforcement and court documents may have been stored in the practical obscurity of a file room—now must coexist in a world where information is subject to rapid and mass dissemination, for example through the internet.
>
> In light of common law and constitutional principles protecting free speech, and with the expungement statute as a backdrop, the Court holds that the traditionally recognized defense of truth to a defamation action was not lost in this case because of the existence of an expungement order. The expungement statute does not transmute a once-true fact into a falsehood; it cannot banish memories. The right to speak freely on matters of public concern and the right to criticize a candidate for public office implicate core values protected by our federal and state constitutions. Truth may be personally embarrassing and offensive to some, but it remains a defense in a defamation action, even when the truth revealed concerns information contained in an expunged record. Here, for purposes of the defamation action, it would make no difference that the speaker knew of the expungement order or how he obtained it.[31]

A law requiring commercial information vendors to include a notation in their criminal background reports if a reported conviction has been expunged, sealed, pardoned, or vacated might pass constitutional muster. It would further the government's legitimate interest in promoting the accuracy of criminal record reports without suppressing speech. However, such a policy would be feasible only if the commercial vendor can readily find out about an expungement, sealing, or pardon. The best solution would be an electronic database of sealed and expunged convictions and pardoned record-subjects that commercial vendors could search when preparing criminal background reports.[32] Ironically, however, making expungements easily accessible would readily bring expunged convictions to light, thereby undermining the goal of expungement.

The Right to Lie?

Expungement and sealing would not mean much if public and private employers, licensing boards, and others could require applicants to divulge expunged convictions on pain of firing or prosecution. Thus, to be effective, expungement and sealing statutes must (1) prohibit employers and others from asking job seekers about expunged and sealed convictions or (2) authorize the beneficiary of the expunction to (falsely) deny having ever been arrested, prosecuted, or convicted.[33] The first option, a version of which exists in New York State, raises serious First Amendment problems. The second option is authorized in other countries and some U.S. states.*

> Expungements are based on the premise that those with criminal records will have trouble reintegrating into society and may face barriers from participating in public life unless they have a legitimate means of being able to honestly deny that

* In the United Kingdom, according to the Rehabilitation of Offenders Act (1974), a conviction becomes "spent" after a specified time without a new crime. Spent convictions are not deleted from police records when they become spent, but they remain on the Police National Computer until the individual's 100th birthday.

A person whose conviction is spent is referred to as a "rehabilitated person." Under section 4 of the act, the general rule (subject to a number of exceptions) is that a rehabilitated person is treated for all legal purposes as if he had never committed the offense that led to the spent conviction or caution. Exceptions to the general rule are set out in the Rehabilitation of Offenders Act 1974 (Exceptions) Order 1975, SI 1975/1023, which lists a number of jobs, professions, and other activities known as "excepted positions." Excepted positions cover (for example) work with children or vulnerable adults or roles in certain licensed occupations or positions of trust (e.g., police officers, solicitors). If a person wishes to undertake an excepted position, then she can be required to disclose full details of her criminal record, including details of any spent convictions or cautions. These details are confirmed through a criminal background check conducted by the Disclosure and Barring Service (formerly the Criminal Records Bureau).

> they have ever been charged with a crime or possessed a criminal record. As a result, most states permit individuals who have had their records expunged to answer in the negative if asked whether they have been arrested or charged for a crime. Therefore, if asked on a job or school application, an applicant with an expunged record may honestly answer "no" to having been charged with a crime. Additionally, for those states that permit expungements after convictions, some permit the same negative answer to be given for questions concerning conviction.[34]

Of the sixteen states that allow expungement or sealing of convictions, thirteen permit an individual to deny, at least under some circumstances, ever having been convicted.[35] For the expungement beneficiary, there is uncertainty about when the expunged conviction can be denied and when it must be disclosed.

Florida allows some individuals with expunged convictions to deny having ever been convicted, but it requires them to truthfully disclose convictions on applications for employment to state and local criminal justice agencies, the Department of Education, and the Florida Bar Association's Character and Fitness Committee. The New York State Bar Committee on Character and Fitness asks lawyers applying for bar admission to divulge "all convictions, even if expunged." (Because the Bar Committee asks for this information, so do law school admissions applications.) Answering falsely is grounds for rejecting the applicant's bar admission and, if already admitted to the bar, grounds for disbarment. This policy not only creates confusion, but undermines the legitimacy of expungement. If judges and lawyers, who control bar admissions, can require people to disclose expunged convictions, won't other professional associations, businesses, volunteer organizations, and individuals claim an equally important need for disclosure?

"Unexpunging" Records?

If expunging required actual destruction or erasure of the criminal record, the record would not be retrievable. That would create serious problems in a number of contexts. The police may need to examine an old conviction to solve a recent crime or to rectify another person's unjust conviction. Both the prosecutor and the defense attorney, in deciding whether to call (or how to cross-examine) a witness, need to examine that potential witness's rap sheet and prior criminal case files.

In *Davis v. Alaska* (1974),[36] the Supreme Court considered whether a criminal defendant has a constitutional (confrontation clause) right to cross-examine a prosecution witness about that witness's sealed juvenile criminal record. Alaska, like many states, did not allow lawyers to impeach a witness by exposing prior delinquency adjudications. The state asserted a compelling interest in protecting a person from having his juvenile criminality disclosed. In *Davis*, the court held that a criminal defendant's Sixth Amendment right to impeach a juvenile prosecution witness outweighed the state's interest in protecting that witness from disclosure of his juvenile criminality. Chief Justice Burger's majority opinion said, "Whatever temporary embarrassment might result to Green [the prosecution's witness] or his family by disclosure of his juvenile record—if the prosecution insisted on using him to make its case—is outweighed by petitioner's right to probe into the influence of possible bias in the testimony of a crucial identification witness." It concluded "that the State's desire that Green fulfill his public duty to testify free from embarrassment and with his reputation unblemished must fall before the right of petitioner to seek out the truth in the process of defending himself." (In accordance with the *Davis* decision, the Federal Rules of Evidence, like state evidentiary rules, now provide that a juvenile adjudication is admissible to impeach a witness other than the defendant if an adult's conviction for that offense would be admissible to attack the adult's credibility, and admitting the evidence is necessary to fairly determining guilt or innocence.[37]) The prosecution does not have a similar constitutional confrontation right, but treating the scope of the prosecution's impeachment differently from the scope of the defendant's impeachment would undermine the adversarial trial ideal.

Some non–criminal justice organizations and individuals also have a legitimate need for access to expunged records. The resurrection of an expunged conviction is sometimes necessary because it is relevant to defend against a defamation lawsuit. In *Bahr v. Statesman Journal Company & George Rede* (1981),[38] a candidate for county commissioner in Oregon denied having ever been convicted of a crime. The local newspaper called him a liar, citing an expunged perjury conviction. Bahr sued the newspaper for defamation on the ground that his sealed conviction was a nullity.[39] The court granted the newspaper's motion to dismiss the complaint because the statute "was intended to remove the stigma associated with the conviction of a crime and to give [convicted] individuals another chance . . . unencumbered by that stigma. . . . [However, although] the statute authorizes certain persons to misrepresent their own past, it does not make that misrepresentation true." Oregon's sealing statute explicitly stated that "for purposes of any civil action in which truth is an element of a claim for relief or affirmative defense, the provisions of this section providing that the conviction, arrest or other proceeding be deemed not to have occurred do not apply."[40] Truth being a complete defense in a defamation lawsuit, the court ruled that, in defending against the defamation suit, the newspaper was entitled to reveal the plaintiff's conviction.

Because the Oregon statute explicitly permitted a conviction that had been set aside to be disclosed by a civil defendant, the court did not opine on the newspaper's First Amendment defense—that it is unconstitutional to hold a newspaper criminally or civilly liable for disclosing true information about a set-aside conviction.[41] The U.S. Supreme Court's decisions striking down state statutes prohibiting newspapers from publishing the names of juvenile defendants and rape victims in order to protect their privacy would seem to doom a state's attempt to prohibit disclosure of the names of convicted individuals.[42]

Adding Rehabilitative Achievement to the Criminal Record

Although the best-known and most effective mechanism for neutralizing a criminal record is an executive (gubernatorial or presidential) pardon, pardons are rarely granted.[43] President Obama granted only fifty-two pardons in his first five years in office, the lowest number for any modern president. Some governors serve an entire four-year term without granting a single one.[44] A pardon does not expunge the criminal record but, in effect, pronounces the ex-offender forgiven. For a convicted offender, receiving formal forgiveness from the chief executive probably mitigates social stigma and, in many states, relieves the ex-offender of certain disabilities and disqualifications.

Certificates of Rehabilitation

A certificate of rehabilitation is an alternative to expungement and sealing. Rather than hiding the prior conviction, it places the prior conviction in a more favorable light. Eleven states (Alabama, Arizona, California, Connecticut, Hawaii, Illinois, Iowa, New Jersey, New York, North Carolina, and Ohio) issue some type of certificate of rehabilitation or restoration of rights.[45] These certificates indicate that previously convicted persons have not been convicted of any new offenses (for a certain period of time) since they completed their sentence and are therefore deemed rehabilitated. Here, we again confront the question encountered in our earlier discussion of expungement. What should be the criteria for recognizing rehabilitation? No new felony convictions? No convictions period? No pending criminal charges? What about the charges that were dismissed because evidence was suppressed due to an unlawful search, the victim refused to testify, or because the speedy trial law was violated? (Professor Al Blumstein, the leading scholar of recidivism/desistance, uses arrest as the indicator of recidivism.)

Some people may think that the award of a certificate of rehabilitation should be based on something more than the absence of a new conviction, perhaps the presence of some commendable conduct such as completing a treatment program, holding a job, earning a degree, or supporting a spouse, partner, child or parent. Piling complexity on complexity, if we required a petitioner to have a legitimate job for a specified period of time, white-collar offenders would have a much better chance of obtaining a rehabilitation certificate. That would rightly strike many people as unfair and discriminatory.

In order that a certificate of rehabilitation be an effective tool in combating criminal record stigma, it needs to be recorded on the offender's rap sheet or at least be made easily available to criminal background checkers. Ideally, it would be recorded on the rap sheet and added to the case file so that a commercial information vendor will find the information and report it to customers.[46] The problem is that it is very difficult to guarantee that the certificate will actually be added to the rap sheet, much less the court record that may have been archived years earlier. An effective alternative would be to record all certificates in a publicly accessible state-level "rehabilitated offenders database," which commercial information vendors would be required to search as part of every criminal background check. But that proposal would be effective only if (1) the certificate-issuing court or agency reliably submitted information to the database and (2) criminal background checkers routinely checked that database and reported certificate information in their criminal background reports. Alternatively, the certificate beneficiary could submit a copy of her rehabilitation certificate to prospective employers and others. However, that would call attention to the prior conviction.

New York State's Certificates of Rehabilitation

New York State has been the leader in use of certificates of rehabilitation. It provides for a Certificate of Relief from Disabilities (CRD)[47] and a Certificate of Good Conduct (CGC).[48] The Certificate of Relief from Disabilities is supposed to appear next to the relevant conviction on the rap sheet.[49]

A CRD may be issued by courts or by the Department of Corrections and Community Supervision.* Individuals convicted of an unlimited number of misdemeanors, but no more than one felony, are eligible to apply for the CRD immediately after conviction. Thus,

* The certificate shall be considered a "temporary certificate" when (1) issued by a court to a holder who is under a "revocable sentence" as defined in §700 of the Correction Law and the court's authority to revoke such sentence has not expired or (2) issued by the State Board of Parole and the holder is still under the supervision of the Board.

this certificate is meant to encourage and facilitate rehabilitation, rather than to mark its achievement. Ex-offenders with more than one felony conviction, subject to waiting periods, are eligible to apply to the Board of Parole for a CGC. For class C, D, and E felonies, the waiting period is three years from termination of sentence. For class A and B felonies, the waiting period is five years. A CGC covers all prior convictions.

Both types of New York State certificates of rehabilitation provide an across-the-board restoration of rights, that is, relief from "any forfeiture or disability" and "any barrier to . . . employment that is automatically imposed by law by reason of conviction of the crime or the offense." They also create a judicially enforceable "presumption of rehabilitation" that must be recognized by employers and licensing boards. However, the presumption is easy for employers to overcome.

> The certificates are not dispositive, whether the ex-felon is qualified or barred from the job by reason of past conviction. In the end, an employer still may consider a prior conviction as a good reason not to employ an individual even when a certificate has been issued. None of this is to suggest, however, that relief should not be sought or celebrated when it is secured. It is an important form of self-validation and may open doors to advancement throughout the career of its holder.[50]

Even though the criteria do not seem difficult to meet, historically very few certificates have been granted. The Board of Parole issued only 281 certificates in 2003. However, since 2007, there has been a marked increase, to more than 1,000 per year. Courts grant an additional 2,500 certificates each year.[51] Given that approximately 350,000 defendants are convicted in New York State courts each year,[52] the two procedures affect only a small fraction of convicted offenders. Perhaps more aggressive notification of convicted offenders about how to apply for a certificate could increase the number,[53] but one suspects that ex-offenders do not regard them as worth the time and effort.

Conclusion

Expungement, sealing, and certificates of rehabilitation reflect the view that a criminal conviction should not be a permanent stigma and disability.[54] There should be a path back to full citizenship and restored reputation. Expungement aims to wipe the record clean after a sufficient period of law-abiding behavior. Sealing makes the record inaccessible, except to those with statutory authorization or a court order. Expungement critics make a forceful point that rewriting history is characteristic of dictatorships, not democracies. Although a strong advocate for ameliorating collateral consequences of conviction, former U.S. Pardons Attorney Margaret Colgate Love opposes expungement for that reason:

> Though expungement still finds its occasional champion in the academic literature, in theory and practice it is an unsatisfactory solution to the problem of restoring rights and status. There are at least four reasons for this, and all relate to its reliance on concealment and denial. First, the concept of "expungement" requires a certain willingness to "rewrite history" that is hard to square with a legal system founded on the search for truth. Second, to the extent expungement involves an effort to conceal an individual's criminal record from public view, it tends to devalue legitimate public safety concerns. Third, the expungement concept ignores the technological realities of the information age; a process whose benefits depend upon secrecy will surely be frustrated by the trend toward broader public posting and private dissemination of criminal history information. Finally, because it is premised on a fiction, expungement fails to afford an opportunity for the offender to be reconciled to the community and helps society to evade its obligation to change its views toward former offenders.[55]

Love makes an important point. Altering public records in pursuit of goals considered more important sets a dangerous precedent. Moreover, it would make no sense to erase convictions, but require truthful answers to queries about past convictions. Thus, purging the record leads inexorably to authorizing expungement beneficiaries to lie about their prior record. If that is considered desirable, it opens the door to "justifiable lying" in other contexts.[56] In drafting its prestigious Model Penal Code, the American Law Institute, rightly in my view, rejected the idea of expunging criminal convictions.[57]

Expungement that takes place many years after the expiration of a sentence could be understood as recognition of successful rehabilitation and reason to terminate legal disqualifications and disabilities. What societal interest could there be in continuing to impose disqualifications and disabilities on an ex-offender after a decade (or more) of law-abiding behavior following termination of sentence? At that point, we ought to consider the earlier criminality no longer relevant to assessing character or risk of future offending.

However, if expungement and sealing are meant to facilitate (rather than recognize) rehabilitation, they should occur much sooner. Ex-offenders need the most assistance immediately after release from prison or termination of sentence. Most recidivism occurs within the first three years after completion of sentence, predominantly in the first year.[58] Furthermore, if the purpose of expungement and sealing is to facilitate rehabilitation, making convictions for serious offenses ineligible for expungement does not make sense. Individuals convicted of serious offenses bear the most stigma and have the most difficulty reintegrating into society. Contrariwise, those convicted of minor offenses face fewest barriers to successful reentry. In any event, it is doubtful that criminal record information can be effectively suppressed in this day and age. Once a conviction has been public for several years, it will likely have been copied to a number of proprietary databases. In addition, a person who has served substantial prison time will have a gap in her résumé likely to lead to disclosure of the conviction. For these reasons, I prefer certificates of rehabilitation to expungement, sealing, and lying. However, the effectiveness of certificates of rehabilitation depends on employers considering them credible. The certificate will not be regarded as a reliable indicator of character or risk if every ex-offender is awarded one.

Rehabilitation certificate schemes must grapple with the difficult question of criteria for issuance. If the bar is too low, for example, sixty days without being arrested for a crime of violence, the certificate will lack credibility. If employers know that the certificate is awarded because it might be helpful to the ex-offender rather than because of sound prediction that this particular ex-offender presents a low risk of reoffending, it will be disregarded. However, if the bar is too high, for example, ten years without any arrest or conviction, the certificate will not facilitate rehabilitation. A convicted person who has not reoffended for ten years after termination of sentence is obviously rehabilitated. If we want the prospect of a certificate of rehabilitation to serve as an incentive to encourage convicted offenders to desist from crime, it should be available sooner. The credibility of rehabilitation certificates might be bolstered by adding more information, for example, enrollment in school, participation in a treatment program, meeting financial obligations to children. Finally, it is important that the certificate of rehabilitation be recorded in a way that is easily accessible to a criminal background checker. Recording it on the rap sheet is problematic given the historical struggle to record case dispositions on rap sheets. It would also be impractical to insert a copy of the certificate into the criminal court case file. The obvious solution is an easily accessible database of certificate of rehabilitation recipients.

8 ERRONEOUS RECORDS PROBLEMS

> FBI rap sheets are considered the gold standard of criminal background checks for employment because they include criminal history information from the federal government and all states, and they are far less vulnerable to mistaken identification. In reality, however, the records themselves do not live up to this reputation, as roughly 50 percent of the FBI records are incomplete or inaccurate.
>
> —National Employment Law Project (2013)[1]

> K. worked as a retail store department clerk after he finished his stint in the military. He was let go after the holiday season and didn't think much of it. He knew he could get other clerk jobs easily. But he was wrong. He applied for job after job and was turned down. Without employment, he lost everything and eventually became homeless. He got another job opportunity selling men's clothing. But when he showed up, he was told they changed their mind. He demanded to know why he was let go. That's when he learned of his erroneous criminal record. He was listed in a database used by all the department stores in that part of the state that he was wanted for arson and shoplifting. When he put two and two together, he realized that the individual who stole his wallet several years ago had been using his identifying information when arrested and released. K. contacted us in 1996 and has been instrumental in our learning about this worst-case scenario of identity theft and in working with the legislative process to pass laws to prevent his situation from happening to others.
>
> —Beth Givens, Director of the Privacy Rights Clearinghouse (2000)[2]

GIVEN THEIR IMPORTANCE for establishing an individual's public identity and reputation, and therefore opportunities for employment, housing, and immigration, intelligence and investigative databases, rap sheets, and court records must be accurate and reliable. Erroneous records can cause innocent people to be arrested and searched. They can result in innocent people being wrongly charged and held in pretrial confinement. Outside the criminal justice context, erroneous records cause people to be passed over for jobs and to lose other opportunities.

Rap Sheet Accuracy

In 1973, Congress passed a law requiring that federally funded state and local criminal records repositories maintain records that are secure, complete, reviewable, and challengeable by the record-subject.[3] Three years later, the U.S. Department of Justice (DOJ) issued implementing regulations that included the aspiration that, through "a process of data collection, entry, storage and systematic audit . . . no record containing criminal history record information shall contain erroneous information."[4] Toward that end, the DOJ required the states to adopt operational procedures to ensure that individual criminal history records are complete and accurate. Dispositions must be added to rap sheets within ninety days. Law enforcement agencies must check with the central repository before disseminating criminal history information. When an error is identified, the repository must notify all criminal justice agencies known to have received the erroneous information. There must be a procedure that, "without undue burden," permits an individual to review and challenge her criminal history record and to appeal a criminal justice agency's refusal to correct an alleged error. States must certify to DOJ their compliance with the federal requirements to the "maximum extent feasible" (defined as "actions which can be taken to comply with the procedures set forth in the plan that do not require additional legislative authority or involve unreasonable cost or do not exceed existing technical ability"). Noncompliance can be punished by reductions of federal funding, but the DOJ has never imposed that punishment.

The states responded to the federal statute and regulations by passing laws governing the maintenance and dissemination of individual criminal history information.[5] The number of states with statutes addressing accuracy and completeness of criminal history records increased from fourteen in 1974 to forty-one in 1978.[6] By 1991, all states and territories, except the Virgin Islands, had laws of varying specificity.[7] Some are quite specific. For example, Alaska requires inclusion of prosecutorial declinations, time limit for reporting, and specific agencies' or officials' reporting responsibilities.[8] Other states' reporting requirements are quite general.[9]

Notwithstanding standard-setting legislation, assuring the accuracy of individual criminal history records is still a challenge. According to the 2010 Bureau of Justice Statistics' Survey of State Criminal History Information, twenty-seven states reported a backlog with regard to entering court dispositions into their criminal history databases; eighteen states reported nearly 1.8 million unprocessed or partially processed court dispositions, ranging from 100 in Kentucky to 761,462 in Utah. The average length of time between a final felony disposition and its receipt by the repository ranged from less than one day in Delaware and New York to 555 days in Kansas. Moreover, the average number of days between a disposition's receipt and its recording on the rap sheet ranged from less than one day in Delaware, Hawaii, and New York to 665 days in Kansas.

A 2005 study found that "[a]lthough state systems are improving, record accuracy and completeness continue to be the most serious problems affecting criminal history databases."[10]* A scathing 2013 National Employment Law Project (NELP) report called the rap sheet system "broken."[11] According to NELP, roughly 50 percent of rap sheet records in the Interstate Identification Index (Triple I) lack information on final disposition. NELP estimated that, of 14.4 million FBI background checks conducted for employment purposes, 1.8 million were based on erroneous or incomplete information.† The most common problems are (1) failure to record an arrest's disposition, (2) attributing to an individual the wrong

---

* One study by the Bronx Defenders found that 62 percent of a random sample of New York State rap sheets contained at least one significant error; 32 percent contained multiple errors. The number of errors ranged from one to nine, with a median of two. According to data from the New York State Department of Criminal Justice Services, approximately seven million New Yorkers have rap sheets. Applying a relatively conservative 30 percent error rate, the Legal Action center estimated that at least 2.1 million New Yorkers have rap sheets that contain errors. Legal Action Center, *The Problem of Rap Sheet Errors: An Analysis by the Legal Action Center*, 2013.

† Criminal history inaccuracies are also a problem in other countries. In the United Kingdom, the *Guardian* newspaper reported that, over a five-year period, inaccurate background checks saddled 12,000 people with erroneous criminal records. Press Association, "Criminal Records Wrongly Name 12,000 people: Almost £2m Paid Out in Compensation as a Result of Errors," *Guardian*, December 27, 2012, http://www.theguardian.com/uk/2012/dec/28/criminal-records-errors.

criminal history record, and (3) multiple entries for the same arrest or conviction.

Rap Sheet Errors

A criminal background check based on rap sheet information may fail to identify a person's criminal record (a false negative error). This can occur because commercial vendors do not search court records in every state; a truly nationwide search is rarely financially feasible.[12] "False positive" errors occur when people are identified as having a criminal record when they actually do not. This happens because more than one person can have the same name and even same birthday. In addition, an explosive increase in identity theft has significantly increased the risk of misidentification. The 2005 Report of the BJS/SEARCH National Focus Group on Identity Theft Victimization and Criminal Record Repository Operations observed that:

1. First, victims may be stopped, detained, or even arrested and charged by law enforcement officials *on the basis of other persons' criminal history records.*
2. Second, victims may be denied employment, licenses, housing, loans, or other services or entitlements because criminal history checks indicate that they have criminal records when, in fact, those records belong to other persons who have *intentionally impersonated the victims* when arrested or who have used names and other identifying information that are identical to or similar to the victim's name and other identifying information.[13]

Mismatching people with rap sheets is more likely to occur when rap sheets are searched by name rather than by fingerprints. Imagine Individual A, who has never been arrested or convicted of a crime, being saddled with the criminal record of Individual B, who has been arrested and convicted many times. Perhaps A and B have the same name, even the same birthday. Or perhaps police personnel, at booking, mistakenly spelled B as A. In either case, A would be tarred with B's rap sheet.

If Ronald Roe is stopped by the police and presents someone else's (John Q. Smith's) driver's license or other identity documents, he may be able to keep the suspicious officer from finding out that he is a fugitive or wanted by police in connection with an unsolved crime. Suppose, at booking, Roe identifies himself with John Q. Smith's name and produces Smith's stolen driver's license (a subterfuge that illuminates the importance of requiring driver's licenses to include photos).* The booking personnel transmit that information, along with Roe's fingerprints, to the state criminal records repository. If Roe's fingerprints are in the database, his ruse will be quickly discovered and the new arrest information will be added to his rap sheet, but John Q. Smith will be added to the rap sheet as an alias. If Roe has no fingerprints on file, the state repository will create a rap sheet in the name of John Q. Smith, but linked to Roe's fingerprints.

It is not likely that the real John Q. Smith (the identity theft victim) will immediately find out that he has a criminal record. If Smith is passed over for a number of jobs, he may suspect a problem and probe for an explanation. Perhaps a human resources officer will tell Smith that he wasn't hired on account of his criminal record. Smith, now realizing that he is the victim of identity theft, seeks to have his name erased from the rap sheet system so that future employers, landlords, and others will not misidentify him as having a criminal record. Unfortunately for Smith, the police will not make the correction that he requests. They will explain that very few people possess a unique name. The police cannot erase the rap sheets of

---

* Title II of The Real ID ACT of 2005 established standards for driver's licenses that would be eligible for federal identification purposes. One of the standards is inclusion on the license of a facial photo. The law encountered a great deal of resistance and enforcement has been several times delayed. In 2011, the Department of Homeland Security issued final rules on implementing the act. See http://www.gpo.gov/fdsys/pkg/FR-2008-01-29/pdf/08-140.pdf

The National Driver Register is a computerized database of names and identifying information about individuals whose driver's licenses have been suspended or revoked. It can be accessed for free by anyone. It does not include information about lost or stolen driver's licenses or of serious driving offenses, such as DWI. See http://www.nhtsa.gov/Data/National+Driver+Register+(NDR).

every criminal-recordless person who has the same name as a person with a criminal record. They will recommend that Smith explain the situation to prospective employers and volunteer his fingerprints or as many pieces of identification as possible (i.e., birthday, place of birth, social security number) when applying for future jobs.

Congress and state legislatures have responded to identity theft with new criminal laws.[14] Some make it a separate crime to offer false (stolen or modified) identity documents to the police.[15] A few are experimenting with identity theft "passports," documents that can be presented to police as proof of identity theft and true identity. To be effective, the passport has to be carried at all times, like an identity card or internal passport. To say the least, Americans have historically objected to identity documents. The National Crime Information Center (NCIC) has the Identity Theft File, a database populated with confirmed identity theft victims' names, social security numbers, dates of birth, photographs, and passwords chosen by the victims. If an identity theft victim is stopped by the police, the police can ask her for this password and thus avoid making an erroneous arrest.[16] California and a few other states have also created databases of identity theft victims. Victims can authorize prospective employers to access the database to verify that they are identity theft victims, thereby alerting them to the likelihood of a mistaken criminal background check.[17]

Identity confusion would be ameliorated if non–criminal justice organizations' access to the rap sheet system was expanded, which in turn would require a substantial increase in FBI and state criminal repository personnel as well as a solution to the problem of incomplete (dispositionless) rap sheets. (Currently, authorized non–law enforcement organizations' access to the Triple I is indirect; background checking requests must be sent to the state repository or, in some cases, to the FBI.) One could easily imagine a system of publicly accessible rap sheets based on names plus additional "soft" identifiers or even on routinized electronic fingerprinting. In 2006, the U.S. Attorney General's Report on Criminal History Background Checks recommended a big step in this direction.

> When a private employer or entity can inquire into whether an applicant or employee has a criminal history, a process should be available that allows the employer to determine whether the response to the question is truthful and complete. We think that the fingerprint-based criminal history information maintained by the FBI and state record repositories should be one of the authorized sources of information for this purpose, as system capacity allows, so long as the process provides appropriate privacy protections to the individual and respects state and federal laws designed to ensure that criminal records are not used to unfairly deny employment.[18]

The Attorney General's proposal recognizes the fact that many businesses and other organizations already have statutory authorization to obtain criminal record information from the Triple I. Adoption of the proposal would go far in transforming law enforcement's rap sheet system into an all-purpose public identity system. It would be more efficient, cheaper, faster, and more reliable than searching state (or county) court records. It is a good idea if, and only if, the problem of dispositionless rap sheets is solved and if rap sheets become more user friendly (easier for laymen to read and comprehend). That this proposal has not achieved any political traction indicates a deep reluctance to admit what has long been a reality—that individual criminal history records are already essentially public.

Failure to Seal or Expunge

Another type of criminal record mistake occurs when criminal record information that should be sealed or expunged is not.* New

---

* A parallel, even more egregious, example of dissemination of sealed investigative information is that some police departments sell the names of arrestees in cases that should have been sealed. In Onondaga County, New York, the sheriff's office sells reports containing arrest information from a Criminal History Arrest Incident Reporting System. A study conducted by a nonprofit organization found that 65 percent of the sheriff's reports contained information about arrests that should have been sealed. See Chapter 10.

York law, for example, requires sealing the record when an arrest or charge is resolved "favorably to the defendant."* Nevertheless, information that should be expunged or sealed often remains on the rap sheet.† Such mistakes are not easy to remedy. Suppose Jane Jones, having obtained a copy of her criminal record, sees a notation for an arrest that should have been sealed. Upon requesting a correction, she is told that she will have to file an application for record correction supported by certified copies of police and court records. This might mean traveling to the courthouse where her case was adjudicated. If the case was never brought to court, it would require correspondence, and perhaps meetings, with prosecutors and/or police officials who themselves might be unfamiliar with the disputed arrest. Other errors that infect rap sheets include multiple recordings of the same incident and recording the wrong criminal offense or wrong disposition or sentence. Such errors can be corrected if the record-subject finds out about errors and has sufficient

---

* New York Criminal Procedure Law § 160.50 provides: "Upon the termination of a criminal action or proceeding against a person in favor of such person . . . unless the district attorney upon motion with not less than five days notice to such person or his or her attorney demonstrates to the satisfaction of the court that the interests of justice require otherwise, or the court on its own motion with not less than five days notice to such person or his or her attorney determines that the interests of justice require otherwise and states the reasons for such determination on the record, the record of such action or proceeding *shall be sealed* and the clerk of the court wherein such criminal action or proceeding was terminated shall immediately notify the commissioner of the division of criminal justice services and the heads of all appropriate police departments and other law enforcement agencies that the action has been terminated in favor of the accused, and unless the court has directed otherwise, that the record of such action or proceeding *shall be sealed*" (emphasis added).

In most states, arrests that do not result in a conviction are not automatically sealed. Nevada requires a petition to a court to seal the record in the event of a dismissal or acquittal. The court must find that there has been an acquittal or a dismissal of charges and that there is no evidence that any further action will be brought against the person who is requesting the record sealing. NRS 179.255.

† An analysis conducted by the Legal Action Center of nearly 3,500 New York State rap sheets found that between 5.1 percent and 10.4 percent of them included information about dismissed cases that should have been sealed and that between 8 percent and 15 percent of them reported violations that should also have been sealed. Legal Action Center, *The Problem of Rap Sheet Errors: An Analysis by the Legal Action Center* (2013).

persistence and competence to pursue the remedial process, but those are big ifs.

Negative Criminal Justice System Consequences of Rap Sheet Errors

Rap sheet errors lead to mistaken decisions by police, prosecutors, and judges. An individual might be wrongly arrested because a record check, after a routine stop, mistakenly indicates that he is subject to an outstanding arrest warrant. The error will "eventually" be sorted out but perhaps not until after the arrestee has been searched and spent some hours, even a day or two, in lockup. If the search produced drugs, an unlawful weapon, or other contraband, the consequences of the information system error will be even more drastic.

In *Arizona v. Evans* (1995),[19] a criminal record check pursuant to a routine traffic stop mistakenly indicated an outstanding arrest warrant. The police officer arrested and searched Evans, finding marijuana. Evans moved to suppress the evidence on the ground that the search was unlawful because it resulted from failure to update the computer information system to reflect that the arrest warrant had been quashed. The trial court accepted that argument, but the appeals court reversed. The U.S. Supreme Court held that the exclusionary rule should not have applied because its purpose is to deter police misconduct, not to deter a judge's or court clerk's negligence in failing to update a computer information system. In her concurring opinion, Justice O'Connor explained that she would have reached a different conclusion if the defendant had shown that the police relied "on a recordkeeping system, their own or some other agency's, that has no mechanism to ensure its accuracy over time and that routinely leads to false arrests."[20] In other words, in her view, the police must not rely on an information system that they know or should know is dysfunctional and then ask to be excused for wrongful arrests caused by that dysfunctional system.

In 2009, the Supreme Court was asked to reverse a conviction based on a search that was attributable to erroneous information in *the police information system.* Bennie Herring had gone to the local police station to retrieve property from his impounded vehicle. When a police officer, who harbored suspicions about Herring, ran a routine criminal background check, it showed an outstanding arrest warrant in a neighboring county. The officer arrested and searched Herring, turning up amphetamine and an unlawful firearm. Herring moved to suppress this evidence on the ground that the neighboring town's police department had failed to update its computer records to show that the arrest warrant, on which the search had been predicated, had been recalled several months earlier. The Supreme Court (5–4) held that the court should not have suppressed the fruits of the search because an IT system mistake is not the kind of police misconduct that the exclusionary rule is meant to deter. For the exclusionary rule to be applicable, "police conduct must be sufficiently deliberate that exclusion can meaningfully deter it, and sufficiently culpable that such deterrence is worth the price paid by the justice system."[21] The rule is meant "to deter deliberate, reckless, or grossly negligent conduct, or in some circumstances recurring or systemic negligence."[22] Justice Ginsburg wrote a spirited dissent:

> Inaccuracies in expansive, interconnected collections of electronic information raise grave concerns for individual liberty. The offense to the dignity of the citizen who is arrested, handcuffed and searched on a public street simply because some bureaucrat has failed to maintain an accurate computer database is evocative of the use of general warrants that so outraged the authors of our Bill of Rights.[23]

Justice Ginsburg makes a good point. Citizens should not have to endure unreasonable searches and seizures because the police operate an IT system that isn't reasonably current or accurate. However, it is also true that the exclusionary rule is very strong medicine, created to deter deliberate police abuse of Fourth and Fifth Amendment rights. The exclusionary rule was not meant to punish the police (by letting a guilty defendant go free) for every mistake. Every error in entering or failing to enter data into the

IT system does not require suppressing relevant evidence of criminal conduct. The police desire to have accurate records for law enforcement purposes provides a strong incentive to maintain a reliable IT system. Justice O'Connor was on the right track in *Evans;* suppression is appropriate only when the police have recklessly relied on a flawed IT system that repeatedly produces serious errors.

Suits for false arrest due to police mistaken interpretation of criminal records have not been successful either. Consider *Ainsworth v. Norris* (2012).[24] Officer Norris stopped Michael Ainsworth's vehicle and ran his name through the NCIC and Florida's criminal records database. The search revealed a thirty-three-year-old outstanding warrant matching Ainsworth's name, race, and date of birth. Ainsworth explained that the arrest warrant actually "belonged" to another person with the same name and that the county sheriff's office had given him a letter stating that the outstanding warrant did not apply to him. Unfortunately, he did not have the letter with him. Meanwhile, the Tampa Police Department's dispatcher sent a text message to Norris's squad car pointing out inconsistencies between Ainsworth's identity information and identity information about the person with the outstanding warrant. (Ainsworth did not have a grim reaper tattoo, which was included in the arrest warrant's description of the record-subject. His driver's license showed a different social security number.) The dispatcher advised Officer Norris that "[i]f you cannot be positive that subject is our wanted person do not arrest." Norris, claiming not to have seen this text message, forcibly removed Ainsworth from his vehicle and threw him to the ground, causing injuries. When a fingerprint check confirmed that Ainsworth was not the warrant subject, he was released from custody. The Eleventh Circuit Court of Appeals affirmed the district court's dismissal of Ainsworth's false arrest and unlawful battery suit, finding that Officer Norris could have reasonably concluded that Ainsworth was the person named by the outstanding arrest warrant. It is hard to accept that Ainsworth should be left without compensation for this police misuse of the IT system.

Prosecutorial and Judicial Errors Based on Erroneous Records

While a criminal case is pending, a rap sheet error can significantly impact bail, plea, and sentencing decisions. The judge might set a high bail (or deny bail altogether). The prosecutor might refuse the defense's request for a diversion program on account of mistaken information about prior arrests and convictions. However, in these situations, a defendant will know (almost) right away that a mistake has been made; hopefully, when his defense lawyer immediately calls the error to the attention of the prosecutor and judge, the mistake will be corrected.

In 2008, the Supreme Court considered a case where a criminal record error resulted in extended pretrial detention.[25] When, pursuant to a routine police stop, police searched Walter A. Rothgery, they found a firearm which, on the basis of a criminal background check, they determined he possessed illegally owing to a prior felony conviction. Unable to make bail, Rothgery sat in jail for six months before he was finally assigned a court-appointed defense lawyer who quickly discovered that Rothgery had never been convicted of a felony. The felony charges on Rothgery's rap sheet had actually been dismissed after Rothgery completed a diversion program. Thus, Rothgery's firearm possession was not a violation of the felon-in-possession law. Rothgery sued the county for violating his Sixth Amendment right to expeditious appointment of counsel. The Supreme Court found in his favor. While the decision is an important contribution to right-to-counsel jurisprudence, for our purposes it shows how criminal record errors can lead to serious rights violations.[26]

The FBI's (Non)responsibility for Ensuring Accurate and Reliable State Rap Sheets

That no disposition is recorded on the rap sheet for as many as 50 percent of arrests in some jurisdictions creates the risk that rap sheet users will assume a conviction when, in fact, a felony arrest was resolved by a guilty plea to a misdemeanor or by outright dismissal. Usually police and prosecutors will be able quickly to determine the prior arrest's disposition, but employers have no easy way to get this supplementary information. Therefore, they are likely to assume that the arrest reported by a commercial information vendor resulted in a conviction. This problem has long generated complaints.[27] Several bills have been proposed to Congress to resolve the problem of dispositionless arrests on rap sheets.[28] The most obvious remedy would be for state courts promptly to transmit dispositions to the state's criminal record repository. Indeed, this is now done automatically in a few states where the court IT system is linked to the rap sheet system. However, in the large majority of states, it does not occur automatically and often not at all. Thus, in response to a criminal record inquiry, the FBI sends along whatever information it has, including dispositionless arrests.

In *Menard v. Mitchell* (1970), the D.C. Court of Appeals considered a lawsuit initiated by a young man who had been arrested in Los Angeles on suspicion of burglary but never charged.[29] Pursuant to the arrest, California's criminal record repository recorded his name, photo, fingerprints, and arrest information on a rap sheet and sent a copy to the FBI. Although the LAPD concluded that Menard had been mistakenly arrested, California authorities did not instruct the FBI to remove the arrest information from its database. Understandably, the FBI's policy was to expunge fingerprints and rap sheet information only when so instructed by the state authority holding the original record. Meanwhile, the FBI would respond to inquiries by passing along the information in its database.

Menard sought a court order requiring the FBI to destroy his fingerprints and arrest information. The District of Columbia Circuit Court of Appeals reversed the district court's summary judgment for the FBI and, in its remand order, explained:

> Since "probable cause" necessarily implies substantially less than absolute certainty, it follows that a significant number of those arrested will not in fact have committed the offense for which they have been detained. But this by no means exhausts the scope of the problem. Many individuals have unjustly acquired arrest records without even the excuse of an honest and unavoidable mistake by the police. In the District of Columbia

> alone, literally thousands of persons were once arrested "for investigation" and then released; but their records often remain. Dragnet arrests are at best matters of recent memory. Even worse are those occasions, far more common than we would like to think, where invocation of the criminal process is used—often with no hope of ultimate conviction—as a punitive sanction. Hippies and civil rights workers have been harassed and literally driven from their homes by repeated and unlawful arrests, often made under statutes unconstitutional on their face. Innocent bystanders may be swept up in mass arrests made to clear the streets either during a riot or during lawful political demonstrations. Use of the power to arrest in order to inflict summary punishment is, of course, unconstitutional; but even if the arrest was made lawfully and with the best of intentions, if the person arrested has been exonerated it is difficult to see why he should be subject to continuing punishment by adverse use of his "criminal" record.[30]

On remand,[31] the district court ordered the FBI not to release Menard's arrest information to anyone other than federal and state law enforcement and other governmental agencies. The court found that "[t]here is a compelling necessity to furnish arrest data to other law enforcing agencies for strictly law enforcement purposes" because arrest information is relevant for uncovering criminal acts and for decisions throughout the criminal adjudicatory process. Furthermore, the court deemed the use of arrest records for law enforcement purposes acceptable because they "are subject to due process limitations within the criminal process, and misuse may be checked by judicial action." It conceded that "[t]he same safeguards are not present when an arrest record is used for [governmental] employment purposes," but it approved the federal government's use of arrest records (for employment purposes) as appropriate because it amounts to "discreet use of . . . information already in its possession for its own limited employment purposes in aid of national security." I do not find this reasoning persuasive. Why should the fact that arrest information is held by the FBI give the Department of Agriculture (for example) a greater interest or right to access it than a private agribusiness? Several years later, the District of Columbia Court of Appeals ordered the FBI to destroy Menard's record because of the unusual facts in Menard's case:

> We are not in this case enjoining the FBI from maintaining Menard's fingerprints in its neutral non-criminal files, provided there is no reference of any kind to indicate that the prints originated in a source for criminal files. We do not discern any reasonable claim of legal injury from being included in such general identification files, which also include, e.g., the prints voluntarily submitted by tourists, and which are not translated into the FBI's centralized "rap sheets" reporting to all participating agencies on a person's criminal record. However, our order does protect Menard from the injury portended by inclusion of his record and prints in the FBI's centralized criminal files, for their continued inclusion in those files is, in our view, inconsistent with the intent of Congress. . . . [T]he chief threat to the individual who has been unlawfully arrested arises from the inclusion of his records in the police department's central criminal files, as contrasted with a mere stationhouse record, which is needed to avoid secret police arrests (and harassments and shakedowns) and to protect police against unfounded lawsuits. Absent clear expression of legislative intent, we cannot conclude that Congress intended the individual to be threatened by inclusion in the central criminal files, which are kept to facilitate indexing and future reference.[32]

The District of Columbia Circuit Court of Appeals rejected the FBI's claim not to be responsible for inaccurate state rap sheets: "The FBI cannot take the position that it is a mere passive recipient of records received from others, when it in fact energizes those records by maintaining a system of criminal files and disseminating the criminal records widely, acting in effect as a step-up transformer that puts into the system a capacity for both good and harm."[33] The Court of Appeals instructed the district court to order the FBI to expunge Menard's burglary arrest from its database. The FBI complied but still insisted that it had no responsibility or capacity to ensure the accuracy of state rap sheets. To this day, it continues to tell people who complain about an FBI-held state-created arrest record that they should contact the state criminal records repository that created and holds the original rap sheet; if that repository instructs the FBI to purge the complainant's arrest record, the FBI will do so.

In a subsequent case, the District of Columbia Court of Appeals backed away from its *Menard* decision, holding that the FBI had only a "limited duty" to ensure the accuracy of state-created rap sheets. It instructed the district court to determine "to what extent, if any, does the FBI have a duty to take reasonable measures to safeguard the accuracy of information in its criminal files which is subject to dissemination?"[34] It again sent the case back to the district court, which essentially approved the FBI's position: that individuals challenging the accuracy of an individual criminal history record held by the FBI must ordinarily first file a request with the appropriate local police agency or state court; that the FBI need not record on the rap sheet the existence of a pending challenge to the accuracy of a criminal record; and that year-old arrest records without dispositions may be disseminated for law enforcement purposes.[35]

In a vigorous criticism of the FBI's hands-off policy, the NELP (an NGO that advocates on behalf of persons with criminal records) argued that the FBI, which manages the National Instant Criminal Background Check System (NICS), has to find missing disposition information when it responds to a federally licensed firearms dealer's inquiry about a prospective firearms purchaser whose rap sheet shows a dispositionless arrest.[36] NELP would require the FBI to assume the same responsibility for employer background checks. It recommends that the FBI create a new database populated with information about incomplete or inaccurate state-submitted rap sheets that comes to light in the course of NICS, criminal, and other records checks. That supplemental database could be routinely checked whenever a state repository or the FBI non–law enforcement criminal records check finds a missing disposition. A hit on the proposed supplemental database would spare the FBI and other agencies the effort of chasing down the missing information. In 2013, two bills were introduced into the House of Representatives to implement NELP's recommendation.[37]

In 2013, the FBI conducted a little over twenty-one million background checks for firearms purchases. In the overwhelming majority of cases, the checks do not reveal a disqualifying conviction (since it is a federal crime for a person with a felony conviction to purchase or possess a firearm). However, when there is a felony arrest on the rap sheet, approximately 50 percent of the time there is no disposition and the relevant police department, prosecutor's office, or court must be contacted.[38] The same problem arises when the FBI conducts employment and other non–law enforcement criminal background checks, about eighteen million per year. NELP quite persuasively argues that when a rap sheet shows a dispositionless arrest, the FBI could do the same kind of followup that it does in the NICS context. This would entail significant costs, but they could presumably be covered by increasing the fee employers pay the FBI for criminal background checks. (The FBI charges between $16 to $24 per background check.[39] Employers routinely pass the cost along to the job applicant.)

Court Records Containing Sealed or Expunged Information

Although court records are more complete and less error-prone than rap sheets,[40] they are vulnerable to identification errors because they are not linked to or searchable by fingerprints. Because sealing or expungement orders are often not promptly (if ever) carried out, commercial vendors may obtain such information from court records or, for that matter, from newspapers, social networks, neighbors or friendly police officers, prosecutors, or judges. Private detectives and commercial vendors could take the position that it is their responsibility to provide clients all information they can legally find about the person of interest's prior criminality. Even accepting that argument, a court might still approve a governmental requirement that the report should inform the client that reported information was subsequently ordered sealed or expunged.

Erroneous Criminal Background Reports Prepared by Commercial Information Vendors

The vast majority of employers that use criminal record information for hiring purposes rely on commercial information vendors. The vendors' searches, mostly based on court records, are susceptible to error because court records are not linked to fingerprints and multiple people often share the same name, sometimes even the same birthday.* In addition, information vendors sometimes make administrative and clerical errors. An employee might make a mistake in searching a particular name or in reading or transcribing the court record. A 2012 National Consumer Law Center (NCLC) report claims that, in addition to reporting arrests and convictions that should have been sealed or expunged, commercial information vendors routinely disseminate criminal history information that is (1) inaccurate or incomplete; (2) belongs to a different person, and/or (3) is misleading or prejudicial in its presentation (e.g., multiple entries of the same offense).[41] Consider Catherine Taylor's story as told by the NCLC:[42]

> Ms. Taylor [who is from Arkansas] has no criminal history, but on several occasions, she has had her housing and employment threatened because of mismatched background checks. . . . Choicepoint allegedly reported the criminal record of another Catherine Taylor with the same date of birth. That Catherine Taylor lived in Illinois. According to Ms. Taylor's complaint, Choicepoint had access to other identifying information which would have distinguished these two women; however, the particular Choicepoint product in this case was designed to give an

---

* Background checking firms may also make false negative errors (intentionally or inadvertently), failing to properly check court records and therefore missing criminal records that should be reported. Recently, the U.S. government has accused U.S. Investigation Services, a private firm that conducts security checks for the government, of fraud for systematically reporting no criminal history when, in fact, there were arrests and convictions. See Matt Apuzzo, "Security Check Firm Said to Have Defrauded U.S.," *New York Times*, January 23, 2014, http://www.nytimes.com/2014/01/23/us/security-check-firm-said-to-have-defrauded-us.html?_r=0.

> instant result, and thus not designed to access that information. Choicepoint acknowledged that next time the company generates a report on the Arkansas Catherine Taylor, the same thing will happen again.

The chance of mistake is reduced significantly if several identifiers are used, for example, birth date, residence, and social security number. The problem is that they cannot be used to confirm identity if they are not available in the court records being searched.[43]

Regulating Commercial Information Vendors

The Fair Credit Reporting Act (FCRA) requires credit reporting agencies (CRAs), which include criminal background checking companies, to follow "reasonable procedures" to ensure the "maximum possible accuracy of the information concerning the individual about whom the report relates."[44] The information vendor is entitled to reply on a current public record (e.g., court record or rap sheet).[45] The FCRA requires CRAs to explain to their customers (i.e., employers) that the FCRA requires employers to notify a record-subject when a criminal background report is the cause, wholly or in part, of a negative employment decision. The FCRA also requires the CRA to verify the accuracy of information that relates to an indictment, arrest, or conviction within a period of thirty days prior to the report's dissemination.[46] The extent of compliance is unknown.

When reporting to an employer or other client public record information that is likely to have an adverse effect on a job applicant, the FCRA requires that the CRA either notify the record-subject (that it has issued an adverse report to a named employer) or "maintain strict procedures designed to insure" data accuracy and completeness.[47] CRAs prefer the second option because it is cheaper and, in any event, good business practice.

The FCRA requires CRAs that provide consumer reports to employers to obtain an employer certification that it (1) has disclosed to the job applicant or employee that a report on him is being sought, (2) will notify the job applicant if the report becomes the basis for an adverse action, and (3) will not use the consumer report in violation of any state or federal equal employment opportunity laws.[48]

The FCRA also regulates the CRAs' customers (employers) by requiring the customer to (1) obtain the job applicant's or employee's permission before commissioning a background check, (2) notify the potential employee (in writing and separate from other documents) that the report may have negative consequences, (3) notify the CRA that provides the report that it (the employer) has complied with the FCRA, and (4) before taking negative personnel action based on a consumer report notify the report-subject that she has a right to dispute the report's accuracy.[49] However, employers need not delay a hiring decision until resolution of a dispute about a report's accuracy. According to a Federal Trade Commission (FTC) staff statement from July 2011: "There is no specific period of time an employer must wait after providing a pre-adverse action notice and before taking adverse action against the consumer. Some reasonable period of time must elapse but the minimum length will vary depending on the particular circumstances involved."[50] Although the 1996 Consumer Credit Reporting Reform Act amended the FCRA by setting a thirty-day time limit for a CRA to investigate a job applicant's (or other record-subject's) claim that the consumer report contained inaccurate information, the correction of an erroneous report is unlikely to benefit the complainant with respect to the job for which she was most recently passed over because that job will already have been filled.[51] However, it will be helpful with respect to future job applications.

ENSURING REPORT ACCURACY VIA FTC ENFORCEMENT OF THE FCRA

Historically, the FTC was not an aggressive enforcer of the FCRA. Thus, to encourage more vigorous enforcement, Congress enhanced the FTC's FCRA enforcement authority with the 2003 Fair and Accurate Credit Transactions Act (FACTA) and in 2010 transferred some of the FTC's FCRA enforcement authority to the new Consumer Financial Protection Bureau (CFPB).

Apparently, the FTC got the message. In 2012, it settled its first-ever case involving charges that an information vendor had, in violation of its FCRA obligations, provided erroneous criminal record information to its customers. In its enforcement action against Hire-

Right Solutions, the FTC alleged that "[i]n numerous instances," HireRight "failed to follow reasonable procedures" to avoid duplicative entries of the same criminal offense and failed to report expungements.[52] Moreover, it alleged that HireRight failed to provide consumers with reasonable access to information with which to investigate disputed information, and failed to provide record-subjects with reasonable notice of disclosure of adverse information. The lawsuit was settled with HireRight agreeing to pay a $2.6 million fine (the second largest FCRA enforcement penalty in history) and to hire an FCRA-compliance monitor.[53]*

In June 2012, the FTC entered into a settlement agreement for an $800,000 civil penalty against Spokeo, Inc., a data broker defining itself as "a people search engine that organizes White-pages listings, Public Records and Social Network Information to help you safely find & learn about people."[54] The FTC alleged that Spokeo failed to ensure that the information it provided was accurate and used for a legally permissible purpose.

In 2013, the FTC settled charges against Filiquarian Publishing LLC and Choice Level LLC for selling mobile apps that allow users to obtain individual criminal history information. Filiquarian's advertisements boasted that its app permitted a "quick criminal background check for convictions."[55] The FTC insisted that Filiquarian was a CRA subject to the FCRA. The parties signed a consent agreement that requires Filiquarian to take "reasonable steps" to maximize the accuracy of its criminal background reports. It also mandates that Filiquarian inform its customers of their FCRA obligations. Violations of the consent agreement are punishable by civil penalties of up to $16,000 per violation.

---

* A *New York Times* editorial praised the FTC's activism: "For far too long, the federal government has neglected its responsibility for regulating the companies that provide criminal background checks. . . . The damage done to job seekers by flawed and unreliable data—a common problem with such services—can be devastating. The F.T.C. and the Consumer Financial Protection Bureau, which share jurisdiction, need to step up their scrutiny of the entire industry, which is playing a bigger and bigger role for employers in hiring decisions." Editorial, "Accuracy in Criminal Background Checks," *New York Times*, August 10, 2012, at A18; see also Editorial, "Faulty Criminal Background Checks," *New York Times*, July 25, 2012, at A24.

ENSURING REPORT ACCURACY VIA PRIVATE FCRA ENFORCEMENT

The FCRA gives CRAs immunity from liability for defamation, invasion of privacy, and negligence, unless the plaintiff can prove that the CRA acted "with malice or willful intent to injure."[56] To prove "malice," the plaintiff must show that the CRA "either knew that the [information it disclosed] was false or it acted in reckless disregard of its truth or falsity."[57] Thus, there are no monetary damages available to someone turned down for a job on account of a report containing information copied from public records or negligently transcribed or reported by the CRA.

Despite the obstacles, a few lawsuits have achieved important successes.[58] In *Wiggins v. Equifax*,[59] the plaintiff sued Equifax for providing a consumer report to Wiggins's employer (Cablevision) erroneously showing a felony conviction for cocaine possession. The parties agreed that Equifax's investigator's report mistakenly attributed to Wiggins the criminal record of someone else with the same name but a different date of birth. (There was a discrepant middle name.) When Wiggins disputed the report, Equifax's local office agreed and so notified the main office. Meanwhile, however, the main office had sent the erroneous report to Cablevision, which fired Wiggins. The court rejected Equifax's motion to dismiss the lawsuit, ruling that a reasonable jury could find that Equifax's reporting procedures constituted reckless disregard for the truthfulness of the consumer report. The lawsuit was resolved by a substantial monetary settlement.

To take another example, Infotrack Information Services issued a criminal background check that reported that Samuel M. Jackson had been convicted of several sex offenses. In fact, these offenses belonged to three different registered sex offenders who shared Jackson's name (although not his birth date). One of the convictions occurred when Jackson was three years old. Jackson filed a lawsuit against Infotrack, alleging that the company, in violation of the FCRA, failed to maintain reasonable procedures to ensure the accuracy of its reports.[60] The complaint alleges that, before reporting sex offense convictions, Infotrack did not attempt to match the birth dates of record-subjects with those of individuals listed on the national sex offender database. Infotrack's alleged policy is to include sex offender information on a criminal history report for anyone with the same name as a registered sex offender. The lawsuit was settled for a negligible $35,000.[61]

Three class action claims against IntelliCorp Record, Inc., one of the biggest criminal background screening companies, and Insurance Information Exchange LLC, both units of Verisk Analytics, Inc., alleged that the defendants failed to report expungements and disposition data and misattributed other individuals' criminal history records to the plaintiffs. Moreover, plaintiffs allege that the companies did not notify the record-subjects that these reports were being sent to employers. Plaintiffs maintained that the companies failed to follow reasonable procedures to guarantee maximum possible accuracy of the reports. The parties settled, with defendants agreeing to pay plaintiffs over $18 million.[62]

Conclusion

Criminal records are widely (but exaggeratedly) regarded as a reliable indicator of character, reliability, integrity, and self-discipline. Many more people commit crimes than are convicted or even arrested. Self-report studies show that the "true" extent of criminality is far larger than that represented by number of arrests, prosecutions, and convictions. In fact, a surprisingly high percentage of anonymous respondents usually admit the commission of undetected crimes, even quite serious ones.[63] Putting undetected criminality to the side, recorded and reported criminal records and databases have significant accuracy problems.

Failure to record dispositions on state rap sheets has been a problem for at least four decades. Perhaps as many as 50 percent of rap sheets in the Interstate Identification Index do not show ultimate disposition. Thus, they may leave the rap sheet consumer with the false impression that the record-subject was convicted when, in fact, the prosecution was dismissed or ended in an acquittal or misdemeanor guilty plea. This problem can be solved by linking judicial information systems with the record repositories' rap sheet databases as is done in New York State. It "only" requires resolve and resources.

Alternatively, the responsibility could be placed on the FBI to find out whether there was a disposition before reporting a dispositionless arrest to employers and other non–law enforcement agencies. Perhaps the same responsibility could be placed on the state repositories. They certainly are in a better position to obtain the missing information than employers and others who purchase the background checks. If the FBI and state repositories had this responsibility, they would undoubtedly lobby police, prosecutors, and courts to send them dispositions expeditiously.

Court files overwhelmingly contain accurate information about the adjudication of criminal cases. However, criminal record searches by commercial information vendors sometimes match a person to the wrong court record. Criminal background checks based on names alone are very risky and should be strongly discouraged. If court personnel and commercial vendors used names plus other identifiers (e.g., birth date, address, social security number), mismatching should be rare.

Reporting information that should have been sealed or expunged could be significantly reduced if states created easily searchable databases of persons with arrests and convictions that should have been sealed or expunged. Of course, it would be a travesty if commercial vendors then used that database to report to customers information that they otherwise would not have found. But the First Amendment does not permit the government to prohibit commercial vendors from transmitting information legally obtained from a government database or another source.

Regulation of the commercial information industry should focus on ensuring that individual criminal history reports are accurate and reliable. The CFPB, which shares with the FTC responsibility for regulating commercial information vendors, should actively enforce FCRA violations (including, for example, failures to verify information, inadequate accuracy controls, failures to provide notice to consumers, and inaccessible and/or inadequate procedures for challenging report inaccuracies). It should require licensing of criminal background checking companies. It should urge states that sell court records and other data to CRAs to impose, as a condition of sale, that CRA purchasers frequently update their records. Perhaps the CFPB or state regulators could require CRAs to hire auditors who annually report to the regulator on CRAs' regulatory compliance. The National Association of Professional Background Screeners (NAPBS) could play a constructive role by strengthening its voluntary accrediting program. If it did so, over time, employers would have a strong incentive to purchase criminal background checking services from accredited companies. A country where criminal records play such a significant role should place a very high priority on reliable and accurate criminal records and criminal record reports.

PART III

U.S. CRIMINAL RECORD EXCEPTIONALISM

U.S. CRIMINAL RECORDS LAW and practice is a powerful example of American criminal justice exceptionalism. In Europe, individual criminal history records created and held by the police are not available to non–police agencies, much less the media and general public. Each European country records convictions in its own National Conviction Register (NCR).* The NCR is prohibited from disclosing conviction information to anyone other than certain police officials, prosecutors, judges, and the record-subject. Moreover, in European countries, court files on criminal cases are not available to the media or public. Indeed, in some European countries, published judicial opinions in criminal cases anonymize the defendant's name and other identifying information. This preference for treating individual criminal history information as confidential is reflected and reinforced by the European Convention for the Protection of Individuals with Regard to Automatic Processing of Personal

* When an EU member state convicts a citizen of another member state, it is supposed to notify the defendant's home state's NCR. The home state is supposed to enter the conviction into its NCR. Thus, each member state's NCR should have a record of its citizens' convictions in every EU member state. See James B. Jacobs and Dimitra Blitsa, *Sharing Criminal Records: The United States, the European Union and Interpol Compared*, 30 Loy. L.A. Int'l & Comp. L. Rev. 125 (2008).

Data, which requires EU member states to exercise control over the collection, storage, and transfer of personal data. Article 6 states: "Personal data revealing racial origin, political opinions or religious or other beliefs, as well as personal data concerning health or sexual life, may not be processed automatically unless domestic law provides appropriate safeguards. *The same shall apply to personal data relating to criminal convictions*" (emphasis added). The European Court of Human Rights has steadfastly enforced the Convention.

While there are some national differences, European countries' criminal records policies have much in common. In addition, the European Union and the European Court of Human Rights have issued directives and opinions significantly harmonizing national policies. Importantly, unlike in the United States, European employers, landlords, and voluntary associations may not obtain criminal history information from the NCR or from courts. There is no equivalent of U.S. federal and state laws that provide non–law enforcement government agencies and some private employers and volunteer organizations with access to rap sheets.

Chapter 9 compares the accessibility of conviction records in the United States and Spain. It contrasts the U.S. commitment to governmental, especially judicial, transparency with the Spanish commitment to protecting informational privacy and reputation as well as promoting rehabilitation. I do not claim that Spanish law and policy is identical to that of every other European country, but Spain is not an outlier. Even if it were, it would still be valuable for showing that American policy is not inevitable.

Chapter 10 shines a light on the status of arrest records. No other country routinely makes arrestee information public. The U.S. position is dictated by the First Amendment and by constitutional, political, and cultural commitment to governmental, especially judicial, transparency. Some police departments, however, go beyond what constitutional and statutory law requires, aggressively disseminating arrestee information, not to facilitate scrutiny of their operations, but to employ naming and shaming as a deterrent strategy.

Policy and jurisprudence of arrest records is interesting and complex. It is one thing for an arrest that results in a conviction to remain on the rap sheet, but quite another thing to include on the rap sheet arrests that were not prosecuted or that were dismissed or that resulted in acquittals. We will consider whether it is legally possible, or even desirable, to purge certain arrest information from rap sheets, or to prohibit arrest information from being reported to non–criminal justice organizations and individuals.

Chapter 11 examines what the jurisprudence of punishment has to say about public disclosure of criminal records. We consider whether any of the prevailing theories of punishment—retribution, deterrence, incapacitation, rehabilitation—require criminal records to be public. Is the publicness of a conviction essential to the purpose of criminal law? Even if not required, are publicly accessible criminal records justifiable under prevailing punishment theories?

9 TRANSPARENCY OF CRIMINAL CONVICTIONS

> Court records exist at the confluence of two strong currents in liberal democratic societies. One current is the demand for openness. Because court records provide an essential window into the functioning of one of the three pillars of government, citizens are presumed to have a right to inspect them to ensure that courts are exercising their powers not only competently and fairly but also within the limits of their mandate. The other current is privacy. The courts are a stage where many of life's dramas are performed, where people may be shamed, vindicated, compensated, punished, judged, or exposed.
>
> —Amanda Conley et al., *Sustaining Privacy and Open Justice in the Transition to Online Court Records* (2012)[1]

> [T]he Court . . . emphasises that although data contained in the criminal record are, in one sense, public information, their systematic storing in central records means that they are available for disclosure long after the event when everyone other than the person concerned is likely to have forgotten about it, and all the more so where, as in the present case, the caution has occurred in private. Thus as the conviction or caution itself recedes into the past, it becomes a part of the person's private life which must be respected.
>
> —European Court of Human Rights, *Case of M.M. v. the United Kingdom* (2012)[2]

AMERICAN CRIMINAL RECORD policy exceptionalism is illustrated by a comparison with Spain, which, like other continental EU member states, treats criminal records as personal data entitled to privacy protection.* Access to police and court records is restricted in order

---

* The United Kingdom's criminal records are not as transparent as those of the United States, but they are far more transparent than those in continental Europe. See Nicola Padfield, *Judicial Rehabilitation? A View from England*, 3(1) European Journal of Probation 36 (2011); Terry Thomas, *Criminal Records: A Database for the Criminal Justice System and Beyond* (Basingstoke, UK: Palgrave Macmillan, 2007); Terry Thomas and David Thompson, *Making Offenders Visible*, 49(4) Howard J. Criminal Justice 340 (2010);

to protect the convicted person's privacy and dignity and to promote rehabilitation. Although Spain's Constitution requires public access to criminal trials, the verdict is not usually announced in open court; rather, the defendant is informed of the judgment in writing, perhaps several weeks after completion of the trial. If there is a published opinion, a government agency first anonymizes the defendant's name and other identifying information. Case files are not available for public inspection. The following cases illustrate the stark difference between criminal record policy in the United States and Spain.

Illustrative Spanish Cases

CASE 1: TRIBUNAL SUPREMO (SALA DE LO CONTENCIOSO-ADMINISTRATIVO, SECCIÓN 1ª), MARCH 3, 1995

Desirous of obtaining business information from court records, Grupo Interpres S.A., a supplier of financial information to business clients, sued to obtain access to civil judgments containing information that its clients wanted to see. In support of its position, it pointed out that Spain's constitution and statutes provide that (1) "judicial proceedings will be public with the exceptions foreseen by the procedural laws" and (2) "any interested person can have access to the court's judgment." According to Grupo Interpres, these laws mandate public access to court records. The lower court was not persuaded.

On appeal, the Spanish Supreme Court ruled that, although the right to public trial gives citizens a presumptive right to attend court proceedings, only litigants have a right to see the court's judgment.[3] (In other words, the courts are open to the public, but verdicts and judgments are not a matter of public record.) Although the statute says that a signed judgment must be made available for "any interested person's inspection," the Supreme Court ruled that "interested" does not mean merely curious; rather, an "interested person" is someone who can demonstrate a "concrete and singular connection" to the case. The court ruled that Grupo Interpres's commercial

---

Elena Larrauri, Criminal Record Disclosure and the Right to Privacy, *Criminal Law Review* (forthcoming, 2014).

interest in the judgment did not qualify as a "concrete and singular connection."[4]

An individual or organization that passes the "concrete and singular connection test" (which the court did not explain) must also satisfy two additional requirements: (1) that release of the desired court-held information would not affect the litigants' fundamental privacy rights; and (2) that the disclosed information will be used only for judicial purposes (like sentencing). In effect, civil and criminal case files will not be available to journalists, employers, or anyone else. Had the Grupo Interpres case arisen in the United States, it would quickly have been resolved in favor of the company because the public has a right to inspect and copy court records, including dockets and case files. U.S. judges, political scientists, and legal academics regard judicial transparency as an important feature of democratic government.[5] The U.S. political tradition considers secret court proceedings and rulings dangerous. The people should be able to monitor and critique what transpires in "their" courts.

CASE 2: SENTENCIA TRIBUNAL CONSTITUCIONAL (STC), JULY 22, 1999 (NO. 144)

The Spanish Supreme Court affirmed H.'s (the anonymized defendant's) criminal libel conviction, sentenced him to prison for one month and one day, and suspended his right to run for office. The victim of H.'s libel urged the Electoral Commission to disqualify H. from running for elective office. In the course of deciding that issue, the Electoral Commission requested and received H.'s criminal record from the National Conviction Register (NCR). It then disqualified H. from running for elective office. H. appealed to the Constitutional Court, arguing that the NCR violated his rights by disclosing his conviction to the Electoral Commission. The Constitutional Court agreed, holding that a criminal conviction is "personal information" protected by the constitutional right to privacy. Accordingly, the NCR must not disclose, even to another government agency, that a named individual has been convicted of a criminal offense because "the constitutional right to privacy guarantees anonymity, a right not to be known, so that the community is not aware of who we are or what we do."

U.S. law would have dictated the opposite result. A governmental agency, like an election commission, would be authorized to obtain information about an individual's previous criminal convictions from that state's criminal records repository. In addition, federal and state laws authorize the criminal record repositories to disclose criminal history information to many categories of private employers and volunteer organizations. Of course, anyone can go to the courthouse where a criminal case was adjudicated and examine the case file.

CASE 3: TRIBUNAL SUPREMO (SALA DE LO CONTENCIOSO-ADMINISTRATIVO, SECCIÓN 6A), JUNE 26, 2008

The director of police complained to the Spanish Data Protection Agency (DPA) that the Association Against Torture (the Association) had posted on its website the names of Civil Guard officers, police officers, and politicians who had previously been found guilty of torture or whose torture prosecutions were presently pending. Along with each name, there was posted information about the place where the torture was allegedly committed and, if there was a conviction, its date. The DPA ruled that this website violated the Personal Data Protection Law (PDPL), because personal data includes any information that relates to an identified physical person. It therefore fined the Association and ordered it to remove from its website the list of torture defendants. On appeal, the Association argued that (1) the posted information is a report, not a database; (2) information about individuals accused and convicted of torture is not personal data because it does not pertain to an individual's "private sphere"; (3) the information was obtained from publicly accessible sources; and (4) the right of free speech should protect the Association when identifying people found guilty of torture. Rejecting these arguments, the court held that (1) information about accusations and convictions of named individuals is personal data; (2) the PDPL makes it illegal to post such information on a website; (3) information contained in court judgments is not publicly accessible; (4) only an authorized government agency can maintain a database of criminal convictions; and (5) the privacy rights of persons named on the list of torturers outweighs the Association's right of free speech. (The court added that a journalist's free speech right, although stronger than a private individual's or organization's free speech right, would also not be strong enough to outweigh the listed torturers' privacy rights.)

This decision is shocking to an American lawyer. It is hard to imagine a matter of greater public interest than who was and was not brought to justice for committing torture. In the United States, with limited exceptions for defamation and obscenity, an individual or organization has an absolute First Amendment right to publish or post whatever they like. American law makes no distinction between printed and electronic expression. It also makes no distinction between free speech rights of journalists and nonjournalists.

CASE 4: SENTENCIA DE LA AUDIENCIA NACIONAL, FEBRUARY 10, 2010

An officer in the Melilla Police Department was convicted and sentenced to two years' imprisonment (suspended) for sexual assault. After the Supreme Court upheld the conviction, the department fired him. For that administrative sanction to become effective, city hall officials had to notify the officer, but his police colleagues prevented notification by helping him elude the officials seeking to deliver notice. Finally, city hall officials posted notice of his dismissal on their Legal Bulletin website, an accepted means of providing notice of an administrative sanction. The fired police officer filed a complaint with the DPA, charging that the local government violated his privacy right by publicizing his sexual assault conviction. The DPA agreed with him.

The appellate court affirmed the DPA's decision because posting the officer's name and conviction offense on the city hall website, even though not part of a database, constituted "processing personal data" under the PDPL. Although city hall officials had acted properly in posting the termination of service order on the website, the posting should not have disclosed the officer's criminal conviction. Even if a newspaper had previously reported the conviction, it would still be unlawful to post the information on a website because conviction information is personal data entitled to protection from disclosure by anyone.

U.S. law does not consider a criminal conviction to be personal or private information. Indeed, a criminal prosecution, brought in the name of "the people," is a quintessentially public matter. Although there are statutes regulating government officials' disclosure of information stored in governmental databases, the First Amendment absolutely protects private persons and organizations from publishing (or otherwise disclosing) true information about an individual's criminal history.

CASE 5: THE DOMESTIC VIOLENCE WEBSITE

In 2001, in order to deter domestic violence against women, Castilla-La Mancha passed a law authorizing a local government agency to publish a list of names of men convicted of domestic violence against female partners. The law's proponents argued that publicizing offenders' identities would deter violence against women. The law's preamble has an American sound to it: "The sentence must be imposed by the judge, but the government has a responsibility to encourage victims not to remain silent and to make offenders' sentences known." Legal and lay commentators immediately charged that the law violated convicted batterers' constitutional rights of honor, privacy, and rehabilitation.[6] The DPA ruled that it is unlawful to post conviction information unless that information is available from a public source. However, a court judgment is not a public source. Moreover, the DPA pointed out that no statute authorized a local government to create a database of convicted offenders.

U.S. law does not regulate print or electronic publication of convicted offenders' names. Indeed, federal and state laws require posting convicted sex offenders' names and offense details (often including photos and addresses) to online registries. In addition, some states post to websites the names and offenses of prison inmates. A few states (e.g., Texas[7] and Minnesota[8]) make the names and offenses of all convicted defendants accessible via the Internet. In Minnesota,[9] criminal convictions remain accessible online for fifteen years following the completed sentence.[10] Private individuals and organizations are free to publish or post any true information about convicted offenders and their conviction offenses. For example, the National Domestic Violence Registry is an online database of names of persons convicted of domestic violence offenses and those subject to protection orders on account of domestic abuse.[11] There is no charge for searching the registry by name or location.

The Controlling Spanish Principles

The key legal principles that explain the difference between Spanish and U.S. law and policy on access to and dissemination of individual criminal history information are publicity of the judgment and access to court records; protection of honor and privacy; and protection of personal data, free speech, and rehabilitation.

PUBLICITY OF THE JUDGMENT

There is a tension in Spanish law between commitment to public courts and free speech on the one hand and to a defendant's right of informational privacy on the other. Spanish scholars and judges believe that criminal judgments are public based on the Constitution (article 120), which states that "1. Judicial proceedings will be public with the exceptions foreseen by the procedural laws; 2. The trial will be mostly oral, especially in criminal law cases; 3. Judgments will always be rendered and justified in a public hearing." However, there is no mechanism for compelling judges to comply with the constitutional requirement. In practice, criminal convictions rarely become public. Lower court judgments are not published. Only the Supreme Court's and appellate courts' decisions are published; even then, the Center for Judicial Documentation anonymizes the defendant's name and identifying information. Moreover, a 2003 amendment substantially weakens the commitment to public judgments by providing that "*access to judgments may be restricted when an individual's privacy is affected.*"[12] Arguably, disclosure of conviction information always affects the convicted person's privacy (i.e., personal sphere, reputation). Judges (and the legal establishment) believe that disclosing discrediting information is wrong.

THE RIGHT TO HONOR

The constitutional right to honor encompasses respect for the individual's sense of self-worth and community standing. According to the Constitutional Court, the right to honor encompasses the right to a good reputation, the right not to be despised, and the right not to be humiliated in front of others. Because honor can be impugned by both truthful and untruthful information, whether the communicator had a right to disclose discrediting information about the aggrieved person turns on the disclosed information's newsworthiness and relevance. The court has attempted to reconcile a criminal justice process that condemns the defendant as a law violator with the individual's constitutional right to honor. Imposition of a criminal sentence does not violate the right to honor, since "injury to honor is not due to the judgment and sentence, but to the individual's own conduct; neither the Constitution nor statutory law can guarantee honor to a person who has blighted his reputation through his own conduct."[13] Disseminating prosecution and conviction information must be supported by a very weighty interest.

Spanish judges and law professors overwhelmingly disapprove of some U.S. police departments' practice of publishing the names of persons convicted (or, even worse, just arrested) for offenses such as prostitution and patronizing a prostitute. They consider public naming and shaming to be degrading punishment, akin to the Spanish Inquisition's practice of posting a convicted person's name and crime at a village's entrance.[14]

There is no right to honor in American constitutional or statutory law. Under U.S. constitutional law, "punishment" refers to sanctions imposed by the government; it does not include a private person's shunning, disrespecting, or discriminating against another private person. Moreover, the First Amendment provides absolute protection for speech that communicates true facts. It would be unconstitutional to impose liability on a speaker who made discrediting, but factually accurate, comments about someone. Truth is an absolute defense to defamation and libel.

THE RIGHT TO PRIVACY

The Spanish constitutional privacy right protects and promotes individual dignity. It guarantees the individual a private sphere protected from public exposure. The disclosure of information about an individual's personal life, whether by a government official, news organization, or a private party, violates this right. Neither Spanish judges nor treatise writers have squarely addressed whether a criminal conviction constitutes private information, that is, information belonging to the individual's private sphere.[15] However, we saw in Case 2 that the Constitutional Court found that H.'s privacy right was violated when the NCR disclosed his criminal record to the Electoral Commission.

THE RIGHT TO PERSONAL DATA PROTECTION

The 1981 Council of Europe's Convention for the Protection of Individuals with Regard to Automatic Processing of Personal Data aims to protect European citizens from misuse of personal information stored in electronic databases, explicitly including criminal conviction information. In 1995, the European Parliament and the Council of Europe augmented the Convention so that "processing of data relating to offenses, criminal convictions or security measures may be carried out only under the control of official authority. . . . [A] complete register of criminal convictions may be kept only under the control of official authority."[16]

The Spanish PDPL, passed to comply with the Convention, provides that (1) personal data can be maintained in a database from which information can be retrieved only with the consent of the record-subject, except when a law provides otherwise; (2) judicial judgments are not a public source of information; and (3) only authorized government agencies can create criminal offender databases. The Spanish Constitutional Court has held that the constitutional right to personal data protection provides broader protection than the Constitution's right to privacy.[17] An individual has a right to know which agencies possess his or her personal data and for what purposes. The PDPL protects personal data, which, if used by third parties, may affect an individual's rights. Disclosing on a website a named individual's criminal conviction violates that individual's right to personal data protection and is punishable by an administrative fine.

THE RIGHT TO FREE SPEECH

The Spanish Constitution's guarantee of free speech is much weaker than the U.S. First Amendment. The Spanish Constitutional Court and Supreme Court have held that publishing criminal conviction information infringes honor and privacy but that free speech prevails if the published conviction information is (1) true or the result of a good faith and reasonable effort to determine the truth; and (2) newsworthy, that is, relevant to informing public opinion and germane to the news story in which it is embedded. Disputes usually center on whether information about a particular conviction is "newsworthy." In the last few years, the Supreme Court has several times found a criminal judgment to be newsworthy, even though it did not involve a "public person." The trend seems to be in the direction of greater press freedom with respect to disclosing the names of convicted persons but, other than cases involving famous persons, journalists have limited ability to obtain conviction information since courts do not make criminal judgments available.

RIGHT TO REHABILITATION

The preference for keeping an individual's criminal history information confidential is reinforced by Spanish law's commitment to rehabilitation as the primary goal of criminal sentencing. The Spanish Constitution provides that criminal punishments should aim toward rehabilitation and social integration. Spanish lawmakers and scholars believe that the rehabilitative goal would be seriously undermined if the public had access to criminal conviction information.[18] Therefore, only judges, prosecutors, certain police agencies, and the record-subject may obtain conviction information from the NCR. Interestingly, although employers cannot obtain criminal record information directly from the NCR, they are not prohibited from asking job applicants about prior convictions and/or requesting them to provide a *certificado de antecedentes penales*, an official summary of past convictions or, if they have none, an official document attesting to that fact. Spanish academics believe that private employers rarely ask job applicants to submit a certificate, but their impression has not been empirically verified.[19] Spanish law has long provided that persons with unexpunged convictions are ineligible to hold public sector employments.

The U.S. Preference for Transparency over Privacy

POLICE RECORDS AND RAP SHEETS

U.S. police records and rap sheets are not publicly accessible, but they are much more accessible than the Spanish NCR. As we saw in

Chapter 3, federal and state statutes require that rap sheet information be disclosed to government agencies (for employment purposes) and to private employers and volunteer organizations authorized by law. Police stationhouse blotters have, historically, been publicly accessible.

FREEDOM OF INFORMATION ACT AND ITS LAW ENFORCEMENT EXCEPTION

Federal and state Freedom of Information acts are the most important embodiment of U.S. commitment to governmental transparency. With respect to public access to criminal records, these laws necessarily balance transparency and privacy. The federal Freedom of Information Act (FOIA), passed in the 1940s and substantially amended in 1966, establishes a strong presumption that federal government records will be available to the public.[20] However, the FOIA exempts law enforcement records from disclosure if release (1) could reasonably be expected to interfere with law enforcement proceedings; (2) would deprive a person of a right to a fair trial or an impartial adjudication; (3) could reasonably be expected to constitute an unwarranted invasion of personal privacy; (4) could reasonably be expected to disclose the identity of a confidential source; (5) would disclose techniques, procedures, or guidelines for law enforcement investigations or prosecutions; or (6) could reasonably be expected to endanger an individual's life or physical safety.[21]

In *U.S. Department of Justice v. Reporters Committee for Freedom of the Press et al.* (1989), the Supreme Court considered whether protection of informational privacy protected criminal record information from FOIA disclosure.[22] The media plaintiffs filed an FOIA lawsuit after the U.S. Department of Justice (DOJ) refused to provide arrest, charge, and conviction information regarding four persons whom the Pennsylvania Crime Commission had linked to organized crime. The DOJ argued that it had a strong interest in protecting the privacy interests of the persons whose criminal record information it holds. The federal district court supported DOJ's position, but the Court of Appeals reversed, seeing only a weak DOJ interest in protecting the confidentiality of individual criminal history information that originated in public proceedings and that is available for examination at one or more courthouses. The Supreme Court agreed with the DOJ.

> Because events summarized in a rap sheet have been previously disclosed to the public, respondents contend that Medico's privacy interest in avoiding disclosure of a federal compilation of these events approaches zero. We reject respondents' cramped notion of personal privacy. Where, as here, the subject of a rap sheet is a private citizen and the information is in the Government's control as a compilation, rather than as a record of what the Government is up to, the privacy interest in maintaining the rap sheet's "practical obscurity" is always at its apex while the FOIA-based public interest in disclosure is at its nadir. *Thus, as a categorical matter, rap sheets are excluded from disclosure . . . in such circumstances. The government's asserted interest in protecting the record subject's privacy is reasonable.*[23]

In determining whether individual criminal history information is exempt from FOIA disclosure on account of privacy, courts balance the public interest in disclosing the information against the personal privacy interest of the individual who is referred to in the document.[24] Investigators, witnesses, informants, and suspects named in an investigative file may have a privacy interest. Should their identities be revealed, they might be subject to harassment or danger; even "the mention of an individual's name in a law enforcement file will engender comment and speculation and carries a stigmatizing connotation."[25] Once a privacy interest is established, the FOIA requester must show a "significant public interest in shedding light on the actions of the agency from which documents are being sought."[26] This is consistent with the fact that the FOIA's main purpose is to allow for public scrutiny of federal agencies' and officers' performance of statutory duties.[27]

Applying these principles, courts have upheld judicial and government agencies' withholding identifying personal information about law enforcement personnel, prison inmates, informants, witnesses, and other nonsuspects.[28] The DOJ has for years resisted FOIA requests and lawsuits brought by the Transactional Records

Access Clearinghouse (TRAC),* a data-gathering organization whose primary purpose is reporting data on federal prosecutions.[29]

A 2013 case brought by the American Civil Liberties Union (ACLU) against the Department of Homeland Security (DHS) and the U.S. Immigration and Customs Enforcement agency (ICE) illustrates how criminal record information can be disclosed in spite of individual privacy interests.[30] The ACLU sought information regarding immigration detainees who had been held in custody more than ninety days, claiming that prolonged detention of immigrants violates regulatory, statutory, and constitutional laws. The ICE redacted from its files many details, including the detainee's criminal history, the location of the detainee's detention facility, how the detainee arrived in the United States, and national security concerns. The ACLU contested the redactions, arguing that the privacy exemption was inapplicable because the requested information did not involve personally identifying information. The ICE and DHS maintained that, despite the absence of names and identification numbers, the information requested "is so collectively unique that even without a name or alien number . . . it is still a personally identifying characteristic." Siding with the ACLU, the District Court for the Southern District of New York held the privacy exemption inapplicable.

---

* "The purpose of TRAC is to provide the American people—and institutions of oversight such as Congress, news organizations, public interest groups, businesses, scholars and lawyers—with comprehensive information about staffing, spending, and enforcement activities of the federal government. On a day-to-day basis, what are the agencies and prosecutors actually doing? Who are their employees and what are they paid? What do agency actions indicate about the priorities and practices of government? How do the activities of an agency or prosecutor in one community compare with those in a neighboring one or the nation as a whole? How have these activities changed over time? How does the record of one administration compare with the next? When the head of an agency or a district administrator changed, were there observable differences in actual enforcement priorities? When a new law was enacted or amended, what impact did it have on agency activities? An essential step in the process of providing this information to the public is TRAC's systematic and informed use of the Freedom of Information Act (FOIA)." Transactional Records Access Clearinghouse, Syracuse University, "About Us," http://trac.syr.edu/aboutTRACgeneral.html.

PROSECUTION RECORDS

In the course of preparing charges and case presentation, prosecutors compile and maintain copious files, which are mostly exempt from disclosure under the FOIA and its state equivalents. However, federal, state, and local prosecutors regularly receive requests for information about past cases. They generally honor the requests of law enforcement and other government agencies. Information requests from lawyers involved in civil litigation are handled on a case-by-case basis.

PUBLICLY ACCESSIBLE COURT RECORDS

Spain's and the United States' criminal records policies differ sharply with respect to public accessibility of court records. In the United States, criminal case files can be examined and copied at the courthouse and, increasingly, downloaded via the Internet. The First Amendment prevents the government from prohibiting the media (or a private citizen) from disclosing information about past and present criminal cases. Indeed, the Supreme Court has repeatedly recognized that judicial transparency is a check on police, prosecutorial, and judicial abuse of power. In *Richmond Newspapers v. Virginia* (1980), the court overturned a lower court's order closing a criminal trial to the press and the public: "Open trials are bulwarks of our free and democratic government: public access to court proceedings is one of the numerous 'checks and balances' of our system, because contemporaneous review in the forum of public opinion is an effective restraint on possible abuse of judicial power."[31] Two years later, the court heard a newspaper's challenge to a Massachusetts law that required closure of certain sexual offense trials. In ruling in favor of the newspaper, the court said:

> Although the right of access to criminal trials is of constitutional stature, it is not absolute. . . . But the circumstances under which the press and public can be barred from a criminal trial are limited; the State's justification in denying access must be a weighty one. Where, as in the present case, the State attempts to deny the right of access in order to inhibit the dis-

> closure of sensitive information, it must be shown that the denial is necessitated by a compelling government interest, and is narrowly tailored to serve that interest.[32]

In 1972, the Supreme Court struck down a Georgia law that prohibited the media from publishing sex crime victims' names because the First Amendment trumped the state's "shield law" and the common law right of privacy.

> The freedom of the press to publish that information appears to us to be of critical importance to our type of government in which the citizenry is the final judge of the proper conduct of public business. In preserving that form of government the First and Fourteenth Amendments command nothing less than that the States may not impose sanctions on the publication of truthful information contained in official court records open to public inspection.[33]

If the First Amendment protects the media's right to disclose the names of rape victims, it certainly protects the media's right to disclose the name of convicted rapists. Neither a federal, state, nor local government agency nor a court could prohibit a private person from posting to a website a convicted person's identity and offense. Disclosing an expunged conviction could not be prohibited or punished as long as the information was lawfully obtained.

The First Amendment, the tradition of open courts, and powerful political support for the public's right to know make European-type data protection, especially for criminal records, inconceivable in the United States. Even prohibiting credit reporting agencies (CRAs) from reporting accurate but arguably "obsolete" information (e.g., arrests more than seven years old) is constitutionally dubious because it constitutes suppression of true information. Nevertheless, some regulation of commercial information vendors is permissible.

In *King v. General Information Services* (GIS), the plaintiffs alleged that a commercial information vendor violated the Fair Credit Reporting Act (FCRA) by regularly reporting outdated or "obsolete" criminal history information—criminal record information, other than convictions, that is more than seven years old.[34] The company argued that the FCRA is unconstitutional, citing *Sorrell v. IMS Health, Inc.* (2011), a Supreme Court case that struck down a Vermont law restricting disclosure, sale, and use of certain pharmacy records.[35] The *Sorrell* court said "fear that people would make bad decisions if given truthful information" does not justify the suppression of true information.[36] The GIS also insisted that (1) the arrest and charge information that the FCRA prohibited it from disclosing is publicly available from courthouse records; (2) the FCRA arbitrarily prohibits GIS from disseminating "outdated" criminal record information, but does not prohibit employers from considering such information; and (3) many federal and state statutes prohibit people with criminal records from working in particular occupations (thus assuming the availability of the very information the FCRA seeks to suppress).[37] The DOJ intervened to defend the FCRA's constitutionality, arguing that consumer reports are entitled only to the lesser First Amendment protection afforded commercial speech. According to the government's brief, the FCRA carefully balances individuals' privacy interests against businesses' interest in obtaining information about people to whom they might offer a loan, a job, or an insurance policy.

> [Commercial information vendors] assemble and disseminate such large amounts of information that they pose a particularly significant threat to individuals' privacy. . . . Easily available compilations of potentially embarrassing information have a power . . . to affect personal privacy that outstrips the combined power of the bits of information contained within. Thus, even though information about past arrests and criminal charges is a matter of public record, an individual retains a privacy interest in maintaining the practical obscurity of that information.[38]*

---

* The Federal Trade Commission joined the DOJ and the Consumer Financial Protection Bureau in filing a brief in support of the FCRA's constitutionality. The brief argues that the *Sorrell* decision "does not change the settled First Amendment standards that apply to commercial speech, nor does it suggest that restrictions on the dissemination of data for commercial purposes [such as those by CRAs] must satisfy stricter stan-

The District Court for the Eastern District of Pennsylvania accepted the government's argument that consumer reports are entitled to only reduced First Amendment protection.[39]

> The disclosure requirements . . . embody Congress' dual interests in meeting business needs and protecting consumer privacy. By barring consumer reporting agencies from disclosing adverse pieces of information after a certain period of time, section 1681c directly advances the governmental interest in protecting individuals' privacy in potentially harmful and embarrassing information. . . . At the same time, however, Congress also advances its substantial interest in meeting the needs of businesses by permitting this excluded information to be furnished in certain exceptional cases: in financial transactions of more than $150,000 and in employment situations with an annual salary of more than $75,000. Balanced against the substantial interest of consumer privacy, the FCRA permits exemptions from the general rule of non-disclosure in circumstances where businesses are faced with high-stake decisions, such as extending a higher paying job or high value loan. As such, the balance is shifted from broad protection of consumer privacy to an allowance of commercial information in these higher-stake situations.

In June 2014, the parties settled. When GIS reports a criminal conviction more than seven years old, with narrow exceptions, it will remove all nonconviction information and remove indication of counts that did not result in convictions. The constitutional issue remains unresolved.*

---

dards." Therefore, the brief concludes, the court should uphold the constitutionality of the FCRA provision, as it "directly advances the government's substantial interest in protecting individuals' privacy, and is no more extensive than necessary to protect that interest while also accommodating businesses' competing interest in obtaining complete information about people to whom they are considering offering a loan, an insurance policy, or a job." See Memorandum of the United States of America in Support of the Constitutionality of §1681c of the Fair Credit Reporting Act, 20–21, http://www.ftc.gov/os/2012/05/120508fcraking-gis.pdf.

* In *Dun & Bradstreet v. Greenmoss Builders* (1985), Dun & Bradstreet (D&B), a credit reporting agency, issued a report that Greenmoss Builders, a construction contractor,

THE JUVENILE COURT EXCEPTION

The juvenile court's policy on confidentiality of proceedings and records differs diametrically from prevailing policy in adult courts. The juvenile court's founders believed that the state should prevent a "youthful indiscretion" (attributable to family problems, immaturity, impulsivity, misjudgment, and mistake) from imposing a lifelong stigma.[40] In 1909, Chicago Juvenile Court's Judge Julian Mack stressed that confidential juvenile court proceedings were necessary "to get away from the notion that the child is to be dealt with as a criminal; to save it from the brand of criminality, the brand that sticks to it for life; to take it in hand and instead of first stigmatizing and then reforming it, to protect it from the stigma—this is the work which is now being accomplished [by the juvenile court]."[41] Accordingly, the first strategy to prevent juvenile offenders from suffering long-term stigma was to keep juveniles' criminal activity confidential and to restrict adjudicatory information to a small

---

had voluntarily filed for bankruptcy. The report was false and misrepresented Greenmoss Builders' assets and liabilities. D&B appealed a state court's approval of a $350,000 compensatory and punitive damages award for defamation. D&B argued that it violated the First Amendment to allow punitive damages for defamation without a finding of actual malice. The Supreme Court (5–4) said that the correct test for evaluating "[w]hether . . . speech addresses a matter of public concern must be determined by [the expression's] content, form, and context, . . . as revealed by the whole record." The court held that D&B's credit report "concern[ed] no public issue" and was entitled to less First Amendment protection—because "[i]t was speech solely in the individual interest of the speaker and its specific business audience." Moreover, D&B's report was particularly undeserving of heightened protection because it was "wholly false and clearly damaging to the victim's business reputation." The court concluded that "[t]here is simply no credible argument that this type of credit reporting requires special protection to ensure that 'debate on public issues [will] be uninhibited, robust, and wide-open.'" However, the court added that its decision did not apply to all credit reports. And defamation does not apply to situations where the speech in question is true. *Dun & Bradstreet, Inc. v. Greenmoss Builders Inc.*, 472 U.S. 749, 762 (1985). In dissenting from the Supreme Court's denial of certiorari in *Trans Union Corp. v. FTC*, Justice Kennedy said: "It is questionable, however, whether this precedent has any place in the context of truthful, non-defamatory speech. Indeed *Dun & Bradstreet* rejected in specific terms the view that its holding 'leaves all credit reporting subject to reduced First Amendment protection.' The Court of Appeals, nonetheless, relied on *Dun & Bradstreet* to denigrate the importance of this speech. A grant of certiorari is warranted to weigh the validity of this new principle" (536 U.S. 915, 916 [2002], internal citations omitted).

number of juvenile court insiders. This would be accomplished by closing the courtroom to outsiders. There would be no jurors, who might leak information about respondents and charges.

The second strategy was to keep the court, insofar as possible, from itself creating stigmatizing criminal records. This was achieved by declaring juvenile court records nonstigmatizing. Delinquency proceedings were defined as civil rather than criminal. The accused youth would be a "respondent," not a criminal defendant. The respondent would not be convicted but "adjudicated as delinquent." The third strategy was to keep juvenile courts' records confidential. The probation officer and other interested parties (parents, school officials, case worker) would assist the judge in working out a plan that was in the respondent's best interests. Juvenile court records would be available only to juvenile court officers and others who could prove good cause. In some states, juvenile court adjudications were not appealable.[42] The fourth strategy was to expunge juvenile court records so that the formerly delinquent youth would embark on adulthood without criminal stigma.* The fifth strategy required anonymization of the juvenile respondent's name (e.g., "*In re* J.B.") in the event that an appellate court did render a written opinion in a juvenile court case. By midcentury there was broad political and legal consensus that juvenile records should be treated confidentially. Nevertheless, this effort to prevent the juvenile from being stigmatized as a criminal was not effective. Purposeful or inadvertent leaks might come from lawyers, witnesses, court personnel, or the judge.

Even though its procedures were informal, the juvenile court required records in order to keep track of and account for detainees, probationers, and reformatory inmates. Furthermore, even a juvenile court judge fully committed to confidentiality needed comprehensive

---

* For example, Massachusetts's law provided that "[c]riminal offender record information shall be limited to information concerning persons who have attained the age of 17 and shall not include any information concerning criminal offenses or acts of delinquency committed by any person before he attained the age of 17; provided, however, that if a person under the age of 17 is adjudicated as an adult, information relating to such criminal offense shall be criminal offender record information." Mass. Gen. Laws Ann. Ch. 6.

information about each juvenile respondent in order to properly assess the child's needs. The probation officer or prosecutor who was pressing the state's case against an alleged juvenile offender certainly wanted to know about the respondent's prior juvenile court adjudications; so did the juvenile court judge in order to craft an appropriate rehabilitation plan. Indeed, in determining the best interests of the child, the juvenile court judge often required comprehensive information, including the youth's prior law enforcement and court contacts as well as information regarding physical and mental problems, family relationships, school experience, and contacts with social service agencies. The probation officer compiled a great deal of such information, including unfounded rumors, in the respondent's "social file." To obtain the necessary information, the probation officer sometimes passed along information to schools, social service agencies, and others.

Confidentiality and secrecy did not necessarily work to the juvenile delinquent's benefit. The U.S. Supreme Court, in the watershed 1967 case *In re Gault*, exposed a kangaroo court whose procedures denied respondents most due process protections enjoyed by adult criminal defendants. The respondents often appeared without legal representation or even notice of the charges. Evidence frequently amounted to no more than rank hearsay. There was no right of confrontation and no protection against compelled self-incrimination. The Supreme Court's majority in *Gault* observed that

> Juvenile Court history has again demonstrated that unbridled discretion, however benevolently motivated, is frequently a poor substitute for principle and procedure. In 1937, Dean Pound wrote: "The powers of the Star Chamber were a trifle in comparison with those of our juvenile courts." The absence of substantive standards has not necessarily meant that children receive careful, compassionate, individualized treatment. The absence of procedural rules based upon constitutional principle has not always produced fair, efficient, and effective procedures. Departures from established principles of due process have frequently resulted not in enlightened procedure, but in arbitrariness.[43]

In response to the state's claim that juvenile court secrecy was necessary to protect young offenders from being tarred with a criminal label, the court questioned the juvenile court's commitment to confidentiality:

> [I]t is frequently said that juveniles are protected by the process from disclosure of their deviational behavior. As the Supreme Court of Arizona phrased it in the present case, the summary procedures of Juvenile Courts are sometimes defended by a statement that it is the law's policy to "hide youthful errors from the full gaze of the public and bury them in the graveyard of the forgotten past." This claim of secrecy, however, is more rhetoric than reality. Disclosure of court records is discretionary with the judge in most jurisdictions. Statutory restrictions almost invariably apply only to the court records, and even as to those the evidence is that many courts routinely furnish information to the FBI and the military, and on request to government agencies and even to private employers.[44]

The *Gault* court's devastating criticism of the juvenile court led many political liberals to question the desirability of keeping the juvenile court's proceedings and records confidential. They argued that secret proceedings invite arbitrariness and that lack of access to records invites abuse of authority and discrimination.

The Supreme Court next considered the desirability and importance of confidential juvenile court records in *Davis v. Alaska* (1974).[45] Alaska, like many states, did not allow lawyers to impeach a witness by exposing delinquency adjudications. In *Davis*, the court held that a criminal court defendant's Sixth Amendment right to impeach a prosecution witness outweighed the state's interest in keeping the witness's juvenile criminal history confidential. The court gave little weight to the state's interest in protecting the witness from the stigma that might follow from disclosure of his delinquency. Writing for the majority, Chief Justice Burger said: "Whatever temporary embarrassment might result to Green or his family by disclosure of his juvenile record, if the prosecution insisted on using him to make its case, is outweighed by petitioner's right to probe into the influence of possible bias in the testimony of a crucial identification witness." Moreover, "we conclude that the State's desire that Green fulfill his public duty to testify free from embarrassment and with his reputation unblemished must fall before the right of petitioner to seek out the truth in the process of defending himself."

Several years later, in a different context, the Supreme Court again found that the state's interest in protecting juvenile offenders from criminal stigma was outweighed by other values. In *Oklahoma Publishing v. District Court* (1977)[46] and *Smith v. Daily Mail Publishing* (1979),[47] the court ruled that a state cannot, either by court order (*Oklahoma Publishing*) or by statute (*Smith*), prevent or punish the media for revealing a juvenile arrestee's identity as long as the media acquired the information legally. Justice Rehnquist's concurring opinion in *Smith* reads like a swan song for the confidentiality of juvenile offending:

> The prohibition of publication of a juvenile's name is designed to protect the young person from the stigma of his misconduct and is rooted in the principle that a court concerned with juvenile affairs serves as a rehabilitative and protective agency of the State. . . . Publication of the names of juvenile offenders may seriously impair the rehabilitative goals of the juvenile justice system and handicap the youths' prospects for adjustment in society and acceptance by the public. . . . Such publicity also renders nugatory States' expungement laws, for a potential employer or any other person can retrieve the information the States seek to "bury" simply by visiting the morgue of the local newspaper. The resultant widespread dissemination of a juvenile offender's name, therefore, may defeat the beneficent and rehabilitative purposes of a State's juvenile court system.

Law-and-order conservatives also favored making juvenile court records more accessible. They argued that prosecutors of adult defendants should have access to a defendant's juvenile delinquency adjudications in order to make sensible decisions on charges, plea bargains, and sentence recommendations. In their view, it was wrong and dangerous to treat a twenty-year-old offender with previous delinquency adjudications as a first-time adult offender. State legislators mostly agreed.[48]

In the mid-1980s, Congress repealed the 1950 Federal Youth Corrections Act, which made eighteen- to twenty-six-year-old federal offenders eligible to have their convictions "set aside" if the court released them early from probation. Moreover, the Federal Sentencing Guidelines (1987) instructed federal judges to assign the same weight to a delinquency adjudication (for conduct that would be criminal if committed by an adult) as to an adult conviction.[49] Twenty-four states, including fourteen with sentencing guidelines, require judges in adult criminal cases to consider prior juvenile adjudications.

Not surprisingly, European countries are committed to the confidentiality of juveniles' criminal records. The 2008 European Rules for juvenile offenders subject to sanctions or measures states that "the imposition and implementation of sanctions or measures shall . . . take account of their age, physical and mental well-being, development, capacities and personal circumstances (principle of individualization) as ascertained when necessary by psychological, psychiatric or social inquiry reports."[50] From this principle, it follows that "[s]anctions and measures imposed on juvenile offenders should not be held against them for the rest of their lives. This implies that they should not be punished more heavily as adults because of their youthful indiscretions. It also follows that records of the offences of juveniles should not be kept for longer than absolutely necessary."[51] The rules further provide that (1) information in case records shall only encompass matters relevant to the community sanction or measure imposed and its implementation; (2) information in a case record shall be disclosed only to those with a legal right to receive it, and any information disclosed shall be limited to what is relevant for the task of the authority requesting information; and (3) after the termination of a community sanction, case records shall be destroyed or kept in archives where access to their contents shall be restricted by rules providing safeguards on revealing their content to third parties.

What about Privacy?

The U.S. Constitution does not specifically mention a right to privacy. However, the Supreme Court has found a "penumbral right of privacy" that protects the individual from government intrusion on sexual and reproductive choice.

> Specific guarantees in the Bill of Rights have penumbras, formed by emanations from those guarantees that help give them life and substance. Various guarantees create zones of privacy. . . . The Third Amendment, in its prohibition against the quartering of soldiers "in any house" in time of peace without the consent of the owner, is another facet of that privacy. The Fourth Amendment explicitly affirms the "right of the people to be secure in their persons, houses, papers, and effects, against unreasonable searches and seizures." The Fifth Amendment, in its Self-Incrimination Clause, enables the citizen to create a zone of privacy which government may not force him to surrender to his detriment. The Ninth Amendment provides: "The enumeration in the Constitution, of certain rights, shall not be construed to deny or disparage others retained by the people."[52]

Even though reputation is not protected by a constitutional privacy right, it would be wrong to say that in the United States there is no legal concern with the dissemination of personal information.[53] For example, the DOJ's guidance on the FOIA's privacy exception for law enforcement records states that law enforcement information should not be disclosed if it could reasonably (1) interfere with a current proceeding; (2) deprive someone of the right to a fair trial; (3) constitute an unwarranted invasion of personal privacy; (4) disclose the identity of a confidential source; (5) disclose law enforcement techniques; or (6) endanger the safety of anyone.[54]

More generally, the 1974 federal Privacy Act[55] prohibits federal agencies and officials from unauthorized disclosure of information maintained in government databases. Unless a specific exception applies, "No agency shall disclose any record which is contained in a system of records by any means of communication to any person, or to another agency, except pursuant to a written request by, or with the prior written consent of, the individual to whom the record pertains."[56] In *Bartel v. Federal Aviation Administration* (1984), the United States Court of Appeals for the District of Columbia reversed the dismissal of a former Federal Aviation Administration (FAA) employee's claim that the FAA had violated the Privacy Act by disclosing records of its investigation of him. According to the court, "The Privacy Act safeguards the public from unwarranted collection, maintenance, use and dissemination of personal information contained in agency records . . . by allowing an individual to participate in ensuring that his records are accurate and properly used."[57]

The Health Insurance Portability and Accountability Act of 1996 (HIPAA) is another example of a data privacy–protecting statute.[58] It restricts to whom and how hospitals, doctors, others who work in the medical sector, and insurance companies disseminate personal medical information.[59] Likewise, the Family Educational Rights and Privacy Act (FERPA) prohibits colleges and universities from disclosing a student's educational records (i.e., grades; class lists; student course schedules; disciplinary records; student financial records; or payroll records for employees who are employed as a direct result of their status as students, for example, work study, assistantships, resident assistants) without the student's consent.[60]* However, if a media organization or private person gets hold of and publishes personal medical information or grades, that disclosure would be protected by the First Amendment's free speech guarantee.

A criminal conviction stands on very different footing from medical information and college grades. There is no public interest in

* FERPA does contain some exceptions to the written consent rule. Those exceptions allow disclosure without consent to university officials (including third parties under contract) with legitimate educational interests; to comply with a judicial order or lawfully issued subpoena; to appropriate parties in a health or safety emergency in order to protect the student or others; to parents in cases of drug or alcohol violation when the student is under the age of twenty-one; to the provider or creator of a record to verify the validity of that record (e.g., in cases of suspected fraud); to organizations conducting research studies on behalf of the university, provided there is a written agreement between the university and the research organization; and last but not least, to officials at an institution in which the student seeks or intends to enroll or is currently enrolled.

an individual's medical condition (and arguably college grades), but a criminal conviction is infused with public interest. More importantly, this is not information produced by governmental officials. By contrast, a criminal prosecution is brought by a public prosecutor in the name of "the people." Evidence in support of the charges is aired in a courtroom open to the public. A judgment and sentence are meant to express community condemnation. Any proposal to treat criminal conviction information like medical or educational information would contradict the long-standing policy of public court records. It would likely also be unconstitutional.

What about Honor and Dignity?

Most U.S. readers probably find the Spanish (and European) "right to honor and dignity" quite strange, especially its prohibition on disclosing true information about criminal convictions. Why should the state seek to guarantee that a convicted person can keep her reputation intact when a prosecution is, in essence, an attack on the defendant's reputation and character? The U.S. Constitution does not mention "dignity," but the Supreme Court has frequently used the word in Fourth, Fifth, and Eighth Amendment cases.* The first

---

* Dignity is a contested concept. Immanuel Kant meant dignity to refer to a kind of intrinsic worth each human has because of his or her capacity for moral reasoning (Immanuel Kant, *Groundwork of the Metaphysics of Morals, Cambridge Texts in the History of Philosophy,* translated by Mary Gregor and Jens Timmermann, 46–47 [Cambridge: Cambridge University Press, 2012]). Jeremy Waldron argues that whatever its moral meanings, dignity in Western law has come to be associated with institutionally specific rights to better treatment for high-status individuals and that the meaning of human dignity as expressed in contemporary human rights law is the normative objective that all individuals should be treated with the solicitude that was once extended to high-status individuals. It is an "upwards equalization of rank" (Jeremy Waldron, *Dignity, Rank, and Rights* [Oxford: Oxford University Press, 2012]). For Christopher McCrudden, the concept of human dignity means "that each human being possesses an intrinsic worth that should be respected, that some forms of conduct are inconsistent with respect for this intrinsic worth, and that the state exists for the individual not vice versa" (Christopher McCrudden, *Human Dignity and Judicial Interpretation of Human Rights,* 19 Eur. J. Int'l L. 655, 722–23 [2008]). In her survey and analysis of the court's use of "dignity," Professor Leslie Meltzer Henry identified five different meanings: "institutional status as dignity," "equality as dignity," "liberty as dignity," "personal integrity as

appearance of "human dignity" in a Supreme Court majority opinion was in *Rochin v. California* (1952).[61] The court held that the police acted unconstitutionally in forcing an emetic down a suspect's throat by means of a tube in order to make the suspect vomit morphine capsules swallowed to prevent seizure by the police. Justice Frankfurter called such police conduct "shock[ing] to the conscience" and violative of human dignity. Recently, the Supreme Court found that a middle school nurse's strip search of a thirteen-year-old girl violated the Fourth Amendment.[62] To determine whether the girl was secretly hiding prohibited pills in her clothing, school officials requested that she remove her outer clothing and searched her underwear. Justice Souter's majority opinion said that the search's "indignity does not outlaw the search, but it does implicate the rule that the search [be] 'reasonably related in scope to the circumstances which justified the interference in the first place.' "[63]

Many decisions interpreting the Eight Amendment's cruel and unusual punishment clause begin by quoting from the Supreme Court's decision in *Trop v. Dulles* (1958): "The basic concept underlying the Eighth Amendment is nothing less than the dignity of man. While the State has the power to punish, the Amendment stands to assure that this power be exercised within the limits of civilized standards."[64] Almost twenty years after that decision, the court again found the concept of dignity indispensable to interpreting the Eighth Amendment's prohibition on cruel and unusual punishment. Various justices invoked dignity in *Gregg v. Georgia* (1976), where the court confirmed that the death penalty was not per se unconstitutional, but the court held that "[a] penalty also must accord

---

dignity," and "collective virtue as dignity." She finds dignity becoming more popular with the current Supreme Court and equally invoked by the conservative and the liberal justices (Leslie Meltzer Henry, *The Jurisprudence of Dignity*, 160 U. Pa. L. Rev. 169, 171, 172 [2011]). Professor Jonathan Simon distinguishes between a Dignity 1.0, which concerned liberty and equality, and an emerging Dignity 2.0, concerned with personal integrity and public virtue. He observes that "[l]ooked at as a long arc, beginning in the 1950s with dignity as liberty and equality, and continuing in this century with personal integrity and public virtue, dignity has emerged as a mature expression not just of individual human rights, but also of the relationship between individuals and government" (Jonathan Simon, *The Second Coming of Dignity*, at 17 [working paper, 2013]).

with 'the dignity of man,' which is the 'basic concept underlying the Eighth Amendment.' "[65]

In 2011, the court used the notion of dignity to uphold a lower court ruling ordering the State of California to alleviate severe prison overcrowding. Justice Kennedy, for the court, wrote that "[a]s a consequence of their own actions, prisoners may be deprived of rights that are fundamental to liberty, yet the law and the Constitution demand recognition of certain other rights. Prisoners retain the essence of human dignity inherent in all persons. Respect for that dignity animates the Eighth Amendment prohibition against cruel and unusual punishment."[66] Moreover, "[a] prison that deprives prisoners of basic sustenance, including adequate medical care, is incompatible with the concept of human dignity and has no place in civilized society."[67]

No Supreme Court justice has yet indicated that he or she believes that dignity protects reputation, much less a convicted offender from reputational injury caused by dissemination of true criminal record information.

Conclusion

Publicly accessible court records are so much a part of the legal system in the United States that American readers will likely be surprised to learn that, even in countries where court proceedings are open to the public, court records are not publicly accessible. In most continental European countries, only a party to the litigation or someone who can prove "good cause" or a "qualified interest" is permitted to see a record of a pending or closed case. Journalistic and academic interests do not qualify as good cause. In Italy, for example, courts usually find that only the defendant and victim's attorney have "good cause." Others have to demonstrate that allowing them access to the record is supported by a strong public interest that outweighs the defendant's privacy interest.

Transparency of governmental operations and especially court proceedings is a hallmark of American democracy and deeply embedded in American political-legal culture. People have a right to know what is and has occurred in the courts. Justice should be done and should be seen to be done. Without access to records showing how criminal cases have been handled, there could be no such confidence. (Maybe minority defendants are being discriminated against? Maybe prosecutions against rich defendants are inexplicably dropped?) Arguably, transparency contributes to confidence in the fairness, integrity, and competence of judges. Even if transparency exposes incompetence and injustice, criticism may trigger or reinforce reform.

The First Amendment right to free speech and press also provides very strong support for publicly accessible court records. To survive First Amendment challenge, a policy proposal that would punish the disclosure of true information requires a compelling state interest. Protecting offender privacy and promoting offender rehabilitation are not considered compelling.

Unlike court records, there is no tradition of publicly accessible police, prosecutorial, and corrections records. Police, prosecutors, and corrections personnel deal with a great deal of sensitive information about suspects and defendants whose cases are being investigated or pending. If investigative information were publicly disclosed, witnesses could be bribed, intimidated, and killed, and suspects could flee. Even after a criminal case has been successfully prosecuted, there is good reason to keep police and prosecutorial files confidential. Much information gathered by police and prosecutors is not introduced in court because it is considered untrustworthy or irrelevant. It may cast aspersions on innocent people. Other information may contain unnecessarily graphic representations of abuse and wounds. In short, police and prosecutors play a screening role in deciding what information will be made public.

There are, of course, critics (e.g., the Reporters Committee for Freedom of the Press) of policies and decisions that keep law enforcement and corrections records confidential. These critics stress the public's right to know. Nevertheless, there are strong reasons to treat police and prosecutorial records as presumptively confidential, especially when so much information is available in court records. One of the strongest reasons is that persons named in these records would have no effective way of rebutting disparaging information were it to be made public. Of course, that is not a reason to withhold the information from the record-subject herself. The FBI's FOIA Document Processing System provides that an individual may obtain certain FBI records pertaining to herself.[68]

European countries conceive of an individual's criminal history record as analogous to information about race, religion, health, and sexual orientation. An individual's criminal history is not other people's business. Government officials, including judges, are best placed to determine what consequences, formal and informal, convictions should have in the short and long run. Spanish law highly values individual dignity, honor, and privacy. Spanish judges, criminal law scholars, and policy makers believe that because criminal history information belongs to the individual's "private sphere," the dissemination of conviction information should be significantly restricted. While Spanish law treats a criminal defendant's past convictions as relevant for sentencing, it does not recognize shaming as a legitimate anticrime or deterrence strategy; indeed, Spanish jurists find that idea appalling.[69] Spain's commitment to confidentiality is reflected in and reinforced by the European Union's PDPL, which prohibits posting databases of named criminal offenders on the World Wide Web.

The European effort to keep individual criminal history information confidential is under pressure from the media and free speech proponents, legal and social science researchers, and advocacy groups. Electronic databases and the Internet make collection, storage, retrieval, and dissemination of information faster, cheaper, more efficient, and more difficult to control. The same kind of fear about recidivating child sex offenders that grips the United States is also evident in Europe.[70] In 2011, Directive 2011/92/EU of the European Parliament and of the Council of December 13, 2011, on combating the sexual abuse and sexual exploitation of children and child pornography requires member states to ensure that those convicted of any specified offenses against children "may be temporarily or permanently prevented from exercising at least professional activities involving direct and regular contacts with children." Member states retain discretion regarding what kind of vetting scheme to adopt (e.g., via a criminal or administrative decision or an occupational licensing law) and how to interpret "direct and regular contacts with children." Additionally, member states are encouraged to consider extending disqualifications to positions in organizations that provide services to children.

The directive, for the first time, recognizes, that an employer who is recruiting staff for professional or voluntary activities involving direct and regular contacts with children has a right to be informed of job applicants' prior convictions for sexual offenses against children and of related employment disqualifications. Thus, an EU member state that does not currently provide for disclosure of criminal records to employers working with children will have to change its national law. The directive also requires member states to exchange child sex offense conviction information for the purposes of (1) enabling the requesting member state to identify and bar sex offenders convicted in other member states from working with children and (2) enabling EU employers to make informed decisions about the suitability of EU job applicants for positions affording close contact with children. It remains to be seen whether the Spanish and European effort to limit the stigma of a criminal record will continue to prevail as part of a distinctive European crime policy or whether technology, politics, emphasis on free speech, and fear of recidivist sex offenders and terrorists will move law and policy further in the direction of making criminal record information available to the public.

10 PUBLIC ACCESS TO ARRESTEE INFORMATION

> [F]ingerprinting is not a punishment. It is a means of identification which is useful in many circumstances some of which relate to the enforcement of our laws. Unless the burdens that this procedure places on the individual are unreasonable, therefore, it will be upheld as one of those annoyances that must be suffered for the common good.
>
> —*Krapf v. United States*, United States Court of Appeals for the Third Circuit (1960)[1]

> Should a citizen be haunted by fingerprints labelled "criminal" or a rogue's gallery photograph, when he has no charges pending against him? I think not. The preservation of these records constitutes an unwarranted attack upon his character and reputation and violates his right of privacy; it violates his dignity as a human being. . . . [W]hen an accused is acquitted of the crime or when he is discharged without conviction, no public good is accomplished by the retention of criminal identification records. On the other hand, a great imposition is placed upon the citizen. His privacy and personal dignity is invaded as long as the Justice Department retains "criminal" identification records, "criminal" arrest, fingerprints and a rogue's gallery photograph.
>
> —*Kalish v. United States*, United States District Court for the District of Puerto Rico (1967)[2]

FROM AN INTERNATIONAL PERSPECTIVE, publicly accessible arrest records are even more exceptional than publicly available conviction records. In the United States, arrestee information becomes public in several ways. Most police departments maintain a publicly accessible chronological ledger ("blotter") of arrestees, which crime beat reporters regularly check for newsworthy arrests. Sometimes police departments, as part of a deterrence campaign, release to the media or post online the names of persons arrested for certain crimes. Some police departments even sell arrestee information. The arrestee's identity may become public when he is displayed to the media ("perp walk") on the way to central booking or on the way from central booking to court. The arrest always becomes public at the arrestee's initial appearance before a magistrate in open court, a hearing that must occur within forty-eight hours of arrest. At that point, a publicly accessible court record is created.

Police "Blotters"

The police record all arrests at the police station in a daily log book called "the police blotter" (in New York City, the "command log"). Even if an arrestee is not formally charged, his name and arrest offense will be memorialized on the blotter, which reporters (and others) can examine for newsworthy crimes or arrestees and publish stories like this:

> A 23-year-old woman was arrested after she allegedly pointed a Taser at another woman who tried to stop her from stealing a cake and a bottle of Sunny Delight juice from 10 Star Deli on Myrtle Avenue on May 2, police reported. Yvette Ray—who was accompanied by her five year-old son to the deli at around 3 p.m.—was charged with robbery in the first and third degrees, menacing in the second degree, petit larceny, criminal possession of stolen property in the fifth degree, endangering the welfare of a child, criminal possession of a weapon in the fourth degree, menacing in the third degree, sale and possession of electronic thumb guns and harassment in the second degree, according to the King's County [Brooklyn] District Attorney's office.[3]

Why do the police make this log available to the public? The intent to inflict reputational punishment on arrestees before the judicial process even begins, for retributive or deterrence purposes, could not be justified on policy grounds and is arguably an unconstitutional denial of due process. The only plausibly justifiable grounds for this policy, although not one that was likely to have motivated the police, is to make policing transparent. It could be argued that the media, advocacy groups, and the public should be able to find out who has been arrested (and not arrested) for what conduct. Such information casts light on which criminal laws are and are not being enforced, whether members of some groups are arrested more often than others, and how frequently classes of arrestees are not prosecuted. Although arrestee information might contribute to answering these questions and thereby contribute to greater police accountability, the case for publicly available police blotters is weak.[4] Sufficient information to assess police performance can be obtained by monitoring the arraignment court. Admittedly, however, it would not reveal information about police arrests that did not lead to filed charges.

Disclosing Arrests as a Deterrence Strategy

Some police departments, from time to time, publicize arrests in order to mobilize community censure for the purpose of deterring high-frequency low-level crimes, for example, soliciting or patronizing a prostitute, drunk driving, and shoplifting.[5] Deterrence depends upon would-be offenders being unwilling to risk the shame (reputational injury) of being exposed as an accused violator of these laws. To implement a shame-based enforcement strategy, the police post to a website or send the media the names of people arrested for particular offenses.[6] One study found 202 examples of police departments publicizing the names (and sometimes photographs) of persons arrested for patronizing a prostitute. The Arlington (Texas) Police Department, for example, posts arrestee information on its website and mails postcards to the arrestee's home in order to activate spousal and familial censure and remedial efforts. In California, the Oakland Police Department's "Operation Shame" placed photos of individuals arrested for soliciting prostitutes on billboards.[7] In February 1995, Boston officials broadcast a twenty-minute television video of arraignments of people arrested for soliciting prostitutes.[8] Kansas City, Missouri, officials aired on television photos, names, dates of birth, and places of residence of individuals arrested on prostitution-related charges;[9] several cities replicated the program.[10] In Florida, the Orlando Police Department posted on its website the names of individuals arrested for prescription drug fraud.[11] The Maricopa County, Arizona sheriff's office posted on its website the mug shots and names of all people arrested in the preceding three days.[12] The mug shots are categorized by type of offense, for example, “Deadbeat Parents,” “Animal Cruelty,” “Arson,” “Sex Crimes,” and “DUI.” If a visitor to this website clicks on a mug shot, detailed information about the arrestee is revealed. This kind of intentional public naming and shaming undermines the core principle of due process of law. In effect, it dispenses with the need for adjudication. Many, perhaps most, of the people arrested for these minor crimes will not be prosecuted or, if prosecuted, will receive only a minor punishment such as a small fine or community service. A cynical criminal justice policy would decide to save the time, effort and money to adjudicate the arrest and just pronounce, explicitly or implicitly, the arrestee guilty.

Sale of Arrestee Information

Some police departments sell arrest information to the public.[13] The Onondaga County, New York sheriff’s office sells arrest information from the Criminal History Arrest Incident Reporting System (CHAIRS) database. CHAIRS is a good example of an investigative database populated with information about criminal incidents.[14] For $10, employers, landlords, volunteer groups, and anyone else can obtain any person’s lifetime record of arrests (without dispositions) in Onondaga County. The Center for Community Alternatives found that 65 percent of a sample of CHAIRS reports issued between 2008 and 2010 contained arrest information that should have been sealed. To take another example, the National Consumer Law Center (NCLC) reported that, in 1998, the Michigan Sheriffs’ Association made a private corporation the exclusive distributor of arrest information to private sector individuals and organizations.

The FOIA and Mug Shots

U.S. federal appeals courts disagree on whether the FOIA requires government disclosure of arrestee mug shots (booking photographs). Federal law enforcement agencies refuse to disclose booking photographs on the ground that mug shots fall within FOIA’s exception for law enforcement records whose disclosure would cause an unwarranted invasion of personal privacy. Only the Sixth Circuit has rejected that argument in *Detroit Free Press v. DOJ* (1996).[15] However, in that case, the defendants had already been indicted and appeared in court. At that point in time, the court reasoned, personal privacy is not infringed "simply because" disclosure of the requested information could cause embarrassment or ridicule. The court stated that mug shots should be afforded less privacy than rap sheets because the latter "are not single pieces of information but, rather, compilations of many facts that may not otherwise be readily available from a single source. Thus, rap sheets both disclose information that extends beyond a particular, ongoing proceeding and recreate information that, under other circumstances, may have been lost or forgotten"; by contrast the mug shot provides much less information.[16] The dissenting judge vigorously disagreed:

> The majority's view that one's mug shot conveys no more than one's appearance misconceives the true nature of a mug shot. While a photograph may not reveal any "private" information, a mug shot conveys much more than the appearance of the pictured individual. Unlike a photograph taken under normal circumstances, it relates a number of facts about a person, including his expression at a humiliating moment and the fact that he has been booked on criminal charges. Furthermore, as this court has recognized, mug shots are widely viewed by members of the public as signifying that the person in the photo has committed a crime. *Eberhardt v. Bordenkircher*, 605 F.2d 275, 280 (6th Cir. 1979) (mug shots convey an "unmistakable badge of criminality"). In my view, these considerations lead to but one conclusion: that the subject of a mug shot has a cognizable privacy interest in preventing its public dissemination.[17]

The Tenth Circuit, in *World Publishing Co.* (2012), and the Eleventh Circuit, in *Karantsalis v. U.S. Department of Justice* (2011), shared Judge Norris's view that mug shots infringe on arrestees' privacy interests and that federal law enforcement agencies therefore should not make them available to the media. According to the district court, whose judgment the Eleventh Circuit affirmed:

> The Court agrees with the U.S. Marshals Service, that a booking photograph is a unique and powerful type of photograph that raises personal privacy interests distinct from normal photographs. A booking photograph is a vivid symbol of criminal accusation, which, when released to the public, intimates, and is often equated with, guilt. Further, a booking photograph captures the subject in the vulnerable and embarrassing moments immediately after being accused, taken into custody, and deprived of most liberties.[18]

Both the Tenth and Eleventh Circuit courts emphasized that disclosure of mug shots provides no insight into how federal law enforcement agencies perform their functions, while infringing arrestees' privacy interests. Therefore, both courts concluded that FOIA's law enforcement exception covered the U.S. Marshals Service's refusal to disclose mug shots to the media and the public.

Because of the circuit split, the U.S. Marshals Service currently discloses mug shots pursuant to FOIA requests filed in the Sixth Circuit regardless of where the mug shot originated. In effect, this renders all mug shots in its possession subject to disclosure even though every federal circuit, except the Sixth would not disclose them.[19] This is an unfortunate result. Mug shot disclosure causes reputational injury, especially in the case of arrestees who were never prosecuted or, if prosecuted, were not convicted.

Should Arrests That Did Not Result in Convictions Be Expunged?

Once an arrest is recorded, expunging it is complicated.* To delete arrest information from the rap sheet system before the prosecutor's

---

* In 1986, the National Conference of Commissioners on Uniform State Laws adopted the Uniform Criminal History Records Act (UCHRA), in an effort to promote uniformity with respect to police recording, storing, and exchanging individual criminal history information. One UCHRA provision authorizes dissemination of arrest information to anyone for any purpose as long as a "reportable event" has occurred in the case within a year preceding the request. The American Bar Association House of Delegates officially approved the UCHRA, despite the Criminal Justice Section's objections. The UCHRA was then recommended to each state's legislature, but only Illinois adopted (a modified version of) it. See Gary T. Lowenthal, *The Disclosure of Arrest Records to the*

office decides whether to file charges would impede or prevent the processing of the case. Likewise, it does not make sense to expunge the information before the judge decides whether the case should go forward. It might take months, sometimes more than a year, for an arrest to be resolved by dismissal, conviction, or acquittal.[20] Adjudication may be interrupted and delayed because the defendant is not available (sick, fled the jurisdiction, etc.). The speedy trial clock may be stopped and thus the time limit extended due to pretrial motions and hearings. The defendant may request a trial postponement to accommodate his defense lawyer's schedule or to await the results of more forensic testing. While the case is pending there must be a record in order to keep track of the defendant and the progress of the case through the adjudication process.

The strongest case for erasing a recorded arrest is that police supervisors or prosecutors concluded that no crime was committed or that, although there was a crime, this arrestee had nothing to do with it. (That was the situation in *Menard v. Mitchell*, discussed in Chapter 8.) However, that is not usually the case. The most common reason why an arrest does not lead to a conviction is lack of victim or witness cooperation. Some victims and witnesses do not want to take time off from work, perhaps because they themselves have a criminal record and fear police and prosecutorial attention. Some victims fear that cooperating with the police or prosecutor would harm their relationship with the defendant whom they count on for financial and emotional support. Some witnesses fear that cooperating with the prosecution would provoke the defendant's retaliation. Sometimes the victim or key witness has died or become too ill to testify.

Some arrests do not result in conviction because the prosecutor or the judge determines that crucial evidence is inadmissible at trial; this certainly does not mean that the arrestee is factually innocent. Likewise, the court may dismiss charges because of a speedy trial

---

Public under the Uniform Criminal History Records Act, 28 Jurimetrics Journal 9, at 9–10 (1987–1988); Nicole Julal et al., *Criminal Records History Scope Proposal to the National Conference of Commissioners on Uniform State Laws Committee on Scope and Program, Mid-Year 2012*, http://www.uniformlaws.org/shared/docs/Criminal%20Records%20Access%20and%20Accuracy/2012jan_Criminal%20Records_Proposal%20to%20Scope%20and%20Program.pdf.

violation. Sometimes the prosecutor decides that a pretrial diversion program is the best disposition for the arrestee. In such cases, police and prosecutors want to retain a record of the arrest and diversion so that if the same person is arrested in the future, she is not assumed to be a first offender. When there is a deferred prosecution, the prosecutor and court need to retain information on the arrest and charges in case the person does not successfully comply with the diversion program. Even if the case is dismissed, the arrest records will be needed in the event that the police department is sued for wrongful arrest.* Records of arrests that were not prosecuted will also be needed to monitor and evaluate police officer conduct, for example, whether a particular officer is regularly arresting innocent people. Finally, if arrest records had to be purged when prosecutors voluntarily dismiss charges, police and prosecutors might be less likely to exercise leniency.

Even if the defendant is not successfully prosecuted, the police retain arrest records in order to identify suspects in unsolved past and future crimes. Moreover, in deciding whether and how to charge a particular defendant, whether to request bail, and whether to offer and/or accept a guilty plea, criminal justice decision makers want to know as much as possible about the suspect's or defendant's criminal career.[21] A defendant with a slew of arrests for serious offenses looks much different than someone with no previous arrests. Indeed, risk assessment instruments, often used in making pretrial detention and parole decisions, usually use previous arrests as an important predictor of future criminality.

Sealing or Purging Arrest Records

It is standard practice for an arrest to remain on the rap sheet even if the case is dismissed, adjourned in contemplation of dismissal, or resolved by a not guilty verdict. However, a few states require that

---

* A wrongful (or false) arrest is a tort that consists of an unlawful restraint of an individual's personal liberty or freedom of movement by another purporting to act according to the law. An action can be instituted for the damages ensuing from false arrest, such as loss of salary while imprisoned or injury to reputation that results in a pecuniary loss to the victim.

arrests that do not result in a conviction within a certain period of time be sealed or expunged. New York State law requires that local police departments and the state's criminal record repository must seal or expunge arrest information from a rap sheet if the arrest does not result in formal charges or if formal charges are dismissed, unless the district attorney or the court "demonstrates to the satisfaction of the court that interests of justice require otherwise."[22]* However, there is some doubt about the extent of compliance. In its analysis of nearly 3,500 New York rap sheets, the Legal Action Center, an NGO that advocates for ex-offenders, found that from 5.1 percent to 10.4 percent revealed information that should have been sealed.[23] Errors with regard to arrests that should have been sealed because either the police decided not to pursue the matter or because the prosecutor declined to prosecute are more difficult to correct, as the record-subject needs to produce records kept by the local police department or prosecutor's office that may be difficult to locate. Sometimes, older records cannot be easily found.

In 1991, the New York Court of Appeals considered a robbery and assault appeal by Charles Patterson, whose mug shot the police used in a photo array, although it should have been destroyed or

* N.Y. CPL. Law § 160.50: "Upon the termination of a criminal action or proceeding against a person in favor of such person . . . unless the district attorney upon motion with not less than five days notice to such person or his or her attorney demonstrates to the satisfaction of the court that the interests of justice require otherwise, or the court on its own motion with not less than five days notice to such person or his or her attorney determines that the interests of justice require otherwise and states the reasons for such determination on the record, the record of such action or proceeding shall be sealed and the clerk of the court wherein such criminal action or proceeding was terminated shall immediately notify the commissioner of the division of criminal justice services and the heads of all appropriate police departments and other law enforcement agencies that the action has been terminated in favor of the accused, and unless the court has directed otherwise, that the record of such action or proceeding shall be sealed. Upon receipt of notification of such termination and sealing . . . all official records and papers, including judgments and orders of a court but not including published court decisions or opinions or records and briefs on appeal, relating to the arrest or prosecution, including all duplicates and copies thereof, on file with the division of criminal justice services, any court, police agency, or prosecutor's office shall be sealed and not made available to any person or public or private agency."

returned to Patterson. Patterson argued that the identification should have been suppressed, but the court disagreed, holding that a defendant identified on the basis of arrest information that should have been purged cannot invoke the exclusionary rule.[24] The dissenting judge persuasively criticized the majority for discounting the importance of purging nonconviction information from rap sheets:

> [T]he majority's refusal to invoke the suppression remedy in this context reflects an overly restrictive application of the law. Although the majority insists that [the law] was not designed "to create a constitutionally-derived right," its assertion is belied by its own acknowledgment that the statute was specifically designed to protect the constitutionally derived presumption of innocence by ensuring that "one who is charged but not convicted of an offense suffers no stigma as a result of his having once been the object of an unsustained accusation. . . ."
>
> The majority's analysis is also lacking because it fails to consider the substantiality of the harm suffered by individuals whose rights under [the law] have been disregarded. Where the individual's confidentiality rights are not protected, "[o]pportunities for schooling, employment, or professional licenses may be restricted or nonexistent as a consequence of the mere fact of an arrest, even if followed by acquittal or complete exoneration.'" Additionally, materials retained from a prior arrest may be "employed as a basis to subsequently suspect, harass or otherwise penalize." The unauthorized retention and use of arrest photographs and fingerprints is particularly pernicious because, as occurred here, they form the basis of a new criminal investigation, subjecting the individual to the attendant humiliation and discomfort. Thus, there can be no doubt that violations of the statutory command result in impairments of constitutional rights that are both real and substantial.[25]

Reputational injury to the arrestee would be much diminished or even entirely avoided if information about arrests that did not result in convictions were not available to non–law enforcement organizations and individuals. In fact, some repositories follow that policy.

Purging the Arrest Charge When Defendant Pleads Guilty to a Lesser Offense

Another important rap sheet question is how to deal with information about an arrest that is resolved by a plea of guilty to a lesser offense. Suppose the defendant was arrested for rape but pled guilty to assault or, at trial, was convicted of assault. Should the fact that the person convicted of assault was arrested and charged with rape remain on his rap sheet, which is now standard practice? If so, the rap sheet consumer might infer that, despite the plea of guilty to assault and battery, the defendant probably committed rape. The police have a legitimate need for this information, but non–law enforcement organizations and individuals do not. If they learn about the dismissed charges, the defendant, to some extent, loses the benefit of his plea bargain.

Employers' Access to Arrest and Arrestee Information

All states and the federal government require their criminal records repository to release rap sheet information to certain designated businesses and organizations. (Each state decides which employers and entities should have this privilege.) That always means access to conviction information, but what about arrest information? Most states' criminal record repositories make no distinction. In nineteen states, a name-based non–criminal justice background check returns the full criminal history record. In eighteen states, the criminal repository provides non–criminal justice agency requesters with information on convictions only for name-based checks.[26] A few states' statutes provide that arrests pending for more than one year should not be reported to non–criminal justice agency requesters. That should be standard policy for all jurisdictions.

The majority of employers and other non–criminal justice agency consumers of criminal records obtain criminal history information, including arrest information, directly or indirectly, from the courts via commercial information vendors. The commercial vendors obtain arrest and charge information from court records.[27] Thus, even if the records repositories did not provide employers with arrest information, it would make little difference as long as private information vendors did not follow that same policy.

Originally, the Fair Credit Reporting Act (FCRA) prohibited credit reporting agencies (CRAs) from reporting arrests, indictments, or convictions more than seven years old. An amendment to the FCRA made criminal convictions reportable indefinitely. However, the FCRA still prohibits reporting arrest records older than seven years, unless the arrest resulted in a conviction or unless the position for which the record-subject is being vetted is reasonably expected to carry an annual salary in excess of $75,000, in which case the arrest information, no matter how old, can be reported. Some state laws have set different thresholds.

Several state laws are more restrictive than the FCRA with respect to reporting old arrests. Montana and Nevada prohibit reporting arrest records that are older than seven years regardless of income level. California, Hawaii, Illinois, Kentucky, Massachusetts, New Mexico, New York, Pennsylvania, Rhode Island, Utah, and Wisconsin prohibit CRAs from reporting arrests unless the case is pending or a conviction resulted.

Arrests and Reputational Injury

It is one thing to label as a criminal an individual who has been convicted of a crime, but quite another to similarly stigmatize a person who was arrested but never formally charged, much less convicted. This smacks of punishment (reputation injury) without due process. The Supreme Court faced the issue in *Paul v. Davis* (1976).[28] Just before Christmas, Louisville's police chief, Edgar Paul, and Jefferson County's police chief, Russell McDaniel, sent to local businesses an "Active Shoplifters" circular containing names and photos of persons who had previously been arrested for shoplifting.

Edward C. Davis, whom the circular identified as an active shoplifter, filed a lawsuit against Chief Paul and Chief McDaniel claiming that, by publicly branding him as a criminal, the two police chiefs had violated his right to due process of law under the Fourteenth Amendment and his constitutional right to privacy. The Sixth Circuit, relying on the Supreme Court's decision in *Wisconsin v.*

Constantineau (1971), held in Davis's favor.[29] *Constantineau* struck down a state statute allowing the posting in liquor stores of the name of any individual "who by excessive drinking produces described conditions or exhibits specified traits such as exposing himself or family 'to want' or becoming 'dangerous to the peace' of the community." The selling or giving of alcoholic beverages to such individuals was forbidden. The Supreme Court found that denial of notice and a hearing violated due process. "Where the State attaches a 'badge of infamy' to the citizen, due process comes into play."[30]

In *Davis*, the Supreme Court distinguished *Constantineau*, finding "no constitutional doctrine converting every defamation by a public official into a deprivation of liberty within the meaning of the Due Process Clause of the Fifth or Fourteenth Amendment."[31] The governmental action in *Constantineau* deprived the plaintiff of a property interest, the opportunity to purchase or receive alcoholic beverages. Davis did not benefit from a legal guarantee of enjoyment of reputation. Reputational damage resulting from dissemination of arrest information did not violate a property or liberty interest protected by the due process clause.

The Supreme Court was also not persuaded by Davis's claim that circulation of the information about the previous arrest violated his constitutional right to privacy. The court rejected the notion that there is a right to informational privacy, opining that constitutional privacy protection is limited to body searches, procreation, marriage, contraception, and child rearing.

> [Davis] claims constitutional protection against the disclosure of the fact of his arrest on a shoplifting charge. His claim is based, not upon any challenge to the State's ability to restrict his freedom of action in a sphere contended to be "private," but instead on a claim that the State may not publicize a record of an official act such as an arrest. None of our substantive privacy decisions hold this or anything like this, and we decline to employ them in this manner.

Moreover, according to the court, because the circular containing Davis's name and photo was not an official criminal record, its potential damage to reputation was minimal.

Conclusion

It seems counterintuitive, indeed outrageous, that every police officer has the power to stigmatize any person with a lifelong arrest record. Yet this is more or less the case, except in a few states where arrests not resulting in convictions must be sealed. This anomalous situation is caused by the fact that police rap sheets have come to be widely used by non–criminal justice agencies, organizations and individuals. Prior arrest information often provides important leads for current investigations. It is also necessary for defensive documentation in case the police are sued for wrongful arrest. However, it is not legitimate for the police or prosecutors to use arrest information to shame arrestees, even if it could be shown that this practice contributes to general or specific deterrence. Naming and shaming is a controversial form of punishment in the sentencing context, but indefensible when meted out by police.

From a law enforcement point of view, arrest and arrestee information is important whether or not it results in a conviction. Neither the police nor the criminal record repositories should disclose to non–law enforcement agencies arrests that have been pending for more than one year, especially when the same information exists in publicly accessible court records.* New York's practice of sealing arrest records when charges are resolved favorably to the defendant (i.e., dismissal) is a sound policy. However, even in New York, the arrestee cannot be sure that the arrest information will actually be removed from the rap sheet and other police databases, much less court records.

The existence of the commercial information sector makes it increasingly likely that arrest information that is pending for months

---

* According to a 2001 Department of Justice report regarding public attitudes toward the uses of criminal history information, about half of American adults are in favor of granting limited access to arrest records to an employer or government licensing agency, depending on the nature of the position. Roughly 15 percent would allow access to arrest records to all employers and government licensing agencies, whereas approximately 30 percent would bar all employers and licensing agencies from accessing the arrest record. See U.S. Department of Justice, Bureau of Justice Statistics, *Public Attitudes toward Uses of Criminal History Information: A Privacy, Technology, and Criminal Justice Information Report* (July 2001), http://www.bjs.gov/content/pub/pdf/pauchi.pdf.

and even years will be downloaded to a proprietary database and thereafter disseminated to employers and other customers. The FCRA restriction on disseminating information on arrests more than seven years old is unsatisfactory. Why should someone who has been arrested but never convicted bear a criminal stigma for seven years (actually much longer, since the information that has been publicly available for seven years remains in the public mind far longer)? The FCRA should be amended to require that arrest information that did not result in a conviction within a year not be circulated to non–criminal justice agencies, organizations, associations, and individuals. Whether such a law would withstand a First Amendment challenge remains to be seen.

11 PUBLICLY ACCESSIBLE CRIMINAL RECORDS AND PUNISHMENT THEORY

> There can be no outrage, methinks, against our common nature,—whatever be the delinquencies of the individual,—no outrage more flagrant than to forbid the culprit to hide his face for shame; as it was the essence of this punishment to do. . . . But the point which drew all eyes, and, as it were, transfigured the wearer,—so that both men and women, who had been familiarly acquainted with Hester Prynne, were now impressed as if they beheld her for the first time,—was that Scarlett Letter, so fantastically embroidered and illuminated upon her bosom. It had the effect of a spell, taking her out of the ordinary relations with humanity, and enclosing her in a sphere by herself.
>
> —Nathaniel Hawthorne, *The Scarlet Letter* (1850)[1]

> Under policies holding that public disgrace is an appropriate component of punishment for crime, past convictions are disclosable to the public.
>
> —National Conference of Commissioners on Uniform Laws, Uniform Criminal History Record Act (1986)[2]

IN ANCIENT TIMES, a criminal conviction was "written" on the offender's body by branding or mutilation. This served a deterrent purpose by inflicting painful punishment[3] and by marking the convict for social ostracism.[4] Branding the convict as a pariah also served a social defense function. It signaled to everyone in the home and neighboring communities that the individual was a disgraced "outlaw" who should be avoided or approached with caution.*

The publicly accessible criminal record is the modern equivalent of branding. It is not burned or carved on the convict's body and

---

* "Outlaw" derives from the old English noun *utlaga*, meaning one who is banished, and has historically been used to describe those who are "outside the law and deprived of its benefits and protection" (*Oxford English Dictionary*, Online Edition, Oxford University Press, 3rd ed., December 2004, at "outlaw"; T. F. Hoad (ed.), *The Concise Oxford Dictionary of English Etymology* [Oxford: Oxford University Press, 1993], at "outlaw").

does not involve physical pain but, thanks to name, fingerprint, and DNA-profile databases and to criminal history records, it is readily connected to the corporeal body. Unlike an emblazoned scarlet letter, an individual's criminal history is not immediately apparent, but with little effort and cost, anyone's criminal record can be located. While identification as a convicted person often involves shaming and reputational injury, it always involves legal and discretionary disqualifications.

This chapter asks whether naming and shaming is an intended and required part of criminal punishment. If it is not required, is it justified by one or more theories of punishment? At first blush, a "yes" answer to the first question seems obvious because criminal law is predicated on community moral condemnation, and there could be no community condemnation if the conviction was secret. Edwin Sutherland, the father of U.S. criminology, famously observed that "stigma"* is an inherent and distinctive feature of criminal law: "[A] civil fine is a financial penalty without the additional penalty of stigma, while a criminal fine is a financial penalty with the additional penalty of stigma."[5] However, the matter continues to provoke lively debate, especially in light of the negative consequences of criminal stigma for employment and successful reentry into legitimate society.

Retributive Justice

Retribution has been the dominant justification for punishment in the United States since the mid-1970s, after rehabilitation lost its luster.[6] A short chapter (much less one section of a short chapter) could not hope to survey the many different versions or explanations of retributive justice or each version's implications for making criminal records public.[7]† According to the eminent philosopher

* Stigma derives from the ancient Greek term στίγμα, meaning "mark or brand." Originally the term had a neutral connotation, but then it progressively evolved to indicate a distinguishing mark of social disgrace.

† John Cottingham, *Varieties of Retribution*, 29(1) Philosophical Quarterly 238 (1979), identifies nine variants of retribution theory: repayment theory, desert theory, penalty

John Rawls, "What we may call the retributive view is that punishment is justified on the grounds that wrongdoing merits punishment. It is morally fitting that a person who does wrong should suffer in proportion to his wrongdoing. . . . [T]he severity of the appropriate punishment depends on the depravity of his act."[8] I have in mind "positive retributivism," the theory that a convicted offender should receive a punishment that reflects his just desert. Antony Duff, the leading advocate of positive retributivism, explains that

> [p]ositive retributivism is typically expressed in the language of penal desert. The guilty, those who commit criminal offences, deserve to be punished. . . . For the positive retributivist, not merely that we must not punish the innocent, or punish the guilty more than they deserve, but that we *should* punish the guilty to the extent that they deserve: penal desert constitutes not just necessary, but an in principle sufficient reason for punishment (only in principle, however, since there are very good reasons—to do with the costs, both material and moral, of punishment—why we should not try to punish all guilty persons). A striking feature of penal theorizing during the last three decades of the twentieth century was a revival of positive retributivism—of the idea that the positive justification of punishment is to be found in its intrinsic character as a deserved response for criminal conduct.[9]

The key question for us here is whether a publicly accessible criminal record is meant to be part of the convicted offender's punishment. Publicizing the conviction is not invariably necessary to satisfy the requirements of positive retributivism. In a particular case, a fine, a prison term, or capital punishment could satisfy just deserts, without additional reputational and emotional injury resulting from naming and shaming. But a public criminal record that evokes a negative community response is justifiable under retributive justice, at least

theory, minimalism, satisfaction theory, fair play theory, placation theory, annulment theory, and denunciation theory.

in some cases. In Italy, for example, where publicly accessible criminal records are not the norm, the Penal Code (art. 36) provides that for certain serious convictions, publication of the conviction is a deserved additional punishment.

In the United States, the majority of convictions are for misdemeanors,[10] which are usually "punished" by a suspended sentence or small fine. The most serious punishment that the convicted defendant will experience is the judge's words of censure in imposing sentence and any verbal or nonverbal disapprovals from correctional personnel and members of the community. In some cases, community censure could be too harsh, thus violating retributive justice's proportionality principle. When it comes to the most severe sentences (e.g., long-term imprisonment), community members' censure would not add much, if any, desert.

A criminal prosecution is a public accusation of wrongdoing brought in the name of "the people." A criminal judgment and sentence communicate deserved censure.[11] At the sentencing stage, it is the judge's duty, on behalf of the community, to make clear to the convicted defendant in open court that his or her criminal conduct was wrongful and condemnable. However, for that censure to be effective, doesn't the judge's message need to be recommunicated or echoed by at least some members of the community? Even assuming that the judge gives an effective lecture, the defendant who hears only from the judge on a single occasion may not internalize the community's censure. Indeed, the convicted offender might believe that his conviction matters only to the judge, and dismiss the judge's censure as personal opinion.* Interestingly, there is no empirical study on judges' sentencing lectures.

The renowned legal theorist Henry Hart said in his classic essay "The Aims of the Criminal Law" that he thought it unacceptable

* Professor Dan Markel argues that it is preferable for the public to be informed of the defendant's conviction and sentence, but that a censorious response from the public is not desirable. Community shaming, in his view, is inconsistent with the state's responsibility to function as retribution's public agent. Markel thinks that public censoriousness is an unwarranted infringement on the convicted defendant's dignity. Dan Markel, *Are Shaming Punishments Beautifully Retributive? Retributivism and the Implications for the Alternative Sanctions Debate*, Vand. L. Rev. 2157, 2211–12 (2001).

that a judge friend of his did not feel comfortable expressing society's condemnation to convicted defendants.[12] Hart observed that the criminal law gives expression to the community's values and, in addition, shapes those values. Unless there is community condemnation of a particular species of conduct, there should not be a criminal law prohibiting that conduct. Unless there is community condemnation of a particular offender's criminal law violation, no criminal sanction should be applied.

Fifty years later, Professor Andrew Taslitz expressed it this way:

> [D]isesteem-imposition, even if not phrased quite this way, is a clear goal of our criminal justice system. The system assumes that conviction carries stigma with it and that the degrees of, and actual imposition of, various sentences reflect degrees of disesteem.[13]

Both law professors assume that retributive justice requires that community members know about the conviction and participate in censoring the convicted person. If so, criminal convictions must be a matter of public record. Moreover, for censure to be experienced as a punishment, the convicted offender must perceive community disesteem and experience it as undesirable.

Disesteem Implementation Problems

Putting philosophical debate to the side, there are serious practical problems in assigning community censure a role in implementing criminal punishment. Consider that, when it comes to imposing a jail or prison term, the sentencing judge controls (in some states, subject to a parole board) how many days, months, or years the offender will serve. She also fully controls, down to the dollar, the amount of a financial sanction. By contrast, the judge cannot impose X or Y units of community censure. Imagine a sentencing judge saying, "I advise members of the community, for the next three years, upon encountering the defendant, to hiss at him for ten seconds." Community censure cannot be turned on and off like that. It is determined by members of the community who, to be sure, will not be of one mind in their attitude toward the crime and the criminal. Some will be highly censorious, others indifferent, still others, perhaps, admiring. Because the judge does not control the quantity or quality of community censure, there is a serious risk that the community's censure would violate the proportionality principle.*

For those who favor a role for community censure, what should it consist of and who, in addition to the sentencing judge, should communicate it? Is it desirable or justifiable for members of the community to proactively shun, disparage, or discriminate against the convicted person? If so, for how long? Does a majority or substantial minority of the community have to take part, or can appropriate censure be conveyed by just a few people? And how likely is it that the censured defendant will internalize or even hear the censure? The offender might be more influenced by the opinion of his relatives, friends, and acquaintances.

Professor John Braithwaite favors *reintegrative shaming*.[14] He believes that the breakdown of social ties in modern society means that the convicted criminal is not ashamed of his conduct and is not remorseful; therefore, he continues to victimize others. Braithwaite thinks it desirable that the convicted person believes that community members are "gossiping about the conviction." However, he does not say whether gossip actually needs to occur. It seems likely that if no one were gossiping, convicted defendants would soon realize that they have no reason to feel shamed in the eyes of others. If reintegrative shaming were to be operationalized as policy, members of the community would need guidance about what such gossip should consist of, how many people should participate, how often it should occur, how the gossiping should be made known to the convicted person, and how long it should continue. Posing these questions exposes the weaknesses of the theory for purposes of criminal justice policy making.

---

* Professor James Whitman opposes shaming punishments because they violate the offender's dignity as "[t]here is no way to predict or control the way in which the public will deal with him, no rhyme or limit to the terms the public may impose." James Q. Whitman, *What Is Wrong with Inflicting Shame Sanctions?* 107 Yale L.J. 1055, 1090–91 (1997); see also Andrew von Hirsch et al., *Punishments in the Community and the Principles of Desert*, 20 Rutgers L.J. 595 (1989).

The philosopher Antony Duff believes that punishment should be conceived as communication of deserved censure to offenders from a democratic political community. He has advanced a *communicative theory of punishment* that would involve the offender in a moral dialogue about her previous criminal conduct. Punishment "should communicate to offenders the censure they deserve for their crimes and should aim through that communicative process to persuade them to repent those crimes, to try to reform themselves and reconcile with those whom they wronged."[15] Do imprisonment and fines provide this persuasion? Or does communication refer to the judge's lecture at sentencing, which is likely the last time that judge will see that defendant? Presently, judges' lectures probably do not invite a moral dialogue. Perhaps corrections officials (probation, jail, prison personnel) are in a better position to engage in moral dialogue because they see the convicted person regularly, but their roles do not carry as much moral authority as the judge's role. Indeed, defendants often hold them in contempt.

If retributive theory requires or justifies community censure, the censure's intensity and duration should vary according to the seriousness of the conviction offense. Just as conviction for a minor offense does not deserve the same jail term as conviction for a serious offense, the degree and intensity of censure should be proportional. The rapist deserves greater censure than the shoplifter. Likewise, repeat offenders deserve greater censure than first offenders. What constitutes greater and lesser censure? Harshness of message? Tone of voice? Decibel level and duration of censorious expression? If censure involves nonverbal communication (turning a cold shoulder once, twice, etc.), how could that be calibrated?

Consequentialist Theories of Punishment

The goal of consequentialist theories of criminal punishment is nicely illuminated by a Latin quote from Seneca: *nemo prudens punit, quia peccatum est, sed ne peccetur* ("no wise man punishes because a wrong has been done, but rather in order that no future wrong will be done").[16] For consequentialists, the goal of punishment is prevention of future criminal conduct by the punished offender and others. Different consequentialist theories emphasize different crime prevention strategies: (1) moral education of the community, (2) general deterrence, (3) specific (sometimes also called special) deterrence, (4) incapacitation, and (5) rehabilitation. What position would proponents of these different strategies have on whether criminal records must/may be public?

THE MORAL-EDUCATIVE JUSTIFICATION FOR PUNISHMENT

According to the moral-educative justification for punishment, the purpose of punishment is to reinforce the importance and legitimacy of criminal laws in the eyes of the community.[17] If the community does not hear about convictions for criminal conduct that it believes occurs frequently, it may conclude that society (or the government or its courts) does not consider that criminal conduct to be wrong. Perhaps that misimpression could be corrected if government, from time to time, announced summary conviction and punishment statistics? Or the government could announce convictions using anonymized names? In a mass society like ours, only a tiny fraction of the populace personally knows any particular convicted offender. To everyone else, using a pseudonym would be just as effective as using a real name, unless it became widely known that a conviction does not actually result in naming and shaming. Spain and some other continental European countries use pseudonyms (or defendants' initials) in reporting criminal court judgments and sentences. In the United States, juvenile court respondents are identified by initials.

The moral education rationale for punishment does not require that individual criminal histories be publicly accessible. The populace could internalize the importance of criminal laws and the values they seek to uphold without knowing the convicted offender's real identity. However, disclosing the names of the persons who are convicted is not inconsistent with the moral education strategy of crime prevention. Whether real names are used or not, the public learns that violation of criminal law is wrong and condemnable.

GENERAL DETERRENCE

From the perspective of deterrence theory, people obey the law because they believe that the expected costs of violating the law are greater than the expected benefits.[18] Costs (negative consequences) include direct consequences like capital punishment, imprisonment, and fines as well as a range of collateral consequences like shame, social ostracism, loss of employment opportunities, and deportation.[19] Jeremy Bentham, the most famous proponent of the general deterrence rationale for criminal punishment, proposed that criminal punishment include public shaming.[20] Contemporary research confirms that fear of being publicly exposed and shamed is a strong inhibitor of criminal conduct. On the basis of tax noncompliance scenarios administered to a sample of middle-class adults, Steven Klepper and Daniel Nagin concluded that[21]

> [a]s with all criminal cases, criminal prosecutions for tax evasion are a matter of public record. Here we found evidence of a different decision calculus . . . if the evasion gamble also involved putting reputation and community standing at risk, our middle-class respondents were seemingly unwilling to consider taking the non-compliance gamble.[22]

Deterrence is significantly furthered by expected public shaming. Suppose a significant number of people in the community regarded the conduct for which the defendant was convicted as morally neutral or even commendable? What if they tell the convicted defendant that he still enjoys their respect and admiration, even respect him more for his criminal conduct? This would certainly weaken punishment's general and specific deterrent effects (and it is what makes it difficult, if not impossible, to deter terrorists who enjoy community support).

As Professor Henry Hart observed in "The Aims of the Criminal Law," "[A legislator] will be likely to regard the desire of the ordinary man to avoid the moral condemnation of his community . . . as a powerful factor influencing human behavior which can scarcely with safety be dispensed with."[23] For individuals, especially first offenders, who are contemplating committing low-level offenses that are unlikely to be punished by prison or jail time, the formal and informal consequences of the recorded conviction will be of greatest concern.

Publicizing criminal convictions in order to deter others from violating the law is not uncommon. For example, at a small train station on the outskirts of Birmingham, England, I saw a notice board listing the names and hometowns of people who had recently been convicted of riding on the train without purchasing a ticket. At a country pub, I saw a posted list of names of people who had been convicted for drunken behavior. Naming and shaming is meant to deter by threatening public exposure, embarrassment, and collateral consequences.

Convicted defendants vary in their sensitivity to formal and informal community censure. Strongly socialized individuals will most fear the anticipated community knowledge of and reaction to a publicized conviction, even an arrest. By contrast, threat of public disclosure will have little marginal deterrent effect on an individual who does not believe that the community or, more specifically, that segment of the community whose opinion he cares about, would react negatively to his conviction and punishment.

If legislators, prosecutors, and judges are going to rely on community censure to deter criminality, public policy should encourage community shaming. At a minimum, this requires publicizing the names of convicted persons and their offenses. Beyond that, it might require some instruction on how the community should act toward convicted persons. Again, this brings us face to face with the intractable problem that policy makers cannot calibrate or control community censure. There is no obvious way for policy makers (even if they could reach agreement) to persuade community members to express "X" censoriousness toward this offender or group of offenders and "Y" censoriousness toward that offender or group of offenders. In any event, such an instruction would only be advisory; it could not be monitored or enforced.

SPECIFIC DETERRENCE

While general deterrence refers to the impact of the threat of legal punishment on the general public, specific or special deterrence is concerned with the impact of punishment on the punished individual. The object is to make the punishment sufficiently unpleasant so that she will not decide to commit future crimes.[24] Perhaps the convicted offender will be told that members of the community will forgive a first offense (especially one that is not very serious), but not a second offense.[25] The convicted offender will be warned that future criminal conduct will elicit harsher punishment, including harsher community censure. Specific deterrence does not require a threat to make a future conviction publicly accessible, but such a threat is not incompatible with specific deterrence theory.

High rates of recidivism cast doubt on the effectiveness of specific deterrence. The potency of punishment, including community censure, as a deterrent diminishes with use. Individuals who have been repeatedly convicted and censured have little reason to fear additional community censure. Moreover, the stigma associated with a conviction diminishes considerably if the offender's peers also have conviction records.[26] Sociological labeling theorists persuasively argue that one of the most dysfunctional consequences of criminal labeling is pushing stigmatized offenders into closer association with each other, thereby reinforcing their antisocial attitudes and values.[27]

INCAPACITATION

The aim of incapacitation is to render an individual incapable of committing future crime.[28] While retributive justice calibrates punishment according to defendants' moral culpability and harm caused, incapacitation assigns punishments based on risk of future dangerousness. Because of limited criminal justice resources, this requires predicting which convicted offenders pose the greatest threat to recidivate and then imposing an incapacitative sanction, historically including execution or banishment and, in more recent times, incarceration, home detention, and electronic monitoring.[29] Making criminal records publicly accessible is irrelevant to incapacitation.

However, making criminal records publicly accessible facilitates avoidance of victimization. A person who is marked as a criminal will have fewer criminal opportunities because people who know about his past convictions will be less likely to give him the opportunity to victimize them. Sex offender registries are an excellent example. Since the mid-1990s, Congress and every state passed Megan's Laws requiring convicted sex offenders to register with the police or other designated government agency. The agency in charge of administering the registration program is required to bring to the attention of "the community" the names, photos, and whereabouts of previously convicted sex offenders who reside in their area. Community notification is accomplished by contacting those who are most likely to encounter the registered sex offender and by making some convicted sex offenders' identities and personal information available on the Internet. This is not meant to encourage vigilantism but to facilitate evasive action.[30] According to Wayne Logan, the leading scholar of U.S. sex offender registration laws:

> The public, in short, came to feel that it was entitled to registrant information not only as a moral matter, but also due to practical necessity. Government had shown that its historic monopoly on information was unjustified; community members needed access to such information so that they could take self-protective measures.[31]

Liberal access to individual criminal history information reflects the same cultural values as liberal access to firearms, that is, that the individual has the right to protect herself from possibly dangerous people based on her own assessment. She should not have to rely on government officials to decide what criminal record information she and other community members should have access to. This does not mean that consumers of criminal record information are accurate predictors of future criminality. They make decisions based on intuition, hunches, and common sense. Empirical research on recidivism is far too complicated and unsettled for the vast majority of criminal record consumers to master. Indeed, it does not give clear direction on how to assess the risk of future criminality posed by persons with prior convictions.

REHABILITATION

Rehabilitation is sometimes said to be a purpose (or even *the* purpose) of criminal punishment. (In my view, this is a mistake. A person should not be punished in order to be helped, although if punishment is deserved, providing rehabilitative opportunities to a prisoner or probationer serves the public interest as well as the defendant's interest.) Like special deterrence and incapacitation, rehabilitation is a crime prevention strategy for reducing the probability that the convicted offender will commit future crimes. While special deterrence works via threat, rehabilitation works via persuasion or "conversion" to prosocial attitudes and values. Judges, who stress the primacy of rehabilitation, seek to impose a sentence that maximizes the likelihood that the defendant will voluntarily desist from future criminal conduct.

In Europe, offender rehabilitation is the reigning purpose of sentencing. For example, the Spanish Constitution expressly requires legislatures, judges, and criminal justice system policy makers to give priority to rehabilitation in formulating and implementing criminal justice policies.[32] "Punishments entailing imprisonment and security measures shall be aimed at rehabilitation and social reintegration and may not consist of forced labor." Likewise, the Italian Constitution mandates rehabilitation as the goal of the criminal justice process; criminal convictions are made public only when publicity is explicitly intended as part of the punishment. Because publicly accessible criminal records stigmatize those who have been convicted, disclosing information about individual criminal history is regarded as substantially impeding the rehabilitative goal.

In the United States, rehabilitation dominated sentencing theory in the 1950s and 1960s but declined thereafter.[33] Liberals attacked rehabilitation for being arbitrary, capricious, and for facilitating discrimination. Retributivists criticized rehabilitation for treating the offender as a moral infant rather than as a responsible individual deserving punishment. Conservatives attacked rehabilitation for being unrealistic, romantic, ineffective, and insufficiently protective of the law-abiding public. It was supplanted by retributive justice, general and specific deterrence, and incapacitation. Recently, however, rehabilitation has been making a comeback.[34]

Treating individual criminal history records as public is incompatible with rehabilitation. Empirical criminologists have repeatedly identified legitimate employment as the most important determinant of whether a convicted offender reoffends.[35] When past convictions are part of the public record, ex-offenders are easily identified and easily discriminated against. Surveys and field studies show that employers do discriminate against job applicants with a criminal record. A recent survey on employer willingness to accept an applicant with a criminal record found that 43 percent of employers indicate that they would "probably not" or "definitely not" be willing to hire the individual, while approximately 35 percent of employers responded that that their willingness would depend on the job applicant's crime.[36] With opportunities for legitimate employment and social connections restricted, the formerly convicted person will be more likely to turn to crime again. This is hardly surprising given the myriad laws that require employment and other discrimination against formerly convicted persons.

Proponents of rehabilitation have been and are well aware of the negative impact of publicly accessible criminal records on desistence from future crime. Therefore, in the 1960s and 1970s, they urged that criminal records be sealed or expunged after some period of crime-free behavior. In effect, they were proposing that adult criminal records be treated the same way that juvenile criminal records had long been treated—confidentially. According to this view, an expungement process will provide an incentive to rehabilitate and will remove barriers to successful integration into legitimate society.[37] However, as we have seen, expungement eligibility that requires many crime-free years cannot facilitate rehabilitation.

Conclusion

General deterrence is the only punishment theory that requires criminal records to be public. A sentencing scheme that seeks to maximize general deterrence would threaten criminal law violators with public exposure and community censure. Specific deterrence also depends on making future crime too costly to commit when compared with the expected benefit. Some convicted persons may be anxious to convey the message that they are reformed and regard a subsequent publicly accessible conviction as highly undesirable, but others will not be concerned about further injury to their reputation in mainstream society. Even if making criminal convictions publicly accessible does not deliver a big specific deterrent effect, it is certainly not incompatible with the theory of specific deterrence.

Incapacitation is a crime control strategy completely in the hands of government officials. It doesn't make sense to speak of private citizens incapacitating a convicted offender. Consequently, incapacitation does not require publicly accessible individual criminal history records. However, it does require that police, prosecutors, judges, and corrections personnel have ready access to defendants' criminal histories in order to evaluate risk of future criminality. Moreover, victimization avoidance is furthered by providing the public with information about individuals who have been found guilty of various types of crimes. Individuals and organizations can then make their own decisions about how best to protect themselves from criminal risks. Publicly accessible sex offender websites enable private individuals to avoid associations and situations that they think pose a risk to their children and themselves. Other publicly accessible offender websites might be proposed for the same reason.

Rehabilitation is clearly incompatible with publicly accessible criminal records. Indeed, it is best furthered by the opposite, keeping criminal records confidential, as in European countries. Theorists and policy makers who advocate rehabilitation favor eliminating as many barriers as possible to the offender's postconviction employment and smooth reentry into mainstream society. Publicly accessible criminal records are clearly a barrier. A criminal law regime seeking to maximize rehabilitative outcomes would minimize the creation of criminal records, keep criminal records confidential, eliminate or at least scale back collateral consequences of conviction, and provide liberal opportunity for sealing and expunging records of arrests and convictions.

Because there are so many different versions of retribution, it is the most difficult punishment theory to analyze. Retributive justice does not require individual criminal history records to be public. Just deserts could be satisfied by incarceration, a fine, or some other punishment or combination of punishments. In some cases, naming and shaming provides too much punishment, therefore violating retributive justice's proportionality principle. In other cases, especially those where no other punishment is delivered, naming and shaming could be justified as providing just desert.

PART IV

DIRECT AND COLLATERAL CONSEQUENCES OF A CRIMINAL RECORD

PART IV DEALS WITH the consequences of criminal record policies. Chapter 12 focuses on how criminal records are used in investigations, adjudication, and sentencing. A prior criminal record plays a crucial role at every stage of law enforcement and criminal justice in determining the treatment of suspects, arrestees, defendants and convicted persons. It sounds odd to call this "discrimination on the basis of criminal record," but that is essentially the reality. It is a species of discrimination widely considered to be entirely reasonable—it is taken as noncontroversial that the longer and more serious the criminal record the more the criminal justice system is justified in treating them with suspicion and severity. Likewise true first offenders should be shown leniency.

Chapter 13 illuminates the pervasive governmental discrimination against convicted persons, even after they finish serving their sentence and have been released from prison. The sheer volume of statutorily prescribed forfeitures, disqualifications, and ineligibilities imposed on convicted persons constitutes a huge body of law and jurisprudence that is just now being comprehensively documented and catalogued. Moreover, it cannot go without saying that debate concerning the legality and morality of these practices is significantly complicated by the disproportionate impact they have on African Americans and Hispanics.

If public policy requires and supports so much criminal record–based discrimination, it is not surprising that private employers, volunteer organizations landlords, and other entities and individuals also choose to discriminate against convicted persons. Chapter 14 examines discretionary, mostly private employment discrimination based on criminal records. Employment discrimination has always made it especially difficult for an ex-convict to avoid resorting to crime as a necessary means of survival. As such, the strong link between pervasive employment discrimination and high recidivism rates is unsurprising, albeit extremely frustrating, in light of statutorily sanctioned policies that seem specially designed to facilitate private sector bias against convicted persons. In this chapter, I argue that private sector discrimination is the logical consequence of unforgiving and lengthy employment restrictions and disabilities imposed on convicted persons, coupled with largely unfettered public access to criminal record information. It follows that reformers should target governmental discrimination before its private sector analogues.

12 CRIMINAL JUSTICE CONSEQUENCES OF A CRIMINAL RECORD

> Today's philosophy of individualizing sentences makes sharp distinctions for example between first and repeated offenders. . . . [Probation reports] have been given a high value by conscientious judges who want to sentence persons on the best available information rather than on guesswork and inadequate information. To deprive sentencing judges of this kind of information would undermine modern penological procedural policies that have been cautiously adopted throughout the nation after careful consideration and experimentation.
>
> —U.S. Supreme Court, *Williams v. New York* (1949)[1]

> All the studies—from parole prediction to selective incapacitation contexts—showed that prior correctional contacts (arrests, convictions, and incarcerations) were the single best predictor of recidivism. The result was the development of sentencing schemes that were more simplistic but easier to administer, relying predominantly on prior criminal history, such as sentencing guidelines, mandatory minimums, and "three-strikes" laws that enhanced punishment for prior offenders.
>
> —Bernard Harcourt, *Against Prediction* (2007)[2]

CRIMINAL JUSTICE AGENCIES sort and categorize those whom they investigate and process on the basis of their criminal records. Every significant contact with law enforcement, courts, and corrections is recorded on one or more criminal records. These records produce categories such as "professional criminals," "drug traffickers," "fraudsters," "violent drunks," and "petty offenders."[3]

Readers are probably most familiar with the use of prior criminal records at the sentencing stage, but a defendant's criminal record is of critical importance for investigation, prosecution, plea-bargaining, trial, and corrections. At every step of the criminal justice system, persons with criminal records are treated more severely than those with no criminal record; the more serious the record, the more severe the treatment. The centrality of criminal records for criminal justice system decision makers has spilled over into the wider society, so that employers and other decision makers treat the criminal record as a powerful, often determinative, predictor of future conduct.

Police Use of a Prior Criminal Record

One of the important consequences of a criminal record is that, in the future, law enforcement will regard the record-subject as more suspicious than the non-record-subject. In general, police focus greater attention on individuals with a criminal record or quasi-criminal record and are less likely to give those individuals the benefit of the doubt. In investigating a crime, the police often begin by looking through their records for individuals living in the vicinity who have previously been convicted or arrested for similar crimes. Such individuals are likely to be monitored and questioned.[4] This makes sense. It reduces the pool of possible suspects by giving special attention to those who have acted similarly in the past. But it also amplifies the attention that police give to African Americans and Hispanics, who are disproportionately likely to have a criminal record.[5] An individual's prior record is an important factor in a police officer's decision to make an arrest rather than release an individual with a warning or summons.[6]

Pretrial Detention and the Criminal Record

At the arrestee's initial court appearance, the judge decides whether the arrestee will be released on recognizance or bail while the charges are being adjudicated. Some state statutes require the judge to consider an arrestee's prior criminal record.[7] A growing number of courts and pretrial services agencies use "risk assessment instruments" to determine, if released, the arrestee's risk of flight and risk of further criminality. These risk assessments give great weight to prior criminal records, and notably include arrests as well as convictions.[8] Even without a statutory requirement or use of a formal risk assessment instrument, the judge is likely to give significant weight to the arrestee's criminal record. Empirical research has shown that, for defendants charged with the same offense, defendants with one or more prior felony convictions are more than twice as likely to be denied bail.[9] If bail is set, the dollar amount will depend, to a significant extent, on the criminal record.

Prosecutorial Charging, Plea-Bargaining, and the Criminal Record

Prosecutors have virtually unreviewable discretion to decide whether to charge an arrestee with a crime and, if so, what the charge(s) will be.[10] A prior record is almost always considered. States that have statutorily prescribed deferred prosecution options often deny eligibility to arrestees with prior records. If the prosecutor does not have a bright line rule against offering deferred prosecution to recidivists, the arrestee's criminal history, including prior arrests, will be an important factor in the decision to offer the arrestee a diversion program in lieu of prosecution.[11]

If the prosecutor decides to file charges against an arrestee, the existence of a prior criminal record has a strong influence on the type and number of charges. Because of their prior criminal record, some offenders can, or even must, be charged with a more serious offense than would otherwise be applicable. For example, if a person with a prior drunk driving conviction is rearrested for drunk driving within a statutorily prescribed number of years, she can be charged with felony (rather than misdemeanor) DUI. To take another example, the federal "felon-in-possession of a firearm offense" makes it a felony for a person with a prior felony conviction to possess a firearm. Another good example is the federal Racketeer Influenced and Corrupt Organizations Act (RICO). It requires proof that the defendant "conducted the affairs of an enterprise through *a pattern of racketeering activity*."[12] "A pattern of racketeering activity" is defined as commission of at least two of a long list of federal felonies or their state equivalents within a ten-year period. Prosecutors satisfy RICO's predicate offenses element by introducing the record of the defendant's prior state and federal convictions.

The defendant's prior criminal record is an important factor in the prosecutor's plea offer and willingness to accept a compromise settlement. Sometimes this is governed by explicit policy. In

Manhattan, for example, how the district attorney's office handles a marijuana possession arrest is largely determined by the arrestee's prior record. If this is the defendant's first marijuana arrest, the prosecutor usually agrees to an adjournment in contemplation of dismissal (ACD). For a second-time marijuana possession arrest, the prosecutor usually must press for a guilty plea to a "violation." For a third marijuana possession arrest, office policy calls for a guilty plea to a misdemeanor. A prior criminal record that subjects the defendant to a substantial statutory sentence enhancement strengthens the prosecutor's position in plea-bargaining.

The Criminal Record at Trial

Over 90 percent of criminal cases are resolved by guilty pleas, but if a case goes to trial, the admissibility of the defendant's and witnesses' criminal records presents a major evidentiary issue. Until 1918, a witness with a prior felony conviction was not permitted to testify at all. In *Rosen v. United States*, the Supreme Court abolished that rule.[13] The court reasoned that anyone with relevant information should be eligible to testify, allowing the fact finder, having heard about the witness's prior criminal record, to decide how much to credit the witness's testimony. After *Rosen*, a witness's prior convictions do not bear on competency, but rather on credibility.

English and American common law and later evidentiary codes provided that a defendant's prior convictions and other "bad acts" were inadmissible to prove the defendant's propensity to commit the crime for which she is on trial. This rule reflected two concerns. First, if jurors learn about the defendant's prior criminal record, they might, consciously or unconsciously, conclude that "if he did it before, he probably did it this time as well." Second, jurors might consciously or unconsciously conclude that the defendant is a bad and/or dangerous person who, regardless of guilt on present charges, should be punished and/or incapacitated.

Although judges and legal scholars recognized that exposing a jury to the defendant's prior conviction is prejudicial, they also recognized that, at least under some circumstances, the relevance of prior criminal conduct cannot be denied. Thus, the defendant's prior convictions and uncharged criminal conduct ("bad acts") became admissible at trial under a number of evidentiary exceptions, for example, if that prior criminality shows that the defendant has "specialized knowledge" relevant to the present crime. For example, if a defendant charged with using sophisticated techniques to break into a bank vault previously had been convicted for the same type of break-in, the previous conviction would be admissible. Moreover, a prior criminal record can be disclosed to impeach a witnesses, including the defendant; that is, opposing counsel can cite the prior conviction as a reason why the jury should not believe the witness's testimony. Today, the admissibility of the defendant's prior crimes is usually determined at a pretrial hearing. If the judge rules in the prosecutor's favor, the defendant will have a strong disincentive to testify at trial, fearing that the jury will hold his prior conviction against him when assessing the credibility of his testimony and his guilt. Even a defendant with a plausible defense may decide that it is in his best interest to accept a plea-bargained lesser sentence rather than risk a more severe sentence if convicted. A guilty plea will be especially attractive if, by pleading guilty, the defendant can avoid imprisonment. Moreover, the defendant may rationally conclude that, given his criminal record, the additional reputational injury that will result from the new conviction is insignificant.

Special Admissibility of Prior Sex Offense Convictions

The most serious criminal stigma attaches to a sex offense conviction.[14] Convicted sex offenders face a whole range of statutory restrictions (e.g., where they may not reside) and disqualifications (e.g., employment involving contacts with children). Historically, trial judges often found a defendant's prior sex offense conviction admissible in a current prosecution for a sex offense under the "motive" exception, that is, the previous conviction is relevant to the defendant's motive (sexual compulsion) for committing the current sex offense. In 1994, Congress approved amendments to the Federal Rules of Evidence (FRE), addressing the admissibility of prior sex crimes.[15] "In a sexual assault prosecution, the court may admit evidence that the defendant committed a previous sexual assault. The evidence may be considered on any matter to which it is relevant."[16] FRE 415 adds an even more specific admissibility exception for a prior sexual assault against a child.[17]

Importance of the Criminal Record for Sentencing

The French magistrate and penal reformer Arnould Bonneville de Marsangy (1802–1894) campaigned for creation of systematic conviction records, which would allow judges to sentence recidivists more severely for incapacitation purposes.[18]

> [His] simple but practical solution suggested the assembling of all the reports of sentences imposed on a given individual by having such reports sent to the clerk of court in the district of his birthplace. The proposed system would create at each district tribunal a "mobile card-index cabinet" where, henceforth, certificates of final sentences pronounced anytime and anywhere against people born in that district would be centralized and classified there in alphabetical order by the names of the convicted persons. Such a penal register could easily and promptly answer an inquiry by the prosecuting authorities.[19]

Bonneville believed that a national register of criminal convictions would contribute to specific and general deterrence because many potential offenders would abstain from committing crimes if they feared that their conviction would be publicized.[20] Eventually all European countries created national criminal registers that record convictions.[21] Importantly, European conviction registers were created to serve the judiciary, while the U.S. rap sheet system was created to serve the police.

Sentencing according to the Criminal Record

Judges in the United States, as in other countries, sentence recidivists more severely: the more serious and lengthier the prior record, the harsher the sentence.[22] Sometimes, statutes dictate sentence enhancement for recidivists and sometimes it is left to judicial discretion; either way, recidivists are punished more severely, sometimes much more severely, than first offenders. While a sentence premium for recidivists is so deeply ingrained in our legal culture, criminal law theorists do not agree on whether there is a convincing rationale for it.[23] The problem is particularly acute for retributivist (just deserts) theorists, since a fundamental tenet of this sentencing theory is that a law violator should be punished proportionate to the harm that he or she attempted or inflicted. This suggests that a defendant's prior record should have little, if any, impact on the current sentence.[24] However, some desert theorists are willing to accept a limited role for prior record on the ground that the first offender deserves a sentence discount, rather than the recidivist deserving an enhancement. Even a second offender might deserve a small discount, but at some point the offender exhausts his claim to mitigation.[25] Some retributive theorists who do not subscribe to just desert theory argue that a recidivist is more blameworthy than a first offender,[26] because he has disregarded the clear, emphatic, and official message embodied in his previous sentence. (The analysis becomes more complex when considering how much extra punishment, if any, a defendant with two or three prior convictions deserves.)

The most frequently made objection to the retributivist sentencing premium is that the defendant has already been punished for his previous offense. He paid his debt to society. Thus, it is unfair, indeed a kind of double jeopardy, to punish him again for the previous offense with a more severe sentence than he would otherwise deserve. As we will see in Chapter 13, the same kind of argument is made against collateral punishments (e.g., disenfranchisement, license revocation, denial of welfare benefits). Nevertheless, the Supreme Court has upheld enhancing a sentence on account of previous convictions, because the recidivist's enhancement is not punishment for a previous offense but punishment for the current offense based on the defendant's unsympathetic character and need for incapacitation. As early as 1895, *Moore v. Missouri* held that a defendant who received a sentence enhancement on account of prior convictions "is not again punished for the first offence . . . because the punishment is for the last offence committed, and it is rendered more severe in consequence of the situation into which the party had previously brought himself."[27] Chief Justice Shaw rejected a constitutional attack on a state statute that imposed a higher punishment for a recidivist, on the grounds that the defendant's continued criminal activity demonstrated that the former punishment did not result in his reform.

> *People v. Stanley* [held that] the punishment for the second [offense] is increased, because, by his persistence in the perpetration of crime, he has evinced a depravity, which merits a greater punishment, and needs to be restrained by severer penalties than if it were his first offense; and in *Kelly v. People*, that it is just that an old offender should be punished more severely for a second offense—that repetition of the offense aggravates guilt. It is quite impossible for us to conclude that the Supreme Court of Missouri erred in holding that [the defendant] was not twice put in jeopardy for the same offense, or that the increase of his punishment by reason of the commission of the first offense was not cruel and unusual.[28]

One hundred years later, Justice John Paul Stevens reaffirmed *Moore v. Missouri:*

> We have of course held that a State is justified in punishing a recidivist more severely than it punishes a first offender. But in order to avoid double jeopardy concerns, we have repeatedly emphasized that under recidivist sentencing schemes the enhanced punishment imposed for the [present] offense is not to be viewed as . . . [an] additional penalty for the earlier crimes, but instead as a stiffened penalty for the latest crime, which is considered to be an aggravated offense because a repetitive one.[29]

Utilitarian criminal law theorists justify recidivist sentence enhancement on both specific deterrence and incapacitation grounds. They argue that the recidivist has already shown that the ordinary punishment threat is not sufficient to deter his criminal conduct. Therefore, he needs to be threatened with enhanced punishment in order to deter him from committing criminal offenses in the future. If that future offense occurs, the enhanced threat must be carried out for general deterrence purposes so other potential recidivists will believe that the enhanced punishment threat is credible. The twice convicted and twice punished offender should be threatened with even greater punishment in order to deter a third offense. This argument leads to escalating sentence enhancements for each successive conviction.

Those who believe that incapacitation is the best justification for enhancing the punishment of recidivists argue that an individual who willfully assumes the risk of getting rearrested after serving his first prison sentence has shown himself to have strong criminal propensities (even more true for the multirecidivist). To prevent him from committing even more crimes, he must be incarcerated (or otherwise incapacitated). The most forceful objection to the incapacitation rationale for recidivist sentence enhancement is that it, in effect, punishes the defendant for crimes he has not yet committed, a violation of due process of law. (That same criticism is leveled at collateral consequences as well.) Moreover, critics argue that predicting future criminality is not sufficiently accurate and routinely exaggerated. Nevertheless, the courts have emphatically rejected those criticisms.

Accepting the justifiability of assigning punishments according to prior criminal record requires facing a slew of further policy issues: What should be the magnitude of the recidivist enhancement? To what extent should the recidivist-sentencing premium vary with the number, type, and seriousness of past convictions? Is the defendant who repeats the same offense a more appropriate candidate for a recidivist enhancement than the defendant who commits different offenses? Should the sentence-enhancing effect of a prior conviction diminish as time passes? Do/should past convictions in other jurisdictions count the same as convictions in the sentencing court's jurisdiction? What impact, if any, should juvenile delinquency adjudications have? Such questions have produced a substantial corpus of Supreme Court and lower court decisions as well as scholarly commentary.

Statutory Enhancements for Recidivists

Statutes authorizing or mandating enhanced sentences for recidivists are very common. New York State's "predicate felon" law dates back to the nineteenth century. In its current version, the law provides that a convicted defendant is subject to a mandatory minimum term of one and a half to three years in prison if, within the last ten years (excluding prison time), she had been convicted of certain "predicate" felonies.[30] A defendant who has two previous violent predicate felony convictions is subject to a significant recidivist premium. For example, if the predicate felon's current conviction is for a class B felony, she must be sentenced to a determinate prison sentence of not less than ten years nor more than twenty-five years. If the current conviction is for a class E felony (the lowest), the judge must impose at least a three-year prison term. In California, a defendant with a single "serious or violent" prior conviction must be sentenced to twice the term otherwise provided for that current offense.

In *Rummel v. Estelle* (1980), the Supreme Court rejected the defendant's argument that a life (with possibility of parole) sentence imposed under Texas's three-strikes law amounted to unconstitutional cruel and unusual punishment in violation of the Eighth Amendment. Rummel had been convicted in 1964 of felony theft for fraudulent use of a credit card to obtain $80 worth of goods or services. In 1969, he was convicted of another felony, passing a forged check in the amount of $28.36. His third felony conviction was rendered in 1973, obtaining $120.75 by false pretenses. Pursuant to Texas's law, he was sentenced to life imprisonment. Rummel argued that no jurisdiction in the Western world provided for a sentence this severe for a series of low-level property crime convictions. The court rejected Rummel's contention that his sentence constituted cruel and unusual punishment because

> the interest of the State of Texas here is not simply that of making criminal the unlawful acquisition of another person's property; it is in addition the interest, expressed in all recidivist statutes, in dealing in a harsher manner with those who by repeated criminal

> acts have shown that they are simply incapable of conforming to the norms of society as established by its criminal law.[31]

Just two years later, the court heard another Eighth Amendment challenge to a habitual offender statute in *Solem v. Helm.* Defendant Helm was convicted of issuing a check for $100 on a nonexistent bank account, an offense punishable in South Dakota by a maximum five-year prison term. However, because Helm had six previous convictions, albeit for nonviolent offenses, state law mandated life imprisonment without the possibility of parole. The Supreme Court, in a 5–4 decision, found his sentence unconstitutionally cruel and unusual because it was "grossly disproportionate" to his offenses.[32] Although a majority of justices said that *Rummel* was not overruled, the decision placed a cloud over the fate of draconian sentencing statutes.

Washington voters passed the first of a new wave of "three-strikes" law in 1993. California passed its draconian three-strikes law in 1994. The idea swiftly spread to other states. By 2004, twenty-six states and the federal government had laws that satisfied criteria for designation as three-strikes statutes—namely, that a third felony conviction brings a sentence of life in prison, without possibility of parole for at least twenty-five years. (In Fall 2012, California voters passed an initiative that significantly reined in the reach of the three-strikes law.) States' three-strikes laws vary significantly with respect to which felonies count as a first, second, and third strike. They also vary with respect to whether the three-strikes sentence is a term of years or life with or without the possibility of parole. The federal three-strikes law provides for a mandatory life sentence for a federal defendant convicted of "a serious violent felony," who already has two or more prior federal or state convictions. One of the prior convictions must be for a serious violent felony. The other prior conviction must be for a serious violent felony or serious drug offense.[33]

In 2003, the Supreme Court considered an Eighth Amendment challenge to California's three-strikes law. Over the years, Gary Ewing had accumulated numerous convictions for robbery and burglary, as well as a drug conviction. While on parole, he attempted to steal three golf clubs (valued at approximately $1,200). This constituted "grand theft," an offense that California classified as a "wobbler," a crime that the prosecutor had discretion to charge either as a misdemeanor or as a felony. The prosecutor charged felony theft and, upon conviction, the judge sentenced Ewing to twenty-five years to life for his third strike. On appeal, Ewing argued that his sentence, like Helm's, was so grossly disproportionate to his crime (theft of golf clubs) that it amounted to cruel and unusual punishment. The Supreme Court disagreed:

> Throughout the States, legislatures enacting three strikes laws made a deliberate policy choice that individuals who have repeatedly engaged in serious or violent criminal behavior, and whose conduct has not been deterred by more conventional approaches to punishment, must be isolated from society in order to protect the public safety. Though three strikes laws may be relatively new, our tradition of deferring to state legislatures in making and implementing such important policy decisions is longstanding.[34]

Ewing's case makes it exceedingly unlikely that future Eighth Amendment challenges to recidivist sentence enhancements will be successful. Thus, a prior criminal record can have devastating direct consequences, transforming the sentence for a minor crime into a life sentence.

Sentencing Guidelines and the Recidivist Premium

Sentencing guidelines, like other forms of structured sentencing, place great weight on the defendant's prior criminal record.* The Federal Sentencing Guidelines (FSG), for example, provide a "recommended"† sentencing range based on an offense severity

---

* For example, in *Nichols v. United. States*, 511 U.S. 738, 748–49 (1994), the Supreme Court upheld a sentence under the Federal Sentencing Guidelines, which added 25 months to a federal drug sentence because of an uncounseled misdemeanor drunk driving conviction several years earlier.

† The FSG were mandatory for federal courts until the Supreme Court declared them unconstitutional in *United States v. Booker*, 543 U.S. 220 (2005). After *Booker*, the FSG

score and a prior criminal record score. In calculating a defendant's criminal history score, the FSG manual states that points should be assigned according to the following schedule: three points for each prior sentence of imprisonment exceeding one year and one month; two points for each prior sentence of imprisonment of at least sixty days but not more than thirteen months; one point for each prior sentence of less than sixty days; two points if the defendant committed the instant offense while in prison or on probation, parole, supervised release, imprisonment, work release, or escape status; two points if the defendant committed the instant offense less than two years after release from imprisonment on a sentence of sixty days or more or while in imprisonment or escape status on such sentence; and one point for each prior sentence resulting from a conviction of a crime of violence that did not receive any points because such sentence was counted as a single sentence, up to a total of three points.

To appreciate the significance that the FSG accords a prior criminal record, consider that a defendant convicted of residential burglary is assigned an offense severity score of seventeen. However, if that defendant has no or just a minor criminal record, he will be assigned to Criminal History Category I (the lowest) and face twenty-four to thirty months of imprisonment. However, a defendant with a substantial criminal record who committed the same crime will be assigned to the highest Criminal History Category VI and faces a sentence of fifty-one to sixty-three months.

To take another example, stalking or domestic violence has a base offense level of eighteen, which means a twenty-seven- to thirty-three-month prison sentence for a defendant in criminal history category I and a fifty-seven- to seventy-one-month sentence for a defendant in criminal history category VI. Kidnapping, abduction, and unlawful restraint have a base offense level of thirty-two, which leads to a minimum of 121–151 and a maximum of 210–262 months of imprisonment, respectively, at the different ends of the Criminal History Score. In other words, under the FSG, a serious criminal record at least doubles the defendant's sentence.

---

are simply recommended. However, most federal sentencing judges accord them presumptive authority.

State sentencing guideline schemes all link sentence severity to a prior criminal record. Minnesota's sentencing guidelines, like the FSG, compute a presumptive sentence based on the seriousness of the offense and the seriousness of the offender's prior record. Unlike the FSG, the Minnesota guidelines assign different point values to prior convictions according to their seriousness, determined by the offense's inherent dangerousness and depravity.

Juvenile Records

Many studies have found that a juvenile record is predictive of adult offending. Thus, should a juvenile delinquency record enhance the sentence of a convicted adult defendant?[35] When an adult, especially a young adult, is arrested, the police, prosecutors, and adult court judges want access to his or her juvenile offending history in order to inform their decision making. From a law enforcement perspective, this makes good sense. Confidentiality was meant to protect an individual from lifelong negative consequences of adolescent indiscretions and bad decisions. If the former delinquent is rearrested as an adult, the rationale for concealing the prior delinquency no longer applies. To the contrary, the juvenile record confirms that the young adult offender should be treated as a recidivist. The prior criminal adjudication places the current case in a different light.

Every state provides adult criminal court judges with access to at least some delinquency adjudications for purposes of pretrial release or detention and sentencing. Some states, including fourteen with sentencing guidelines, require criminal court judges to consider juvenile adjudications.[36] The FSG instructs federal judges to assign the same weight to a delinquency adjudication (for conduct that would be criminal if committed by an adult) as to an adult conviction. If a delinquency record is to be available for calculating the adult defendant's sentence, it cannot be expunged.*

---

* A delinquency adjudication is considered equivalent to an adult conviction for purposes of some collateral consequences. For example, the 1993 Handgun Violence Control Act (Brady Law) imposed a lifetime disqualification from firearms ownership on individuals who had been adjudicated delinquent for conduct that would be a felony if

Convictions in Other States

State and federal sentence enhancement statutes for recidivists make no distinction between prior conviction in the home jurisdiction and prior convictions meted out in other states or in federal court. The defendant's prior convictions in other states count as predicate offenses or "strikes" as long as they constitute felony offenses in the home jurisdiction. Determining whether a prior conviction in another jurisdiction would have constituted an offense with the same name in the home jurisdiction can be an interpretative challenge. While the definitions of criminal offenses in the fifty states and federal jurisdiction are quite similar, they are not identical. In *Shepard v. United States*, a federal defendant was convicted of being a felon in possession of a firearm. The maximum statutory punishment was ten years. However, the prosecutor moved to sentence Shepard under the Armed Career Criminal Act, which provides that a convicted felon with three prior convictions for violent felonies or drug offenses must be sentenced to a fifteen-year minimum sentence. The question was whether a prior Massachusetts burglary conviction counts as a violent felony under federal law.[37] Shepard argued that, while federal law considers a federal burglary conviction to be a violent conviction, Massachusetts's definition of burglary is broader and encompasses less serious conduct; consequently, he argued, it should not count as a violent felony for federal sentencing purposes.[38] The Supreme Court ruled that a federal judge, at sentencing, should analyze the indictment, plea agreement, and sentencing allocution in order to determine whether the defendant's conduct would have constituted "generic burglary" as defined by federal law.[39]

---

committed by an adult. Likewise, immigration officials can consider a delinquency adjudication in decision making regarding deportation, assigning an alien to secure detention pending deportation and whether to "adjust" immigration status. In many states, a juvenile sex offense adjudication bars the record-subject from working with children and other vulnerable populations. Every state has a "Megan's Law" that requires juvenile as well as adult sex offenders to register with a designated state agency. The federal Adam Walsh Child Protection and Safety Act requires that state sex offender registries include juveniles convicted in adult court of sex offenses. A delinquency adjudication for a drug offense can disqualify a person from living in public housing.

Convictions in Foreign Countries

For sentencing purposes, all federal and state courts treat all prior convictions originating in any U.S. jurisdiction equally, regardless of which jurisdiction they were rendered in.[40] Extending full faith and credit to the criminal judgments of another jurisdiction's criminal judgments is an important and probably underappreciated dimension of federalism.[41] But how are criminal records from other jurisdictions regarded?

Under the FSG, convictions rendered in other countries do not count toward the defendant's criminal history score. However, the sentencing court may impose a more serious sentence than the FSG would otherwise prescribe if the judge thinks that the criminal history score significantly underrepresents the seriousness of the defendant's criminal history or likelihood of recidivism. A defendant's foreign convictions are relevant to that question.* In *U.S. v. Korno* (1993), the defendant was convicted of defrauding a federally insured bank. Korno's single prior state conviction for check forgery placed him in criminal history category II; under the FSG, the appropriate sentence was an eight- to fourteen-month imprisonment. However, the pre-sentence report recommended an upward departure because the defendant's criminal history category significantly underrepresented the seriousness of his criminal record, due to numerous Canadian convictions for fraud, burglary, possession of stolen property, use of counterfeit documents, possession of stolen credit cards, and assault. Had these convictions occurred in U.S. courts, Korno's criminal history score would have placed him in category VI, with a sentence range of twenty-four to thirty months.

---

* The Supreme Court held in *Small v. United States*, 544 U.S 385 (2005), that federal law prohibiting gun possession by a person convicted of "any felony" did not include a foreign (Japanese) conviction. The court emphasized that this was a matter of statutory interpretation and that the authors of the federal felon in possession law had not considered its application to defendants with foreign convictions. By contrast, the FSG states that the defendant's criminal history score significantly understated his criminality on account of foreign convictions, an upward departure is authorized. See Dionna K. Taylor, Note, *The Tempest in a Teapot: Foreign Convictions as Predicate Offenses under the Federal Felon in Possession of a Firearm Statute*, 43 Washburn L.J. 763 (2004).

The court specifically found that Korno's Canadian convictions were valid, that Korno had been represented by counsel, and that the Canadian justice system is "sufficiently close to the American system as to make those convictions reliable." Consequently, the judge sentenced him to twenty-four months' imprisonment. The Seventh Circuit Court of Appeals affirmed.[42]

Sentence Enhancement for Arrests and Uncharged Conduct

Perhaps many readers will be surprised to learn that arrests and uncharged conduct can also contribute to an enhanced sentence. Presentence reports routinely provide sentencing judges with information about the convicted defendant's prior arrests and uncharged conduct.[43] Thus, sentencing judges, consciously or unconsciously, can and do sentence convicted defendants to more severe sentences on account of nonconviction entries on their criminal record. In *Williams v. New York* (1949), the Supreme Court rejected a due process challenge to a judge's consideration of prior arrests and uncharged crimes in determining that the defendant deserved a death sentence. In explaining his decision to impose a death sentence, the judge said that he was taking into account that Williams had committed thirty uncharged burglaries. The U.S. Supreme Court upheld the sentence and the New York law allowing sentencing judges to consider all relevant information about the defendant, including prior uncharged criminal conduct. According to the Williams court, this practice was deeply embedded in U.S. sentencing jurisprudence.

Use of the Criminal Record in Corrections and Parole

Criminal records also affect and play a major role in the corrections context. If an individual is placed on probation, the number and type of previous convictions (and perhaps arrests) will be an important factor in the type and intensity of probationary supervision that is assigned to him. If the defendant is sent to prison, corrections officials will examine his entire criminal record before making an institutional assignment (the so-called correctional classification). For example, a defendant with convictions for violent crimes and attempted escapes will almost certainly be assigned to a maximum-security institution. Even within the prison, work and cell assignment depend on past convictions. Moreover, certain prior convictions render a prisoner ineligible for work release and some in-prison programs.

The parole board will also take a hard look at a prisoner's criminal record when deciding whether to grant an early release.[44] Some parole boards use risk assessment instruments. For instance, according to the Massachusetts Parole Board, "[a] validated risk assessment tool provides the Board with statistical risk information about the risk of a particular offender based upon factors such as age, prior criminal history, and substance abuse issues."[45]

Conclusion

Prior criminal records are relevant at every decision point in the law enforcement and criminal justice process. To an extent rarely appreciated, criminal justice agencies' decision making depends on the business of creating and using criminal record biographies. Punishing individuals more seriously because they have a prior criminal record raises extremely important and thorny policy and jurisprudential issues. Does a convicted person deserve more punishment because she has been previously convicted? Is it fair (desirable?) to enhance a defendant's sentence because of a prediction of future criminality based on their past criminality? My own conclusion is that defendants should be sentenced for their crime of conviction, not for their previous offending. However, I would permit some mitigation for first offenders when their criminal conduct was not premeditated. I do not think that sentences should be enhanced using predictions of future criminality based on prior criminality because such predictions are often seriously exaggerated. Professor Harcourt would go farther, rejecting the use of prediction in deploying investigative and prosecutorial resources. He argues that such targeting is inefficient because it pays insufficient attention to people without criminal records (or at least serious records), thereby inefficiently weakening deterrence and apprehension. While this counterintuitive argument should be given serious consideration and tested empirically, I continue to believe that it is sensible and legitimate for investigators to devote disproportionate attention to persons who, by their past conduct (especially if recent), have demonstrated the willingness and ability to commit crimes.

The pervasive use of a prior criminal record in law enforcement, adjudication, and correction creates a reality that radiates far beyond the criminal justice system. The direct consequences of a criminal record are inextricably linked to the collateral consequences of conviction. Because it is considered normal and sensible to treat arrested, charged, and convicted persons more severely because of their prior criminal records, the same prejudice reigns in other social, political, and legal contexts. There is an inextricable link between the way that criminal records are regarded in criminal justice and non–criminal justice decision making.

13 SECOND-CLASS CITIZENS BY LAW

In the prison reform movement, it's called the "mark of Cain," but contrary to the biblical injunction, God's mercy isn't attached. Rather, it shackles former offenders like me with restrictions barring us—often permanently—from the means to live a normal life. Legally, these restrictions are called "civil disabilities." More realistically, they are called "civil death," a condition that, for many of us, offers little option but to return whence we came: to prison.

—Webster Hubbell, former U.S. associate attorney general, convicted of mail fraud and tax evasion (2001)[1]

Individuals who have shown they are unwilling to follow the law cannot claim the right to make laws for the rest of us. We don't let everyone vote—not children, for instance, or noncitizens, or the mentally incompetent. We have certain minimum standards of trustworthiness before we let people participate in the serious business of self-government, and people who commit serious crimes don't meet those standards.

—Roger Clegg, General Counsel, Center for Equal Opportunity (2004)[2]

[W]hen we consider the expanded reach of the network of invisible punishment, we detect a social impulse distinct from the robust retributivism that has fueled harsher sentencing policies over the past twenty-five years. In this brave new world, punishment for the original offense is no longer enough; one's debt to society is never paid. The National Council on Crime and Delinquency summarized the effects this way: "Even when the sentence has been completely served, the fact that a man has been convicted of a felony pursues him like Nemesis."

—Jeremy Travis, "Invisible Punishment: An Instrument of Social Exclusion" (2002)[3]

THE ANCIENT GREEKS punished certain offenses with "infamy," the forfeiture of all citizenship rights. Some Germanic tribes pronounced those convicted of certain serious crimes "outlaws," who were deprived of all their rights. They were banished from their community and could be killed with impunity.[4] In medieval England, a felony conviction rendered the defendant civilly dead; all his rights and property were forfeited.[5] This conception of the convicted felon as a noncitizen carried over into U.S. law, particularly with respect to prisoners, who were treated as "beyond the ken of the courts."[6] Even persons who had completed their sentences were denied certain citizenship rights. In *Wolff v. McDonnell* (1974), the Supreme Court held that prisoners were not beyond the protection of the Constitution. Writing for the court, Justice Byron White said: "But though his rights may be diminished by the needs and exigencies of the institutional environment, a prisoner is not wholly stripped of constitutional protections when he is imprisoned for crime. There is no iron curtain drawn between the Constitution and the prisons of this country."[7] This legal position is now well entrenched in U.S. prisoners' rights jurisprudence, although there has been much litigation over what limitations on rights the exigencies of incarceration require. The more complicated question is what forfeitures, restrictions, and disqualifications can justifiably be placed on persons who have completed their criminal sentences.[8]* Felony, and a few misdemeanor, convictions trigger disqualifications for voting and political participation, firearms ownership, adoption, occupational licensing, social welfare benefits, and immigration status. The prisoner reentry movement in the last decade of the twentieth century shined a bright light on these statutorily imposed disabilities. Consider Professor Gabriel Chin's observation:

> To this day the legacy of civil death for felons is perpetuated in an array of federal, state and local prohibitions, disqualifications and ineligibilities.[9] In the last decade or two, collateral consequences of conviction have attracted a great deal of critical attention. [C]ivil death has surreptitiously reemerged. It no

---

* Judges have always had discretion to impose additional sanctions as conditions of probation, for example, to cease driving for six months in a case of reckless driving, to forgo visitation in case of child abuse, or to give up all interests in the nursing home industry in a case of nursing home fraud or abuse. By definition, such case-specific requirements and restrictions are more closely tailored to the defendant's risk of future criminality than collateral consequences that are applicable to all convicted felons.

> longer exists under that name, but effectually a new civil death is meted out to persons convicted of crimes in the form of a substantial and permanent change in legal status, operationalized by a network of collateral consequences.[10]

The Supreme Court's decision in *Padilla v. Kentucky* (2010), holding that a defendant's right to effective assistance of counsel was violated by his defense lawyer's failure to advise him on the immigration consequences of a guilty plea,[11] spawned heroic attempts by the American Bar Association (ABA) and others to identify all federal and state "collateral consequences of conviction." The Uniform Law Commission recommended a Uniform Collateral Consequences of Conviction Act that would require states to make all collateral consequences easily accessible.[12] The American Bar Association's National Inventory of the Collateral Consequences of Conviction (NICCC) website and Margaret Colgate Love et al.'s Collateral Consequences of Conviction treatise are impressive compilations.[13] The NICCC is an interactive website that enables the visitor to see for every state all collateral consequences. Love's treatise is a comprehensive practice manual that will assist defense lawyers seeking to advise clients on the collateral consequences of a particular guilty plea.

Love has also traced the history of proposals to scale back or eliminate collateral consequences. In 1956, the National Conference on Parole, held under the joint auspices of the attorney general of the United States, the United States Board of Parole, and the National Council on Crime and Delinquency, called laws depriving convicted persons of civil and political rights "an archaic holdover from early times" and urged their repeal.[14] The American Law Institute's 1962 Model Penal Code included a provision authorizing the sentencing judge, after the defendant successfully completed the sentence, to enter an order eliminating legal disabilities stemming from the conviction. Moreover, "[i]n the states, efforts had been underway since the 1960s to dismantle the statutory apparatus of 'civil death,' and by the end of the 1970s, a majority of states provided for automatic restoration of civil rights upon completion of sentence."[15] (At that point, the trend reversed; collateral consequences proliferated.)

There is also a body of academic criticism. In a seminal 1970 *Vanderbilt Law Review* article, William Grant and colleagues observed that "until the harsh injustices presently embodied in civil disability law are eliminated, ex-convicts will continue to pass through the gates of freedom only to find the doors of opportunity hopelessly closed."[16] They argued that because the only proper justification for laws imposing forfeiture, disqualification, and ineligibility is public safety; collateral consequences should not be imposed as punishment for criminal conduct. This is a sound principle. If the legislature means a particular forfeiture, disqualification, or ineligibility to be part of the punishment, it should be included in the sentence the judge imposes.

Grant et al.'s principle for imposing collateral consequences is helpful as far as it goes, but it doesn't go very far. It covers felon disenfranchisement and a few other high-visibility collateral consequences, but it does not provide a methodology for determining which collateral consequences are justifiable on public safety grounds.[17] There are plausible, but disputable, public safety grounds for most all collateral consequences. This was the conclusion of comparative law scholar Mirjan Damaška, whose classic 1969 article on the subject concluded that

> [t]he usefulness of a *general restatement* is increasingly questioned. If disqualifications are imposed to counter a danger emanating from the offender, or in order to protect another public interest, then these disqualifications should be removed only when the reasons prompting their imposition have ceased to exist. The removal of each disqualification should be considered on its merits by competent bodies or person.[18]

Forfeiture of Constitutional Rights

Forfeiture of constitutional rights upon conviction, especially forfeiture that remains in force after the defendant has completed his felony sentence, is the lowest hanging fruit for collateral consequences reformers. Felon disenfranchisement became a salient issue after the controversial 2000 *Bush v. Gore* presidential election; arguably, Florida's draconian felon disenfranchisement law cost Gore the presidency. According to the Sentencing Project, about six million people, or 2.5 percent of eligible voters, are disenfranchised on account of a criminal record.[19] All but two states disenfranchise incarcerated prison inmates. Some states disenfranchise convicted felons for their entire sentence, including probation, parole, and unsupervised released. Florida and a few other states impose lifetime disenfranchisement.[20] In Kentucky, permanent disenfranchisement also applies to "high misdemeanors."[21]

Sociologists Jeff Manza and Christopher Uggen found that, after the Civil War, felon disenfranchisement was adopted as a strategy to keep blacks from voting.[22] That, of course, is a strong reason for repealing those laws. Law professor Pamela Karlan identifies and rejects deserved punishment as the only modern-day rationale for felon disenfranchisement.[23] However, in support of disenfranchisement, former federal election commissioner Hans von Spakovsky argues that "[t]he proposal to automatically restore felons' right to vote as soon as they have completed their sentences is shortsighted and bad public policy. . . . It takes time to establish a track record. Yet it is the only method to find out if the felon is now participating in the social compact that governs our country and complying with the rules of a civil society."[24] To say the least, his is a minority view.

European democracies (e.g., Czech Republic, Denmark, Germany, Iceland, the Netherlands, Portugal, Sweden, Switzerland, Ukraine) mostly permit even incarcerated felons to vote. In 2005, the European Court of Human Rights affirmed a lower court (chamber) ruling striking down as disproportionate punishment the United Kingdom's disenfranchisement of prisoners.[25] By contrast, the U.S. Supreme Court upheld the constitutionality of felon disenfranchisement in *Richardson v. Ramirez* (1974). The court considered whether a provision of the California Constitution, which disenfranchised those convicted of "infamous crimes," violated the Equal Protection Clause of the Fourteenth Amendment.[26] The court found a textual basis in section 2 of the Fourteenth Amendment for postsentence felon disenfranchisement. Section 2 reduces congressional representation for states that deny the right to vote to males twenty-one years and older, "except for participation in rebellion, or other crime."[27] The court found, by negative implication, constitutional support for disenfranchising felons.

> The exclusion of felons from the vote has an affirmative sanction in U.S. Const. amend. XIV, § 2, a sanction not present in

> the case of other restrictions on the franchise. The understanding of those who adopted the Fourteenth Amendment, as reflected in the express language of U.S. Const. amend. XIV, § 2 and in the historical and judicial interpretation of the Amendment's applicability to state laws disenfranchising felons, is of controlling significance in distinguishing such laws from those other state limitations on the franchise which have been held invalid under the Equal Protection Clause.[28]

In dissent, Justice Marshall, who was joined by Justice Brennan, vigorously disagreed, stating:

> I think it clear that the State has not met its burden of justifying the blanket disenfranchisement of former felons presented by this case. There is certainly no basis for asserting that ex-felons have any less interest in the democratic process than any other citizen. Like everyone else, their daily lives are deeply affected and changed by the decisions of government. As the Secretary of State of California observed in his memorandum to the Court in support of respondents in this case: "It is doubtful . . . whether the state can demonstrate either a compelling or rational policy interest in denying former felons the right to vote. The individuals involved in the present case are persons who have fully paid their debt to society. They are as much affected by the actions of government as any other citizens, and have as much of a right to participate in governmental decision-making. Furthermore, the denial of the right to vote to such persons is a hindrance to the efforts of society to rehabilitate former felons and convert them into law-abiding and productive citizens."[29]

Putting constitutional law aside, this ruling is not good crime policy. Don't we want convicted misdemeanants and felons to be politically active? Shouldn't that be seen as a positive step toward reintegration into the community? A survey conducted by Jeff Manza and Christopher Uggen found that a majority of American survey respondents favor reinstating voting rights for convicted felons who are on probation and parole; 31 percent support restoring voting rights to those who are incarcerated.[30] The recent trend in the United States is toward eliminating barriers to voting for previously convicted persons who have completed their sentence. Since 1997, twenty-three states have, in one manner or another, reenfranchised some ex-offenders. In California, convicted felons are automatically reenfranchised when they have completed their sentences, including parole.[31]

Disqualification from Jury Service

Most states and the federal government permanently ban convicted felons from jury service.[32] The rationale is that a felony conviction demonstrates lack of integrity and prosocial values necessary for an impartial juror.[33] Perhaps a convicted felon will be so hostile to the prosecution that she will refuse to vote guilty no matter how strong the evidence? However, that assumption would bar millions of Americans (including approximately 30 percent of African American males)[34] from jury service. This is clearly undesirable and unwarranted. Effective voir dire (prospective juror questioning) should be able to weed out biased jurors.

Loss of the Right to Keep and Bear Arms

Not only do federal and state laws prohibit ever-convicted felons from purchasing or possessing a firearm, they *make it a felony* for an ever-convicted felon to possess a firearm.[35] (The federal felon-in-possession law carries a ten-year maximum sentence.) Reformers and commentators almost universally accept or are silent about forfeiture of Second Amendment firearms rights upon conviction of a felony and some misdemeanors.[36]

At first blush, firearms disqualification seems justifiable on community safety grounds, since a firearm can be used to commit crimes. Indeed, the Supreme Court's *Heller* decision, recognizing that the Second Amendment guarantees an individual right to keep and bear arms, said that "nothing in our opinion should be taken to cast doubt on longstanding prohibitions on the possession of firearms by felons."[37] However, granting that there is good reason to deny some convicted offenders (those who committed crimes with guns) the right to keep and bear arms, that justification does not apply to offenders who did not use a firearm or even any violence. The federal felon-in-possession law itself includes a narrow exception for persons convicted of antitrust and unfair trade practices offenses. This recognizes that there are forms of criminality that have no relationship to firearms dangerousness or unreliability. Moreover, even when forfeiture of Second Amendment rights is reasonable for societal protection, lifetime disqualification is unreasonable.[38] Moreover, such a drastic constitutional disqualification has implications for other collateral consequences. For example, since Congress has concluded that all convicted felons and some misdemeanants are too risky and irresponsible to ever exercise Second Amendment rights, isn't it reasonable for an employer to conclude that ex-offenders are too risky and irresponsible to employ?

Contrariwise, eliminating the bar to ex-felons possessing firearms would be a powerful precedent for eliminating most other collateral consequences. If ex-felons are deemed responsible enough to have their gun rights restored, shouldn't it follow that they should be deemed responsible enough to have many other rights and eligibilities restored? Interestingly, many states (but not the federal government) seem more willing to restore felons' firearms rights than to restore other rights and opportunities. Indeed, *New York Times* journalist Michael Luo argues persuasively that some states' firearms restoration programs make it too easy for ex-offenders to regain the right to keep and bear firearms:

> Today, in at least 11 states, including Kansas, Ohio, Minnesota and Rhode Island, restoration of firearms rights is automatic, without any review at all, for many nonviolent felons, usually once they finish their sentences, or after a certain amount of time crime-free. Even violent felons may petition to have their firearms rights restored in states like Ohio, Minnesota and Virginia. Some states, including Georgia and Nebraska, award scores of pardons every year that specifically confer gun privileges.[39]

If states are willing to trust convicted felons with firearms, shouldn't they have similar trust with respect to voting and jury service?

Loss of Political Rights

By "political rights" I am referring to non–constitutionally based rights to political participation in the affairs of the community, for example, the right to run for and hold public office.[40] For noncitizens, the most important political right is the right to remain in the country.

RIGHT TO REMAIN IN THE UNITED STATES

In 1917, Congress passed the first statute authorizing deportation of lawful immigrants convicted of a state or federal crime involving *moral turpitude*.[41] The courts, not surprisingly, had difficulty determining which crimes indicated moral turpitude. Periodically, Congress specifically designated moral turpitude offenses.* The Anti-Drug Abuse Act of 1988 added to the list of crimes warranting deportation a new category—"aggravated felonies."[42] At the time, murder and drug and firearms trafficking were the only aggravated felonies. Subsequently, Congress added dozens more offenses, including rape, sexual abuse of a minor, money laundering, unlawful possession of explosive materials, diverse crimes of violence, certain theft offenses, possession of child pornography, racketeering offenses, human trafficking, treason, offenses relating to the transmission of classified information, fraud, tax evasion, alien smuggling, passport fraud, various obstruction of justice offenses, absconding offenses, and certain attempt and conspiracy offenses.[43] Some misdemeanor convictions (e.g., prostitution, theft, burglary, perjury, or obstruction of justice) also qualify for deportation if the value of stolen property is at least $10,000 or if the defendant is sentenced to at least one year of imprisonment.[44]

In *Padilla v. Kentucky*, the Supreme Court recognized that, for noncitizen criminal defendants, deportation is usually a greater concern than the criminal sanction.[45] Jose Padilla had been a permanent

* This subsection focuses primarily on removals of lawful permanent residents on account of criminal record. A criminal conviction also jeopardizes the status of temporary visa holders and undocumented aliens. See Alina Das, *The Immigration Penalties of Criminal Convictions: Resurrecting Categorical Analysis in Immigration Law*, 86 NYU L. Rev. 1669, 1682 (2010).

resident of the United States for more than forty years when police arrested him for transporting marijuana.[46] Relying on his defense lawyer's (erroneous) advice that he did not have to worry about deportation because he had been in the country so long, Padilla pleaded guilty to three state drug offenses (including trafficking in more than five pounds of marijuana). Unfortunately for Padilla, his guilty plea to these aggravated felonies made deportation "virtually inevitable."[47] On appeal, Padilla successfully argued that his conviction should be reversed because his Sixth Amendment right to effective assistance of counsel was violated by his defense lawyer's erroneous advice. Writing for the majority, Justice Stevens explained that "changes to our immigration law have dramatically raised the stakes of a noncitizen's criminal conviction. . . . These changes confirm our view that as a matter of federal law, deportation is an integral part—indeed, sometimes the most important part—of the penalty that may be imposed on noncitizen defendants who plead guilty to specified crimes.[48]

The *Padilla* court did not opine on the fundamental policy issue—which, if any, convictions justify terminating a permanent resident's right to remain in the United States? If a conviction justifies deportation, is it because the offender has shown himself to be a future threat to community safety, or because deportation is deserved punishment for criminal conduct? If it is the former, each criminal offense's relevance for predicting future conduct should be assessed, which would be a massive and unresolvable challenge. How much risk is too much? Should Congress or immigration authorities determine which convictions warrant deportation? Should we abjure categorical assessments and give immigration judges discretion to make case-by-case determinations, taking into account everything they think relevant to deportation?

ELIGIBILITY FOR NATURALIZATION

Equating lack of a conviction record with good character and the presence of a conviction record with bad character is deeply embedded in American law, policy and culture. Since 1790, in order to exclude "disruptive" applicants and "to assure a virtuous polity," applicants for naturalization have had to demonstrate good moral character.[49] In recent times, a criminal record has become a greater impediment to naturalization.[50] An aggravated felony conviction is automatically disqualifying.[51] Aggregate incarceration for more than 180 days in the five years prior to submitting the naturalization application renders an alien ineligible for citizenship consideration.[52] Convictions older than five years are not automatically disqualifying but are relevant to assessing good moral character. (This is an example of differentiating a collateral consequence according to the age of the past conviction, a factor that should always matter.)

To my eye, a presumption that aliens who have committed certain crimes while residing in the United States cannot remain in the country or become citizens is reasonable and much more workable (efficient) than case-by-case assessments by scores of different decision makers. But how should bright lines be drawn? Which convictions should trigger deportation and ineligibility for naturalization? Clearly, every conviction ought not to be disqualifying and age of conviction should matter. There must be some room for administrative discretion. However, discretion invites arbitrariness, discrimination, and subversion of congressional intent. Case-by-case adjudication is time-consuming, expensive, and dependent on the expertise of the lawyer representing the alien.

RIGHT TO RUN FOR AND HOLD ELECTIVE OFFICE

States typically bar certain categories of ex-offenders from holding elective office,[53] apparently reflecting the view that persons holding office must be honest and must be perceived as honest in order to support the legitimacy of governmental decision making and government itself.

Alabama permanently bars convicted felons from holding state office.[54] In New York State, a person sentenced to prison is disqualified from holding public office but becomes reeligible upon completion of sentence.[55] In California, a person with a prior felony conviction must have her voting rights restored in order to be eligible for appointed or elective office.[56] (Voting rights are automatically restored when the sentence has been served.)

Should eligibility to hold elective or appointed office be limited to persons whose integrity is beyond reproach or at least not marred by a (recent) conviction bearing on character? On the one hand, official corruption is not an imaginary problem. It wastes and distorts government resources, breeds cynicism, and undermines democracy. On the other hand, all convictions do not warrant lifetime disqualification from all elective and appointed positions.* Moreover, disqualifying individuals from running for elective office overrides the right of the electorate to choose representatives. What if the people prefer the scoundrel they know to the scoundrel they don't know? Should that choice be denied them?

Ineligibility for Social Welfare Benefits

Requiring that convicted felons forfeit social welfare benefits, a product of the "tough on crime" politics of the 1980s and 1990s, is clearly intended for retributive and deterrent purposes. The Anti-Drug Abuse Act of 1988 established the Denial of Federal Benefits Program.[57] The law allows federal and state courts, as a sentencing option, to disqualify defendants convicted of drug possession or trafficking from receiving some or all federal benefits, including "any grant, contract, loan, professional license, or commercial license."[58]† These disabilities are clearly intended as supplementary punishment for drug offenders; between 1990 and the second quarter of 2004, 8,300 offenders were denied federal benefits.[59]

The 1996 Personal Responsibility and Work Opportunity Reconciliation Act ("Welfare Reform Act") disqualified persons convicted of drug offenses from receiving food stamps and Temporary Assistance to Needy Families (TANF).[60] However, the act permits states to opt out of these disqualifications, or to limit their scope. In fact, only ten states comply with the food stamps disqualification in its entirety; fifteen states and the District of Columbia have opted out.

---

* Despite his conviction for violating the Sedition Act of 1798, Matthew Lyon served as a member of the House of Representatives from 1803 to 1811. Marion Barry, a former Washington, DC, mayor, was convicted of cocaine possession in 1990 (while still mayor). In 2004, he was elected to the Washington, DC, City Council.

† But disqualification does not apply to "retirement, welfare, Social Security, health, disability, veterans benefit, public housing, or other similar benefit, or any other benefit for which payments or services are required for eligibility" (21 U.S.C. § 862).

Only eleven states comply with the TANF disqualification without modification, while thirteen have rejected it.[61] The Agricultural Act of 2014 disqualifies from food stamp eligibility persons convicted of murder, aggravated sexual abuse, sexual assault, and offenses involving the sexual abuse and exploitation of children if they are not in compliance with the terms of the sentence.[62] These misguided disqualifications have nothing to do with public safety. They are purely punitive.

DISQUALIFICATION FROM PUBLIC HOUSING

Federal law disqualifies from federally supported public housing authorities (1) individuals reasonably believed to be using illegal drugs and (for at least three years) those previously evicted from public housing as a result of a drug conviction;[63] (2) individuals convicted of sex offenses who are subject to lifetime sex offender registration;[64] and (3) individuals convicted of manufacturing methamphetamine on public housing premises.[65] In addition, it permits local housing authorities extensive discretion to consider all criminal convictions in making eligibility and eviction determinations.

The first thing to notice about the federal law is that it is overinclusive. Drug use, especially marijuana use, is common throughout society and hardly indicative of being a bad tenant or neighbor. The second thing to notice is that the list of disqualifying convictions is underinclusive; only drug and sex offenses trigger public housing disqualification. Despite the lack of close fit between the statutory exclusions and bad tenancy, there is an important nonpunitive rationale for rejecting disruptive individuals and families. Public housing projects are frequently plagued with gangs, crime, drugs, and guns. Irresponsible and antisocial tenants can impose havoc and misery on their neighbors. Treating criminal convictions as a warning sign is not irrational. Given the number of needy deserving people who want to live in public housing, it is rational and responsible for housing administrators to prefer individuals and families with a history of good citizenship. Nevertheless, here as elsewhere, conclusively assuming that a prior conviction presents an unacceptable risk is problematic.[66]

Bright-line rules are always overinclusive, but what is the alternative? Suppose public housing officials "merely" took criminal records "into consideration"? Would that mean that officials consider certain prior convictions "a negative factor" that can be overcome by strong countervailing evidence of good citizenship (rehabilitation)? In addition to being time-consuming and expensive, case-by-case decision making that takes account of every biographical details is vulnerable to subjective, arbitrary, and even corrupt decision making. It would be preferable to relax eligibility requirements but more aggressively enforce evictions of bad tenants. Contrariwise, the harder it is to evict a tenant, the more reason there is to rigorously screen applicants.

DENIAL OF VICTIMS' COMPENSATION

Some state compensation programs for crime victims disqualify claimants on the basis of a criminal record. According to the National Association of Crime Victim Compensation Boards, nine states consider felony convictions in determining eligibility for compensation.[67] For example, the Louisiana Crime Victims Reparations Fund compensates victims of violent crime for costs that are not covered by insurance.[68] The fund reimburses up to $5,000 of murder victims' funeral expenses. However, a felony conviction within the last five years renders a victim ineligible, an important exclusion given that two-thirds of murder victims in New Orleans have prior felony arrests. Furthermore, a victim who was serving a sentence or on probation in the five years preceding the crime may also be disqualified, although the Crime Victims Reparations Board has some discretion.[69] One Louisiana Commission on Law Enforcement staff member explained to a *Times-Picayune* journalist that persons with criminal records "are not as deserving as what we would call truly innocent victims."[70] That conclusion is not justified.

INELIGIBILITY FOR STUDENT FINANCIAL AID

Convicted drug offenders are ineligible for federal education loans, grants, and scholarships. In 1988, amendments to the Anti-Drug Abuse Act permitted judges to suspend eligibility for federal financial aid as part of an offender's sentence.[71] In reauthorizing the Higher Education Act in 1998, Congress added the Drug-Free Student Loan Provision, disqualifying for a specified period of time from a grant, loan, or work assistance individuals convicted of sale or possession of a controlled substance.[72] The law's sponsors claimed that it would deter the use and sale of drugs on college campuses, impose student accountability, and encourage student drug abusers to get treatment.[73] How much deterrence was achieved is unknown.[74] In 2005, the act was amended to apply only to those individuals convicted of a drug offense while receiving student loans.[75] Some states also deny educational aid to persons with criminal convictions.[76] This is another misguided punitive policy unconnected to community safety. A sensible policy would encourage ex-offenders to stay in school.

Disqualification from Public Contracting

Various federal and state laws bar convicted individuals from eligibility to serve as government contractors. Under federal law, a conviction for specified offenses, including fraud in obtaining or performing a public contract, antitrust violations, embezzlement, forgery, bribery, or tax evasion, can result in contract debarment.[77] In addition, a person convicted of fraud or any other felony arising out of a contract with the Department of Defense is ineligible to serve on the board or act as a manger, supervisor, consultant, or representative of a defense contractor or first-tier subcontractor for at least five years from date of conviction.[78]

New York City created a database (VENDEX) for use by New York City contracting officers in assessing whether a firm is a "responsible" public contractor.[79] VENDEX is populated with criminal intelligence, individual criminal histories, debarments, cautions, findings of nonresponsibility, and bankruptcies. If a New York City agency's chief contracting officer believes the would-be contractor is corrupt or "irresponsible," the contract must be denied.[80] Ultimately, agency officials and the mayor must decide whether too many doubts about a contractor's integrity have been raised. If the agency gives the contractor the benefit of the doubt, it risks being excoriated by the media, the comptroller, law enforcement officials, and political opponents and rivals. It is understandable that risk-averse agency officials believe that the safer course is to disqualify a contractor against whom there is any negative entry in VENDEX or in the files or minds of law enforcement investigators. This policy is not motivated by a desire to punish but by a desire to ensure that public contracts will be obtained and performed honestly. That certainly is reasonable given the vulnerability of public contracts to fraud and numerous cases of fraudulent contract performance. However, it is predicated on a prediction that prior criminality poses a significant risk of future criminality. At least a partial alternative to debarment is requiring contractors to hire a government-approved contract monitor, who will report to the contracting authority any suspicions of fraud or other misconduct.[81]

Disqualification from Public and Private Employment

Legally imposed employment (de jure employment discrimination) bars on ex-offenders are long-standing and deeply rooted. Thousands of federal and state laws and administrative regulations prohibit individuals with all or some convictions from (1) holding appointed offices and civil service positions; (2) serving in the military; (3) working in some private sector industries, agencies, and positions; and (4) obtaining or retaining occupational licenses.

DISQUALIFICATION FROM CIVIL SERVICE POSITIONS

A felony conviction is a permanent bar to public employment in seven states.[82] Many other states also disqualify felons from public employment but allow for restoration of eligibility.[83] Disqualifications can apply to all or some felony convictions and even to some misdemeanors. For example, in Rhode Island, a state employee who discloses a worker's compensation report is guilty of a misdemeanor and is barred from public employment for a year.[84] In some cases, a felony conviction can lead to automatic disqualification from civil service, while in other instances disqualification is discretionary. The New Jersey "Forfeiture Act" is one of the strictest laws governing disqualification from public office. It provides that upon conviction of a serious offense or a crime of dishonesty involving one's position as a civil servant, this position is immediately forfeited and the individual is "forever disqualified from holding any office or position of honor, trust or profit under this State or any of its administrative or political subdivisions."[85]

Federal hiring policy provides for discretion with respect to excluding those with a criminal record from civil service jobs. Though a felony conviction may constitute a bar to certain positions, such as in law enforcement, federal agencies generally do not automatically disqualify people with prior convictions.[86] Rather, the federal Office of Personnel Management (OPM) imposes "suitability requirements" for federal civil service jobs. Under OPM's rules, federal agencies may bar individuals from federal employment for up to three years on account of prior criminal or dishonest conduct. Suitability is based on "a person's character or conduct that may have an impact on the integrity or efficiency of the service." Whether a particular ex-offender is suitable is a subjective judgment. If arrived at without rules or some kind of scoring criteria, decisions are likely to vary greatly from case to case and decision maker to decision maker. Is this fairer than a bright-line rule that excludes whole categories of ex-offenders from certain agencies or jobs for a specified number of years? Probably bright-line eligibility (disqualification) rules need to be combined with a certain amount of agency discretion.

In 2013, the House of Representatives approved a sensible bright-line bill that prohibits public schools from employing teachers and other personnel with certain criminal convictions, including sexual offenses against children, rape, spousal abuse, murder, and kidnapping. The bill enjoyed bipartisan support in Congress, but the National Education Association and the American Federation of Teachers charged that it would undermine contractual rights and have a disparate impact on minorities.[87]

DISQUALIFICATION FROM PRIVATE SECTOR EMPLOYMENT

Congress and state legislatures bar certain categories of ex-offenders from working in some private sector employments. For example, federal laws prohibit ex-offenders from holding union offices or working in banking, financial securities, and nuclear power plants. Texas makes a slew of convictions, ranging from forgery to tax evasion, a bar to working for a private security company.[88] All jurisdictions have laws barring some or all sex offenders from working in certain organizations, occupations, and jobs.

One might legitimately ask why government should be in the business of ordering *private organizations* to discriminate on the basis of a criminal record? Why shouldn't private organizations be permitted to make their own decisions? After all, it is in their self-interest to employ honest, reliable and productive employees. Indeed, they must internalize the costs of dishonest and unreliable employees and compensate victims for injuries inflicted by their employees.

PROTECTING THE PUBLIC

Legislators may believe that some private businesses (e.g., nuclear power plants, airport security, ports) pose so much risk to the public that the government must ensure that they operate safely and honestly. The costs of a nuclear accident, for instance, would not just (or even primarily) be absorbed by the firm operating the power plant. Tens of thousands of lives and billions of dollars of other peoples' property might be lost. Thus, government is justified in ensuring that these power plants are managed safely. Safe management might well include employing technically and morally qualified employees.

A similar argument could be made about banks and financial institutions, especially because the government itself might have to cover extensive losses if the financial institution is run dishonestly or recklessly. Government has a good reason for ensuring that the top employees of financial institutions do not have a history of embezzlement and fraud.

What about protecting the public from physical and sexual victimization? The public certainly has a strong interest in the reliability and moral integrity of child and elder care providers, masseurs, doctors, nurses, and physical therapists. But for reasons of resources and efficiency this argument cannot be stretched so far that the government assumes responsibility for supervising the operation of all organizations, even all service-providing organizations. Members of the public must be presumed capable of protecting themselves by relying on the reputation of the service providers and their right to sue for injuries that the service providers cause. Of course, the service providers themselves have a strong reputational and financial interest in operating safely. Ordinarily, they can be expected not to hire employees whose backgrounds indicate a risk, even a modest risk, of injuring customers, clients, and fellow employees. However, some employers might be willing to hire employees that others will not hire because they believe themselves better judges of character, because they believe that their management model can effectively monitor employees, or because they are committed to giving ex-offenders job opportunities. In my view, the government's interference with private hiring choices ought to require a very strong showing of public interest and as narrow regulation as necessary to satisfy the public interest. This is especially true if the government's expertise in evaluating the risk posed by a prior criminal record is dubious.

It is certainly reasonable to seek to protect customer, clients, and employees from victimization by barring convicted persons from certain employments. The problem is that there is no science for assessing the risk that a particular convicted person poses for a particular job. (Indeed, we could make the problem even harder by considering a conviction that was plea-bargained down from a greater crime or an individual with several previous convictions.) Consider private security work. Private security guards often have unsupervised access to residential and business property, posing a risk of theft. How can we assess whether a three-year-old burglary conviction poses an undue risk for a security guard position? What if, in addition, the applicant had also been convicted of shoplifting a couple of years before the burglary or six months after being sentenced for burglary?

Analysis is further complicated by the fact that many ex-offenders are not one-time convictees, much less one-time arrestees.[89] If it is unreasonable to exclude a first-offense tax evader from a high school teaching position, what if originally, in addition to tax evasion, that person was charged with (indicted on) two counts of fraud that were dropped as part of the plea bargain? What if there were two counts of tax evasion relating to two different years? One tax conviction and one embezzlement conviction? Two convictions for low-level sex offenses? Three convictions for drunk driving? At some point, it must be reasonable for the government to step in to protect potential customers, clients, and the general public. But working out what that point is and for which organizations and jobs is a herculean task. Ubiquitous plea-bargaining makes the task much harder. (In this chapter we are considering the reasonableness of the government barring persons with certain records from certain employments. In the next chapter we ask whether it is reasonable for private individuals and firms to make such assessments themselves.)

PROTECTING THE PUBLIC AGAINST CRIMINAL ENTERPRISES

Legislators may believe that some organizations are vulnerable to corruption at the top (e.g., casinos) and that, if left unregulated, they would operate as criminal enterprises. Some organizations and business sectors have such a notorious history of organized crime involvement that, as a remedial measure, Congress barred persons with felony records from employment. For example, in 1953, following newspaper exposés and public hearings revealing organized crime influence throughout the Port of New York and New Jersey, Congress passed a bistate compact (ratified by both states) that establishes a bistate Waterfront Commission to police and regulate the port in a manner that would eradicate corruption and racketeering.[90] The legislation included prohibitions and restrictions on employing convicted felons. These disqualifications from working at the port were least restrictive for the longshoremen who load and unload the cargo ships and most restrictive for the shipping companies and their executives.

The compact requires that longshoremen not "constitute a danger to the public peace or safety."[91] While the commission may "in its discretion" deny a longshoreman applicant who has been convicted of specified offenses, the compact does not require the Waterfront Commission to disqualify an applicant with a criminal record. Workers in supervisory positions are required to be of "good character and integrity."[92] An individual could not serve as a pier superintendent, hiring agent, or port watchman if ever convicted of an attempt or conspiracy to commit, treason, murder, manslaughter, or any felony or high misdemeanor or any of the following misdemeanors or offenses: illegally using, carrying, or possessing a pistol or other dangerous weapon; making or possessing burglar's instruments; buying or receiving stolen property; unlawful entry of a building; aiding an escape from prison; unlawfully possessing, possessing with intent to distribute, sale, or distribution of a controlled dangerous substance (controlled substance) or, in New Jersey, a controlled dangerous substance analog (controlled substance analog); and violation of the Waterfront Commission Compact.[93] However, an applicant could obtain a waiver by proving to the commission that he has "conducted himself as to warrant the grant of such license" for at least five years.[94] Moreover the commission can refuse to hire an applicant who lacks "good character and integrity," a judgment that could be based on convictions not explicitly enumerated above.[95]

The compact required the commission to license the shipping companies (stevedores) that want to do business in the port. The stevedore executives and the companies themselves are disqualifiable for the same criminal convictions as pier superintendents, hiring agents, or port watchmen.[96]

The high-profile U.S. Senate (McClellan Committee) hearings (1957–1959) revealed widespread corruption and racketeering in a number of unions, especially the Teamsters.[97] The hearings exposed organized-crime-affiliated union officers exploiting their unions, union pension, welfare funds, and union members (e.g., by accepting employer bribes to ignore the terms of the collective bargaining contract). Proponents of the Labor Management Reporting and Disclosure Act (LMRDA) argued that without congressional action to prohibit convicted persons from serving as union officials, a convicted union officer who dominated his union's politics could continue to direct union affairs, even from jail. In passing the LMRDA, Congress meant to remove "the criminal element" from labor unions and prevent future organized crime infiltration.* Consequently, the LMRDA disqualified convicted felons from serving as union officers, union consultants, and labor relations consultants for thirteen years from conviction or completion of sentence, whichever comes

* In some cases, even disqualifying the convicted labor racketeer from union office was not enough to extinguish his influence over the union. The convicted person exerted influence on the union from a nominally low-level union position or, even without a union position, through a surrogate. James B. Jacobs and Kerry T. Cooperman, *Breaking the Devil's Pact: The Battle to Free the Teamsters from the Mob* (New York: New York University Press, 2011).

later. (Obviously, there is no magic in thirteen years.)[98] However, the LMRDA provides that a convicted person's eligibility to hold union office can be restored after three years if the convicted person can persuade the sentencing court she has been rehabilitated since commission of the disqualifying crime and will not endanger the labor organization in which she proposes to hold office.[99]

Because of gambling's historic connection with organized crime, casino gambling laws in Nevada and New Jersey prohibit anyone with a criminal record from working in a casino. In Nevada, the Gaming Commission "may revoke or suspend the gaming license or finding of suitability of a person who is convicted of a crime . . . if the crime or conviction discredits or tends to discredit the state of Nevada or the gaming industry."[100] Moreover, casino employees must register with the Nevada Gaming Commission and State Gaming Control Board; a criminal record can render an individual ineligible to register.[101]

UPHOLDING THE PRESTIGE OF AN OCCUPATION

One of the rationales for excluding ex-offenders from some professions and occupations is the desire to protect the public's confidence in the profession and the profession's prestige. For example, a person previously convicted of a felony cannot serve as a military officer, unless she obtains a "moral waiver."[102] Some convictions are not waiver eligible, for example, domestic violence, sexual assaults, and kidnapping. Is it reasonable for Congress to categorically exclude certain ex-offenders from the officer corps in order to promote the officer corps' reputation, image, and prestige? If this rationale were widely adopted, it could disqualify previously convicted persons from a large number of professions and occupations. Of course, the military would argue that for officers to be effective leaders, their character and conduct needs to be above reproach. The same could be asserted, and similarly not demonstrated empirically, for positions in all sorts of organizations. This "promotion of confidence in the occupation" rationale could, in some cases, be a convenient way to protect the occupation's incumbents from competition.

State laws give the professions (accounting, architecture, law, medicine) self-governing authority, which they exercise by licensing their practitioners. The legal profession, as governed by a state character and fitness committee, requires that lawyers be honest and trustworthy. Bar association committees license lawyers who meet criteria of "good character," good reputation," or "honesty and trustworthiness."[103] If people doubt the integrity of lawyers generally, they will be less willing to confide in them. In New York State, an applicant for a license to practice law must have "good moral character."[104] An applicant must disclose whether, as an adult or juvenile, she has ever been arrested, cited, or charged with the violation of any law, "except minor parking violations."[105] Applicants must even disclose expunged convictions (thereby undermining the value of expungement). Unlike in some other states, in New York a felony conviction is not automatically disqualifying but is grounds for inadmissibility.[106] Moreover, an attorney who is convicted of a felony is automatically disbarred.[107] However, a disbarred attorney may have her license reinstated if "it appears consistent with the maintenance of the integrity and honor of the profession, the protection of the public and the interest of justice."[108]

New Jersey law requires all applicants for a real estate salesperson or broker license to possess good character, trustworthiness, honesty, and integrity. A felony conviction is grounds for, but does not automatically require, disqualification.[109]

Protecting the Public from Convicted Sex Offenders

Convicted sex offenders are subject to unique legal disqualifications and disabilities. In addition to registration and community notification requirements, discussed in Chapter 2, sex offenders face extraordinary statutorily imposed employment and housing restrictions. For example, they are disqualified from working in federally operated or funded child care facilities. Similar state laws prohibit employment in organizations that provide children's services, a category that can be defined very broadly.[110] In Alabama, a convicted sex offender is prohibited from working or volunteering within 2,000 feet of a school or child care facility.[111] Some states prohibit convicted sex offenders from residing near a location frequented by children, such as a school, park, or school bus stop.

There are no hard data to justify these laws. Indeed, numerous studies have found lower recidivism rates for convicted sex offenders than for felonies generally. When the government imposes such disqualifications in the name of protecting children, it is not surprising that private individuals and organizations adopt the same policy.

In *Doe v. Miller* (2005), a federal district court in Iowa found unconstitutional the statute prohibiting a person convicted of a sex offense against a minor from residing within 2,000 feet of a school of child care facility.[112] The judge pointed out that practically all of Des Moines and Iowa City are off-limits to previously convicted sex offenders.[113] The Eighth Circuit Court of Appeals reversed, holding that the statute did not violate the sex offenders' right to procedural due process, right to travel, or right to privacy and choice with regard to family matters.

Sex offenders can also be subject to lifelong community supervision and involuntary civil confinement. At least thirty-nine states have implemented GPS or other electronic monitoring for sex offenders; sometimes this monitoring remains in effect even after a sentence has been fully and successfully served, sometimes for life.[114] The federal government and nineteen states provide that sex offenders can be preventatively detained after release from prison.[115] Such laws certainly send a signal to the public that convicted sex offenders are forever dangerous and should be avoided. The online sex offender registries are an even more explicit message.

Strategies for Scaling Back Collateral Consequences

There are many critics of the web of collateral consequences that limit opportunities for persons with criminal records.[116] Law school dean Nora Demleitner has written:

> [E]xile in penal colonies abroad for citizens has long been abolished. Nevertheless, upon release from prison or discharge from non-incarcerative sentences, many ex-offenders find themselves internally exiled. They are saddled with restrictions that exclude them from major aspects of society. An increasing

> number of mandatory exclusions from the labor force and governmental programs have followed a temporary decrease of some collateral consequences during the 1960s and early 1970s. . . .
>
> Ultimately, exclusions from the political, economic and social spheres of life undermine the notion that offenders can ever be successfully rehabilitated. In conjunction with the exponential increase in the number and length of incarcerative sentences during the last two decades, collateral sentencing consequences have contributed to exiling ex-offenders within their country, even after expiration of their maximum sentences. The impact of collateral consequences is especially disturbing since such consequences frequently lack penological justification. They merely add to the overall severity of the sentence without being grounded in theories of retribution, prevention, deterrence, or rehabilitation.[117]

The 2003 American Bar Association Standards for Criminal Justice recommend not imposing collateral sanctions unless "the conduct constituting that particular offense provides so substantial a basis for imposing the sanction that the legislature cannot reasonably contemplate any circumstances in which imposing the sanction would not be justified." According to the ABA's commentary:

> The imposition of collateral penalties has serious implications, both in terms of fairness to the individuals affected, and in terms of the burdens placed on the community. If promulgated and administered indiscriminately, a regime of collateral consequences may frustrate the chance of successful re-entry into the community, and thereby encourage recidivism.[118]

The criticisms are clear, but the remedy is not. It is easy to categorically state, and I join the chorus, that employment disqualifications based on a criminal record should be cut back to those that can be justified by public, consumer, or client safety. Employment disqualifications triggered by any felony conviction (e.g., robbery, tax evasion, car theft, computer hacking) is always overbroad, but achieving a consensus about which convictions properly disqualify a person from which jobs is extremely difficult. It is even more difficult because many people with criminal records have more than one conviction. Perhaps two marginally disqualifying convictions are sufficient to justify a disqualification where one would not be? Reform must also take into account the duration of any disqualification or ineligibility. A lifetime disqualification is rarely reasonable. But the proper duration of a particular license disqualification is very difficult to specify. (A lawyer convicted of stealing from his client? A doctor's sexual assault of a patient?) Scaling back collateral consequences is a daunting task because of different disqualifications and ineligibilities and lack of data on risk.

Ban the Box

More than sixty states, counties, cities, and towns, including Boston, San Francisco, Chicago, New York, Philadelphia, Baltimore, Austin, Seattle, Durham, Atlanta, Minneapolis, and St. Paul, have adopted initiatives to ameliorate public sector discrimination against job applicants with criminal records.[119] In San Francisco, an ex-offender group, All of Us or None (AUN), led a "Ban the Box" campaign to end discrimination against ex-offenders applying for city and county jobs. The "box" refers to the question on the city's employment application form asking whether the job applicant has ever been convicted of a crime. AUN argued that, in addition to promoting employment discrimination against ex-offenders, the question deters ex-offenders from even applying for city jobs. After several rallies and vigorous lobbying with the city's Human Rights Commission and Department of Human Resources, AUN persuaded the San Francisco Board of Supervisors to pass a resolution calling on the city and county to eliminate the criminal record question from the job application form, except when state or local law expressly bars certain ex-offenders from a particular job. The resolution would prohibit any criminal background check or inquiry until after a tentative offer of employment has been made. At that point in the hiring process, a criminal record would be relevant if it posed an unacceptable risk that the applicant could not fulfill the job's requirements.

Boston has taken the Ban the Box initiative further. Boston requires background checks only for city positions involving contact with children, the elderly, and the disabled, as well as for law enforcement positions. The background check, however, is not conducted until after an applicant initially applies for a position, is interviewed by the hiring department, and is selected as a finalist for the position. The department refers finalists' names to Human Resources, which conducts background checks. If a conviction is revealed that does not disqualify the applicant from the position, the department will be told that the applicant is cleared for the position. If there is a disqualifying conviction, the applicant has an opportunity to meet with the Human Resources Department to explain mitigating circumstances. The department head may ask for a formal review of the denial.[120] Boston is not the only city that restricts background checks to only certain positions; so do Minneapolis, Baltimore, Hartford, Oakland, and Seattle, among others.[121]

At least twelve states have adopted a Ban the Box policy.[122]* Four out of these ten (Hawaii, Massachusetts, Minnesota, and Rhode Island) have even extended Ban the Box to government contractors. In Hawaii, which in 1998 became the first state to pass Ban the Box legislation applicable to both private and public employers, an employer can inquire about an applicant's criminal record only after extending a tentative job offer, which can be rescinded if the applicant has a conviction rationally related to the responsibilities and duties of the position.

The Ban the Box campaign does not involve costly regulation and enforcement. It constitutes a creative experiment that might turn out to benefit ex-offenders and society generally. If it works, Ban the Box will provide an important example that second (and third) chances assist rehabilitation without endangering the community.

---

* These states are California, Colorado, Connecticut, Delaware, Hawaii, Illinois, Maryland, Massachusetts, Minnesota, Nebraska, New Mexico, and Rhode Island. See National Employment Law Project, *Statewide Ban the Box, Reducing Unfair Barriers to Employment of People with Criminal Records* (May 2014).

Obviously, Ban the Box reaches only ex-offenders who are job ready and job capable. It will be of most help to ex-offenders with the most social capital: education, skills, competent presentation of self, and a less serious (perhaps white-collar) criminal record. It will be of little, if any, help to those hundreds of thousands of ex-offenders who lack psychological and emotional stability, education, job skills, social skills, and a work history; those with an extensive record of recidivism; and those who have been convicted of horrific crimes. Time will tell how aggressively local governments implement Ban the Box. The states and cities that have voluntarily adopted Ban the Box have not said that a criminal record is wholly irrelevant. They have said that ex-offenders should be encouraged to apply for public sector jobs; the criminal record will be considered only after the agency has formed a favorable impression of the applicant.

Conclusion

The current prohibitions, disqualifications, and exclusions on ex-offenders are overinclusive (i.e., there are too many). The ABA Commission on Effective Criminal Sanctions recommends that governmental units at all levels eliminate employment and licensing restrictions that are not "substantially related to the particular employment" and are "not designed to protect the public safety."[123] As a general rule, that makes good sense. Collateral consequences ought not to be used as punishment, but only for forward-looking protective purposes. The problem is in determining which conviction records are relevant to which jobs. If the legislature decides that a particular disability should be included in the punishment for particular crimes, those consequences should be spelled out in the penal code. For example, why not include in the authorized sentence for a Medicare or Medicaid fraud conviction that the defendant must or may be debarred from participating in these government programs for up to ten years?[124] Of course, most convictions are not so obviously program or employment related.

When, if ever, should Congress step in to protect government programs and operations and the public from risks posed by ex-offenders? Arguably, the public needs special protection from white-collar offenders—corrupt politicians and cops, fraudsters of all types, embezzlers, environmental polluters, and others whose criminality defrauds or injures clients, consumers, and the public. Even when there is good reason for the government to impose hiring restriction, it is unreasonable to apply them for life, especially for first convictions. But convictions reflecting dishonesty appropriately trigger occupational exclusions, at least until the ex-offender has demonstrated a turn toward honesty and integrity. There is no alternative to considering the reasonableness of every exclusion and disqualification. Even then, we need to get beyond the simplistic matching of abstract offense with general job categories.

The United States is not the only country to exclude convicted felons from government employment. Continental European countries generally ban persons with unexpunged convictions from employment in "public administration," roughly equivalent to our "civil service."[125] In Spain, for example, a conviction-free record is required to work as a teacher, university professor, medical doctor, and civil servant. In recent years, the European Union has passed a number of laws requiring member states to commit to excluding convicted sex offenders from positions that afford access to children.

Governments can lead by example by voluntarily ignoring past criminal convictions for many public sector jobs. If government agencies can demonstrate that persons with a criminal record can be good employees, they will establish a strong case for repealing many de jure restrictions on ex-offender licensing and employment and also strong encouragement to private employers not to discriminate against ex-offenders.

14 EMPLOYMENT DISCRIMINATION BASED ON A CRIMINAL RECORD

> It is no argument against the validity of this statute that it considers a criminal conviction as a showing of unfitness, for it is not open to doubt that the commission of crime, the violation of the penal laws of a State, has some relation to the question of character. A professional license is a high privilege from the State, and the State can attach to its possession conditions onerous and exacting.
>
> —*Barsky v. Board of Regents* (1953)[1]

> I have worked hard to turn my life around. I have remained clean for nearly eight years, I am succeeding in college, and I continue to share my story in schools, treatment facilities and correctional institutions, yet I have nothing to show for it. . . . I have had numerous interviews and sent out more than 200 resumes for jobs which I am more than qualified. I have had denial after denial because of my felony.
>
> —Anonymous (2011)[2]

IN ADDITION TO facing legally imposed forfeitures, disqualifications, and ineligibilities, people with criminal records face extensive discretionary (de facto) discrimination, especially employment discrimination. Given the importance of legitimate employment for desisting from further criminal conduct, de facto discrimination is a serious obstacle to postconviction success.* Harvard sociologist

---

* While conviction-based employment discrimination (CBED) impedes a convicted person's success, its impact ought not to be exaggerated. Most ex-offenders suffer from one or more employment handicaps, such as educational deficiency, mental illness, drug dependency, and little or no legitimate work history. In 2008, over 36 percent of ex-prisoners lacked a high school or general equivalency diploma, compared with 10 percent of the general population. Sixty percent of all state prisoners report using illegal drugs in the month prior to their offense. Sixteen percent of adult prisoners report having either a mental disorder or an overnight stay in a psychiatric facility. John Schmitt and Kris Warner, Center for Economic and Policy Research, *Ex-offenders and the Labor Market*, November 2010, http://www.cepr.net/document/publication/ex-offenders-2010-11.pdf.

Devah Pager echoes the mainstream view of criminologists in observing that,

> [i]n our frenzy of locking people up, our "crime control" policies may in fact exacerbate the very conditions that lead to crime in the first place. Research consistently shows that finding quality steady employment is one of the strongest predictors of desistance from crime. The fact that a criminal record severely limits employment opportunities—particularly among blacks—suggests that these individuals are left with few viable alternatives.[3]

We saw in Chapter 13 the large number of federal and state laws restricting ex-offenders' rights and eligibilities. These statutes should be the first target of reformers. When so many federal and state laws *require* public and private employers to discriminate on the basis of a criminal record, it would be hypocritical for federal and state governments to prohibit private sector employers from discriminating against ex-offenders. With the important exception of race, sex, religion, handicap and age, federal law* permits employers to hire and fire employees for any reason or for no reason.[4] Freedom of contract is a core constitutional and political value.† It is

---

* German law is representative of continental European approaches to employment discrimination based on a criminal record. Employers generally do not have access to criminal history information. An employer may ask a job applicant about previous convictions only if a specific type of criminal propensity would be incompatible with carrying out a particular job's duties successfully. Thus, for example, an applicant for an accountant or cashier position may be asked about previous convictions for property offenses, or an applicant for a truck driver position may be asked about previous convictions for drunk driving. The job applicant, however, does not have to disclose convictions that have been expunged. Moreover, the applicant is not obliged to answer inadmissible questions. To prevent the employer from concluding that the applicant's refusal to answer is itself an admission, the applicant is allowed to answer unlawful questions with a lie. See also Elena Larrauri, *Legal Protections against Criminal Background Checks in Europe*, 16 Punishment & Society 50–73 (2014).

† Law professor Richard A. Epstein argues that all antidiscrimination laws should be repealed. In his view, the antidiscrimination statutes not only violate freedom of contract but also result in inefficient employment practices and ultimately cause more

important that entrepreneurs be encouraged to start and expand their businesses.

Why Do Private Employers Discriminate against Persons with Criminal Records?

Employers want to hire the job candidate most likely to succeed in a particular job and in the company generally. Therefore, employers attempt to make the best prediction of future performance based on information that can be obtained at reasonable cost. Other things being equal, a job applicant with an unblemished record of honesty, reliability, and self-discipline will be preferred to one who has a criminal record.* In one survey, 92 percent of responding employers stated that they required criminal background checks for some or all jobs.[5] Their reasons include preventing theft and workplace violence and avoiding liability for injuries and damages caused by employees.[6]

Suppose that an employee who installs appliances assaulted a customer while doing work at his home. Under civil tort law, employers are liable for injuries caused by employees within the course of employment. In some states, employers are also liable for injuries traceable to negligent hiring. Suppose the employer had not commissioned a criminal background check, and suppose that a background check would have revealed a recent conviction (perhaps several convictions) for assault. The injured customer would sue, claiming that the employer should have known that the assaulting

---

discrimination than they prevent. See *Forbidden Grounds: The Case against Employment Discrimination Laws* (Cambridge, MA: Harvard University Press, 1992).

* In *El v. Southeastern Pennsylvania Transportation Authority* (SEPTA), the plaintiff challenged SEPTA's policy of excluding all job applicants who had ever been convicted of a violent felony. El (now fifty-five), who applied for a job as a para-transit driver, had been convicted of second-degree murder forty years earlier. The Third Circuit observed that some level of risk is inevitable in all hiring and that, "in a broad sense, hiring policies . . . ultimately concern the management of risk." Title VII requires employers to justify criminal record exclusions by demonstrating that they "accurately distinguish between applicants who pose an unacceptable level of risk and those who do not." Nevertheless, the court affirmed dismissal of El's lawsuit because para-transit drivers have unsupervised access to vulnerable adults. 479 F.3d 232 (3d Cir. 2007).

employee was potentially dangerous. While courts generally held that employers do not have a duty to obtain a criminal background report on every employee, the duty depends on the nature of the job and whether there is anything in the job applicant's background that would have put a reasonable employer on notice that a background check is prudent.[7] Given the modest cost of a background check, and the ease of passing the cost to the job applicant, the cautious employer will routinely check all new hires.

Suppose the criminal background check reveals an assault conviction several years ago. After interviewing the job applicant, the hiring officer may be inclined to regard the old conviction as aberrational, but legal counsel may caution that if the ex-offender does injure a customer, client, or fellow employee, a jury might reach the opposite conclusion.[8] Thus, the risk-averse employer will prefer to hire someone with a spotless record. Indeed, even if the job applicant's record is not for assault but for drunk driving or drunk and disorderly conduct, the rational employer might think it more prudent to hire someone whose record has no black mark that might expose the employer to liability for personal injuries and property damage.

Ex-offender advocates propose abolishing the negligent hiring tort by legislation. A New York State statute protects employers from negligent-hiring liability if the employer proves due diligence in hiring the injury-causing ex-offender.* A 2012 Ohio law provides that an employer is immune from negligent hiring liability if it hired a job applicant who has a Certificate of Qualification for Em-

---

* The 2008 New York State Human Rights law states that New York's public policy is to encourage the employment of persons previously convicted of one or more criminal offenses. Toward that end, it creates a rebuttable presumption in favor of excluding evidence of prior conviction(s) in a negligent hiring case where the employer considered the following factors: the specific duties and responsibilities related to the employment sought or held; the bearing the criminal offense(s) will have on the person's ability or fitness to perform the job; how much time has elapsed since the conviction(s); age at time of conviction; seriousness of the conviction(s); information regarding the person's rehabilitation; and the employer's legitimate interest in protecting property, and the safety and welfare of specific individuals or the general public.

ployment.[9] However, in New York and Ohio, the employer cannot avoid liability under the *respondeat superior* doctrine—employers are strictly liable for the injuries caused by their employees in the course of their employment.

The Extent of De Facto Employment Discrimination

In the early 1960s, sociologists Richard Schwartz and Jerome Skolnick conducted a field experiment to determine the impact of a criminal record on employment opportunity.[10] They sent one of four applications from fictitious job seekers to random employers. Twenty-five employers received application number 1, twenty-five received application number 2, and so forth. The "job seekers" had identical curricula vitae (race not identified), except for a criminal record. Applicant 1's résumé included an assault conviction. Applicant 2's application indicated an assault acquittal. Applicant 3 submitted a fictitious trial judge's letter explaining an assault acquittal in a light favorable to the job applicant. Applicant 4 had no criminal record. The employers' responses demonstrated substantial conviction-based employment discrimination (CBED). Applicant 4 (no criminal record) received favorable responses from 36 percent of employers. Applicant 3 (assault acquittal plus the letter from the judge) received positive responses from 24 percent of employers. Applicant 3 (assault acquittal) received positive responses from 12 percent of employers, and Applicant 1 (assault conviction) received a positive response from just 4 percent of employers. The authors concluded that

> [f]rom a theoretical point of view, the finding leads toward the conclusion that conviction constitutes a powerful form of "status degradation" which continues to operate after the time when, according to the generalized theory of justice underlying punishment in our society, the individual's "debt" has been paid. A record of conviction produces a durable if not permanent loss of status. For purposes of effective social control, this state of affairs may heighten the deterrent effect of conviction—though that remains to be established. Any such contribution

> to social control, however, must be balanced against the barriers imposed upon rehabilitation of the convict. If the ex-prisoner finds difficulty in securing menial kinds of legitimate work, further crime may become an increasingly attractive alternative.[11]

The authors correctly note the fateful negative consequences of an assault conviction for the ex-offender, but they do not comment on the reasonableness of the employer's lack of interest in a job applicant with a prior assault conviction. The employer does not and cannot know how much risk is indicated by the prior assault conviction, but will reasonably conclude that it indicates greater risk than an applicant with a spotless criminal record. Unless the ex-offender has special qualifications that outweigh the risk of future misconduct, the employer will likely prefer to hire one of the many job applicants with no assault convictions on their record. While there is a substantial public interest in ex-offenders being hired, the particular employer has no such interest.

Almost forty years after Schwartz and Skolnick, sociologist Devah Pager launched a more sophisticated field experiment.[12] She sent pairs of student job applicants to contact employers. Two white students comprised one pair and two black students the other. The students in each pair were matched on all attributes and had identical curricula vitae, except that one student of each pair disclosed having served an eighteen-month prison term for a drug crime. The two pairs contacted different randomly selected employers. The white job seeker with no criminal record received twice as many positive employer responses as his white matched colleague with a drug conviction and prison sentence (34 percent vs. 17 percent). The African American job seeker with no criminal record received positive interest from 14 percent of employers, while his African American matched colleague with a prior drug crime conviction and prison sentence received positive responses from just 5 percent of employers. The experiment clearly demonstrated that a felony drug conviction reduced employer interest by 50 percent for whites and 65 percent for blacks. *Strikingly, the experiment also revealed even greater racial discrimination than conviction-based discrimination.*

Both Schwartz and Skolnick's and Pager's field experiments provide powerful evidence that even a single conviction (indeed, even an acquittal) is a powerful barrier to obtaining employment. Their findings are confirmed by Professor Harry Holzer and colleagues' employer surveys. They interviewed 3,000 employers from 1992 to 1994 in Atlanta, Boston, Detroit, and Los Angeles, followed by a survey of 600 L.A. employers. Of these employer respondents, 42.1 percent said that they would "definitely not" or "probably not" hire a person with a criminal record; 35 percent said that their willingness would depend on the particular crimes.[13] (Thus, we can assume that for prior serious offense convictions, at least 77.1% of employers would not hire the ex-offender.) A 2002 survey of 122 California employers found that, while 84 percent of respondents would consider hiring someone with a misdemeanor conviction, just 23 percent would consider hiring someone with a drug-related felony, 7 percent would consider hiring someone with a property-related felony, and less than 1 percent would consider hiring a person with a violent felony conviction.[14] The significance of a criminal record as a barrier to employment is strikingly illuminated by comparing employers' attitudes toward hiring applicants with different "black marks" on their résumés. While just 20 percent of employers were definitely or probably willing to hire an ex-offender, the comparable figure for welfare recipients was 93 percent; general equivalency diploma, 97 percent; spotty employment history, 66 percent; and unemployment for a year or more, 80 percent.[15]

Employer surveys should be treated with caution.* As Pager points out, employers' hiring practices are often less generous to ex-offenders than their survey answers indicate. She and Lincoln Quillian compared employers' expressed willingness to hire ex-offenders with their actual hiring practices. Employers who told

* On account of ideological and moral preference or on account of their business models, some employers are happy to hire ex-offenders. Respondent to a survey of companies that intentionally hire ex-offenders praised ex-offenders' enthusiasm, desire to succeed, and appreciation and loyalty. See Jennifer Fahey et al., *Employment of Ex-offenders: Employer Perspectives,* at 12 (Crime and Justice Institute, October 31, 2006, Final Report).

survey researchers that they were ready and willing to hire people with criminal records were, in practice, no more likely to hire an ex-offender than those employer respondents who said they would not.[16]

Should Conviction-Based Employment Discrimination Be Prohibited?

Title VII of the 1964 Civil Rights Act prohibits public and private employers from discriminating against job applicants and employees on the basis of race, ethnicity, religion, or gender, unless the employer can demonstrate a business necessity for such discrimination.[17] Other laws prohibit employment discrimination on the basis of age and physical disability. These discriminations are widely, almost universally, condemned as immoral and irrational. There is a strong societal consensus in support of laws prohibiting discrimination based on a person's race, religion, ethnicity, gender, age, or physical disability. However, CBED is looked at differently because the former list represents innate characteristics beyond a person's control (or, in the case of religion, a person should not have to make a choice on account of other people's prejudices). Public policy strongly condemns criminal conduct. Punishing and deterring criminal conduct is necessary for public order and community life. Government has a legitimate interest in protecting the public, especially vulnerable elements of the public, from threats to safety and well-being. Moreover, government itself engages in pervasive discrimination against persons with criminal records. It would be hypocritical to compel businesses, volunteer organizations, and other entities to put aside prejudices against persons with criminal records when the legislature mandates the exercise of discrimination and disqualification.

Government certainly has a legitimate concern in promoting ex-offender employment. However, while ex-offenders need jobs, so do people with no criminal record. When an ex-offender is passed over for a job, that job does not disappear, but is filled by someone who may be equally or even more needy. Job seekers with a spotless criminal record biography would have a valid complaint against a government policy that compelled private employers to treat a criminal record as irrelevant. Such a policy might undermine a person's commitment to obeying the law. Imagine the incentives that would be created by a publicly announced policy of job preferences for ex-offenders! One might persuasively argue that to bolster popular commitment to law-abiding conduct, job applicants with an unblemished record of law-abiding conduct should get a preference (reward).

Regulating CBED

While neither federal nor state laws absolutely prohibit employment discrimination based on a criminal record, a few states do restrict such discrimination. Hawaii, New York, and Wisconsin make employment discrimination against ex-offenders unlawful,[18] unless an employer can show that successful performance of the job would be jeopardized by a person with a propensity for the kind of crime of which the job seeker had previously been convicted.[19]

New York law states that

> [n]o application for any license or employment, and no employment or license held by an individual, to which the provisions of this article are applicable, shall be denied or acted upon adversely by reason of the individual's having been previously convicted of one or more criminal offenses, or by reason of a finding of lack of "good moral character" when such finding is based upon the fact that the individual has previously been convicted of one or more criminal offenses, unless:
>
> (1) There is a direct relationship between one or more of the previous criminal offenses and the specific license or employment sought or held by the individual; or
>
> (2) the issuance or continuation of the license or the granting or continuation of the employment would involve an unreasonable risk to property or to the safety or welfare of specific individuals or the general public.

While, at first blush, this statute would seem to prohibit CBED, the two caveats are quite expansive. The employer is free to discriminate if "there is a direct relationship between one or more of the previous criminal offenses and the specific license or employment sought." Direct relationship means that "the nature of criminal conduct for which the person was convicted has a direct bearing on his fitness or ability to perform one or more of the duties or responsibilities necessarily related to the license, opportunity, or job in question." Might an employer be able to say that the defendant's conviction for a property or drug offense renders him unfit to handle money or valuable property? Likewise, might the employer be able to plausibly say that the job applicant's conviction for either a property or violent crime makes him an unreasonable risk to the employer's property and to the safety of customers, clients and fellow employees? Alternatively, the employer might deny being influenced by the prior conviction, saying only that it preferred another candidate with better work experience, education, or interpersonal skills as demonstrated at the interview. In other words, the ex-offender who is not hired will have a very difficult time proving that the reason was CBED; even if he could prove it, the two affirmative defenses available to the employer seem relatively easy to satisfy.

The New York statute and similar anti-CBED laws and proposals erroneously assume that offenders are specialists who present only a specific type of risk, but research shows that many individuals who engage in criminal conduct are generalists and opportunists.[20] Today's burglar may be tomorrow's drug dealer. The person who beat up his girlfriend may fight with fellow employees and sell drugs.

Couldn't an employer reasonably and legitimately consider honesty, reliability, and self-discipline to be highly desirable qualities for every job? Moreover, isn't it reasonable for a company that is hiring for an entry-level job to prefer applicants who will be capable of filling in where needed and who will, in time, be candidates for promotion? If so, the company ought to be permitted to consider the conviction's relevance for a number of possible positions, in addition to the one applied for.

Focusing on the fit between the conviction offense and a job's requirements ignores plea-bargaining. The offense for which the job applicant was convicted may not accurately reflect the underlying criminal conduct. Perhaps a person with an assault conviction was originally charged with attempted rape? Perhaps a defendant who pled guilty to a drug charge was originally charged with illegal possession of a firearm as well? To add complications, we cannot assume, as many CBED critics do, that ex-offender job seekers have only one prior conviction. Surely, the employer is entitled to consider all previous convictions, separately and cumulatively.

CBED's Disparate Impact on Blacks and Hispanics

While discrimination on the basis of a criminal record is neither immoral nor illegal, discrimination on the basis of race is both. If CBED is a pretense for racial discrimination, it is and should be unlawful. But how will fact finders be able to determine if the employer's preference for employees without a criminal record is a pretense for racial discrimination?

In *Griggs v. Duke Power Co* (1971),[21] the Supreme Court interpreted Title VII of the Civil Rights Act of 1964 to prohibit use of hiring tests or other employment screening devices which, while neutral on their face, have a *disproportionate or disparate impact* on a protected group.[22] Proof of disparate impact establishes a presumption of racial discrimination, which the employer can overcome by showing that its screening device is justified by business necessity. *Griggs* and its progeny have generated massive litigation over hiring tests and screening criteria, like a criminal record.[23]

The use of a criminal record to screen job applicants has a disparate impact on African Americans and Hispanics because they are disproportionately likely to have criminal records.[24] African Americans constitute approximately 13 percent of the U.S. population but account for 28 percent of arrestees[25] and 45 percent of persons convicted of crime.[26] Thus, screening out job applicants with criminal records would violate the Title VII rights of Blacks and Hispanics unless the employer demonstrates that its CBED is justified by business necessity. (An employer could, of course, screen out whites, Asians, and others on the basis of a criminal record without raising any Title VII issue.)

In *Albemarle Paper Co. v. Moody* (1975), the Supreme Court handed down an employer-friendly decision on business necessity.[27] According to the court, to prove business necessity, the defendant-employer has to show that a hiring criterion resulting in a disparate impact "is predictive of or significantly correlated with important elements of work behavior which comprise or are relevant to the job or jobs for which candidates are being evaluated." In another Title VII decision, *New York City Transit Authority v. Beazer* (1979), the court approved the Transit Authority's disqualification of individuals who use or possess methadone from any transit job, including "non-sensitive" positions, because there is a "manifest relationship to the employment in question"; the methadone disqualification serves legitimate safety and efficiency goals.[28] The court seemed to accept the employer's commonsense rationale: for a mass transit company, drug-using employees pose a greater risk than non-drug-using employees. Had the court required the Transit Authority to prove statistically that methadone users cause more workplace accidents and other problems than non–methadone users, the company probably would not have prevailed. Such statistics are much harder to find or produce than many critics assume. Ten years later, in *Wards Cove Packing Co. v. Antonio* (1989), the Supreme Court further weakened the disparate impact doctrine by holding that a hiring standard or test meets the business necessity test if it "serve[s], in a significant way, the legitimate employment goals of the employer."[29]

Congress stopped the erosion of the disparate impact doctrine with 1991 amendments to Title VII that restored the pre–*Wards Cove* understanding of disparate impact and business necessity.[30] However, federal district courts continued to find the disparate impact doctrine confusing. Some judges give short shrift to attacks on the use of a criminal record to screen out job seekers, holding either that disparate impact analysis does not even apply to criminal record employment screening or, if it does apply, that employers can easily prove a valid business necessity. For example, in *Scott v. Genuine Parts Co.*, a federal court in Indiana upheld the company's refusal to hire a job applicant who had several drug trafficking convictions and had failed a drug test while employed by a previous company.[31]

> In cases similar to this, courts have upheld the employer's decision not to hire or to terminate. *See, e.g., Kehrer v. City of Springfield*, (female applicant's criminal history, among other factors, was a legitimate, non-discriminatory reason for removing ap-

> plicant's name from employment eligibility); *Redding v. Chicago Transit Authority*, (applicant's positive drug test was a legitimate, non-discriminatory reason for refusing to hire); *Matthews v. Runyon* (At best, the plaintiff charges that [the employer] places inordinate weight on an applicant's prior convictions and/or pending criminal charges, a claim clearly not cognizable under Title VII); *Heerdink v. Amoco Oil Co.*, (employer's business decision to hire a more experienced truck driver did not violate female truck driver's right under Title VII); *Grooms v. Wiregrass Electric Cooperative, Inc.*, (commercial driver's positive drug test conducted pursuant to the DOT regulations was a legitimate, non-discriminatory reason for adverse employment action).

Likewise, in *EEOC v. Carolina Freight Carriers*,[32] a federal district court in Florida upheld a company's lifetime employment bar on individuals ever incarcerated for felony theft.[33] The court dismissed out of hand a Hispanic plaintiff's argument that disparate impact of the company's policy violated Title VII.

> Obviously a rule refusing honest employment to convicted applicant is going to have a disparate impact upon thieves. That some thieves are going to be Hispanic is immaterial. That apparently a higher percentage of Hispanics are convicted of crimes than that of the "White" population may prove a number of things such as: (1) Hispanics are not very good at stealing, (2) Whites are better thieves than Hispanics, (3) none of the above, (4) all of the above. . . . If Hispanics do not wish to be discriminated against because they have been convicted of theft, *they should stop stealing*.[34]

It would have sufficed and been less tendentious for the judge to have said that an employment policy screening out persons convicted of theft substantially serves an employer's legitimate interest in protecting its business and staff.

Some courts have been more sympathetic to claims of disparate impact caused by CBED. For example, In *Green v. Missouri Pacific Railroad Company*,[35] the Eighth Circuit Court of Appeals, having previously expressed doubts about using prior convictions to screen employees,[36] criticized a railroad company's policy of refusing to hire persons with prior convictions. The court noted that African Americans are 2.2 to 6.7 times as likely as whites to be convicted and that, in urban areas, 36.9–78.1 percent of African Americans would be convicted of a crime at some point in their lives, compared with 11.6–16.8 percent of whites. The court concluded that these statistics establish a prima facie case of disparate impact because the railroad's policy denied employment to 5.3 percent of African-American applicants compared to 2.23 percent of white applicants.

The railroad claimed business necessity, offering several risks posed by job applicants with prior criminal convictions for theft: (1) cargo theft, (2) handling company funds, (3) bonding qualifications, (4) impeachment if called as a witness, (5) liability for negligent hiring, (6) missing work if charged with new crime, and (7) lack of moral character. The court rejected these justifications because the company had not empirically validated its hypothesis that persons without a recorded conviction have a higher probability of being successful employees than those with a recorded conviction. Its opinion observed that if all employers followed the railroad's policy, ex-offenders would be permanently unemployed. However, it said that a narrower criminal record exclusion policy would be justifiable. For example, an individual with an embezzlement conviction might be excludable from a position that involved handling money.[37] The court then sent the case back to the trial court to determine whether, under that interpretation, the company's policy was justifiable.

The company amended its policy. Henceforth, it would treat criminal history as a "factor" rather than an absolute disqualification. The Eighth Circuit affirmed the district court's approval of this policy as long as the employer considered the nature and gravity of the prior convictions, the time elapsed since the completion of the sentence, and the nature of the job for which the applicant has applied.[38] The opinion does not define "consider"—that is, how much weight the employer can give to a job applicant's criminal record. Can the employer consider a felony conviction in the past five years presumptively disqualifying unless the record-subject has an extraordinary postconviction record of rehabilitation? Can the employer consider the pre-plea-bargained charges rather than conviction to which the job applicant pled guilty? Suppose the employer said "we considered the rejected job applicant's prior conviction(s) a minor negative because the person we hired had outstanding qualifications?"

The U.S. Equal Employment Opportunity Commission and CBED

The U.S. Equal Employment Opportunity Commission (EEOC) can enforce Title VII. Toward that end, it issues "guidances" on various aspects of federal employment law.[39] A guidance is not legally binding, but it is influential with courts, commentators, and human resources departments. The guidance on criminal records states:

> The following are examples of best practices for employers who are considering criminal record information when making employment decisions.
>
> *General*
>
> - Eliminate policies or practices that exclude people from employment based on any criminal record.
> - Train managers, hiring officials, and decision-makers about Title VII and its prohibition on employment discrimination.
>
> *Developing a Policy*
>
> - Develop a narrowly tailored written policy and procedure for screening applicants and employees for criminal conduct.
> - Identify essential job requirements and the actual circumstances under which the jobs are performed.
> - Determine the specific offenses that may demonstrate unfitness for performing such jobs.
> - Identify the criminal offenses based on all available evidence.
> - Determine the duration of exclusions for criminal conduct based on all available evidence.
> - Include an individualized assessment.

- Record the justification for the policy and procedures.
- Note and keep a record of consultations and research considered in crafting the policy and procedures.
- Train managers, hiring officials, and decision-makers on how to implement the policy and procedures consistent with Title VII.

Questions about Criminal Records

- When asking questions about criminal records, limit inquiries to records for which exclusion would be job related for the position in question and consistent with business necessity.

Confidentiality

- Keep information about applicants' and employees' criminal records confidential. Only use it for the purpose for which it was intended.

On a number of points, the EEOC's guidance is not clear. Consider: "When asking questions about criminal records, limit your inquiries to records for which exclusion would be job related for the position in question and consistent with business necessity." How many offenses could the employer ask about? Would the EEOC object to an employer asking a minority job applicant to disclose all convictions in order to identify convictions relevant to the sought-after position?

When the EEOC has sued employers who discriminate on the basis of a criminal record, it has sometimes met substantial judicial resistance. For example, the U.S. District Court in Maryland dismissed an EEOC suit against Freeman, Inc. The EEOC alleged that Freeman unlawfully relied on credit and criminal background reports that had a disparate impact on African American and Hispanic job applicants. The court first observed that credit and criminal background checks are legitimate and important:

> Because of the higher rate of incarceration of African-Americans than Caucasians, indiscriminate use of criminal history infor-

> mation might have the predictable result of excluding African-Americans at a higher rate than Caucasian. Indeed, the higher rate might cause one to fear that any use of criminal history information would be in violation of Title VII. However, this is simply not the case. Careful and appropriate use of criminal history information is an important, and in many cases essential, part of the employment process of employers throughout the United States. As Freeman points out, even the EEOC conducts criminal background investigations as a condition of employment for all positions, and conducts credit background checks on approximately 90 percent of its positions.[40]

The court criticized the EEOC's effort to prove disparate impact based on statistical disparities, calling the EEOC's expert reports "laughable," "based on unreliable data," and "rife with analytical error." According to the court, these reports contained "a plethora of errors and analytical fallacies" and a "mind-boggling number of errors." It went on to call the reports "completely unreliable," "so full of material flaws that any evidence of disparate impact derived from an analysis of its contents must necessarily be disregarded," "distorted," "both over and under inclusive," "cherry-picked," "worthless," and "an egregious example of scientific dishonesty." The court held that the EEOC failed to meets its prima facie burden because it failed to identify specific policy or policies causing the alleged disparate impact and made "no effort to break down what is clearly a multi-faceted, multi-step policy."

CBED Based on Previous Arrests

Some employers choose not to hire job seekers or to retain employees on the basis of an arrest that did not (or has not yet) resulted in a conviction. At first blush, it seems preposterous that a police officer has the de facto power to saddle an individual with a lifelong employment disability.[41] In fact, however, drawing a negative inference about a person because of an arrest for a serious crime is common. For example, liberal New York senator Charles Schumer recently introduced a bill that would render an individual who had ever been arrested for a drug offense ineligible to purchase a firearm.[42]

An employer is clearly not required to consider a job applicant "innocent until proven guilty," an evidentiary rule that applies to the prosecutor's burden of proof at trial.[43] An employer might rationally think that if the police had probable cause to arrest X, and a prosecutor believed it was proper to charge X, and a grand jury indicted X, his company could pass over X's job application and move on to consider other job seekers.

It may seem odd that an employer can base its hiring decision on a recorded arrest, but it is no more odd than an employer basing its hiring decision on a previous employer's suggestion or hint that the applicant had been dismissed for dishonesty. Suppose a detective told an employer that a job applicant's neighbors considered the applicant to be involved in gang or organized crime activity? Must the employer ignore that information because it has not been proved beyond a reasonable doubt? Isn't it widely believed that Catholic Church leaders should have defrocked or at least isolated priests against whom there were credible complaints of sexual misconduct? Church critics would rightly scoff at the notion that it was not incumbent on church leaders to act until a priest was found guilty beyond a reasonable doubt.

What inference can be drawn from an arrest? It depends. An arrest occurs when a police officer, believing that she has probable cause to assume that an individual has committed or is about to commit a crime, takes the suspect into custody. The police officer's judgment might be wrong or even maliciously motivated. However, in the vast majority of cases, it has a basis in fact. Couldn't an employer reasonably assume that an arrest was based on probable cause? If not, can the employer reach that conclusion once the prosecutor files formal charges based on the officer's arrest report? If not, once a judge finds probable cause? Once a grand jury issues an indictment? Must employers ignore pending charges?

The principal reason for not filing or for dropping charges is the victim's unwillingness to testify, perhaps because the process is too time-consuming or perhaps due to fear of retaliation by the perpetrator or his friends. Sometimes the victim herself has reasons to avoid involvement with the police. Sometimes key evidence may have been held inadmissible because of an unlawful search, but that does not mean that an employer or any other organization or individual must consider the defendant to be factually innocent. Some prosecutions are dismissed because the prosecutor failed to obtain an indictment in compliance with the speedy trial act; that doesn't mean that the dismissal beneficiary is factually innocent. In many jurisdictions, a significant percentage of cases are dismissed (either before or after charges are filed) through deferred prosecution (pretrial diversion), the parties agreeing that if the defendant does not "get into trouble" for a specified period (typically six months), charges will be dropped; that, too, does not call into question the likelihood that the arrested person committed the crime for which she was arrested.

Title VII and Arrests

Title VII's disparate impact doctrine provides a remedy for African American and Hispanic (but not white or Asian American) job applicants who are automatically disqualified for employment on account of prior arrests. According to the EEOC's Enforcement Guidance on the Consideration of Arrest and Conviction Records in Employment Decisions under Title VI, "since the use of arrest records as an absolute bar to employment has a disparate impact on some protected groups, such records alone cannot be used to routinely exclude persons from employment."[44] However, the guidance advises employers that it can reject the minority job applicant on the basis of "*conduct* which indicates unsuitability for a particular position . . . where it appears that the applicant or employee engaged in the conduct for which he was arrested and that the conduct is job-related and relatively recent, exclusion is justified." What could this mean? The guidance explains that

> [a]n employer may deny employment opportunities to persons based on any prior conduct which indicates that they would be unfit for the position in question, whether that conduct is evidenced by an arrest, conviction or other information provided to the employer. It is the *conduct*, not the arrest or conviction *per se*, which the employer may consider in relation to the position sought.

The guidance provides examples:

> Example 1:
>
> Wilma, a Black female, applies to Bus Inc. in Highway City for a position as a bus driver. In response to a pre-employment inquiry, Wilma states that she was arrested two years earlier for driving while intoxicated. Bus Inc. rejects Wilma, despite her acquittal after trial. Bus Inc. does not accept her denial of the conduct alleged and concludes that Wilma was acquitted only because the breathalyzer test which was administered to her at the time of her arrest was not administered in accordance with proper police procedures and was therefore inadmissible at trial. Witnesses at Wilma's trial testified that after being stopped for reckless driving, Wilma staggered from the car and had alcohol on her breath. Wilma's rejection is justified because the conduct underlying the arrest, driving while intoxicated, is clearly related to the safe performance of the duties of a bus driver; it occurred fairly recently; and there was no indication of subsequent rehabilitation.

How is the employer supposed to find out this information? Must it conduct an investigation, that is, ask Wilma where she was arrested, then contact the police and/or prosecutor's office for an account of the case? Suppose the harried prosecutor's office doesn't take the call (not a farfetched assumption if a large number of employers began deluging the office with queries about previously arrested persons) or can't/won't locate the person who prosecuted the case (maybe the assistant prosecutor left the office). Suppose the relevant prosecutor is located but doesn't remember this case and says she's too busy to dig out the file. If the prosecutor does provide the employer with an explanation as far as she recalls, is that good enough for a negative hiring decision, or must the employer contact the defense lawyer to get Wilma's explanation?

Suppose Wilma admits the arrest but says the charges ended in an acquittal. (As we saw in Chapter 2, rap sheets frequently lack dispositions.) Must the employer ask Wilma to provide proof of the acquittal? If so, this is likely to take weeks, even if Wilma is willing to spend the time and bear the expense of obtaining the required document. By that time, the position may already have been filled.

Let's look at Example 2.

Example 2:

Lola, a Black female, applies to Bus Inc. for a position as a bus driver. In response to an inquiry whether she had ever been arrested, Lola states that she was arrested five years earlier for fraud in unemployment benefits. Lola admits that she committed the crime alleged. She explains that she received unemployment benefits shortly after her husband died and her expenses increased. During this period, she worked part-time for minimum wage because her unemployment check amounted to slightly less than the monthly rent for her meager apartment. She did not report the income to the State Unemployment Board for fear that her payments would be reduced and that she would not be able to feed her three young children. After her arrest, she agreed to, and did, repay the state. Bus Inc. rejected Lola. Lola's rejection violated Title VII. The commission of fraud on the unemployment system does not constitute a business justification for the rejection of an applicant for the position of bus driver. The type of crime which Lola committed is totally unrelated to her ability to safely, efficiently and/or courteously drive a bus. Furthermore, the arrest is not recent.

Must the employer accept Lola's explanation as true? Can the employer choose not to hire Lola because the company has experienced a good deal of bus driver embezzlement? Would it make a difference that the candidate whom the employer wishes to hire is also an African American female?

The EEOC's guidance requires the employer to consider Lola's application. What does "consider" mean? Suppose the bus company says that it considered Lola's job application, but her admitted fraud made her slightly less desirable than another candidate? Suppose the bus company says that Lola wasn't "rejected," but that the company was more impressed with another applicant? Many employers will be tempted to evade the guidance by providing other reasons (e.g., lack of experience, poor interview) why the candidate with the criminal record was not selected.

Acquittals

A background check based on court records may reveal an acquittal. (However, in New York and a few other states, dismissals, acquittals, and other dispositions favorable to the defendant are supposed to be sealed.)[45] Must an employer regard a not guilty verdict as equivalent to factual innocence? The Supreme Court considered a version of this issue in *Watts v. United States*, where the issue was whether a federal judge at sentencing could enhance a defendant's sentence on the basis of conduct for which the defendant had previously been acquitted. In reviewing the Federal Sentencing Guidelines and pre-Guidelines case law, the court stated: "Indeed, under the pre-Guidelines sentencing regime, it was "well established that a sentencing judge may take into account facts introduced at trial relating to other charges, even ones of which the defendant has been acquitted. The Guidelines did not alter this aspect of the sentencing court's discretion."[46] The court explained that "acquittal on criminal charges does not prove that the defendant is innocent; it merely proves the existence of a reasonable doubt as to his guilt." If a sentencing judge is entitled to enhance a sentence on the basis of criminal conduct for which the defendant was acquitted, can't an employer decide not to hire the acquitted job seeker? Surely an employer does not need to have proof beyond a reasonable doubt in order to decide that a job applicant is likely to be unreliable, dishonest, or dangerous.

Government Can Lead by Example

Government (federal, state, local) is a huge employer. If it were to decide, for policy reasons, to ignore job seekers' past criminal convictions, it could vastly increase job opportunities for ex-offenders without violating anyone's right to make their own business decisions and personal choices. The Ban the Box movement has persuaded more than forty counties and municipalities as well as ten state governments to cease asking job applicants to disclose prior convictions on their initial employment application.[47] When and if the applicant passes the initial screening and becomes a serious candidate for a position, she will be asked to disclose her criminal record, and/or a criminal background check will be conducted. In initially ignoring past criminal convictions for most public sector jobs, government employers could set a persuasive example, which if successful, many private sector employers and voluntary associations might be persuaded to emulate.

Target Stores' Ban the Box

Target Stores, the nation's second largest retailer, decided in late 2013 to ban the box. This is an excellent example of the influence that voluntary CBED reform in the public sector can have on voluntary CBED policy change in the private sector. In 2013, in response to intense lobbying by the NAACP and a grassroots advocacy group, TakeAction Minnesota, Minnesota passed a law prohibiting state employers from asking job applicants about prior arrests and convictions until after they are selected for an interview. After succeeding with the state law, TakeAction Minnesota launched a series of protests at Target's national headquarters (located in Minneapolis) and filed ten unfair labor practices against Target. After meeting with the protesters, Target announced that it would follow the state's Ban the Box policy and look at additional ways to boost hiring of ex-convicts. This signals a major development in changing attitudes toward ex-convicts. It remains to be seen how much actual impact it will have since Target and public sector Ban the Box adopters reserve the right to ask about a criminal record after the job applicant has passed the initial screening.

Conclusion

Legitimate employment is nearly a prerequisite for successful rehabilitation. The first aim of public policy should be to scale back de jure discrimination against persons with criminal records. The second aim should be for government employers to set an example. The third aim should be to encourage private sector employers to give ex-offenders a second (or third or fourth) chance. Encouragement does not mean compulsion. Absent invidious discrimination, private employers should be free to hire whomever they like. With three-year recidivism rates as high as 68 percent,[48] the government ought not to prohibit employers from considering a criminal conviction predictive of future dishonesty, unreliability, and lack of compliance with company policies and rules, certainly not within that three-year time frame. (Admittedly, recidivism would be lower if ex-offenders had legitimate jobs. It is also true that recidivism is not likely to take place on the job.)

In his 2004 State of the Union address, President George W. Bush surprised many observers by declaring: "We know from long experience that if they can't find work, or a home, or help, they are much more likely to commit more crimes and return to prison. . . . America is the land of the second chance, and when the gates of the prison open, the path ahead should lead to a better life."[49] The Second Chance Act of 2007 contained a number of provisions meant to improve the employability of ex-offenders.[50] The act authorized federal grants to government agencies and nonprofit organizations to provide employment assistance, housing, substance abuse treatment, family programming, mentoring, and related services. It also established the National Offender Re-entry Resource Center to manage, monitor, and disseminate information to service providers and community organizations delivering services. The federal government has also encouraged employers to hire ex-offenders by offering them tax incentives.

Race is a complicating factor. African Americans and Hispanics are disproportionately arrested and convicted. Therefore, employment discrimination based on a criminal record will disproportionately impact members of these minority groups. This, too, is highly undesirable from a societal standpoint; it is and should be unlawful to use the criminal record as a pretext for a racist hiring policy. However, the aggressive application of Title VII's disparate impact doctrine to strike down discrimination on the basis of a criminal record is unfair and undesirable. It may also not benefit African Americans and Hispanics as a group. Professor Shawn Bushway, an economist specializing in criminology, has persuasively argued that a policy prohibiting employers from using a prior criminal record in hiring would advantage minority group members who have a criminal record while disadvantaging minority group members who do not have a criminal record. He believes that if employers were denied access to criminal record information, consciously or unconsciously, they would assume that minority job applicants have a criminal record and be reluctant to hire them.[51]

Courts should normally consider hiring policy that screens for honesty, integrity, sobriety, and self-discipline to be a business necessity for all positions. Employers should not be required to show the relevance of a particular past conviction for a particular job. It is reasonable for an employer to insist on an expectation that over time every person hired will move on to other jobs within the firm. Even if a past theft conviction is not relevant to the successful performance of duties in a current job, it might be relevant to a future position in the firm. Choosing not to hire or do business with a previously convicted defendant is no more immoral than discriminating on the basis of previous unsatisfactory job performance or poor educational achievement. Ex-offenders, like school dropouts or dishonorably discharged soldiers, but unlike members of minority groups, are responsible for their tainted biography. An employer should not be condemned for preferring to hire a person who has performed well at her last job to one who has performed poorly or preferring to hire a person who has been successful in school and college to a person with a poor educational record.

It is important to remember that when an ex-offender is not hired, the job does not disappear. It goes to another job seeker who may be equally or even more in need of legitimate employment. In fact, if the society's interest in preventing crime is behind the impulse to give preference to ex-offender job applicants, it should be pointed out that the non-ex-offender who is passed over might himself turn to crime to make money. This hypothesis is even more plausible if the out-of-work job seeker with no criminal record comes to feel that there is no reward for following a law-abiding path. Indeed, the law-abiding job seeker might think that public policy gives ex-offenders an advantage in the competition for employment. This does not mean that government should not encourage hiring ex-offenders with tax incentives and similar benefits. However, it would be better to extend such incentives to disadvantaged workers generally, rather than focusing them particularly on ex-offenders.

15 CONCLUSION

WE MUST STOP assuming that our policies regarding the dissemination and use of criminal records are the only ones possible. The criminal records that we have and how they are used are the product of policy choices, sometimes explicit and sometimes implicit, but always choices. Focusing on criminal records opens a window on the labeling, marking, and biography-creating role of the criminal justice system and its profound impact on social stratification. The main purpose of individual criminal history records may once have been to keep track of criminal cases, but as record keeping evolved into criminal biography making, criminal records came to determine how suspects are identified, investigated, arrested, detained, typed, charged, negotiated with, sentenced, monitored on probation, and classified in prison. It evolved further to become a crucial marker of public identity.

The revolution in information technology has impacted the criminal justice system, just as it has impacted every other societal sector. It has forced legislatures, law enforcement agencies, and courts to decide whether court records should be digitized and made accessible to the public; whether the names, photographs, and addresses of "sex offenders" should be posted on the Internet; and whether police officers should populate a database with suspicions about gang membership that can be accessed by thousands of police officers. Intelligence databases are expanding to include noncriminals, like visa violators and persons subject to protection orders. Law enforcement agencies have practically unfettered authority to collect, store, collate, and retrieve information about people who might have committed crimes in the past or who might commit crimes in the future. Concern about such overreach has been voiced by many mental health advocates, who are opposed to expanding the National Instant Criminal Background

Check System (NICS) database to include the names of persons who, for reasons of past or current mental illness, should not be permitted to purchase firearms.

First Amendment purists and open government advocates believe that more information is always better than less information. They argue that when it comes to combatting crime, criminal justice agencies and courts do a better and fairer job of preventing and solving crime when they have more information at their disposal. I agree, but take seriously the admonitions of many criminologists who caution against overestimating our capacity to predict future criminality. They also remind us that criminality (at least street crime) declines with age, whether or not the individual has a lengthy criminal biography. Moreover, Bernard Harcourt's *Against Prediction* raises the possibility that focusing law enforcement attention on people with prior convictions might not be the most efficient crime control policy if it diverts attention away from those without a criminal record, thereby reducing their expected cost of criminality. In addition, we should keep in mind the labeling theorists' thesis: treating people with prior records more severely at every stage of the criminal justice process creates an "us and them" reality. People are indelibly typed, indeed stereotyped as "usual suspects" and criminals. So labeled, they are reinforced in their criminal identities, roles, and self-conceptions.

The debate over whether the criminal justice system assigns too much significance to prior criminal records mostly arises in the context of sentencing. Current sentencing regimes give prior convictions a great deal of weight; under the Federal Sentencing Guidelines, a defendant in the highest criminal history category is likely to be punished two to three times more severely than a defendant who has no prior convictions. An even more extreme example can be found in the controversial three-strikes laws, which catapult a third conviction for a marginal felony, otherwise deserving of probation or a short jail term, into a life sentence. Debate about the impact that prior record should have on sentencing is important, but should be broadened to include other decision-making contexts, including law enforcement's decision to arrest, judges' decision to release or detain pretrial, prosecutors' decisions on what charges to bring and what pleas to offer and accept, and correctional officials' classification decisions.

It is extraordinary how criminal records have migrated from their birthplaces in law enforcement, adjudication, and corrections to every nook and cranny of society. Public and private employers, governmental and professional licensing bodies, armed services, public and private landlords, volunteer organizations, and some colleges and universities routinely commission criminal background checks. Some individuals hire criminal background checking companies or themselves conduct criminal background searches to find out about the possible criminal past of potential business associates, personal services providers, friends, and lovers.

Fifty years ago, practically no one, other than the police, knew anything about someone's criminal record. These days, pretty much anyone can find out anything about anybody's prior criminal history. In fact, the FBI actually conducts more fingerprint-based criminal records checks for non–criminal justice entities than for criminal justice agencies. And FBI records searches constitute a fraction of total non–criminal justice agency criminal background checking. Technology and a booming background checking industry, mostly utilizing court records, have put this information within everybody's reach. The information vendors aggressively encourage demand for individual criminal history information. Additionally, ordinary individuals carry out their own criminal background checking on publicly accessible websites, recently with the assistance of easy-to-use apps. In fact, a person's criminal record is a more easily accessible "credential" than his or her educational record and employment history.

What has migrated into society generally is not just raw information on convictions and arrests, but also the criminal justice system's classification of that information. Categories like felon and misdemeanant, violent offender, sex offender, white collar offender, drug trafficker, organized crime member, chronic offender, and career criminal are used by all manner of decision makers, despite the fact that they were created primarily for sentencing purposes. It is not an exaggeration to say that the criminal record is, for many, the most important marker of their public identity.

It is not irrational for businesses, not-for-profits, volunteer organizations, and individuals to commission criminal background checks on those with whom they do business or employ. It is desirable to enter business and social relationships with more information rather than less. In the business context, failure to search out such information might later be the basis for civil liability. It is a matter of due diligence for company officials to find out about the possible criminal histories of the officers of companies with whom they are considering a relationship. They have a legitimate interest and responsibility to minimize risk of harm to their businesses. Employers and landlords would be foolish to ignore potential tort liability that might result from hiring or renting to a person who has previously victimized someone in a similar context. Each of us wishes to minimize the risk of being victimized by crime. Character and personality are not chimeras. While some people's attitudes, values, characters, and personalities do change over time, past behavior is usually a good predictor of future behavior. In our daily interactions, we assume that a person who was generous and kind yesterday will act similarly tomorrow and the day after (we may be less willing to bet on how he will behave ten years from now); likewise, yesterday's bully and wise guy will probably be equally obnoxious next week and next month. Social life would be incredibly confusing if people did not act "in character."

Would we knowingly hire a previously convicted embezzler or fraudster as a financial adviser, a convicted drunk driver as a chauffeur or school bus driver, or a convicted thief as a housekeeper or babysitter? In general, we would prefer to hire and associate with people whose biographies indicate honesty, reliability, and self-control. Of course, common sense and experience tell us that some criminal biographies are more predictive of future conduct than others. Some crimes (e.g., smoking marijuana) are so common as to be normative, while others (e.g., armed robbery) are highly deviant. That an applicant to law school has smoked marijuana tells me nothing important about the likelihood that she will make a good lawyer, because it doesn't distinguish her from the majority of her peers. Telling me that she was recently convicted of insurance fraud or forgery places her in a very different category from her peers and raises a serious question about her character, propensities, and judgment.

The more recent a conviction, the more relevant it is to character assessment. If an ex-convict manages to remain crime-free for years without committing a new offense, it suggests that the earlier criminality was aberrational and not predictive of future conduct. This is especially true in cases where a person's first conviction(s) occurred during adolescence, a stage of human development often marked by impulsivity, poor judgment, and susceptibility to peer influence. Thus, there is good reason to discount or ignore adolescent criminality that did not recur in the years following adolescence.

We cannot be sure that a recent conviction was aberrational; we will need to wait and see. Repeated criminal behavior tells us more about an individual's character than a single criminal episode. Crimes that are planned are a better indicator of character than crimes that occurred on the spur of the moment; a complex multiyear fraud shows motivation, planning, and frequent consideration. It tells us much more about character than an assault stemming from a bar fight.

The usefulness of a criminal record as an indicator of character assumes that and depends on criminal record information being accurate. If we knew that criminal record information was seriously flawed and often mistaken, it would have little, if any, usefulness. Our criminal record information systems are not fundamentally flawed, but they are not accurate enough. Lack of dispositions on rap sheets can cause serious police and prosecutorial mistakes that lead to wrongful arrests, searches, and detention. However, in the criminal justice context, erroneous record information is usually quickly disputed by the defendant or his defense lawyer. By contrast, it is not easy to discover an erroneous record that is being used by employers and other non–criminal justice system decision makers who do not tell the record-subject why she was not chosen for a position. Even if discovered, it is difficult to correct errors that have been copied in numerous databases. Thus, it is important to strengthen and enforce the Fair Credit Reporting Act's requirements. Federal regulation is much more efficient and effective than state regulation.

Public policies have different goals than individual decision makers. While individuals seek to minimize their own risk of criminal victimization, government policy makers need to minimize the total amount of crime. From a societal standpoint, it is highly desirable, indeed crucial, that offenders desist from further offending. Toward that end, ex-offenders need to have a path back into law-abiding society. The absence of such a path defines convicted offenders as outlaws and consigns them to a life of crime. That is a terrible outcome for society.

Criminalization is meant to remediate and prevent injuries and threats to people, property, and social order, but punishment processes also create social problems, that is, a pool of people labeled criminal and relegated to a criminal subculture or effectively exiled to the periphery of legitimate society. Decriminalizing where possible (e.g., drugs, prostitution, minor assaults) would spare people a criminal record and perhaps reduce their marginalization. Years ago, this was done with "traffic violations," previously defined as criminal offenses. Dangerous driving certainly should be discouraged by hefty administrative fines, but imagine the problems (including the costs) that would result from treating traffic code violators as criminals. Overuse of criminal law undermines its deterrent potential.

Even where criminalization is necessary for retributive, deterrence, and incapacitative purposes, public policy need not and should not emphasize maximum feasible criminal enforcement. Consider that only a minuscule percentage of tax and insurance fraud violators are prosecuted; administrative fines and civil liability are by far the more common response to these criminal law violations. To take another example, although medical malpractice could often be prosecuted criminally, it almost never is. We saw in Chapter 6 that recognition of the negative consequences of a criminal record has led to the increasing popularity of pretrial diversion programs and deferred prosecution (adjournment in contemplation of dismissal). This is a salutary development.

Many legal commentators favor more criminal record confidentiality. Some steps in this direction are feasible. There is no need for law enforcement agencies to post offender registries online, much less attempt to deter crime by publishing the names of arrestees.

This is doubly true when it comes to mug shots. Police departments should not disclose mug shots as punishment or for deterrence. While the First Amendment makes it difficult to shut down websites that seek to extract fees from mug shot subjects, federal and state governments should continue to explore ways to address this form of blackmail.

Even if access to rap sheets could be cut back, and even if the police did not disclose their daily blotter to reporters and/or publish or post it online, almost all of the same information could be obtained from court records. The constitutional and political commitment to publicly accessible court records makes confidential convictions impossible and confidential arrests very unlikely. Of course courts do not have to sell their databases in bulk to commercial information vendors or make records electronically accessible via the Internet.

However, I believe that the momentum toward ever more public criminal records is inexorable. In the future, there will likely be continuing lobbying and legal challenges from the media and others who want access to still more information (e.g., presentence reports, cooperation agreements, probation and parole files) from police, prosecutors, courts, probation, jails, prisons, and parole agencies. Moreover, information security will become an even greater problem. It is extremely difficult to keep information confidential in the information age. We have seen extraordinary leaks of personal information from banks, retailers, and other private organizations as well as from government agencies, including the National Security Agency. It is very unlikely that budget-strapped law enforcement and correctional agencies will be able to devote significant resources to keeping information secure against internal leakers and external hackers. Once information is recorded, we should presume that it will or at least might become public. Thus, we should focus on such questions as what criminal justice system information to record and what databases to create. We should be particularly concerned with intelligence databases that implicitly label persons as crime risks although there is not enough evidence to arrest them. We should also be concerned about expanding the subject matter of police databases to include such categories as visa violators, "deadbeat dads," and persons subject to protection orders, not to mention categories for those who have done nothing even morally wrong, such as firearms owners, the mentally ill, and political dissidents.

The United States would benefit from creating different criminal records systems for criminal justice agencies and non–criminal justice agencies. Criminal records designed by and for police and prosecutors' use are not well suited to routine use by employers, landlords, voluntary associations, and other non–criminal justice consumers. Rap sheets are difficult for laypeople to read and often give an exaggerated impression of the record-subject's criminality. Moreover, if rap sheets are going to be disclosed to the general public, expeditiously recording dispositions is critical. New York and a few other states have already adopted information technology that transmits court judgments to the criminal record repository. Every jurisdiction should follow suit. If rap sheets are going to be routinely used by laypersons, they should be redesigned to be more user-friendly and they should provide more information about the charges than a bare notation of "assault" or "theft."

Expunging or sealing criminal records is largely futile. Contrary to what the word "expunge" implies, criminal records are not destroyed or erased. Some record of a conviction and an arrest must be retrievable for several purposes, including retrials and civil litigation. A serious problem with sealing documents in the digital age is that the information to be sealed is unlikely to exist only in the sealed file, record, or database. In addition, sealing only one or a few documents in the case file often results in mistaken disclosure of that information. Moreover, a sealing policy requires the support of subsidiary policies regarding how the beneficiary of the expunged or sealed record can/should respond to governmental agencies' and nongovernmental organizations' questions about the sealed information. Instructing the individual to lie is bad public policy. Even when the ex-offender has permission to lie, savvy employers will sometimes expose them as liars and sometimes assume that they are lying.

Widespread public access to criminal records would not be so important if the information did not carry such negative consequences for those with criminal records. The explosion of collateral consequences is the result of tough-on-crime politics, especially the war on drugs. Public policy should focus on significantly reducing the number of laws requiring discrimination against ex-offenders. These laws signal to society generally that ex-offenders represent a disreputable and dangerous caste. Reform should start with the principle that it is not desirable or justifiable for the government to inflict further punishment via collateral consequences on the convicted defendant after the sentence has been served.

This is easier stated than implemented because, with a few obvious (and important) exceptions (disenfranchisement, food stamps, student loans), it is extremely difficult to determine the purpose behind a particular criminal record disability or disqualification. For the vast majority of disabilities and disqualifications, a plausible safety and security rationale can be concocted. Each must be examined to determine whether there is a bona fide and reasonable relationship between the conviction(s) and the forfeiture, disqualification, or ineligibility. The result of such inquiry will, to a significant degree, turn on the level of scrutiny to which the disability is subjected.

If all that is required to justify an ex-offender disqualification is a plausible relationship between the disqualification and a public interest other than punishment, very few disqualifications will be eliminated. For example, disqualification of drug traffickers from public housing can be justified on the ground that drug users or sellers make bad neighbors and attract bad elements to buildings where tenants are struggling. Thus, the onus needs to fall on those arguing for the maintenance of collateral consequences. They should have to present a convincing case that the de jure discrimination against the person with a prior record is necessary to protect society against a significant risk of significant harm. What risks should be considered significant and which too speculative to worry about? Suppose X, who applies for a nurse's license, was convicted two years ago for possessing crack cocaine? How much risk is there that she might steal hospital drugs? Might sell drugs to staff or patients? Might be high on the job? Might negligently harm or kill a patient? There is no empirical evidence that can help us estimate such risks. It makes sense for a hospital and patients to prefer nurses without such convictions.

Congress and state legislatures are certainly not equipped to engage in a comprehensive examination of the justifiability of statutes mandating discrimination against all or some ex-offenders. Such work might be done by a single national commission (not commissions in every state) composed of criminologists, lawyers, and ex-offender and victims advocates. The commission would have to judge the magnitude and seriousness of the risk and then how much risk is tolerable. Perhaps a 10 percent risk of a repeat insurance fraud is more tolerable than a 10 percent risk of a repeat drunk driving?

Commentators who demand a "close relationship" between a conviction and a job oversimplify. Most often they choose an easy case—a job applicant or jobholder with an otherwise exemplary résumé and just one decade-old conviction. Although such cases do exist, there are more record-subjects who have accumulated more than one conviction, often many more. Drunk driving is a good conviction to consider because (1) it occurs frequently; (2) injury usually does not result, although serious and fatal injury is always possible; (3) drunk driving may be indicative of a serious alcohol problem that could manifest itself in other antisocial or dangerous conduct; and (4) a first offense is usually classified as a misdemeanor and a second offense (within, say, ten years) as a felony. Should two drunk-driving convictions in the past ten years disqualify one from adopting a baby? Serving as a police officer? Purchasing a firearm? Driving a bus? Suppose the record showed, in the last ten years, one DWI conviction, one domestic assault, and one embezzlement? There is an infinite combination of arrests and convictions to match up against a massive number of occupational licenses. On what basis could we say that a person with one of the above criminal records poses sufficient risk to be disqualified from one or more rights, opportunities, or employments?

Some ex-offender advocates urge government to prohibit private sector discretionary or de facto discrimination. In effect, they would treat private employment (and housing) discrimination based on criminal record in the same way as antidiscrimination laws prohibit race, gender, handicap, and age discrimination. Probably, they would make discrimination based on criminal record presumptively illegal unless the private employer could demonstrate a business necessity for discriminating.

I think that such a prohibition would be undesirable. People who have been convicted of crimes are not victims; in fact, they often are victimizers. They violated laws passed by legislatures and were prosecuted in the name of the people. Their condemnation and punishment served legitimate political interests and the ends of justice. To place convicted criminals on the list of protected groups would demean and perhaps weaken efforts to eradicate discrimination based on race, gender, physical disability, age, and sexual orientation. Those forms of discrimination are immoral and indefensible. By contrast, a morally acceptable case for discriminating against convicted persons can be made. Of course, that is why such discrimination is ubiquitous, not just in the United States. Every country imposes at least some disqualifications on some ex-offenders for some period of time. Given that they must bear the costs of poorly performing business partners, employees, and tenants, private businesses, employers, landlords, voluntary associations, colleges and universities, and others should be permitted to discriminate on the basis of criminal record just as they are free to discriminate on the basis of prior experience, education, personality, and impression.

Title VII's disparate impact doctrine is complex, confusing, and controversial, especially as applied to using criminal record as an employment disqualification. It is one thing to employ some arcane screening device to exclude a disproportionate number of protected minorities from the hiring pool, but quite another thing to consider criminal record an indicator of dishonesty and reliability. A prior criminal record, in many if not most cases, is relevant to honesty, reliability, and self-discipline, qualities that are always relevant for a job. Moreover, it bears emphasizing that when ex-offenders are not hired, the job in question does not evaporate. Other people who also need work are hired. Public policy should concentrate on eliminating unnecessary de jure restrictions on ex-offenders and leave private employers free to making their own decisions about hiring ex-offenders.

The government could do much to promote ex-offender transition to law-abiding citizenship other than compelling private sector employers to hire individuals whom they do not want to employ. Government entities could start by cutting back their own discrimination. Indeed, as long as federal, state, and local governments have so many mandatory felon disqualifications and exclusions, they will reinforce the public perception that individuals with prior criminal records are irredeemably flawed and likely to commit future crimes.

Beyond simply repealing de jure prohibitions, disqualifications, and ineligibilities on persons convicted of felonies, federal, state, and local government units could demonstrate their confidence in ex-offenders via their own employment policies. Banning the box is a compromise. Criminal record is not asked for until after a job applicant has passed the initial screening. At that point, having judged the job applicant favorably, the hiring authority may view the job applicant's prior conviction as less important than it might have on first encountering the application. If government hiring can successfully dispense with initial screening on the basis of criminal record, nongovernmental employers may be persuaded to adopt the same policy.

It may be ironic that so much needs to be done to undo the negative effects of punishments, but that is the reality. Government should support programs aimed at promoting ex-offender employment. The Chicago-based Safer Foundation provides a model for getting ex-offenders "job-ready" and then placed with willing employers to whom the applicant's full criminal record is disclosed. Because the Safer Foundation seeks to builds long-term relationships with employers, its hiring recommendations need to be credible; no lying here. When an ex-offender is placed, Safer maintains contact with both employer and employee. If problems emerge, Safer provides an experienced response. The availability of monitoring and assistance has persuaded employers to take a chance. A federal tax incentive for employers who hire ex-offenders also provides an incentive.

Public policy could aim to assist ex-offenders in building a positive résumé or curriculum vitae. Governments could provide transitional employment after termination of sentence. A credible government-run work program could certify that an ex-offender had performed successfully for a period, say a year. Supervisors and foremen could serve as future references for those ex-offenders who worked under their supervision. However, for these recommendations to be credible, *they need to be earned*, not just handed out automatically.

Rather than trying to force employers, landlords, volunteer organizations, colleges and universities, and others not to discriminate on the basis of criminal record, the government should seek to persuade private and volunteer sector decision makers "to do the right thing," to give job applicants with blighted records a chance to make a case for their selection.* There have always been employers who voluntarily choose to employ ex-offenders. They may be motivated by religious values, their own personal entanglements with the criminal justice system, or other idiosyncratic reasons.

Government would be more effective in persuading employers and others to give ex-offenders another chance if it could credibly assert that conviction and punishment have substantially positive, rather than negative, effects on future conduct. To make this true, government would need to vastly improve its community corrections and prison programs, so that "graduation" from the Department of Corrections would generally be seen to be a positive credential, or at least not such a negative credential. We have a long way to go.

Many academic books end with a recommendation for future research; that is certainly appropriate when it comes to criminal records. Although there is much more information about criminal records than many (including me) might have initially thought, much more needs to be illuminated. There is pressing need to know more about what criminal intelligence and investigatory databases exist, how they are populated, and who has access to them. Being named in one of these databases can have nearly the same effect as a conviction, depending on who has access to the information.

---

* In 2004, Singapore's legislature launched the Yellow Ribbon Project, an initiative aimed at educating the public on the desirability of giving ex-convicts a second chance. The project explains the stigma faced by ex-offenders and urges compassion and assistance. Since its inauguration, the project has received praise from international experts and an honorable mention at the 2007 United Nations Grand Award. According to the project's website, "The best rehabilitation regime during incarceration is of no use if ex-offenders find themselves rejected at every turn when they are released into the larger community. Through the Yellow Ribbon Project, we hope to promote a more accepting society, one that is willing to give ex-offenders a second chance at making good. It is important that we help unlock the second prison for our inmates, even as we let them out of the physical one." See http://www.yellowribbon.org.sg.

Almost no research has been done on criminal records other than those generated by the police and courts. Probation files are an important example. They contain very detailed and often very personal information, including social and psychological assessments, drug test results, and interview notes. It is important to know how these files are compiled, who has access to them, how, if at all, they are shared with other government agencies, and what happens to them after probation is completed. Similar questions should be asked about jail and prison records, including intelligence files, disciplinary files, and social-psychological assessments.

With respect to all criminal record databases, we need to know much more about information security. To what extent are criminal justice agencies and courts protecting their records from purposeful and inadvertent disclosure? How vulnerable are criminal record databases to leakers and hackers?

In the future, it will be important to come up with ways to make businesses and ordinary citizens more sophisticated consumers of criminal records. Getting accurate information into the public domain about recidivism rates, aging out, and the impact of employment on rehabilitation can potentially ameliorate the worst effects of criminal record stigma. President George Bush was on the right track when, in calling for assistance to ex-offenders, he called the United States "the land of the second chance." My guess is that Americans are more willing to give ex-offenders a second chance than some commentators assume. In fact, while the problems that ex-offenders have obtaining legitimate employment should not be minimized, they also should not be exaggerated. Many ex-offenders, especially those who are "job-ready," do obtain employment and do succeed in overcoming their negative curriculum vitae. We should not minimize the influence that public policy could have if government demonstrated willingness to employ ex-offenders and otherwise eliminate mandatory disabilities imposed on them.

APPENDIX

NOTES

INDEX

APPENDIX: SUPREME COURT CASES DEALING WITH CRIMINAL RECORDS

***Moore v. Missouri*, 159 U.S. 673 (U.S. 1895)** Enhancing sentence on account of prior convictions does not violate the double jeopardy clause. It does not impose new punishment for the previous offense. It increases the punishment for the present offense because defendant has shown himself to be incorrigible and because previous punishment proved inefficacious.

***Hawker v. New York*, 170 U.S. 189 (U.S. 1898)** A New York statute prohibiting convicted felons from practicing medicine, even when applied to those convicted prior to the enactment of the statute, does not violate the Ex Post Facto Clause of the Constitution. The statute does not impose additional punishment for past offenses as the state can regulate what qualifications are needed for the practice of medicine and exclude those it deems of bad character.

***Rosen v. United States*, 245 U.S. 467, 471 (1918)** A prior conviction does not disqualify a witness from testifying at a criminal trial. "[T]he truth is more likely to be arrived at by hearing the testimony of all persons of competent understanding who may seem to have knowledge of the facts involved in a case, leaving the credit and weight of such testimony to be determined by the jury or by the court."

***Michelson v. United States*, 335 U.S. 469, 476 (1948)** It is not necessarily unconstitutional to introduce at trial for impeachment purposes the defendant's prior criminal record. However, "the overriding policy of excluding such evidence, despite its admitted probative value, is the practical experience that its disallowance tends to prevent confusion of issues, unfair surprise, and undue prejudice."

***Williams v. New York*, 337 U.S. 241 (1949)** Sentencing judge can consider a defendant's prior arrests and uncharged crimes in deciding whether to impose the death penalty.

***Schware v. Board of Bar Examiners*, 353 U.S. 232 (1957)** The bar applicant's prior arrest record and use of aliases did not raise substantial doubts about his present good moral character. Therefore, refusing him the right to practice law violated due process. "The mere fact that a man has been arrested has very little, if any, probative value in showing that he has engaged in any misconduct."

***DeVeau v. Braisted*, 363 U. S. 144 (1960)** New York law barring a labor union from collecting dues from stevedores if any officer of that union has ever been convicted of a felony does not violate the federal supremacy clause and is not an unconstitutional Ex Post Facto law. The union violated the law because one of its officers had been convicted of grand larceny thirty-six years earlier.

***Spencer v. Texas*, 385 U.S. 554 (1967)** A habitual offender statute that requires the prosecutor to prove and the jury to find that the defendant was previously convicted of another offense does not violate due process, despite potential prejudice to the defendant.

***Davis v. Alaska*, 415 U.S. 308 (1974)** Notwithstanding the state's interest in protecting the confidentiality of juvenile criminal records, prohibiting defendant from impeaching a prosecution witness by disclosing that witness's probation status following adjudication as a juvenile offender violates the defendant's constitutional right to confront witnesses against him.

***Richardson v Ramirez*, 418 U.S. 24 (1974)** State law that disenfranchises felons after they have completed their sentences is not unconstitutional. There is a textual basis in the Fourteenth Amendment for felon disenfranchisement.

***Paul v. Davis,* 424 U.S. 693 (1976)** Despite the reputational injury inflicted on defendant by police chief's dissemination of a circular listing defendant as an "active shoplifter" due to a prior shoplifting arrest, there is no due process violation because defendant has no property or liberty interest in his reputation. Distributing the circular also did not violate defendant's right to privacy.

***Oklahoma Publishing v. District Court,* 430 U.S. 308 (1977)** As long as information was obtained lawfully, prohibiting the media from disclosing a juvenile's arrest and prosecution violates the First Amendment.

***Nixon v. Warner Communications, Inc.,* 435 U.S. 589 (1978)** There is a common law right of access to court records.

***Smith v. Daily Mail Publishing Co.,* 443 U.S. 97 (1979)** Statute prohibiting publication of the name of any youth charged as a juvenile offender violates First and Fourteenth Amendments despite the state's interest in protecting the juvenile from the stigma of a criminal record.

***Rummel v. Estelle,* 445 U.S. 263 (1980)** Habitual offender statute that requires life sentence with possibility of parole for a defendant with three nonserious prior convictions does not constitute cruel and unusual punishment.

***Dickerson v. New Banner Inst., Inc.,* 460 U.S. 103 (1983)** Federal firearms license disqualification due to prior conviction is valid, despite state court having expunged the conviction.

***Solem v. Helm,* 463 U.S. 277 (1983)** Mandatory life sentence without possibility of parole for a defendant with six previous convictions for nonviolent offenses and a current conviction for passing a bad check violates the Eighth Amendment's prohibition of cruel and unusual punishment.

***U.S. Department of Justice v. Julian,* 486 U.S. 1 (1988)** The Freedom of Information Act requires that presentence investigation reports be disclosed to the subject of the report, except for confidential sources, diagnostic opinions, and possibly harmful information. Department of Justice has no valid interest in refusing to disclose presentence report to the subject of the report.

***U.S. Department of Justice v. Reporters Committee for Freedom of the Press et al.*, 489 U.S. 749 (1989)** The Department of Justice may refuse to grant a Freedom of Information Act request for disclosure of an individual's criminal record because the information is not relevant to a government agency's operations. Moreover, the government has a valid interest in protecting the record-subject's reputation.

***Nichols v. United States*, 511 U.S. 738 (1994)** The enhancement of a prison sentence because of a previous uncounseled misdemeanor conviction does not violate the Sixth or the Fourteenth Amendment.

***Arizona v. Evans*, 514 U.S. 1 (1995)** The Constitution does not require suppression of the fruits of a search occasioned by mistaken information in the court's information system. Police officer's reliance on mistaken information from court's information system falls within the good faith exception to the exclusionary rule. The exclusionary rule's purpose does not include deterring unlawful conduct by court personnel.

***Watts v. United States*, 519 U.S. 148, 152 (1997)** Sentencing judge may enhance sentence based on conduct for which the defendant was previously acquitted.

***LAPD v. United Reporting Publishing Corporation*, 528 U.S. 32 (1999)** State statute prohibiting police department from disclosing arrestees' addresses to firms intending to use the information for commercial purposes is not unconstitutional. There is no constitutional right of access to information held by the police.

***INS v. St. Cyr*, 533 U.S. 289 (2001)** Federal law making previously convicted alien ineligible to appeal a removal order does not apply retroactively.

Connecticut Department of Public Safety v. Doe, 123 S. Ct. 1160 (2003) Due process clause does not require a hearing on whether a previously convicted sex offender is currently dangerous before posting the conviction information to the publicly accessible sex offender registry.

Demore v. Kim, 538 U.S. 510 (2003) A rule requiring detention of an alien with a prior conviction, pending a removal hearing, does not violate due process, even without an individualized determination of whether the alien poses a danger to society or a flight risk.

Ewing v. California, 538 U.S. 11 (2003) California's three-strikes law, imposing a mandatory sentence of 25 years to life, does not constitute cruel and unusual punishment as applied to a defendant who was previously convicted of three residential burglaries and one robbery, but whose present conviction is for theft of golf clubs worth $1,200.

Leocal v. Ashcroft, 543 U.S. 1 (2004) For sentencing purposes, a prior drunk driving conviction does not count as a crime of violence, which renders an alien deportable.

Small v. United States, 544 U.S. 385 (2004) A prior foreign conviction does not make defendant ineligible to purchase a firearm.

Shepard v. United States, 544 U.S. 13 (2005) To determine whether a prior state burglary conviction counts as a violent felony for purposes of a federal sentence enhancement, federal judge should examine the state indictment, plea agreement, and sentencing allocution, but not police reports or complaint to decide whether defendant's conduct would have constituted burglary under federal law.

Herring v. United States, 555 U.S. 135 (2009) Application of exclusionary rule is not appropriate when a search resulted from an error in the police information system.

Smith v. Doe, 538 U.S. 84 (2009) Requiring registration by persons convicted of sex offenses before the passage of the Sex Offender Registration Act does not violate Ex Post Facto Clause because the registration requirement is not punishment.

***Padilla v. Kentucky*, 130 S. Ct. 1473 (2010)** Defense counsel has a constitutional duty to provide a client with advice about deportation that would be required if he pleaded guilty.

***Vartelas v. Holder*, 132 S. Ct. 1479 (2012)** With the passage of the Illegal Immigration Reform and Immigrant Responsibility Act of 1996 (IRIRA), lawful permanent residents traveling outside of the country for even brief periods of time, and who have been convicted of certain offenses, must apply for admission to the U.S. upon their return. Admission can be denied because a prior conviction for certain offenses renders the alien removable. However, the IRIRA does not apply retroactively.

NOTES

Preface

1. The sources referred to in the preface are listed here: James B. Jacobs, *Can Gun Control Work?* (Oxford: Oxford University Press, 2002); Howard S. Becker, *Outsiders: Studies in the Sociology of Deviance* (New York: Free Press, 1963); Edwin M. Lemert, *Social Pathology: A Systematic Approach to the Theory of Sociopathic Behavior* (New York: McGraw-Hill, 1951); Edwin M. Lemert, *Human Deviance, Social Problems, and Social Control* (Englewood Cliffs, NJ: Prentice Hall, 1967); Edwin M. Schur, *Labeling Deviant Behavior* (New York: Harper and Row, 1971); Edwin M. Schur, *Labeling Women Deviant: Gender, Stigma, and Social Control* (Philadelphia: Temple University Press, 1983); Erving Goffman, *Stigma: Notes on the Management of Spoiled Identity* (New York: Simon and Schuster, 1963); Shawn Bushway, *Labor Market Effects of Permitting Employer Access to Criminal History Records*, 20 Journal of Contemporary Criminal Justice: Special Issue on Economics and Crime 276 (2004); Shawn Bushway, "Labor Markets and Crime," in Joan Petersilia and James Q. Wilson (eds.), *Crime and Public Policy* 183–209 (New York: Oxford University Press, 2011); Shawn Bushway, *The Impact of an Arrest on the Job Stability of Young White American Men*, 35 Journal of Research in Crime and Delinquency 454–79 (1997); Devah Pager, *Marked: Race, Crime, and Finding Work in an Era of Mass Incarceration* (Chicago: University of Chicago Press, 2007); John H. Laub and Robert J. Sampson, *Shared Beginnings, Divergent Lives: Delinquent Boys to Age 70* (Cambridge, MA: Harvard University Press, 2003); Shadd Maruna, *Making Good: How Ex-Convicts Reform and Rebuild Their Lives* (Washington, DC: American Psychological Association, 2001); Alfred Blumstein and Kiminori Nakamura, *Redemption in the Presence of Widespread Criminal Background Checks*, 47(2) Criminology 327 (2009); Joan Petersilia, *When Prisoners Come Home: Parole and Prisoner Reentry* (Oxford: Oxford University Press, 2003); Jeremy Travis, *But They All Come Back: Facing the Challenges of Prisoner Reentry*

(Washington, DC: Urban Institute Press, 2005); Michelle Alexander, *The New Jim Crow: Mass Incarceration in the Age of Colorblindness* (New York: New Press, 2010); Margaret Colgate Love et al., *Collateral Consequences of Criminal Convictions: Law, Policy and Practice* (Washington, DC: Thomson Reuters, 2013); James Q. Whitman, *The Two Western Cultures of Privacy: Dignity versus Liberty,* 113 Yale L.J. 1151 (2004); Helen Nissenbaum, *Privacy in Context: Technology, Policy, and the Integrity of Social Life* (Stanford, CA: Stanford Law Books, 2010); James B. Jacobs, *Mass Incarceration and the Proliferation of Criminal Records,* 3 University of St. Thomas L.J. 387 (2006); James B. Jacobs and Tamara Crepet, *The Expanding Scope, Use, and Availability of Criminal Records,* 11 N.Y.U. Journal of Legislation and Public Policy 177 (2008); James B. Jacobs and Dimitra Blitsa, *Sharing Criminal Records: The United States, the European Union and Interpol Compared,* 30 Loyola of L.A. International and Comparative L. Rev. 125 (2008); James B. Jacobs and Dimitra Blitsa, *Major "Minor" Progress under the Third Pillar: EU Institution Building in the Sharing of Criminal Record Information,* 8 Chicago-Kent Journal of International and Comparative Law 111 (2008); James B. Jacobs and Dimitra Blitsa, "Paedophiles, Employment Discrimination, and European Integration," in Toine Spapens et al. (eds.), *Universalis: Liber Amicorum Cyrille Fijnaut* 335–46 (Antwerpen: Intersentia Publishers, 2011); James B. Jacobs and Dimitra Blitsa, *US, EU and UK Employment Vetting as Strategy for Preventing Convicted Sex Offenders from Gaining Access to Children,* 20 European Journal of Crime, Criminal Law & Criminal Justice 265 (2012); James B. Jacobs and Elena Larrauri, *Are Criminal Convictions a Public Matter? The USA and Spain* 14 Punishment and Society 3 (2012).

CHAPTER 1
Introduction

1. Howard Becker, *Outsiders: Studies in the Sociology of Deviance* (New York: Free Press, 1963).

2. SEARCH, National Consortium for Justice Information and Statistics, *Report of the National Task Force on the Commercial Sale of Criminal Justice Information,* at vi (2005), http://www.search.org/files/pdf/RNTFCSCJRI.pdf.

3. Sarah Shannon, Christopher Uggen, and Melissa Thompson (April 2011), *Growth in the U.S. Ex-Felon and Ex-Prisoner Population, 1948–2010,* at 12, paper presented at the annual meeting of the Population Association of America, Washington, DC, http://paa2011.princeton.edu/papers/111687.

4. At the federal level, during the fiscal year 2013, 75,718 criminal defendants either pled guilty or were found guilty. See U.S. Department of Justice, Executive Office for United States Attorneys, *Annual Statistical Report. Fiscal Year 2013,* at 8, http://www.justice.gov/usao/reading_room/reports/asr2013/12statrpt.pdf. In 2006, there were 1,132,290 felony convictions in state courts. See U.S. Department of Justice, Office of Justice Programs, Bureau of Justice Statistics, *Felony Sentences in State Courts, 2006—Statistical Tables,* 1 (December 2009), http://www.bjs.gov/content/pub/pdf/fssc06st.pdf. As to misdemeanor convictions, systematic statistics are not available, but it is clear that they are more common than felony convictions. In 2007, public defender offices re-

ported they were assigned 575,770 misdemeanor cases. See U.S. Department of Justice, Office of Justice Programs, Public Defender Offices, *2007—Statistical Tables*, 13 (November 2009), http://www.bjs.gov/content/pub/pdf/pdo07st.pdf.

5. Michael Pinard, *Reflections and Perspectives on Reentry and Collateral Consequences*, 100 J. Criminal Law & Criminology 1213, 1218 (2010).

6. 28 CFR Part 23 provides guidance on operating criminal intelligence information systems effectively while protecting privacy and constitutional rights (C.F.R. T. 28, Ch. I, Pt. 23). See https://www.iir.com/Home/28CFR_Program/; see also *Privacy Impact Assessment for the eGuardian Threat Tracking System*, http://www.fbi.gov/foia/privacy-impact-assessments/eguardian-threat.

7. Over the past two decades, the numbers of estimated arrests of all persons in the United States reached a peak of 15,290,900 in 1997. See FBI Arrest Statistics 1994–2011, http://ojjdp.gov/ojstatbb/ezaucr/asp/ucr_display.asp. In 2012, nationwide police made an estimated 12,196,959 arrests. See Federal Bureau of Investigation, *Crime in the United States 2012*, http://www.fbi.gov/about-us/cjis/ucr/crime-in-the-u.s/2012/crime-in-the-u.s.-2012/persons-arrested/persons-arrested. Over the same period of time, the number of arrests never went below 12,000,000.

8. Michelle Alexander, *The New Jim Crow: Mass Incarceration in the Age of Colorblindness* 7 (New York: New Press, 2010).

9. David Sudnow, *Normal Crimes: Sociological Features of the Penal Code in a Public Defender Office*, 12 Social Problems 255 (1965).

10. Marc Mauer and Meda Chesney-Lind (eds.), *Invisible Punishments: The Collateral Consequences of Mass Imprisonment* (New York: New Press, 2002).

11. Devah Pager, *The Mark of a Criminal Record*, 108 American Journal of Sociology 937, 942 (2003).

12. See generally Byron E. Shafer (ed.) *Is America Different? A New Look at American Exceptionalism* (New York: Oxford University Press, 1991); Seymour M. Lipset, *American Exceptionalism: A Double-Edged Sword* (New York: Norton, 1996); John W. Kingdon, *America the Unusual* (New York: Worth, 1999). With regard to U.S. criminal justice exceptionalism, see Carol S. Steiker, "Capital Punishment and American Exceptionalism," in Michael Ignatieff (ed.), *American Exceptionalism and Human Rights* 57 (Princeton, NJ: Princeton University Press, 2005); Michael Tonry, *Explanations of American Punishment Policies: A National History*, 11 Punishment & Society 377 (2009).

13. James Q. Whitman argues that Europe and the United States have two different conceptions of privacy. For Europeans, protecting privacy is a way to protect a right to respect and dignity. For Americans, privacy is construed as a form of liberty, especially from intrusion by the state. See James Q. Whitman, *The Two Western Cultures of Privacy: Dignity versus Liberty*, 113 Yale L.J. 1151 (2004).

14. See, e.g., LexisNexis, "Resident Screening," http://www.lexisnexis.com/backgroundchecks/business/tenant-screening.aspx; Tenant Verification Service, "Criminal Record Check," http://www.tenantverification.com/criminal-record-check; Goodhire, "10 Reasons to Use Goodhire," http://www.goodhire.com/why-use-goodhire; Talentwise, "Nationwide Employment Background Check," https://fasttrack.talentwise.com/employment-background-.check.html?refers=6075&adword=&trackit=265; Criminal Watch Dog, "What

Is a Criminal Check?," https://www.criminalwatchdog.com/?gclid=CJLK9K2A3bcCFZKk4AodjoIAoQ.

15. SEARCH, National Consortium for Justice Information and Statistics, *Report of the National Task Force on the Criminal Backgrounding of America*, at 1 (2005), http://www.search.org/files/pdf/ReportofNTFCBA.pdf.

16. Society for Human Resource Management, *Background Checking: Conducting Criminal Background Checks*, at 3 (January 2010); Society for Human Resource Management, *Workplace Violence Survey*, at 18 (fig. 17) (January 2004), http://www.shrm.org/research/surveyfindings/documents/workplace%20violence%20survey.pdf (comparing 2003 and 1996 data on criminal background checks); Society for Human Resource Management, *Staffing Research, Getting to Know the Candidate: Conducting Reference Checks*, at 5 (table 2) (2005) (detailing 2004 statistics), http://www.shrm.org/research/articles/articles/documents/getting%20to%20know%20the%20candidate%20-%20conducting%20reference%20checks.pdf.

17. For example: Boy Scouts of America, "Know the Facts: BSA Youth Protection," http://www.scouting.org/sitecore/content/BSAYouthProtection/BSA_Communications/Commitment_to_Youth_Protection.aspx; Ride Connection, http://www.rideconnection.org/ride/SupportUs/Volunteering.aspx; American Red Cross, Louisville Chapter, http://www.redcross.org/ky/louisville/volunteer/faq; Big Brothers, Big Sisters, "Be a Big Sister," http://www.bbbs.org/site/c.9iILI3NGKhK6F/b.5961311/k.2C0A/Be_a_Big_Sister8212help_a_Little_go_a_long_way.htm; see James Jacobs and Tamara Crepet, *The Expanding Scope, Use and Availability of Criminal Records*, 11 N.Y.U. J. Legis. & Pub. Pol'y 177 (2007–2008).

18. Employers Group Research Services, *Employment of Ex-Offenders: A Survey of Employers' Policies and Practices*, San Francisco, SF Works, April 12, 2002.

19. For example, see CBSAtlanta.com, "State House Candidate's Criminal History Exposed," http://www.cbsatlanta.com/story/19125066/state-rep-candidate-stops-interview-when-asked-about-criminal-history; Fox4KC.com, "US Senate Candidate Has Criminal History," http://fox4kc.com/2012/09/17/us-senate-candidate-has-criminal-history/; Oakland Park Patch, "Moraine Candidate Responds to Robo Call Describing Arrest Record," http://orlandpark.patch.com/groups/politics-and-elections/p/moraine-candidate-responds-to-robo-call-describing-area4f4de304; Fox News.com, "63 Days to Decide: New York Senate Candidate Spills Details about Arrest Record," http://www.foxnews.com/politics/2010/08/31/new-york-senate-candidate-spills-details-arrest-record/; The Smoking Gun, "W. Bush DUI Arrest Record," http://www.thesmokinggun.com/documents/celebrity/george-w-bush-dui-arrest-record (webpages retrieved on June 16, 2013).

20. SEARCH, National Consortium for Justice Information and Statistics, *Report of the National Task Force on the Commercial Sale of Criminal Justice Record Information*, at 21 (2005), http://www.search.org/files/pdf/ReportofNTFCBA.pdf.

21. BoyfriendCheck.com, http://www.boyfriendcheck.com; IDHonesty, http://www.idhonesty.com/individual-background-check.html; Check Out a Date, http://www.checkoutadate.com/about/.

22. Margaret Colgate Love et al., *Collateral Consequences of Criminal Convictions: Law, Policy, and Practice* (Washington, DC: Thomas Reuters, 2013).

23. Amy Wax, *Disparate Impact Realism*, 53 Wm. & Mary L. Rev. 621 (2011).

CHAPTER 2
Intelligence and Investigative Databases

1. National Commission on Terrorist Attacks upon the United States, *The 9/11 Commission Report: Final Report of the National Commission on Terrorist Attacks upon the United States*, at 416–17 (July 2004), http://www.9-11commission.gov/report/911Report.pdf.

2. Courtney Bowie, "Wearing a Hoodie While Brown Does Not Mean You Are in a Gang," American Civil Liberties Union Blog of Rights, December 13, 2012, https://www.aclu.org/blog/racial-justice-human-rights/wearing-hoodie-while-brown-does-not-mean-you-are-gang.

3. Justin J. Dintino and Frederick T. Martens, *Police Intelligence Systems in Crime Control: Maintaining a Delicate Balance in a Liberal Democracy* (Springfield, IL: C. C. Thomas, 1983); see also John S. Dempsey, *Introduction to Investigations* (Belmont, CA: Wadsworth/Thompson, 2nd ed., 2003). For an interesting India comparison, see Mrinal Satish, "Bad Characters, History Sheeters, Budding Goondas, and Rowdies": Police Surveillance Files and Intelligence Databases in India" (draft), http://srn.com/abstract=1703762.

4. National Commission on Terrorist Attacks upon the United States, *The 9/11 Commission Report: Final Report of the National Commission on Terrorist Attacks upon the United States*, at 416–17 (July 2004), http://www.9-11commission.gov/report/911Report.pdf.

5. City of New York Office of the Comptroller, *Audit Report on the Development and Implementation of the Omniform System by the New York City Police Department*, at 6 (April 30 2004), http://comptroller.nyc.gov/wp-content/uploads/documents/NYPD_7A04_066.pdf.

6. *Handschu v. Special Servs. Div.*, 349 F. Supp. 766, 767 (S.D. N.Y. 1972).

7. *Handschu v. Special Services Div.*, 605 F. Supp. 1384 (S.D. N.Y. 1985); see also Paul G. Chevigny, *Politics and Law in the Control of Local Surveillance*, 69 Cornell L. Rev. 735 (1983–1984). For a summary of the history of the *Handschu* litigation up until 2010, see *Handschu v. Police Department of the City of New York*, 679 F. Supp. 2d 488, 492–95 (S.D. N.Y. 2010).

8. National Commission on Terrorist Attacks upon the United States, *The 9/11 Commission Report: Final Report of the National Commission on Terrorist Attacks upon the United States* (July 2004), http://www.9-11commission.gov/report/911Report.pdf.

9. *Handschu v. Special Servs. Div.*, 273 F. Supp. 2d 327 (S.D. N.Y. 2003); *Handschu v. Special Servs. Div.*, 288 F. Supp. 2d 411 (2003).

10. Editorial, "LAPD Gets New Guidelines for Handling 'Suspicious Activity Reports,'" *Los Angeles Times*, September 2, 2012, http://articles.latimes.com/2012/sep/02/opinion/la-ed-lapd-suspicious-activity-reports-20120902.

11. Center for Constitutional Rights, *Daniels, et al. v. the City of New York*, http://ccrjustice.org/ourcases/past-cases/daniels,-et-al.-v.-city-new-york (last visited September 18, 2012).

12. *Id.*

13. Bob Herbert, "Big Brother in Blue," Opinion, *New York Times*, March 12, 2010, http://www.nytimes.com/2010/03/13/opinion/13herbert.html.

14. Rocco Parascandola et al., "Gov. Paterson Moves to Sign Bill Ending Frisk Records, NYPD Commish Ray Kelly Says We Lost Key Tool," *New York Daily News*, July 16, 2010, http://articles.nydailynews.com/2010-07-16/local/29440049_1_sign-bill-nypd-commish-ray-kelly-paterson.

15. *Lino v. City of New York*, class action complaint, May 19, 2010, at 2, http://www.nyclu.org/files/releases/S&F_Sealing_Complaint_5-19-10.pdf.

16. *Lino v. City of New York, 2012*, NY SLIP opinion 08783, Appellate Division, 1st Department, December 20, 2012; New York City Police Department, "Stop, Question and Frisk Report Database," http://www.nyc.gov/html/nypd/html/analysis_and_planning/stop_question_and_frisk_report.shtml (emphasis added).

17. Joseph Goldstein, "City Agrees to Expunge Names Collected in Stop-and-Frisk Program," *New York Times*, August 7, 2013, http://www.nytimes.com/2013/08/08/nyregion/city-to-trim-a-database-on-police-stops.html?_r=0; Joseph Ax, "New York City Police to Purge Stop-and-Frisk Database of Names," Reuters, August 7, 2013, http://www.reuters.com/article/2013/08/07/us-usa-newyork-stopandfrisk-idUSBRE97619D20130807.

18. Federal Bureau of Investigation, National Crime Information Center, NCIC Files, http://www.fbi.gov/about-us/cjis/ncic/ncic_history.

19. Federal Bureau of Investigation, National Crime Information Center, NCIC Files, http://www.fbi.gov/about-us/cjis/ncic/ncic_files (last visited June 2, 2012).

20. See Ann Davis, "Data Collection Is Up Sharply Following 9/11," *Wall Street Journal*, May 22, 2003, at B1.

21. Vulnerabilities in the U.S. Passport System Can Be Exploited by Criminals and Terrorists: Hearing before the Senate Comm. on Homeland Security and Governmental Affairs, 109th Cong. 69–74 (2005) (statement of Thomas E. Bush III, Assistant Director, Criminal Justice Information Services Division), at 72.

22. William J. Krouse, Congressional Research Service, Terrorist Identification, Screening, and Tracking under Homeland Security Presidential Directive 6, at 15 (April 21, 2004).

23. *Id.* at 2; see also U.S. Department of Justice Office of the Inspector General Audit Division, *The Federal Bureau of Investigation's Terrorist Watchlist Nomination Practices* (May 2009), http://www.justice.gov/oig/reports/FBI/a0925/final.pdf.

24. U.S. Department of Justice Office of the Inspector General Audit Division, *The Federal Bureau of Investigation's Terrorist Watchlist Nomination Practices* (May 2009), http://www.justice.gov/oig/reports/FBI/a0925/final.pdf.

25. See Timothy J. Healy, Director, Terrorist Screening Center, Federal Bureau of Investigation, Statement before the Senate Homeland Security and Governmental Affairs Committee (December 9, 2009).

26. Timothy J. Healy, Director, Terrorist Screening Center, Federal Bureau of Investigation, Statement before the House Judiciary Committee (March 24, 2010), http://www.fbi.gov/news/testimony/sharing-and-analyzing-information-to-prevent-terrorism; see also Federal Bureau of Investigation, Terrorist Screening Center, *Frequently Asked Questions*, http://www.fbi.gov/about-us/nsb/tsc/tsc_faqs.

27. William J. Krouse, Congressional Research Service, Terrorist Identification, Screening, and Tracking under Homeland Security Presidential Directive 6, at 16 (April 21, 2004).

28. Timothy J. Healy, Director, Terrorist Screening Center, Federal Bureau of Investigation, Statement before the House Judiciary Committee (March 24, 2010), http://www.fbi.gov/news/testimony/sharing-and-analyzing-information-to-prevent-terrorism.

29. *Id.*

30. Federal Bureau of Investigation, Terrorist Screening Center, *Frequently Asked Questions*, http://www.fbi.gov/about-us/nsb/tsc/tsc_faqs.

31. U.S. Department of Justice Office of the Inspector General Audit Division, *The Federal Bureau of Investigation's Terrorist Watchlist Nomination Practices* (May 2009), http://www.justice.gov/oig/reports/FBI/a0925/final.pdf.

32. *Id.*

33. Lizette Alvarez, "Meet Mikey, 8: U.S. Has Him on Watch List," *New York Times*, January 13, 2010 (an eight-year-old boy was repeatedly interrogated at airports—since age two—because he had the same name as someone on the watchlist); see also U.S. Department of Justice Office of the Inspector General Audit Division, *The Federal Bureau of Investigation's Terrorist Watchlist Nomination Practices* (May 2009), http://www.justice.gov/oig/reports/FBI/a0925/final.pdf.

34. U.S. Department of Justice Office of the Inspector General Audit Division, *The Federal Bureau of Investigation's Terrorist Watchlist Nomination Practices* (May 2009), http://www.justice.gov/oig/reports/FBI/a0925/final.pdf.; see also U.S. Government Accountability Office, *Terrorist Watch List Screening: Efforts to Help Reduce Adverse Effects on the Public*, GAO-06-1031 (2006).

35. *Central Statement*, NCIC 2000 Newsletter (Federal Bureau of Investigation), April–May 1996, http://permanent.access.gpo.gov/lps3213/2kv1n3.htm.

36. See David Michael Jaros, *Unfettered Discretion: Criminal Orders of Protection and Their Impact on Parent Defendants*, 85 Ind. L.J. 1445 (2010); David H. Taylor et al., *Ex Parte Domestic Violence Orders of Protection: How Easing Access to Judicial Process Has Eased the Possibility for Abuse of the Process*, 18 Kan. J.L. & Pub. Pol'y 83 (2008).

37. NCIC 2000, Operating Manual—Protection Order File, at 1; see also Womenslaw.com, *How to Get an Order of Protection*, http://www.womenslaw.org/NY/NY_how_to.htm (last visited February 9, 2008).

38. NCIC 2000, Operating Manual—Protection Order File, at 27.

39. 18 U.S.C. 922(g)(8) makes it illegal for anyone to have a gun who was subject to an order that "restrains such person from harassing, stalking, or threatening an intimate partner of such person or child of such intimate partner or person, or engaging in other conduct that would place an intimate partner in reasonable fear of bodily injury to the partner or child."

40. Professor Wishnie argues that disseminating civil immigration information via the NCIC database is both unprecedented and unlawful. See Michael J. Wishnie, *State and Local Police Enforcement of Immigration Laws*, 6 U. Pa. J. Const. L. 1084, 1096 (2004). For more on the Immigration Violator file, see Laura Sullivan, *Enforcing Nonenforcement: Countering the Threat Posed to Sanctuary Laws by the Inclusion of Immigration Records in the National Crime Information Center Database*, 97 Cal. L. Rev. 567 (2009).

41. Testimony of Michael D. Kirkpatrick, Assistant Director in charge of the Federal Bureau of Investigation's Criminal Justice Information Services Division, before the United States Senate Subcommittee on Immigration, Border Security, and Citizenship, November 13, 2003, http://www.fbi.gov/news/testimony/the-fbis-national-crime-information-center.

42. *Nat'l Council of La Raza v. Gonzales*, 468 F. Supp. 2d 429 (E.D. N.Y. 2007) *aff'd sub nom. Nat'l Council of La Raza v. Mukasey*, 283 F. App'x 848 (2d Cir. 2008).

43. Brief of Petitioner-Plaintiff at 2, *Nat'l Council of La Raza v. Gonzales*, 468 F. Supp. 2d 429 (E.D. N.Y. 2007) (No. 03-CV-6324).

44. *Nat'l Council of La Raza v. Mukasey*, 283 F. App'x 848 (2d Cir. 2008)

45. Julie Barrows and C. Ronald Huff, *Gangs and Public Policy: Constructing and Deconstructing Gang Databases*, 8(4) Criminology and Public Policy 675 (2009).

46. Charles M. Katz, *Issues in the Production and Dissemination of Gang Statistics: An Ethnographic Study of a Large Midwestern Police Gang Unit*, 49 Crime & Delinquency 485, 586 (2003).

47. James B. Jacobs, *Gang Databases: Context and Questions*, 8 Criminology and Public Policy 705, 706 (2009).

48. Joshua Wright, *The Constitutional Failures of Gang Databases*, 2 Stan. J. C.R. & C.L. 115 (2006).

49. See Bill S. 744, 113th Congress (2013–2014), S. 3701 and proposed amendment SA 1299 to the bill at http://www.judiciary.senate.gov/legislation/immigration/amendments/Grassley/Grassley43-(ARM13616).pdf and http://beta.congress.gov/amendment/113th-congress/senate-amendment/1299. See also Ashley Parker, "Senate Panel, Getting Punchy on Immigration, Quits for the Night," *New York Times*, May 20, 2013, http://thecaucus.blogs.nytimes.com/2013/05/20/with-disputed-amendments-ahead-senate-panel-returns-to-immigration-bill/; Editorial, "Immigration and Gang Labels," *Los Angeles Times*, May 14, 2013, http://articles.latimes.com/2013/may/14/opinion/la-ed-gangs-20130514.

50. Kristin Henning, *Eroding Confidentiality in Delinquency Proceedings: Should Schools and Public Housing Authorities Be Notified?*, 79 N.Y.U. L. Rev. 520, 544 (2004).

51. Charles M. Katz, *Issues in the Production and Dissemination of Gang Statistics: An Ethnographic Study of a Large Midwestern Police Gang Unit*, 49 Crime & Delinquency 485, 508–9 (2003).

52. Joshua Wright, *The Constitutional Failures of Gang Databases*, 2 Stan. J. C.R. & C.L. 115 (2006).

53. Peggy A. Lautenschlager, Att'y General, Wisconsin Department of Justice, *TIME System Manual*, 285–86, http://www.doj.state.wi.us/dles/cibmanuals/files/TIME/PDF /Time.pdf; see also Memorandum from Richard

A. Weldon, FBI/CJIS Global Initiatives Unit on Violent Gang and Terrorist Organization File Entry Criteria Code (ECR) Change, http://www.acjic.alabama.gov/documents/violent_gang.pdf (describing VGTOF codes pertaining to gang characteristics).

54. Rebecca Rader Brown, *The Gang's All Here: Evaluating the Need for a National Gang Database*, 42 Colum. J. L. & Soc. Probs. 293, 300 (2009).

55. Deborah Lamm Weisel and Tara O'Connor Shelley, *Specialized Gang Units: Form and Function in Community Policing*, Final Report to the National Institute of Justice, NCJRS Doc. No. 207204, 111–12 n.9 (2000) (explaining that San Diego follows CalGang practices); see also CalGang Node Advisory Committee, *Policy and Procedures for the CalGang System*, § 2.21 (September 27, 2007) ("Purge Criteria: Records not modified by the addition of new criteria for a 5-year period will be purged"), http://oag.ca.gov/sites/all/files/pdfs/calgang/policy_procedure.pdf.

56. Civil Rights Complaint for Damages, Declaratory, and Injunctive Relief, *Quyen Pham et al v. City of Garden Grove et al.*, No. 94–3358 21–22 (filed May 20, 1996) at 11–16; Hong H. Tieu, *Picturing the Asian Gang Member among Us*, 11 UCLA Asian Pac. Am. L.J. 41, 50–51(2006); Doreen Carvajal, "O.C. Girl Challenges Police Photo Policy: Lawsuit: Attorneys Contend Youths' Attire, Race Made Them Targets of Mug Shots for Gang File," *Los Angeles Times*, May 20, 1994, http://articles.latimes.com/1994–05–20/news/mn-60111_1_police-department.

57. See James B. Jacobs and Jennifer Jones, *Keeping Firearms Out of the Hands of the Dangerously Mentally Ill*, 47(3) Criminal Law Bulletin 388–409 (2011).

58. National Alliance on Mental Illness, "Where We Stand: Violence, Mental Illness and Gun Reporting Laws," March 2013.

59. Edward G. Lake, *The Anthrax Attacks: Timeline*, http://www.anthraxinvestigation.com/index.html#Timeline; Robert Little, "Long under Suspicion: Suspect Had Been Monitored for More Than a Year," *Baltimore Sun*, August 2, 2008, http://www.baltimoresun.com/news/nation-world/bal-te.anthrax02aug02,0,745330.story.

60. Federal Bureau of Investigation, "Famous Cases and Criminals: Amerithrax or Anthrax Investigation," http://www.fbi.gov/about-us/history/famous-cases/anthrax-amerithrax/amerithrax-investigation

61. On the basis of her own "detective work," Barbara Hatch-Rosenberg, a SUNY Purchase environmental studies professor, became convinced that Hatfill was the anthrax perpetrator and pressed the FBI to pursue him. She met with FBI officials and congressional staffers to discuss her "investigation." Shortly afterward, the FBI began investigating Hatfill in earnest. See Marilyn W. Thompson, "The Pursuit of Steven Hatfill," *Washington Post*, September 14, 2003, http://www.ph.ucla.edu/epi/bioter/pursuithatfill.html; Nicholas D. Kristof, "Connecting Deadly Dots," *New York Times*, May 24, 2002.

62. Transcript, http://www.anthraxinvestigation.com/Hatfill74-F.pdf.

63. Hatfill was placed on a thirty-day administrative leave before being terminated. See Joan McKinney, "LSU Axes Official," *The Advocate*, September 5, 2002, http://www.ph.ucla.edu/epi/Bioter/lsuaxesofficial.html; see also Hatfill's complaint at para. 45.

64. "Anthrax Probe Zeroes in on Scientist," ABC News, January 9, 2003, http://www. anthraxinvestigation.com/abc.html.

65. *Id.*

66. Hatfill settled his libel suit against *Vanity Fair*, *Reader's Digest*, Vassar College, and Foster in February 2007 for $10 million. See http://www.nysun .com/national/ hatfill-settles-10m-libel-lawsuit/49333/. U.S. District Judge Claude M. Hilton dismissed Hatfill's libel suit against the *New York Times* on the ground that the newspaper had not acted with "actual malice," as required by *Gertz v. Robert Welch, Inc.*, 418 U.S. 323, 94 S. Ct. 2997, 41 L. Ed. 2d 789, 1 Media L. Rep. (BNA) 1633 (1974), in suits brought by public figures. *Hatfill v. New York Times Co.*, 488 F. Supp. 2d 522, 35 Media L. Rep. (BNA) 1391 (E.D. Va. 2007), aff'd, 532 F.3d 312, 36 Media L. Rep. (BNA) 1897 (4th Cir. 2008), cert. denied, 129 S. Ct. 765, 172 L. Ed. 2d 755 (2008).

67. U.S.C. § 2680(h).

68. Judge Walton's March 16, 2007, order is available at http://www. anthr axinvestigation.com/Hatfill89.pdf.

69. The Privacy Act of 1974, 5 U.S.C. § 552a (emphasis added).

70. Judge Walton eventually ruled in Hatfill's favor on this issue, ordering the government to amend its answer to Hatfill's complaint, at http://medialaw. org/Content/ Navigation- Menu/Hot_Topics/Reporters_Privilege/Hatfil lOrderonSources(2007).pdf.

71. Defendants' Memorandum in Opposition to Plaintiff's Motion for Leave to File a Motion to Compel Discovery and Overrule Defendants' Assertion of Law Enforcement Privilege, http://www.anthraxinvestigation.com /Hatfill78.pdf.

72. Deposition of Robert Roth, http://www.anthraxinvestigation.com /Hatfill74-B.pdf.

73. Deployed in 1995, the ACS was a mainframe-based electronic investigative system of records. ACS employed technology dating back to the 1980s; critics called ACS obsolete when it was first installed. ACS also drew severe criticism for its lack of security. See Webster Report, U.S. Department of Justice, http://www.usdoj.gov/ 05publications/websterre port.pdf; http://www.9–11commission.gov/staff _statements/ staff_state ment_9.pdf.

74. Several government reports have criticized the system's poor security and operational limitations. See, e.g., U.S. Department of Justice, *Office of Inspector General Report*, September 2007, http://www.usdoj.gov/oig/special /s0710/index.htm.

75. The settlement was announced just weeks before the highly publicized suicide of Dr. Bruce Ivins, another government anthrax researcher whom the FBI eventually claimed had been solely responsible for the anthrax attacks. After Ivins's suicide in July 2008, the FBI determined that he had been responsible for the attacks. On February 19, 2010, the FBI officially closed the investigation, issuing a ninety-two-page report concluding that Ivins "acted alone in planning and executing [the anthrax] attacks." See U.S. Department of Justice, Justice News, "Justice Department and FBI Announce Formal Conclusion of Investigation into 2001 Anthrax Attacks,

Feb. 19, 2010," http://www.justice.gov/opa/pr/2010/February/10-nsd-166.html. See Federal Bureau of Investigation, "Anthrax Investigation: Closing a Chapter," FBI press release, http://www.fbi.gov/page2/august08/amerithrax080608a.html (quoting Assistant Director in Charge of the FBI Washington Field Office Joseph Persichini as saying, "Bruce Ivins was responsible for the death, sickness, and fear brought to our country by the 2001 anthrax mailings").

76. U.S. Department of Justice, Official Statement Regarding the Settlement, http://www.usdoj.gov/opa/pr/2008/June/08-opa-576.html. The settlement agreement is available at http://www.anthraxinvestigation.com/Hatfill162–1.pdf.

77. Federal Bureau of Investigation, "About Us: Frequently Asked Questions," www.fbi.gov/aboutus/faqs/faqsone.htm.

78. See Interim Order, Department Confidentiality Policy, Patrol Guide 203 Series, August 5, 2009 (on file with author).

79. U.S. Department of Justice, Memo, May 7, 2002, http://www.usdoj.gov/ dag/readingroom/dag-memo-05072002.pdf.

80. United States Attorneys' Manual §1–7.530(A), http://ww.usdoj.gov/usao/ eousa/ foia_ read- ing_room/usam/title1/7mdoj.htm.

81. 8 C.F.R. § 50.2, "Release of information by Department of Justice personnel relating to criminal and civil proceedings," http://edocket.access.gpo.gov/cfr_2001/julqtr/pdf/ 28cfr50.2.pdf.

CHAPTER 3
Linking Bodies to Criminal Histories

1. *Time Magazine*, August 4, 1924.

2. President's Commission on Law Enforcement and Administration of Justice, *The Challenge of Crime in a Free Society*, at 286 (February 1967), https://www.ncjrs.gov/pdffiles1/nij/42.pdf.

3. The creation of centralized and systematized criminal record repositories began when large cities in the northeast of the country (e.g., New York and Boston) established formal police departments. For a history of U.S. police, see Robert M. Fogelson, *Big-City Police* (Cambridge, MA: Harvard University Press, 1977); Thomas A. Reppetto, *The Blue Parade* (New York: Free Press, 1978). See also Erin Murphy, *Databases, Doctrine and Constitutional Criminal Procedure*, 37 Fordham Urb. L.J. 803, 805 (2010).

4. John Edgar Hoover, *The Role of Identification in Law Enforcement: An Historical Adventure*, 46 St. John's L. Rev. 613 (1972).

5. See Jane Caplan and John Torpey (eds.), *Documenting Individual Identity: The Development of State Practices in the Modern World* (Princeton, NJ: Princeton University Press, 2001).

6. See Congress of the United States, Office of Technology Assessment, *An Assessment of Alternatives for a National Computerized Criminal History System* 26–28 (Washington, DC: U.S. Government Printing Office, 1982).

7. Francis Galton, *Finger Prints* (London: Macmillan, 1892).

8. Simon Cole, *Suspect Identities: A History of Fingerprinting and Criminal Identification*, chap. 3 (Cambridge, MA: Harvard University Press, 2001).

9. *Maryland v. King*, 569 U.S. – (2013). See also Cole, *Suspect Identities*, at 1–4.

10. "In addition, two-thirds of the arrestee-collection states authorize sampling upon arrest, rather than requiring a judicial determination of probable cause, and most require the sampled individual to seek expungement." See Erin Murphy, *License, Registration, Cheek Swab: DNA Testing and the Divided Court*, 127 Harvard L. Rev. 161, 168 (2013).

11. See http://www.fbi.gov/about-us/lab/biometric-analysis/codis/codis-and-ndis-fact-sheet (retrieved January 23, 2014).

12. See Henry Sontheimer, *Pennsylvania Commission on Crime & Delinquency, Final Report: Comparative Assessment of Three Police Booking Center Projects* (2000), http://www.portal.state.pa.us/portal/server.pt/gateway/PTARGS_0_2_882146_0_0_18/Central%20Booking%20Eval%20Report%20Apr2000.pdf (describing both manual and modern-day automated booking procedures).

13. See Legal Action Center, *Your New York State Rap Sheet: A Guide to Getting, Understanding and Correcting Your Criminal Record* at 11 (2011), http://www.lac.org/doc_library/lac/publications/YourRapSheet.pdf.

14. See U.S. Department of Justice, *Use and Management of Criminal History Record Information: A Comprehensive Report 2001 Update*, U.S. Department of Justice, at 74. Dec. 2001, NCJ 187670, http://www.bjs.gov/content/pub/pdf/umchri01.pdf.

15. See Frank Morn, *The Eye That Never Sleeps: A History of the Pinkerton National Detective Agency* (Bloomington: Indiana University Press, 1982), which examines how the agency filled the gaps of the inadequate public police and their limited jurisdiction.

16. Harry Bratt, Law Enforcement Assistance Administration, United States Department of Justice, *Survey of State Criminal Justice Information Systems*, in George A. Buck (ed.), *Project SEARCH: Proceedings of a National Symposium on Criminal Justice and Statistics Systems* 73, 74 (Sacramento, CA: Search Group, 1970); Paul E. Leuba, *Demand for Criminal History Records by Non-Criminal Justice Agencies*, in Bureau of Justice/SEARCH Conference on Open v. Confidential Records 25 (November 1988).

17. See Bureau of Justice Statistics, U.S. Department of Justice, *Survey of State Criminal History Information Systems* 3 (2012), https://www.ncjrs.gov/pdffiles1/bjs/grants/237253.pdf.

18. International Association of Chiefs of Police, Timeline, http://www.theiacp.org/About/History/Timeline/tabid/101/Default.aspx (last visited April 18, 2012); National Archives, Records of the Federal Bureau of Investigation, http://www.archives.gov/research/guide-fed-records/groups/065.html#65.4 (last visited April 18, 2012).

19. See Richard Gid Powers, *Secrecy and Power: The Life of J. Edgar Hoover*, chap. 6, pp. 144–178 (New York: Free Press, 1987). See also Nathan Douthit, *Police Professionalism and the War against Crime in the United States, 1920s–1930s*, in George L. Mosse (ed.), *Police Forces in History* 317–33 (London: Sage, 1975).

20. Federal Bureau of Investigation, Integrated Automated Fingerprint Identification System, http://www.fbi.gov/about-us/cjis/fingerprints_biometrics/iafis/iafis (last visited May 29, 2012).

21. U.S. Department of Justice, *Use and Management of Criminal History Record Information*, 2001 Update, at 7. See also Athan G. Theoharis, *The FBI & American Democracy: A Brief Critical History* 33–34 (Lawrence: University Press of Kansas (2004); National Archives, *Records of the Federal Bureau of Investigation* (FBI), http://www.archives.gov/research/guide-fed-records/groups/065.html (last visited May 27, 2012).

22. For a history of the FBI's Identification Division, see Federal Bureau of Investigation, *Identification Division of the FBI—A Brief Outline of the History, the Services, and the Operating Techniques of the World's Greatest Repository of Fingerprints* (Washington, DC: FBI, 1991).

23. See U.S. Department of Justice, *Use and Management of Criminal History Record Information*, 2001 Update, at 3; see also James M. Tien, Structured Decisions Corp., *Measuring the Performance of Criminal History Systems: The Records Quality Index* (2005), http://www.sdcorp.net/public/Pub_RQI_Report.pdf; Patricia M. Harris and Kimberly S. Keller, *Ex-Offenders Need Not Apply*, 20(1) J. Contemp. Crim. Just. 6, 15 (2005) (describing problems of data accuracy, especially disposition information, in the state repositories).

24. See U.S. Department of Justice, *Use and Management of Criminal History Record Information*, 2001 Update, at 3.

25. Office of Technology Assessment, *An Assessment of Alternatives for a National Computerized Criminal History System* 31 (Washington, DC: U.S. Government Printing Office, 1982).

26. Omnibus Crime Control and Safe Streets Act of 1968, 90 Pub. L. 351, 82 Stat. 197 (June 19, 1968) at § 101 and § 301.

27. House Resolution 851, November 17, 2009.

28. These include rap sheet standards, Global Justice Information Sharing Initiative, National Information Exchange Model (NIEM), and the FBI's National Data Exchange Project (N-Dex). In 2014, it had a staff of twenty-eight.

29. J. William Holland, Automation of American Criminal Justice, in Mehdi Khosrow-Pour (ed.), *Encyclopedia of Information Science and Technology* 1:197 (Hershey, PA: IGI Global, 2005).

30. Bill Hebenton and Terry Thomas, *Criminal Records: State, Citizen, and the Politics of Protection* 27–36 (Burlington, VT: Ashgate, 1993).

31. Bureau of Justice Statistics' Census of State and Local Law Enforcement Agencies, for 2008 (released in 2011), http://www.bjs.gov/content/pub/pdf/csllea08.pdf.

32. See James B. Jacobs, *Can Gun Control Work?* (Oxford: Oxford University Press, 2002).

33. Crime Identification Technology Act of 1998, 42 U.S.C. § 14601 (1998).

34. Report of the National Task Force on Privacy, Technology and Criminal Justice Information 40, 119 (Sacramento, CA: Search Group, 2001), http://www.bjs.gov/content/pub/pdf/rntfptcj.pdf.

35. See Gerard F. Ramker, U.S. Department of Justice, Bureau of Justice Statistics, *Program Report: Nat'l Criminal History Improvement Program—Improving Criminal History Records for Background Checks*, 2005 (2006), http://www.ojp.usdoj.gov/bjs/pub/pdf/ichrbc05.pdf.

36. Bureau of Justice Statistics, U.S. Department of Justice, *Survey of State Criminal History Information Systems* (2012), at 2.

37. Pub. L. No. 92–544, 86 Stat 1109, 1115 (1972).

38. FBI, *FBI Criminal History Checks for Employment and Licensing*, http://www.fbi.gov/about-us/cjis/background-checks/backgroundchk.

39. 86 Stat. 1115 (1972).

40. See 15 U.S.C. § 78(q)(f)(2) (1982 ed., Supp. V). See also *U.S. Department of Justice v. Reporters Committee for Freedom of the Press et al.*, 489 U.S. 749, 753 (1989).

41. 42 U.S.C. § 2169(a)(2006).

42. National Child Protection Act of 1993, Pub. L. 103-209, 107 Stat. 2490 (1993), and amendments (http://www.ojjdp.gov/pubs/guidelines/appen-a.html).

43. Housing Opportunity Program Extension Act of 1996, Pub. L. 104-120, § 9, 110 Stat. 134 (1996). Additional authorization is required before releasing certain criminal records of juveniles.

44. See Pub. L. 151-205, 112 Stat. 1885 § 221-22 (1998).

45. Uniting and Strengthening America by Providing Appropriate Tools Required to Intercept and Obstruct Terrorism (USA PATRIOT) Act of 2001, Pub. L. 107-56, 115 Stat. 272 (2001); see also SEARCH, *Report of the National Task Force on the Criminal Backgrounding of America* 1 (2005), http://www.search.org/files/pdf/ReportofNTFCBA.pdf.

46. Maritime Transportation Security Act of 2002, Pub. L. 107-295, 116 Stat. 2064 (2002); Pub. L. 151-205, 112 Stat. 1885, § 221-22 (1998).

47. Public Health Security & Bioterrorism Preparedness & Response Act of 2002, Pub. L. 107-188, 116 Stat. 594 (2002).

48. Aviation & Transportation Security Act, Pub. L. 107-71, 115 Stat. 597 (2001).

49. Pub. L. 107-295, 116 Stat. 2064 (2002).

50. 49 CFR § 1572.103, Disqualifying Criminal Offenses.

51. The Private Security Officer Employment Authorization Act (PSOEAA); Pub L. 108-458 § 6403, codified as 28 U.S.C. § 534. DOJ's implementing regulations are at 28 CFR 6402.

52. Intelligence Reform & Terrorism Prevention Act of 2004, Pub. L. 108-458, 118 Stat. 3638 (2004).), sec. 6403(d).

53. U.S. Department of Justice, Office of the Attorney General, The Attorney General's Report on Criminal History Background Checks 76 (June 21, 2006), http://www.justice.gov/olp/ag_bgchecks_report.pdf_p. 76.

54. *Id.* at 78.

55. Pub. L. 92-544 (86 Stat. 1115) (1972).

56. U.S. Department of Justice, Office of the Attorney General, The Attorney General's Report on Criminal History Background Checks 21 (June 21, 2006).

57. E-mail from William Estock to author, July 27, 2012.

58. U.S. General Accounting Office, GAO/GGD-85–4, *Observations on the FBI's Interstate Identification Index* (1984), http://www.gao.gov/products/GGD-85-4.

59. See http://www.fbi.gov/about-us/cjis/cc/quick-links-to-maps/IIImap.

60. Crime Identification Technology Act of 1998, 42 U.S.C. § 14601 (1998); U.S. Department of Justice, Bureau of Justice Statistics, National Crime Prevention and Privacy Compact: Resource Materials 6–7 (1998), http://www.bjs.gov/content/pub/pdf/ncppcrm.pdf; Federal Bureau of Investigation, The National Crime Prevention and Privacy Compact Act of 1998.

61. Federal Bureau of Investigation, National List of Compact/MOU States, http://www.fbi.gov/about-us/cjis/cc/compact-mou-participation/list_of_compact_mou_states.

62. The FBI's Advisory Policy Board for the National Crime Information Center found that the lack of uniformity in state criminal history records made the Triple I less useful and urged greater standardization among states.

63. U.S. Department of Justice, Bureau of Justice Statistics, *Report of the National Task Force on Criminal History Record Disposition Reporting* 13 (1992), https://www.ncjrs.gov/pdffiles1/Digitization/135836NCJRS.pdf.

64. National Criminal History Record Task Force, *Increasing the Utility of the Criminal History Record: Report of the National Task Force* 1 (December 1995), http://www.bjs.gov/content/pub/pdf/IUCHR.PDF.

65. *Id.* at iii.

66. *Id.* at 14.

67. *Id.* at 15.

68. *Id.* at 23.

69. *Id.* at 32.

70. SEARCH, *State Repository Records and Reporting Quality Assurance Programs,* http://www.search.org/programs/policy/qap/ (last visited November 29, 2010).

71. See Employer Access to Criminal Background Checks: The Need For Efficiency and Accuracy, Hearing Before the Subcommittee on Crime, Terrorism and Homeland Security, House Committee on the Judiciary, 110th Congress, 1st Session, April 27, 2007.

72. Karen J. Terry and John S. Furlong, *Sex Offender Registration and Community Notification: A "Megan's Law" Sourcebook* (Kingson, NJ: Civic Research Institute, 2nd ed., 2008).

73. For example, see N.Y. Sex Offender Registration Act § 168-f (Consol. 2011).

74. Wayne A. Logan, *Knowledge as Power: Criminal Registration and Community Notification Laws in America* (Stanford, CA: Stanford University Press, 2009); Wayne A. Logan, *Criminal Justice Federalism and National Sex Offender Policy,* 6 Ohio St. J. Crim. L. 51 (2008); Roxane Lieb, *Washington's Sexually Violent Predator Law: Legislative History and Comparison with Other States* (Olympia: Washington State Institute for Public Policy, 1996), http://www.wsipp.wa.gov/rptfiles/WAsexlaw.pdf.

75. See U.S. Department of Justice, "About NSOPW," http://www.nsopw.gov/Core/About.aspx.

76. See U.S. Department of Justice, "National Sex Offender Quick Search," http://www.nsopw.gov/Core/Portal.aspx?AspxAutoDetectCookieSupport=1; http://www.nsopw.gov/Core/About.Aspx.

77. Adam Walsh Child Protection and Safety Act of 2006, Pub. L. No. 109–248, 120 Stat. 587 (2006), http://www.justice.gov/criminal/ceos/Adam%20Walsh.pdf. The Supreme Court rejected an Ex Post Facto challenge to the law in *Smith v. Doe*, 538 U.S. 84 (2003).

78. See *Sex Offender Registration and Notification—Final Guidelines* (July 2008), http://www.ojp.usdoj.gov/smart/pdfs/final_sornaguidelines.pdf.

79. See http://svcalt.mt.gov/svor/search.asp and http://www.icrimewatch.net/indiana.php for Montana's and Indiana's sexual or violent offender registry, respectively. The New York State Senate passed a bill to create a registry of convicted violent felons—see http://www.nysenate.gov/press-release/senate-passes-bill-create-registry-violent-offenders.

80. See Molly J. Walker Wilson, *The Expansion of Criminal Registries and the Illusion of Control*, 73 La. L. Rev. 509 528–41 (2012–2013); Stacy A. Nowicki, *On the Lamb: Toward a National Animal Abuser Registry*, 17 Animal L. 197 (2010–2011); "Arson Registry Bill Signed into Law," Ohio Senate press release, December 20, 2012, http://www.ohiosenate.gov/schaffer/press/arson-registry-bill-signed-into-law; General Assembly 178, 114th Sess. (S. Carolina 2001).

81. See SEARCH, National Consortium for Justice Information Statistics, Survey, April 9, 2001, http://www.search.org/files/pdf/internet_cch_survey_II.pdf.

82. Kansas Bureau of Investigation, "Kansas Criminal History Record Check," https://www.kansas.gov/criminalhistory.

83. Shawn Bushway, *The Nature of Criminal History Records*, presentation at the Richard Netter Conference on Criminal Records and Employment, December 8, 2011.

84. See, e.g., Terence P. Thornberry and Marvin D. Krohn, *The Self-Report Method for Measuring Delinquency and Crime*, in David Duffee et al. (eds.), *Criminal Justice 2000*, Vol. 4, *Innovations in Measurement and Analysis* 33–83 (Washington, DC: U.S. Department of Justice, 2000); David Lisak and Paul M. Miller, *Repeat Rape and Multiple Offending among Undetected Rapists*, 17 Violence and Victims 73 (2002). The same is true for undetected recidivists: see A. Nicholas Groth et al., *Undetected Recidivism among Rapists and Child Molesters*, 28 Crime & Delinquency 450 (1982).

CHAPTER 4
Court Records

1. *Richmond Newspapers v. Virginia*, 448 U.S. 555, 572 (1980).

2. *Globe Newspaper Co. v. Fenton*, 819 F. Supp. 89, 94 (D. Mass. 1993).

3. *Nixon v. Warner Communications, Inc.*, 435 U.S. 589, 597 (1978) (internal citations omitted).

4. Allan Ashman and Jeffrey Parness, *The Concept of a Unified Court System*, 24 DePaul L. Rev. 1, 2 (1974). Some dimensions of court unification are a simplified organizational structure, centralized court management, centralized rule making, and centralized financing and budgeting. Victor E. Flango, "Court Unification," in David Levinson (ed.), *Encyclopedia of Crime and Punishment* 356 (Thousand Oaks, CA: Sage, 2002).

5. For the complete list of courts described as legally unified, see the National Center for State Courts, "Court Unification," http://www.ncsc.org/topics/court-management/court-unification/state-links.aspx. For a historical account of state court unification and centralized court management, see Allan Ashman and Jeffrey Parness, *The Concept of a Unified Court System*, 24 DePaul L. Rev. 1 (1974); and Victor E. Flango, "Court Unification," in David Levinson (ed.), *Encyclopedia of Crime and Punishment* 356 (Thousand Oaks, CA: Sage, 2002).

6. For a survey of the remote electronic accessibility of court records in state courts, see the Reporters Committee for Freedom of the Press, *Electronic Access to Court Records* (Spring 2007), http://www.rcfp.org/rcfp/orders/docs/EACR.pdf.

7. See, e.g., Judicial Conference Privacy Subcommittee, Conference on Privacy and Internet Access to Court Files, *Panel One: General Discussion on Privacy and Public Access to Court Files*, 79 Fordham L. Rev. 1 (2010–2011); New Jersey Supreme Court Special Committee on Public Access to Court Records, *Report of the Supreme Court Special Committee on Public Access to Court Records*, November 29, 2007. See also Hon. Paul H. Anderson, "Future Trends in Public Access: Court Information, Privacy and Technology," in C. Flango et al., *Future Trends in State Courts 2011* (Williamsburg, VA: National Center for State Courts, 2011); Joint Court Management Committee of the Conference of Chief Justices and the Conference of State Court Administrators, *Public Access to Court Records: Guidelines for Policy Development by State Courts*, July 16, 2002. For a discussion on the computerization of court records and privacy issues, see Amanda Conley et al., *Sustaining Privacy and Open Justice in the Transition to Online Court Records: A Multidisciplinary Inquiry*, 71 Maryland L. Rev. 772 (2012).

8. See Washington Courts, Case Records search page, http://dw.courts.wa.gov/index.cfm?fa=home.home.

9. See, e.g., the CourtConnect system in Arkansas, https://courts.arkansas.gov/administration/acap/courtconnect; and Pennsylvania's Unified Judicial System Web Portal, http://www.pacourts.us/judicial-administration/judicial-automation.

10. See Nancy S. Marder, *From "Practical Obscurity" to Web Disclosure: A New Understanding of Public Information*, 59 Syracuse L. Rev. 441 (2009); Daniel J. Solove, *Access and Aggregation: Public Records, Privacy and the Constitution*, 86 Minn. L. Rev. 1137 (2002). The concept of "practical obscurity" is discussed by Justice Stevens in *U.S. Department of Justice v. Reporters Committee for Freedom of Press*, 489 U.S. 749 (1989).

11. See Peter W. Martin, *Online Access to Court Records—From Documents to Data, Particulars to Patterns*, 53 Vill. L. Rev. 855, 858–59 (2008).

12. United States Courts, Public Access to Court Electronic Records (PACER), homepage, http://www.pacer.gov/; United States Courts, Public

Access to Court Electronic Records (PACER), "Frequently Asked Questions," http://www.pacer.gov/psc/hfaq.html.

13. United States Courts, "Court Records," http://www.uscourts.gov/Court Records.aspx.

14. See Center for Information Technology, Princeton University, RECAP homepage, https://www.recapthelaw.org/privacy/.

15. The National Center for State Courts provides a good explanation of how the public can obtain court records in most states. See National Center for State Courts, "Privacy/Public Access to Court Records, State Links," http://www.ncsc.org/Topics/Access-and-Fairness/Privacy-Public-Access-to-Court-Records/State-Links.aspx.

16. See New York State Unified Court System, eCourts: Webcrims, https://iapps.courts.state.ny.us/webcrim_attorney/Login.

17. See State of Maine Judicial Branch website, http://www.courts.state.me.us/maine_courts/index.shtml.

18. See SEARCH, The National Consortium for Justice Information and Statistics, *Report of the National Task Force on the Commercial Sale of Criminal Justice Record Information* (2005); National Center for State Courts, "Privacy/Public Access to Court Records, Rules on Bulk Data," http://www.ncsc.org/topics/access-and-fairness/privacy-public-access-to-court-records/state-links.aspx.

19. Phone interview with Beth Bickley, June 8, 2012.

20. Rules of Superintendence for the Courts of Ohio, Rule 46, http://www.supremecourt.ohio.gov/Boards/superintendence/PAR/SupR44_47Final.pdf.

21. Supreme Court of New Jersey, Supreme Court Special Committee on Public Access to Court Records, Report of the Supreme Court Special Committee on Public Access to Court Records, at 32–33 (2007).

22. *Id.* at 31–33.

23. Idaho Court Administrative Rule 32, section (g)(29), http://www.isc.idaho.gov/icar32; e-mail correspondence with Taunya Jones, Planning and Research Manager for the Idaho Supreme Court, November 13, 2013.

24. Interview with Stephanie Harris, July 6, 2012. See also Arkansas Judiciary, Administrative Order 19, https://courts.arkansas.gov/rules/admin_orders_sc/index.cfm#19.

25. E-mail correspondence with Stephanie Harris, November 13, 2013.

26. See, e.g., the daily docket of the Clark County Superior Court in Vancouver, WA, http://www.co.clark.wa.us/courts/superior/docket.html; the Maryland Circuit Court for Howard County's docket is available at http://mdcourts.gov/circuit/howard/dockets.html.

27. Meliah Thomas, *The First Amendment Right of Access to Docket Sheets*, 94 Cal. L. Rev. 1537, 1538 (2006).

28. Docket sheet for *U.S. v. Peters*, District Court, Western District of New York (Buffalo) Source: Public Access to Court Electronic Records (PACER), criminal docket sheet for Case# 1:06-Cr-00227-WMS-1.

29. *Hartford Courant Co. v. Pellegrino*, 380 F.3d 83, 93 (2d Cir. 2004).

30. See, e.g., Superior Court of California, County of Santa Clara, "Case Index Search," http://www.scscourt.org/court_divisions/criminal/index_search.asp.

31. New York State Unified Court System, eCourts: Webcrims, https://iapps.courts.state.ny.us/webcrim_attorney/Login.

32. *Id.*

33. See, e.g., Washington Courts, Case search page, http://dw.courts.wa.gov/?fa=home.casesearchTerms.

34. See, e.g., Superior Court of California, County of Santa Clara, "Criminal Index Search," http://www.scscourt.org/court_divisions/criminal/index_search.asp.

35. "The clerk of the district court must enter in the records every court order or judgment and the date of entry," Fed. R. Crim. P. 55; see also 28 James W. Moore et al., *Moore's Federal Practice* § 655.02 (3d ed., 2007): "In every criminal case the clerk maintains a docket in which a record is made of all actions taken in the case. . . . Magistrate judges' proceedings are recorded in a similar fashion."

36. For example, briefs for cases on appeal to the California Supreme Court are available at http://www.courts.ca.gov/2951.htm.

37. N.Y. Cvr. Law § 50-b.

38. For an example of the kind of criteria a pretrial services agency might consider and include in its report, see New York City Criminal Justice Agency, Inc., *CJA: Annual Report 2011* (December 2012), http://www.cjareports.org/reports/annual11.pdf.

39. Other documents that cannot be revealed to the public are information regarding jurors, grand jury records, personal information of victims of sex offenses, and any document that the court specifically marks as sealed or confidential.

40. See New Jersey Courts, *Documents*, http://www.judiciary.state.nj.us/atlantic/criminal/recordrequest.htm#doc (retrieved July 7, 2013).

41. See, e.g., *State v. W.B.*, 205 N.J. 588, 17 A.3d 187 (2011), where the defendant was convicted of offenses relating to the sexual abuse of his stepdaughter.

42. United States Courts, "Privacy Policy for Electronic Case Files," http://www.privacy.uscourts.gov/privacypolicy_Mar2008Revised.htm.

43. *Lugosch v. Pyramid Co. of Onondaga*, 435 F.3d 110, 120 (2d Cir. 2006).

44. N.Y. Cls. Cpl. § 160.50 (d)(ii); see *Matter of Sheriff Officers Assn., Inc. v County of Nassau*, 2012 N.Y. Misc. LEXIS 6057, 2012 NY Slip Op 33159(U) (N.Y. Sup. Ct. November 30, 2012).

45. *McClatchy Newspapers v. United States Dist. Court* (in Re McClatchy Newspapers Inc.), 288 F.3d 369 (9th Cir. Cal. 2001)

46. *Id.* at 374 (internal quotes omitted).

47. Cal. Penal Code § 1203.10 (emphasis added).

48. See Fed. R. Crim. P. 32(e)(2). The Federal Rules of Criminal Procedure (Rule 32(e)(2)) prescribe a presumption of confidentiality for the PSR. The Second Circuit held that the PSR should not be disclosed unless the district court finds "a compelling demonstration that disclosure of the report is required to meet the ends of justice." *United States v. Charmer Indus., Inc.*, 711 F.2d 1164, 1175 (2d Cir. 1983).

49. *U.S. Department of Justice v. Julian*, 486 U.S. 1 (1988).

50. See John P. Higgins, *Confidentiality of Presentence Reports*, 28 Alb. L. Rev. 12, 14 (1964); American Bar Association Project on Standards for Criminal Justice, Standards Relating to Sentencing Alternatives and Procedures 210–12 (approved draft, 1968); Stephen A. Fennel and William Hall, *Due Process at Sentencing: An Empirical and Legal Analysis of the Disclosure of Presentence Reports in Federal Courts*, 93 Harv. L. Rev. 1613 (1979–80). In some states, such as Idaho (Idaho Code G19-5306) and Indiana (Burns Ind. Code Ann. G35-405-6), victims have the right to review the presentence report.

51. *People v. Connor*, 9 Cal. Rptr. 3d 521, 533 (Cal. Dist. Ct. App., 6th Dist. 2004).

52. Phone interview with James Manganello, June 27, 2012.

53. For a discussion of the practices in different states concerning the sealing of plea agreements, see Judicial Conference Privacy Subcommittee, Conference on Privacy and Internet Access to Court Files, *Panel Five: Cooperation and Plea Agreements—Judges' Roundtable*, 79 Fordham L. Rev. 85 (2010–2011).

54. See Caren Myers Morrison, *Privacy, Accountability, and the Cooperating Defendant: Towards a New Role for Internet Access to Court Records*, 62 Vand. L. Rev. 921, 924 (2009).

55. *Id.* at 923: "In response to unwanted scrutiny, prosecutors, sometimes aided by the courts, will attempt to conceal or disguise the information they regard as sensitive or confidential."

56. Department of Justice, *Response to Request for Comments on the Privacy and Security Implications of Public Internet Access to Federal Plea Agreements* (October 26, 2007), http://www.uscourts.gov/uscourts/RulesAndPolicies/Privacy/65.pdf.

57. See Caren Myers Morrison, *Privacy, Accountability, and the Cooperating Defendant: Towards a New Role for Internet Access to Court Records* 62 Vand. L. Rev 921, 969–77 (2009).

58. *Id.* at 925.

59. Commonwealth of Massachusetts, *A Guide to Public Access, Sealing & Expungement*, 45 (Rev. September 2013), http://www.mass.gov/courts/courtsandjudges/courts/districtcourt/pubaccesscourtrecords.pdf.

60. *Commonwealth v. Doe*, 420 Mass. 142, 152 (1995); *Commonwealth v. Stephens*, 75 Mass. App. Ct. 1113 (2009), quoting *Commonwealth v. Roberts*, 39 Mass. App. Ct. 355, 358 (1995).

61. *Commonwealth v. Doe*, 420 Mass. 142. 151 (1995).

62. N.Y. Crim. Pro. Law § 160.50.

CHAPTER 5
Privatizing Criminal Records

1. United States Congress, Senate Committee on Banking and Currency, *Fair Credit Reporting: Report to Accompany S. 823*, S. Rep. No. 91-517, 91st Cong. 2 (Washington, DC: U.S. Government Printing Office, 1969).

2. Quoted in David Segal, "Mugged by a Mug Shot," *New York Times*, October 6, 2013, at BU1.

3. See Neil M. Richards, *Reconciling Data Privacy and the First Amendment* 52 UCLA L. Rev. 1149 (2005).

4. Persis S. Yu and Sharon M. Dietrich, National Consumer Law Center, *Broken Records: How Errors by Criminal Background Checking Companies Harm Workers and Businesses*, at 7–8 National Consumer Law Center (April 2012); see also Editorial, "Accuracy in Criminal Background Checks," *New York Times*, August 10, 2012, at A18 (describing the criminal background checking business as having "grown so quickly that no one seems to know how many companies there are").

5. SEARCH, National Consortium for Justice Information and Statistics, *Report of the National Task Force on the Commercial Sale of Criminal Justice Record Information*, at 7 (2005), http://www.search.org/files/pdf/ReportofNTFCBA.pdf.

6. Montserrat Miller, counsel/lobbyist to NAPBS, *Presentation at the Richard Netter Conference on Criminal Records and Employment*, December 8, 2011.

7. National Association of Professional Background Screeners, *Background Screening PowerPoint Presentation*, slide 14, http://www.napbs.com/i4a/pages/index.cfm?pageid=3280.

8. KPMG Corporate Finance LLC, *2011 Background Screening Industry Survey*, at 7 (April 2011); Sterling Infosystems, Inc., *Press Releases*, http://www.sterlinginfosystems.com/news-and-events/news/press-releases/ (last visited June 20, 2012).

9. HireRight, *On Demand Solutions and Services: Widescreen Plus*, http://www.hireright.com/Widescreen-Plus.aspx.

10. HRO Today, *Top Outsourced Screening Services Provider*, November 2008.

11. Ellen Nakashima and Robert O'Harrow Jr., "LexisNexis Parent Set to Buy ChoicePoint," *Washington Post*, February 22, 2008, http://articles.washingtonpost.com/2008-02-22/business/36857083_1_choicepoint-data-broker-lexisnexis-group.

12. Larry Henry and Derek Hinton, *The Criminal Records Manual* 83 (Lanham, MD: Facts on Demand Press, 3rd ed., 2008); SEARCH, National Consortium for Justice Information and Statistics, *Report of the National Task Force on the Commercial Sale of Criminal Justice Information* 7 (2005).

13. See SEARCH, National Consortium for Justice Information and Statistics, *Report of the National Task Force on the Commercial Sale of Criminal Justice Information* 7, 9 (2005), http://www.search.org/files/pdf/RNTFCSCJRI.pdf.

14. Sterling Infosystems, Inc., *Press Release: Sterling Makes Crain's New York Fast 50 List*, June 26, 2012, http://www.sterlinginfosystems.com/documents/Press-release-Fast-50-List.pdf.

15. HRO Today, *2011 Baker's Dozen Customer Satisfaction Ratings: Employee Screening*, Vol. 10, No. 9, November 2011.

16. First Advantage, *Employment Background Screening*, http://www.fadv.com/screening-and-assessment/employment-background-screening/; see also KPMG Corporate Finance LLC, *2011 Background Screening Industry Survey*, April 2011, at 7.

17. ADP, *Twelfth Annual ADP Screening Index Reveals Nearly 10 Percent of Job Candidates Have Criminal History, Credit Issues or Driving Citations*, December 2009, http://www.adp.com/media/press-releases/archive/2009-news-releases/twelfth-annual-adp-screening-index.aspx; ADP, *Criminal Court Records*, https://www.adpselect.com/ttcs/criminalRecords.htm (last visited June 26, 2012).

18. CoreLogic, National Background Data, http://www.nationalbackgrounddata.com; CoreLogic, National Background Data, *Our Clients, Our Approach*, https://www.nationalbackgrounddata.com/marketing/solution_p_n.html (last visited June 27, 2012). Bloomberg Law, Lexis Nexis, and Thomson Reuters provide online access to court docket information. See Bloomberg Law, *Dockets*, http://about.bloomberglaw.com/product-features/dockets/; Lexis Nexis, *Lexis Nexis Courtlink*, http://www.lexisnexis.com/en-us/products/courtlink-for-corporate-or-professionals.page; Thomson Reuters, *Legal Solutions: Dockets*, http://legalsolutions.thomsonreuters.com/law-products/westlawnext/litigator/dockets.

19. William Hauswirth, President, ISO IntelliCorp Records, *Negligent Hiring: Employer Risk*, ISO Review, http://www.iso.com/Research-and-Analyses/ISO-Review/Negligent-Hiring-Employer-Risk.html.

20. See Bureau of Justice Statistics, U.S. Department of Justice, *Report of the National Task Force on Privacy, Technology, and Criminal Justice Information* 40 (2001), http://www.ojp.usdoj.gov/bjs/pub/pdf/rntfptcj.pdf.

21. In some states, employers who fail to take reasonable steps to screen out risky employees can be held liable for damage caused by the negligently hired employee. See George J. Ramos Jr., Vice President of Diversified Risk Management, Inc., *Employers Can Be Sued for Negligent Hiring* (March 3, 2004), http://www.diversifiedriskmanagement.com/articles/negligent-hiring.html; see also William Hauswirth, President, ISO IntelliCorp Records, *Negligent Hiring: Employer Risk*, ISO Review, http://www.iso.com/Research-and-Analyses/ISO-Review/Negligent-Hiring-Employer-Risk.html.

22. John Monahan and Jennifer L. Skeem, *Risk Redux: The Resurgence of Risk Assessment in Criminal Sanctioning* (forthcoming, 2014). See also John Monahan and Jennifer L. Skeem, *Current Directions in Violence Risk Assessment*, 20 Current Directions Psychol. Sci. 38 (2011).

23. The FCRA was a response to the "database revolution of the 1960s." See Anupam Chander, *Youthful Indiscretion in an Internet Age*, at 127, in Saul Levmore and Martha C. Nussbaum (eds.), *The Offensive Internet: Privacy, Speech, and Reputation* (Cambridge, MA: Harvard University Press, 2010).

24. 115 Cong. Rec. 2411 (January 31, 1969) (introductory statements of Senator Proxmire).

25. Chi Chi Wu et al., National Consumer Law Center, *Fair Credit Reporting*, §§ 1.4.1–1.4.5 (6th ed. 2006).

26. 15 U.S.C. § 1681a(f) (2000) (emphasis added).

27. 15 U.S.C. § 1681a(d)(1) (2000) (emphasis added); 15 U.S.C. § 1681b(a).

28. Consumer Reporting Employment Clarification Act, 15 U.S.C. § 1681c(a)(5).

29. 15 U.S.C. § 1681c(a)(2) (a consumer report may not contain "records of arrest that, from date of entry, antedate the report by more than seven years"); 15 U.S.C. § 1681c (b). See Chi Chi Wu et al., National Consumer Law Center, *Fair Credit Reporting*, §§ 5.2.3.6 (6th ed., 2006): "No special rule exists for criminal complaints, warrants, indictments, parole and probation, and various possible criminal judgments of dispositions other than conviction. These events therefore fall within the general rule for any other adverse item of information, and may be reported for only seven years."

30. See, e.g., US Search Terms of Use, http://www.ussearch.com/consumer/commerce/about/terms.jsp.

31. PublicData.com, *About PublicData*, http://www.publicdata.com/about.html.

32. Universal Background Screening, *Background Screening Solutions*, http://www.universalbackground.com/personal/default.asp.

33. See, e.g., www.KnowX.com (previously Rapsheets.com), a LexisNexis subsidiary that directs site visitors seeking to do background checks for employment to the LexisNexis Risk Solutions site, http://www.lexisnexis.com/risk/solutions/employment-screening.aspx.

34. SEARCH, National Consortium for Justice Information and Statistics, *Report of the National Task Force on the Commercial Sale of Criminal Justice Record Information*, at 60 (2005), http://www.search.org/files/pdf/ReportofNTFCBA.pdf.

35. Cal. Civ. Code § 1786.18(a)(7); N.M. Stat. Ann. § 56-3-6(a)(5); N.Y. Gen. Bus. Law § 380-j (a)(1) ("Prohibited information"); but see N.Y. Gen. Bus. Law § 380-j (b) (outlining limited exceptions related to retailers' shoplifting records);

36. Cal. Civ. Code § 1786.18(a)(7); Mass. Gen. Laws, Ch. 93, Sec. 52(a)(5); Mont. Code Ann. § 31-3-112(5); Nev. Rev. Stat. 5698C.150(2); N.M. Stat. Ann. § 56-3-6(a)(5); N.Y. Gen. Bus. Law § 380-j(f)(5); Texas Bus. & Comm. Code § 20.05(a)(4).

37. Cal. Civil Code § 1786.16(b)(1) (California); 20 Ill. Comp. Stat. Ann. 2635/7(A)(1) (Illinois); Minn. Stat. § 13C.02, subd. 2 (Minnesota); Okla. Stat. Tit. 24 § 148(A) (Oklahoma); see also SEARCH, National Consortium for Justice Information and Statistics, *Report of the National Task Force on the Commercial Sale of Criminal Justice Record Information*, at 61 (2005), http://www.search.org/files/pdf/ReportofNTFCBA.pdf.

38. CA Civil Code § 1785 and § 1786; see also Privacy Rights Clearinghouse, *Fact Sheet 16a: Employment Background Checks in California: A Focus on Accuracy*, http://www.privacyrights.org/fs/fs16a-califbck.htm#4 (detailing California statutes).

39. See Elaine M. Chiu, *That Guy's a Batterer! A Scarlet Letter Approach to Domestic Violence in the Information Age*, 44 Fam. L.Q. 255 (2010); Molly J. Walker Wilson, *The Expansion of Criminal Registries and the Illusion of Control*, 73 La. L. Rev. 509 528–41 (2013); Stacy A. Nowicki, *On the Lamb: Toward a National Animal Abuser Registry*, 17 Animal L. 197 (2010).

40. National Domestic Violence Registry, *About*, http://thendvr.org/about/.

41. National Domestic Violence Registry, *Offender Registry*, http://thendvr.org/offender-registry/.

42. Pet-Abuse.com homepage, http://www.pet-abuse.com/; see Stacy A. Nowicki, *On the Lamb: Toward a National Animal Abuser Registry*, 17 Animal L. 197 (2010).

43. Pet-Abuse.com, *About: Services*, http://www.pet-abuse.com/pages/about/services.php.

44. Pet-Abuse.com, *Database of Criminal Animal Cruelty Cases*, http://www.pet-abuse.com/pages/cruelty_database/name_search.php.

45. *Id.*

46. GIS, *National Retail Mutual Association*, http://www.geninfo.com/nrmastory.asp.

47. GIS, *Our Solution*, http://www.geninfo.com/nrma.solution.asp.

48. Statement from George Slicho from the Zale Corporation, http://www.geninfo.com/theftdatabase.asp.

49. GIS, *National Retail Mutual Association: FAQ*, http://www.geninfo.com/nrmastory.asp.

50. HireRight, *National Theft Database*, http://hirerite.com/National-Theft-Database.aspx.

51. See David Kravets, "Mug-Shot Industry Will Dig Up Your Past, Charge You to Bury It Again," *Wired*, August 2, 2011, http://www.wired.com/threatlevel/2011/08/mugshots/; Associated Press, "Don't Want Mug Shot Online? Then Pay Up, Sites Say," June 23, 2013, http://www.financialexpress.com/news/don-t-want-mug-shot-online-then-pay-up-say-sites/1132780.

52. David Segal, "Mugged by a Mug Shot," *New York Times*, October 6, 2013, at BU1.

53. Internet Crime Complaint Center, *Scam Alerts*, June 19, 2013, http://www.ic3.gov/media/2013/130619.aspx.

54. MugshotsOnline.com, *Terms of Use: Product Pricing and Policies*, http://www.mugshotsonline.com/terms-of-use.

55. Unpublisharrest.com, *About Us*, http://unpublisharrest.com/about-us/.

56. *Id.*

57. See David Kravets, "Mug-Shot Industry Will Dig Up Your Past, Charge You to Bury It Again," *Wired*, August 2, 2011, http://www.wired.com/threatlevel/2011/08/mugshots/.

58. See National Conference of State Legislatures, "Mug Shots and Booking Photo Websites," June 12, 2014, http://www.ncsl.org/research/telecommunications-and-information-technology/mug-shots-and-booking-photo-websites.aspx.

59. Utah H.B. 408, 2013 General Session, enacting Utah Code Ann. § 17-22-30.

60. Colorado House Bill 14-1047, 69th General Assembly, 2014 Regular Session, amending C.R.S. 24-72-305.5.

61. Act 188; see Georgia General Assembly, *2013–2014 Regular Session—HB 150 Law Enforcement Officers; the Reproduction of Arrest Booking Photographs; Enact Provisions*, http://www.legis.ga.gov/Legislation/en-US/display/20132014/HB/150.

62. Wyoming S.F. 0053, 62nd Legislature, 2014 Budget Session, Enrolled Act no. 35, creating Wyo. Stat. § 40-12-601, http://legisweb.state.wy.us/2014/Enroll/SF0053.pdf; Oregon House Bill 3467, 77th Oregon Legislative Assembly, 2013 Regular Session, https://olis.leg.state.or.us/liz/2013R1/Measures/Overview/HB3467.

63. JustMugshots, *Illinois SB0115—What It Really Means*, http://support.justmugshots.com/entries/21672634-Illinois-SB0115-What-it-really-means (emphasis in original).

64. Gene Policinski, *"Mug Shot" Sites Pose First Amendment Dilemma*, First Amendment Center, October 26, 2012, http://www.firstamendmentcenter.org/mug-shot-sites-pose-first-amendment-dilemma.

65. See David Kravets, "Shamed by Mugshot Sites, Arrestees Try Novel Lawsuit," *Wired*, December 12, 2012, http://www.wired.com/threatlevel/2012/12/mugshot-industry-legal-attack/; David Kravets, "Mugshot-Removal Sites Accused of Extortion," *Wired*, July 15, 2013, http://www.wired.com/threatlevel/2013/07/mugshot-removal-extortion/.

66. Associated Press in Toledo, "Mugshot Websites Agree to Stop Charging for Photo Removal," *TheGuardian.com*, January 8, 2014, http://www.theguardian.com/world/2014/jan/08/mugshot-websites-stop-charging-photo-removal; John Caniglia, "Ohio Lawsuit over Online Mug Shots Reaches Settlement; Suit Was One of Several Filed Nationally," *The Plain Dealer*, January 7, 2014, http://www.cleveland.com/metro/index.ssf/2014/01/ohio_lawsuit_over_online_mug_s.html

67. Amended Complaint in *Lashaway et al v. D'Antonio, III et al.*, http://www.wired.com/images_blogs/threatlevel/2013/07/Lashaway-v-Mugshots-Amended-complaint-AS-FILED.pdf.

68. Allen Rostron, *The Mugshot Industry: Freedom of Speech, Rights of Publicity, and the Controversy Sparked by an Unusual New Type of Business*, 90 Wash. U. L. Rev. 1321, at 1328 (2013), citing Ohio Rev. Code Ann. § 2741.02(A) (West 2013).

69. *Id.*

70. *Id.*

71. Ricardo Lopez, "Lawsuit Targets Website That Posts Mug Shots," *Los Angeles Times*, January 22, 2014, http://www.latimes.com/business/la-fi-mug shots-lawsuit-20140121-story.html

72. David Segal, "Mugged by a Mug Shot," *New York Times*, October 6, 2013, at BU1.

73. David Segal, "Mug-Shot Websites, Retreating or Adapting," *New York Times*, November 9, 2013, http://www.nytimes.com/2013/11/10/your-money/mug-shot-websites-retreating-or-adapting.html.

74. SEARCH, *Report of The National Task Force on the Criminal Backgrounding of America* (2005), http://www.search.org/files/pdf/ReportofNTFCBA.pdf.

CHAPTER 6
Whether to Create a Criminal Record

1. *Morrissey v. Brewer*, 443 F.2d 942, 953 (8th Cir. 1971) (en banc), reversed by *Morrissey v. Brewer*, 408 U.S. 471 (U.S. 1972).

2. Erik Luna, *The Overcriminalization Phenomenon*, 54 Am. U. L. Rev. 703 (2005).

3. Jonathan Simon, *Governing through Crime: How the War on Crime Transformed American Democracy and Created a Culture of Fear* (New York: Oxford University Press, 2003).

4. Sun Beale, *The Many Faces of Overcriminalization: From Morals and Mattress Tags to Overfederalization*, 54 Am. U. L. Rev. 747, 748 (2005).

5. John S. Baker Jr., *Revisiting the Explosive Growth of Federal Crimes*, at 1 (Heritage Foundation Memo No. 26, June 16, 2008).

6. John C. Coffee Jr., *Does "Unlawful" Mean "Criminal"? Reflections on the Disappearing Tort/Crime Distinction in American Law*, 71 Boston U. L. Rev. 193, 216 (1991); Edwin Meese III and Paul J. Larkin Jr., *Reconsidering the Mistake of Law Defense*, 102 J. Criminal Law & Criminology 725, 733–36 (2012).

7. John S. Baker Jr., *Revisiting the Explosive Growth of Federal Crimes* (Heritage Foundation Memo No. 26, June 16, 2008).

8. Paul Rosenzweig, "The History of Criminal Law," in Paul Rosenzweig and Brian W. Walsh (eds.), *One Nation under Arrest: How Crazy Laws, Rogue Prosecutors, and Activist Judges Threaten Your Liberty* 131 (Washington, DC: Heritage Foundation, 2010).

9. See, e.g., James B. Jacobs and Kimberly Potter, *Hate Crimes: Criminal Law and Identity Politics* (New York: Oxford University Press, 1998).

10. Donald A. Dripps, *Overcriminalization, Discretion, Waiver: A Survey of Possible Exit Strategies*, 109 Penn State L. Rev. 1155 (2005). Talking about costs, a 2010 study conducted by Heidi Blaine and others found that the marginal cost of prosecuting and convicting a misdemeanor in that state was $1,679. See Heidi Blaine et al., *The Costs Associated with Prosecuting Crime in Oregon* 11 (2010), http://library.state.or.us/repository/2010/201007161627305/index.pdf.

11. See Federal Bureau of Investigation, *Crime in the United States 2012*, http://www.fbi.gov/about-us/cjis/ucr/crime-in-the-u.s/2012/crime-in-the-u.s.-2012/persons-arrested/persons-arrested.

12. See Federal Bureau of Investigation, *Crime in the United States 2012*, http://www.fbi.gov/about-us/cjis/ucr/crime-in-the-u.s/2012/crime-in-the-u.s.-2012/persons-arrested/persons-arrested, plus Table 29, http://www.fbi.gov/about-us/cjis/ucr/crime-in-the-u.s/2012/crime-in-the-u.s.-2012/tables/29tabledatadecpdf.

13. See Douglas Husak, *Overcriminalization: The Limits of the Criminal Law* 4–17 (New York: Oxford University Press, 2008).

14. Internal Revenue Service, *2013 IRS Data Book*, http://www.irs.gov/uac/SOI-Tax-Stats-IRS-Data-Book.

15. Terry Baynes, "More U.S. Doctors Facing Charges over Drug Abuse," Reuters, September 14, 2011, http://www.reuters.com/article/2011/09/14/us-jackson-malpractice-idUSTRE78D3P620110914.

16. Alexandra Natapoff, *Misdemeanors*, 85 S. Cal. L. Rev. 1313, 1327 (2012).

17. Model Penal Code § 2.05 (1985).

18. U.S. Highway Patrol, Driving Citation Statistics, http://www.statisticbrain.com/driving-citation-statistics/.

19. New York Police Department, *Historical New York City Crime Data*, Citywide Violation Offenses, http://www.nyc.gov/html/nypd/downloads/pdf/analysis_and_planning/citywide_historical_violation_offenses_2000-2013.pdf.

20. N.Y. Penal Law § 10.00.

21. N.Y. Crim. Proc. Law § 160.55. See Legal Action Center, *Lowering Criminal Record Barriers* (2013), http://www.lac.org/doc_library/lac/publications/LoweringCriminalRecordBarriers_rev3.pdf.

22. N.Y. Crim. Proc. Law § 160.55. Convictions pronounced after November 1, 1991, must be sealed automatically, whereas prior records require an application to the court in order to be sealed.

23. See New York State Office of Court Administration, Criminal History Record Search, *FAQs*, http://www.nycourts.gov/apps/chrs/faqs.shtml#faqfunction (retrieved January 22, 2014): "As a result of a recent case filed in a New York court, the Unified Court System has reviewed its policy regarding the contents of criminal history summaries that it provides to individuals and businesses upon their request and for a fee. The review has resulted in a change of policy to the extent that the summaries provided will report only convictions on charges that New York State law regards as crimes. Crimes are defined by New York State law as including misdemeanors and felonies only. Convictions on offenses classified as violations and infractions which are not crimes as defined by New York State law will no longer be reported unless the criminal history summary includes a misdemeanor or felony conviction for the same event."

24. 28 CFR §20.32, "Includable Offenses."

25. See James B. Jacobs, "Juvenile Criminal Record Confidentiality," in David Tanenhaus and Franklin E. Zimring (eds.), *Choosing the Future of Criminal Justice* (New York: New York University Press, 2014).

26. See Federal Register, Vol. 71, No. 171, Tuesday, September 5, 2006/Proposed Rules, Department of Justice, Federal Bureau of Investigation, 28 CFR Part 20 [Docket No. FBI 111P; AG Order No. 2833–2006] RIN 1110–AA25, *Inclusion of Nonserious Offense Identification Record*s, at 52303. The new policy will be codified in 2014. See https://www.federalregister.gov/regulations/1110-aa25/inclusion-of-nonserious-offense-identification-records.

27. Proposed Regulation Expanding FBI Rap Sheets to Include "Non-Serious" Offenses for Employment and Licensing Purposes (Docket No. FBI 111P), at 5, http://nelp.3cdn.net/dd4d0466182f8c951e_thm6bnoqb.pdf.

28. On the historical origins of deferred prosecution, see Robert W. Balch, *Deferred Prosecution: The Juvenilization of the Criminal Justice System*, 38 Fed. Probation 46 (1974).

29. According to Margaret Colgate Love, "In twenty states, expungement or sealing of the entire case record is authorized or required following successful completion of probation where judgment has been deferred." See Margaret Colgate Love, *Alternatives to Conviction: Deferred Adjudication as a Way of Avoiding Collateral Consequences*, 22 Fed. Sent. Rep. 6 (2010).

30. American Bar Association, Recommendation 103A, adopted by the House of Delegates on February 12, 2007, http://www.americanbar.org/content/dam/aba/directories/policy/2007_my_103a.authcheckdam.pdf.

31. American Bar Association, Recommendation 103A, adopted by the House of Delegates on February 12, 2007, http://www.americanbar.org/content/dam/aba/directories/policy/2007_my_103a.authcheckdam.pdf.

32. Margaret Colgate Love et al., *Collateral Consequences of Criminal Convictions: Law, Policy and Practice* 7:22, 443 (Washington, DC: Thomson Reuters, 2013).

33. 18 U.S.C. § 3607; 21 U.S.C. § 844 (2012).

34. 18 U.S.C. § 3607(c) (1984).

35. See N.Y. Clp. Law §§170.55 and 170.56.

36. E-mail from eCourts staff, New York State Unified Court System, February 3, 2013, on file with the author.

37. Federal courts are divided on whether dismissals in the interest of justice under N.Y. Crim. Proc. Law § 170.40 constitute a disposition favorable to the accused. Contrast *Singer v. Fulton County Sheriff*, 63 F.3d 110 (2d Cir. 1995) (holding that, as a matter of law, such dismissals are not a disposition favorable to the accused) with *Giannattasio v. Artuz*, 2000 U.S. Dist. LEXIS 3907 (S.D. N.Y. 2000) (holding that, as a matter of law, such dismissals are a disposition favorable to the accused).

38. See Ian Weinstein, *The Adjudication of Minor Offenses in New York*, 31 Ford. Urb. L.J. 1157, 1170–71 and n. 52 (2004).

39. New York State Division of Criminal Justice Services, *Adult Arrests Disposed, New York City*, at 9, http://www.criminaljustice.ny.gov/crimnet/ojsa/dispos/all.pdf.

40. Issa Kohler-Hausmann, *Misdemeanor Justice: The Penal Logic of Dismissal*, Ph.D. dissertation draft chapter, at 370 (2012).

41. *Id.*

42. Texas Code Crim. Proc. Ann. art. 42.12 § 5(c) (West 2009).

43. Md. Code Ann., Crim. Proc. § 6-220 (West 2009); D.C. Code § 16-714.

44. See Md. Code Ann., Crim. Proc. §10-105 (West 2012).

45. On the purposes of the technique of "shock incarceration," see Doris Layton MacKenzie and Robert Brame, *Shock Incarceration and Positive Adjustment during Community Supervision*, 11 J. Quantitative Criminology 111 (1995).

46. See Tex. Code Crim. Proc. Ann. art. 42.12, § 5(c) (West 2011).

47. The Public Information Act, Tex. Gov't Code § 552 (West 2012); Freedom of Information Act, 5 U.S.C. § 552 (1996).

48. Cal. Penal Code §§ 1203.4 and 1203.4a.

49. See California Courts, *Cleaning Your Record*, http://www.courts.ca.gov/1070.htm.

50. N.Y. Executive Law (HRL) §296(15).

51. See Marc Mauer and Ryan S. King, *Uneven Justice: State Rates of Incarceration by Race and Ethnicity*, The Sentencing Project (July 2007), http://sentencingproject.org/doc/publications/rd_stateratesofincbyraceandethnicity.pdf, which finds that African Americans are incarcerated at nearly six times the rate of whites and that Latinos are incarcerated at nearly double the rate. See also Arthur H. Garrison, *Disproportionate Incarceration of African Americans: What History and the First Decade of Twenty-First Century Have Brought*, 11 Journal of the Institute of Justice & International Studies 87 (2011).

52. Steven B. Duke, *Mass Imprisonment, Crime Rates, and the Drug War: A Penological and Humanitarian Disgrace*, 9 Conn. Pub. Intl. L.J. 17 (2010).

53. In New York State, charges can be dropped "in the interest of justice." N.Y. Crim. Proc. Law §170.40. See Mary Fan, *Street Diversion and Decarceration*, 50 Am. Crim. L. Rev. 165 (2013).

CHAPTER 7
Sealing, Purging, and Amending Conviction Records

1. Bernard Kogon and Donald L. Loughery Jr., *Sealing and Expungement of Criminal Records-The Big Lie*, 61 J. Crim. L., Criminology, & Police Sci. 378, 389 (1970).

2. Joan Petersilia, *When Prisoners Come Home: Parole and Prisoner Reentry* 216 (New York: Oxford University Press, 2003).

3. Shadd Maruna, *Making Good: How Ex-Convicts Reform and Rebuild Their Lives* 165 (Washington, DC: American Psychological Association, 2001).

4. For example, Mass. Gen. Laws Ann. ch. 6, § 167 provides that "[c]riminal offender record information shall be limited to information concerning persons who have attained the age of 17 and shall not include any information concerning criminal offenses or acts of delinquency committed by any person before he attained the age of 17; provided, however, that if a person under the age of 17 is adjudicated as an adult, information relating to such criminal offense shall be criminal offender record information."

5. James B. Jacobs, "Juvenile Criminal Record Confidentiality," in Franklin Zimring and David S. Tanenhaus (eds.), *Choosing the Future for American Juvenile Justice* (New York: New York University Press, 2014). See also Markus T. Funk, *The Dangers of Hiding Criminal Pasts*, 66 Tenn. L. Rev. 287, 292–93 (1998), which critically examines expungement schemes enacted by a few legislatures allowing states to permanently seal or even destroy records of serious and chronic juvenile crime (called by the author "aggressive" expungement schemes, as opposed to "nonaggressive" ones limiting the types of crimes that may be expunged to relatively minor and isolated acts).

6. T. Markus Funk and Daniel D. Polsby, *The Problem of Lemons and Why We Must Retain Juvenile Crime Records*, 18 Cato Journal 75, 81 (1998). See also T. Markus Funk and Daniel D. Polsby, *Distributional Consequences of Expunging Juvenile Delinquency Records: The Problem of Lemons* 52 Washington University Journal of Urban and Contemporary Law 161 (1997); T. Markus Funk, *A Mere Youthful Indiscretion? Reexamining the Policy of Expunging Juvenile Delinquency Records*, 29 University of Michigan Journal of Law Reform 885 (1996).

7. Council on Crime and Justice, *The Consequences of a Juvenile Delinquency Record in Minnesota*, http://www.crimeandjustice.org/councilinfo.cfm?pID=157.

8. Howard N. Snyder and Melissa Sickmund, U.S. Department of Justice, Office of Juvenile Justice and Delinquency Prevention, *Juvenile Offenders and Victims: 2006 National Report*, at 108–09, http://ojjdp.ncjrs.org/ojstatbb/nr2006/downloads/NR2006.pdf.

9. Maine State Police, Maine Criminal History Record and Juvenile Crime Information Request Service, http://www5.informe.org/online/pcr/.

10. See, e.g., Memorandum from John Eddy Morrison, to Carlos J. Martinez, Chief Assistant Public Defender, re Florida Department of Law Enforcement's Release of Confidential Juvenile Records, August 21, 2006, http://www.pdmiami.com/cpr/Morrison_Memo_Juv_Confidential.pdf.

11. In 2014, the House of Representatives in Washington State passed a law that reverses a four-decade-old policy of open juvenile records. See Second Substitute House Bill 1651, 63rd Legislative Session, c. 174, Laws of 2014.

12. However, in 1984, Congress repealed the Federal Youth Corrections Act. See *Doe v. Webster*, 606 F.2D 1226, 1234–35 (D.C. 1979); Fred C. Zacharias, *The Uses and Abuses of Convictions Set Aside under the Federal Youth Correction Act*, 1981 Duke L.J. 477 (1981).

13. See also Electronic Privacy Information Center, *Expungement*, http://epic.org/privacy/expungement/. California Penal Code § 17(b) provides a difference between felonies and misdemeanors. Quite interestingly, *wobblers* (offenses that can be sentenced as either felonies or misdemeanors at the court's discretion) can later be reduced from felonies to misdemeanors by petition to the court. Once the conviction has been reduced to a misdemeanor, it is a misdemeanor for all purposes—meaning the person can apply for an expungement under § 11203.4 and can later say that he or she has no felony convictions on job applications.

14. *Dickerson v. New Banner Institute*, 460 U.S. 103, 121–22 (1983) (Justice Blackmun's majority opinion; internal citations omitted). Margaret Colgate Love, who chaired the American Bar Association commission that produced the *ABA Criminal Justice Standards on Collateral Sanctions and Discretionary Disqualification of Convicted Persons*, has called the variety and complexity of approaches among the states "bewildering."

15. Miss. Code Ann. § 41-29-150(d)(2) (2005 & Supp. 2007); Miss. Code Ann. § 99-19-71.

16. 20 ILCS 2630/5.2; Clerk of the Circuit Court of Cook County, *Criminal and Traffic Expungement and Sealing Procedural Guide*, http://12.218.239.52/newsite//GI_NEWS//newscontent/Events/2011/Expungement_Packet_2011.pdf.

17. Six states now single out the prostitution convictions of sex trafficking victims for special expungement eligibility. See Youngbee Dale, "Hawaii: New Law Allows Trafficking Victims to Vacate Prostitution Convictions," *Washington Times*, July 11, 2012, http://communities.washingtontimes.com/neighborhood/rights-so-divine/2012/jul/11/hawaii-new-law-allows-trafficking-victims-expunge-/.

18. Effective May 4, 2012, pursuant to the reform of the Criminal Offender Record Information Act codified at sections 167 to 178, in chapter 6 of the General Laws of Massachusetts.

19. Massachusetts General Laws c. 276 §100A.

20. Utah Code Annotated, 1953 § 77-40-105.

21. R.I. Gen. Laws § 12-1.3-2 (2002).

22. Oregon Revised Statutes § 137.225.

23. Colorado Revised Statues Annotated § 24-72-308.6.

24. House Enrolled Act 1482 (effective July 1, 2013).

25. See 11 Del. Laws, c. 43, §4373.

26. Currently these states include Kentucky (KRS § 431.078), Utah (Utah Code Annotated § 77-40-103), and Wyoming (W.S.1977 § 7-13-1501).

27. R.I. Gen. Laws 1956, § 12-1.3-3.

28. See Stephanos Bibas and Richard A. Bierschbach, *Integrating Remorse and Apology into Criminal Procedure* 114 Yale L.J. 85 (2004).

29. Adam Liptak, "Expunged Criminal Records Live to Tell Tales," *New York Times*, October 17, 2006 (discussing the increased availability of expunged records because of the commercial information vendors). See also Michael D. Mayfield, *Revisiting Expungement: Concealing Information in the Information Age*, Utah L. Rev. 1057 (1997); Viktor Mayer-Schönberger, *Delete: The Virtue of Forgetting in the Digital Age* (Princeton, NJ: Princeton University Press, 2009).

30. Clay Calvert and Jerry Bruno, *When Cleansing Criminal History Clashes with the First Amendment and Online Journalism: Are Expungement Statutes Irrelevant in the Digital Age?* 19 CommLaw Conspectus 123 (2010).

31. *G.D. v. Bernard Kenny and The Hudson County Democratic Organization, Inc.* (A-85-09) (N.J. Supreme Court 2011).

32. See Logan Danielle Wayne, *The Data-Broker Threat: Proposing Federal Legislation to Protect Post-Expungement Privacy*, 102 J. Crim. L. & Criminology 253, 277–81 (2013).

33. Fla. Stat. ch. 943.0585(4)(a)(2008).

34. Electronic Privacy Information Center, *Expungement*, http://epic.org/privacy/expungement/. See also Ben Geiger, *The Case for Treating Ex-Offenders as a Suspect Class*, 94 Cal. L. Rev. 1191, 1200 (2006); Debbie A. Mukamal and Paul N. Samuels, *Statutory Limitations on Civil Rights of People with Criminal Records*, 30 Fordham Urb. L.J. 1501 (2002).

35. Ben Geiger, *The Case for Treating Ex-Offenders as a Suspect Class*, 94 Cal. L. Rev. 1191, 1200 (2006).

36. *Davis v. Alaska*, 415 U.S. 308 (1974).

37. James B. Jacobs, "Juvenile Criminal Record Confidentiality," in Franklin Zimring and David S. Tanenhaus (eds.), *Choosing the Future for American Juvenile Justice* (New York: New York University Press, 2014).

38. *Bahr v. Statesman Journal Company and George Rede*, 51 Or. App. 1776, 624 P.2d 664 (1981).

39. O.R.S. § 137.225.

40. *Id.*

41. Clay Calbert and Jerry Bruno, *When Cleansing Criminal History Clashes with the First Amendment and Online Journalism: Are Expungement Statutes Irrelevant in the Digital Age?* 19 CommLaw Conspectus 123 (2010).

42. See, e.g., *Florida Star v. B.J.F.*, 491 U.S. 524 (1989); *Cox Broadcasting Co. v. Cohn*, 420 U.S. 469 (1975); *Oklahoma Publishing Company v. District Court in and for Oklahoma City* 480 U.S. 308 (1977).

43. Margaret Colgate Love, *The Collateral Consequences of* Padilla v. Kentucky: *Is Forgiveness Now Constitutionally Required?* 160 U. Pa. L. Rev. PENNumbra 113 (2011), http://www.pennumbra.com/essays/12-2011/Love.pdf.

44. On the topic, in general, see Rachel E. Barkow, *The Ascent of the Administrative State and the Demise of Mercy* 121 Harvard L. Rev. 1332 (2008); Austin Sarat and Nasser Hussain (eds.), *Forgiveness, Mercy, and Clemency* (Stanford, CA: Stanford University Press, 2007).

45. Margaret Colgate Love et al., *Collateral Consequences of Criminal Convictions: Law, Policy and Practice* 443–446 (Washington, DC: Thomson Reuters, 2013); see also National Employment Law Project, the National H.I.R.E. Network, *State Reforms Promoting Employment of People with Criminal Records: 2010–11 Legislative Round-up*, at 7 (December 2011), http://www.nelp.org/page/-/SCLP/2011/PromotingEmploymentofPeoplewithCriminalRecords.pdf?nocdn=1.

46. See, e.g., Petition for Relief per Penal Code Section 1203.4 or 1203.4a in California: "If you were convicted of a misdemeanor or a felony and were not sentenced to state prison and you have completed the terms of your sentence, you may file a petition pursuant to Penal Code Section 1203.4 or 1203.4. . . . The relief granted by Penal Code 1203.4 or Penal Code 1203.4a does NOT seal, destroy or remove any entries from the court, law enforcement, Department of Motor Vehicles or Department of Justice records, but is a dismissal of the charges and convictions. Upon granting of the petition, a notation will be entered on the record that relief was granted pursuant to this statute." Available at http://www.monterey.courts.ca.gov/Criminal/CourtRecords.aspx (retrieved January 28, 2014).

47. Codified in N.Y. Corr. L.§§ 701-703.

48. Codified in N.Y. Corr. L.§ 703A-B.

49. The Bronx Defenders, *Certificates That Promote Rehabilitation: Why They Are So Important and How to Get Them* 1 (July 2011), www.reentry.net/ny/library/attachment.172234: "They appear on a person's rap sheet beside relevant convictions."

50. Dora Schriro, *Good Science, Good Sense: Making Meaningful Change Happen—A Practitioner's Perspective*, 11 Criminology & Public Policy 101 (2012), making reference, for example, to the case *Arrocha v. Board of Education* (1999), where the court upheld the New York City Board of Education's refusal to grant a teaching license to an ex-felon who had been convicted of selling drugs, despite the presence of a certificate of relief from disabilities.

51. Margaret Love and April Frazier, *Certificates of Rehabilitation and Other Forms of Relief from the Collateral Consequences of Conviction: A Survey of State Laws* (ABA Commission on Effective Sanctions, 2006).

52. In 2013, the total number of convictions for felonies was 100,886 and for misdemeanors was 206,200. See New York State Division of Criminal Justice Services, *2008–2013 Dispositions of Adult Arrests*, http://www.criminaljustice.ny.gov/crimnet/ojsa/dispos/nys.pdf.

53. Vincent Schiraldi, *A Powerful Tool for Rehabilitation*, New York Law Journal, November 30, 2012, http://www.newyorklawjournal.com/PubArticleNY.jsp?id=1202579748991&A_Powerful_Tool_for_Rehabilitation&slreturn=20130816211502.

54. See, e.g., Meghan L. Schneider, *From Criminal Confinement to Social Confinement: Helping Ex-Offenders Obtain Public Housing with a Certificate or Rehabilitation*, 36 New Eng. J. on Crim. & Civ. Confinement 335 (2010).

55. Margaret Colgate Love, *Starting over with a Clean Slate: In Praise of a Forgotten Section of the Model Penal Code*, 30 Fordham Urb. L.J. 1705, 1726 (2003).

56. See Sissela Bok, *Lying: Moral Choice in Private and Public Life* (New York: Vintage, 1978).

57. Margaret Colgate Love, *Starting over with a Clean Slate: In Praise of a Forgotten Section of the Model Penal Code*, 30 Fordham Urb. L.J. 1705, 1712 (2003).

58. Alan Beck, a National Institute of Justice statistician, found that in the 1980s, "Recidivism rates were highest in the first year—one of four released prisoners was rearrested in the first six months and two of five within the first year after release; the more extensive a prisoner's prior arrest record, the higher the recidivism rate—over 74% of those with eleven or more prior arrests were rearrested, compared to 38% of those with only a single prior arrest." Allen J. Beck and Bernard E. Shipley, U.S. Department of Justice, *Bureau of Justice Statistics Special Report: Recidivism of Prisoners Released in 1983* (1989), http://www.colliersheriff.org/modules/ShowDocument.aspx?documentid=13612.

CHAPTER 8
Erroneous Records Problems

1. Madeline Neighly and Maurice Emsellem, National Employment Law Project, *Wanted: Accurate FBI Background Checks for Employment* (July 2013), http://www.nelp.org/page/-/SCLP/2013/Report-Wanted-Accurate-FBI-Background-Checks-Employment.pdf?nocdn=1.

2. Privacy Rights Clearinghouse, "Identity Theft: The Growing Problem of Wrongful Criminal Records," Speech by Beth Givens, PRC Director, https://www.privacyrights.org/ar/wcr.htm (posted June 1, 2000; revised 2006).

3. U.S. Department of Justice, Bureau of Justice Statistics, *Compendium of State Privacy and Security Legislation: 2002 Overview, Criminal History Record Information*, at 4 (November 2003); Crime Control Act of 1973 (Pub. L. 93-83, August 6, 1973, 87 Stat. 197), amending the Omnibus Crime Control and Safe Streets Act of 1968 (Pub. L. 90–351; 82 Stat. 197).

4. See Code of Federal Regulations, Title 28, Part 20; 40 FR 22114-01; 41 Fed. Reg. 11714; Sharon M. Dietrich, *Expanded Use of Criminal Records and Its Impact on Re-entry* (March 3, 2006), http://meetings.abanet.org/webupload/commupload/CR209800/sitesofinterest_files/Dietrichpaper.pdf.

5. *Id.*

6. U.S. Department of Justice, Bureau of Justice Statistics, *Compendium of State Privacy and Security Legislation: 2002 Overview, Criminal History Record Information*, at 5 (November 2003).

7. *Id.*; Margaret Colgate Love et al., *Collateral Consequences of Criminal Convictions: Law, Policy and Practice*, at 285 (Washington, DC: Thomson Reuters, 2013).

8. U.S. Department of Justice, Bureau of Justice Statistics, *Compendium of State Privacy and Security Legislation: 2002 Overview, Criminal History Record Information*, at 6 (November 2003); Alaska Stat. § 12.62.120 (b)

9. Idaho Code § 67-3005(1)(a) and Idaho Code § 67-3001(4).

10. Patricia M. Harris and Kimberly S. Keller, *Ex-Offenders Need Not Apply*, 20(1) Journal of Contemporary Criminal Justice 6, 16 (2005), describe problems of data accuracy, especially disposition information, in the state repositories. See also citations and summary of state statutes in U.S. Department of Justice, Bureau of Justice Statistics, *Compendium of State Privacy and Security Legislation: 2002 Overview, Criminal History Record Information* (November 2003); U.S. Department of Justice, Bureau of Justice Statistics *Survey of State Criminal History Information Systems, 2006* (October 2008).

11. Madeline Neighly and Maurice Emsellem, National Employment Law Project. *Wanted: Accurate FBI Background Checks for Employment* 5 (July 2013), http://www.nelp.org/page/-/SCLP/2013/Report-Wanted-Accurate-FBI-Background-Checks-Employment.pdf?nocdn=1.

12. Margaret Colgate Love et al., *Collateral Consequences of Criminal Convictions: Law, Policy and Practice*, at 287 (Washington, DC: Thomson Reuters, 2013); see Michael R. Geerken, *Rap Sheets in Criminological Research: Considerations and Caveats*, 10(1) Journal of Quantitative Criminology 3 (1994).

13. Bureau of Justice Statistics and SEARCH National Focus Group on Identity Theft Victimization and Criminal Record Repository Operations, *Report of the Bureau of Justice Statistics/SEARCH National Focus Group on Identity Theft Victimization and Criminal Record Repository Operations* (2005), http://www.search.org/files/pdf/NatFocusGrpIDTheftVic.pdf (emphasis added).

14. See, e.g., Identity Theft Enforcement and Restitution Act of 2008, Pub. L. No. 110-326, §§ 201-09, 122 Stat. 3560, 3560–65 (2008). A bill on this matter is currently being contemplated by Congress (STOP Identity Theft Act of 2013, S. 149, 113th Cong.).

15. See, e.g., 29 O.R.C. 2913.49: "(B) No person, without the express or implied consent of the other person, shall use, obtain, or possess any personal identifying information of another person with intent to do either of the following: (1) Hold the person out to be the other person; (2) Represent the other person's personal identifying information as the person's own personal identifying information."

16. Bureau of Justice Statistics and SEARCH National Focus Group on Identity Theft Victimization and Criminal Record Repository Operations, *Report of the Bureau of Justice Statistics/SEARCH National Focus Group on Identity Theft Victimization and Criminal Record Repository Operations* (2005).

17. State of California Department of Justice, Office of the Attorney General, "Identity Theft," http://caag.state.ca.us/idtheft//; State of California Department of Justice, Office of the Attorney General, "California Identity Theft Registry," http://oag.ca.gov/idtheft/facts/how-to-registry.

18. U.S. Department of Justice, Office of the Attorney General, The Attorney General's Report on Criminal History Background Checks, at 7 (2006).

19. *Arizona v. Evans*, 514 U.S. 1, 115 S. Ct. 1185, 131 L. Ed. 2d 34 (1995)

20. *Id.* at 17.

21. *Herring v. United States*, 555 U.S. 135, 144 (U.S. 2009).

22. *Id.* at 146–48.

23. *Id.* at 155–56 (internal citations omitted).

24. *Ainsworth v. Norris*, 469 Fed. Appx. 775 (11th Cir. Fla. 2012). For a detailed account of the facts of the case, see *Ainsworth v. City of Tampa*, 2011 U.S. Dist. LEXIS 50006 (M.D. Fla. May 10, 2011).

25. *Rothgery v. Gillespie County*, 554 U.S. 191 (2008).

26. See also *Florence v. Bd. of Chosen Freeholders*, 132 S. Ct. 1510 (U.S. 2012).

27. See, e.g., Editorial, "Check It Again," *New York Times*, May 26, 2010, http://www.nytimes.com/2010/05/27/opinion/27thu3.html?_r=0; U.S. Department of Justice, Office of the Attorney General, The Attorney General's Report on Criminal History Background Checks, at 127–129 (2006); Editorial, "Faulty Criminal Background Checks," *New York Times*, July 24, 2012, http://www.nytimes.com/2012/07/25/opinion/faulty-criminal-background-checks.html?_r=2.

28. See, e.g., Fairness and Accuracy in Employment Background Checks of 2013, H.R. 2865, 113th Cong., 1st Session; Accurate Background Check Act of 2013 (ABC Act of 2013), HR 2999, 113th Cong., 1st Session; Fairness and Accuracy in Employment Background Checks Act of 2010, H.R. 5300, 111th Cong. (died in committee).

29. *Menard v. Mitchell*, 430 F.2d 486 (D.C. Cir. 1970).

30. *Id.* at 493–94 (internal citation omitted).

31. *Menard v. Mitchell*, 328 F. Supp. 718 (1971).

32. *Menard v. Saxbe*, 498 F.2d 1017 (D.C. 1974).

33. *Id.* at 1026.

34. *Tarlton v. Saxbe*, 507 F.2d 1116 (D.C. Cir. 1974).

35. *Tarlton v. Saxbe* II 407 F. Supp. 1083 (D.D.C. 1976).

36. Madeline Neighly and Maurice Emsellem, National Employment Law Project, *Wanted: Accurate FBI Background Checks for Employment* (July 2013), http://www.nelp.org/page/-/SCLP/2013/Report-Wanted-Accurate-FBI-Background-Checks-Employment.pdf?nocdn=1.

37. Fairness and Accuracy in Employment Background Checks of 2013, H.R. 2865, 113th Cong., 1st Session; Accurate Background Check Act of 2013 (ABC Act of 2013), HR 2999, 113th Cong., 1st Session.

38. U.S. Department of Justice, Office of the Attorney General, The Attorney General's Report on Criminal History Background Checks, at 17 (2006).

39. *Id.* at 21.

40. See Madeline Neighly and Maurice Emsellem, National Employment Law Project, *Wanted: Accurate FBI Background Checks for Employment* (July 2013), http://www.nelp.org/page/-/SCLP/2013/Report-Wanted-Accurate-FBI-Background-Checks-Employment.pdf?nocdn=1.

41. National Consumer Law Center, *Broken Records: How Errors by Criminal Background Checking Companies Harm Workers and Businesses* (April 2012), http://www.nclc.org/images/pdf/pr-reports/broken-records-report.pdf.

42. National Consumer Law Center, *Broken Records: How Errors by Criminal Background Checking Companies Harm Workers and Businesses*, at 16 (2012).

43. Frank A. Colaprete, *Pre-Employment Background Investigations for Public Safety Professionals* 192 (Boca Raton, FL: CRC Press, 2012).

44. 15 U.S.C. § 1681e(b).

45. 15 U.S.C. § 1681k(a)(2) (2000).

46. 15 U.S.C. § 1681a(e) (defining "investigative consumer report"); 15 U.S.C. § 1681d(d)(3) (outlining verification obligations).

47. 15 U.S.C. § 1681k(a) (2000).

48. 15 U.S.C. § 1681b(b)(1).

49. 15 U.S.C. § 1681 (2000); 15 USC § 1681m.

50. Federal Trade Commission, *40 Years of Experience with the Fair Credit Reporting Act: An FTC Staff Report with Summary of Interpretations*, at 52 (July 2011), http://www.ftc.gov/os/2011/07/110720fcrareport.pdf.

51. Public Law 104-208, the Omnibus Consolidated Appropriations Act for Fiscal Year 1997, Title II, Subtitle D, Chapter 1.

52. *United States v. HireRight Solutions*, No. 12-1313, Complaint for Civil Penalties, Permanent Injunction, and Other Equitable Relief 13 (D.D.C. filed August 8, 2012).

53. *United States v. HireRight Solutions*, No. 12-1313, Stipulated Final Judgment and Order for Civil Penalties, Permanent Injunction, and Other Equitable Relief at 3, 9–10 (D.D.C. filed August 8, 2012); see also Federal Trade Commission, "News Release: Employment Background Screening Company to Pay $2.6 Million Penalty for Multiple Violations of the Fair Credit Reporting Act," August 8, 2012, http://www.ftc.gov/opa/2012/08/hireright.shtm: "The case against HireRight Solutions, Inc. represents the first time the FTC has charged an employment background screening firm with violating the FCRA, and is the second-largest civil penalty that the FTC has obtained under the Act."

54. See Federal Trade Commission Press release, "Spokeo to Pay $800,000 to Settle FTC Charges Company Allegedly Marketed Information to Employers and Recruiters in Violation of FCRA," June 12, 2012, http://www.ftc.gov/opa/2012/06/spokeo.shtm.

55. *In the Matter of Filiquarian Publishing, LLC; Choice Level, LLC; and Joshua Linsk*, individually and as an officer of the companies File No. 112 3195, Docket No. C-4401, http://www.ftc.gov/os/caselist/1123195/130501filquariancmpt.pdf.

56. 15 U.S.C. § 1681h(e); see also Chi Chi Wu et al., National Consumer Law Center, *Fair Credit Reporting*, §§ 1.4.3 (6th ed. 2006); *Feldman v. Comprehensive Information Services, Inc.*, 32 Conn. L. Rptr. 523, 2002 WL 1902994 (Conn. Super. Ct. 2002) (unreported decision) (allegation that CRA was negligent in failing to confirm the truthfulness of the statements in a consumer report was preempted).

57. *Wiggins v. Equifax Services*, Inc., 848 F. Supp. 213 (D.D.C. 1993).

58. Scott Michels, "Advocates Complain of Background Check Errors," ABC News, October 13, 2008; Craig Bertschi, Kilpatrick, Townsend & Stockton, Annual Conference Educational, *FCRA Class Action Lawsuits: The Sharks Are Circling*, at 10–11, NAPBS Journal (January–February 2011).

59. *Wiggins v. Equifax Services, Inc.*, 848 F. Supp. 213 (D.D.C. 1993).

60. Class Action Complaint, *Jackson v. InfoTrack*, Case No. 11-cv-5801 (N.D. Ill. August 23, 2011).

61. National Consumer Law Center, *Broken Records: How Errors by Criminal Background Checking Companies Harm Workers and Businesses*, at 19 (2012);

Lisa Parker, "When the Only Crime Is Having a Common Name," NBC Chicago, July 23, 2013, http://www.nbcchicago.com/investigations/target-5-whats-in-a-name-mistaken-identity-139931853.html.

62. *Jane Roe, et al. v. Intellicorp Records Inc.*, Case No. 1:12-cv-02288; *Michael R. Thomas, et al. v. Intellicorp Records Inc.*, Case No. 1:12-cv-02433; *Mark A. Johnson, et al. v. Insurance Information Exchange LLC*, Case No. 1:13-cv-00616 (District Court of Northern District Of Ohio, Eastern Division); see Anne Bucher, "Background Check Firms Agree to $18M Class Action Settlement, Top Class Actions," http://www.topclassactions.com/lawsuit-settlements/lawsuit-news/5437-background-check-firms-agree-to-18m-class-action-settlement.

63. See, e.g., Terence P. Thornberry and Marvin D. Krohn, "The Self-Report Method for Measuring Delinquency and Crime," in David Duffee et al. (eds.), *Criminal Justice 2000*, Vol. 4, *Measurement and Analysis of Crime and Justice*, 33–83 (Washington, DC: U.S. Department of Justice, 2000); David Lisak and Paul M. Miller, *Repeat Rape and Multiple Offending among Undetected Rapists*, 17 Violence and Victims 73 (2002). The same is true for undetected recidivists: see A. Nicholas Groth et al., *Undetected Recidivism among Rapists and Child Molesters*, 28 Crime & Delinquency 450 (1982).

CHAPTER 9
Transparency of Criminal Convictions

1. Amanda Conley et al., *Sustaining Privacy and Open Justice in the Transition to Online Court Records: A Multidisciplinary Inquiry* 71 Maryland L. Rev. 772, 774 (2012).

2. European Court of Human Rights, *M.M. v. the United Kingdom*, November 13, 2012, Application No. 24029/07.

3. Tribunal Supremo (Sala de lo Contencioso-Administrativo, Seccion 1a), STS, March 3, 1995.

4. See James B. Jacobs and Elena Larrauri, *Are Criminal Records a Public Matter?* 14 Punishment & Society 3, at 6–7 (2012).

5. G. Michael Fenner and James L. Kole, *Access to Judicial Proceedings: To Richmond Newspapers and Beyond*, 16 Harv. C.R.-C.L. L. Rev. 415 (1981).

6. Artemi Rallo Lombarte, *La garantia del derecho constitucional a la proteccion de datos personales en los organos judiciales*, 5 Nuevas Politicas Publicas: Anuario multidisciplinary para la modernizacion de las Administraciones Publicas 97 (2009).

7. Texas Department of Criminal Justice, *Offender Information Search*, http://offender.tdcj.state.tx.us/POSdb2/.

8. Minnesota Bureau of Criminal Apprehension, *Minnesota Public Criminal History*, https://cch.state.mn.us/pcchOffenderSearch.aspx.

9. Minnesota Bureau of Criminal Apprehension, *Public and Private Data*, https://dps.mn.gov/divisions/bca/Pages/criminal-history-public-private-data.aspx.

10. Minnesota Bureau of Criminal Apprehension, *Minnesota Criminal History*, https://cch.state.mn.us/.

11. National Domestic Violence Registry website, http://domesticviolence database.net/.

12. Ley Organica del Poder Judicial, art. 266 (emphasis added).

13. See STC, May 18, 1981, no. 16; and STC, June 14, 1983, no. 50.

14. Rafael Bustos Gisbert, *Sobre la publicacion en paginas web de listados de condenados penalmente: Los casos de las listas de pedofilos, maltratadores, torturadores y errors medicos,* 62 Revista Vasca de Administracion Publica 11 (2002); Justa Gomez Navajas, "Listas de delincuentes: Pena de 'escarnio publico'?," in *Estudios penales sobre violencia doméstica* 493 (Madrid: Edersa, 2002).

15. For an exception, see Veronica del Carpio, *Fiestas, Divulgacion de antecedentes penales y proteccion del derecho al honor y a la intimidad,* 1 Aranzadi Civil 2191 (2005).

16. European Union Directive 95/46/EC, art. 8.5.

17. STC, November 30, 2002, no. 292.

18. Francisco Bueno Arus, *La cancelacion de antecedentes penales* (Madrid: Thomson/Civitas, 2006); Manuel Grosso Galván, *Los antecedentes penales: Rehabilitacion y control social* (Barcelona: Bosch, 1983); Elena Larrauri, *Conviction Records in Spain: Obstacles to Reintegration of Offenders?* 3(1) European Journal of Probation 50 (2011).

19. See Elena Larrauri and James B. Jacobs, *A Spanish Window on European Law and Policy on Employment Discrimination Based on Criminal Records,* in Tom Daems et al. (eds.), *European Penology?* 293 (Oxford: Hart Publishing, 2013).

20. 5 U.S.C. § 552

21. 5 U.S.C. § 552 (b)(7)(C).

22. *U.S. Department of Justice v. Reporters Committee for Freedom of the Press et al.*, 489 U.S. 749 (1989).

23. See U.S. Department of Justice, *Freedom of Information Act Reference Guide* (January 2010), http://www.justice.gov/oip/referenceguide.htm (emphasis added).

24. *U.S. Department of Justice v. Reporters Committee for Freedom of the Press et al.*, 489 U.S. 749 (1989); see U.S. Department of Justice, *Department of Justice Guide to the Freedom of Information Act* (2013 edition), http://www.justice .gov/oip/foia-guide.html.

25. *Fitzgibbon v. CIA*, 911 F.2d 755, 767 (D.C. Cir. 1990).

26. *Rimmer v. Holder,* 700 F.3d 246, 257 (6th Cir. Tenn. 2012).

27. *U.S. Department of Justice v. Reporters Committee for Freedom of the Press et al.*, 489 U.S. 749 (1989).

28. See, e.g., *Rugiero v. United States DOJ,* 257 F.3d 534, 552 (6th Cir. Mich. 2001); *Kurdyukov v. United States Coast Guard,* 657 F. Supp. 2d 248, 255 (D.D.C. 2009); *Librach v. Federal Bureau of Investigation,* 587 F.2d 372 (8th Cir. Mo. 1978); *Brady-Lunny v. Massey,* 185 F. Supp. 2d 928 (C.D. Ill. 2002).

29. *Long v. U.S. Department of Justice,* 778 F. Supp. 2d 222 (N.D. N.Y. 2011); *Long v. U.S. Department of Justice,* 479 F. Supp. 2d 23 (D.D.C. 2007); *Long v. U.S. Department of Justice,* 10 F. Supp. 2d 205 (N.D. N.Y. 1998). See, e.g., *Long v. Office of Pers. Mgmt.*, 692 F.3d 185 (2d Cir. 2012); *Long v. U.S. I.R.S.*, 395 F. App'x 472 (9th Cir. 2010); *Long v. Dep't of Homeland Sec.*, 436 F.

Supp. 2d 38 (D.D.C. 2006); *Long v. Bureau of Alcohol, Tobacco & Firearms*, 964 F. Supp. 494 (D.D.C. 1997).

30. *Am. Civil Liberties Union v. U.S. Department of Homeland Security*, 11 Civ. 3786 RMB, 2013 WL 4885518 (S.D. N.Y. September 9, 2013).

31. 448 US 555, 592 (1980).

32. *Globe Newspaper Co. v. Superior Court*, 457 US 596, 603 (1982).

33. 420 U.S. 469 (1975).

34. *King v. General Information Services, Inc.*, C.A. No. 10-6850, Class Action Complaint (E.D. Pa.) (filed February 14, 2011).

35. *King v. General Information Services, Inc.*, C.A. No. 10-6850, Motion for Judgment on the Pleadings and Supporting Memorandum of Law (E.D. Pa.) (filed September 16, 2011), citing *Sorrell v. IMS Health Inc.*, 131 S.Ct. 2653 (2011).

36. *Sorrell v. IMS Health Inc.*, 131 S.Ct. 2653, 2670–71 (2011).

37. Defendant's Motion and Memo for Judgment on the Pleadings at 8; see also Amended Answer to Amended Complaint at 8: "15 U.S.C. § 1681c(a)(2) and 15 U.S.C. § 1681c(a)(5) . . . violate the First Amendment to the U.S. Constitution to the extent they prohibit consumer reporting agencies from including in consumer reports public record information that is more than seven years old."

38. *King v. General Information Services*, No. 10-cv-6850, Memorandum of the United States of America in Support of the Constitutionality of § 1681c of the Fair Credit Reporting Act, at 13, 15–16 (E.D. Pa.) (filed May 3, 2012) (quoting *U.S. Department of Justice v. Reporters Committee for Freedom of the Press*, 489 U.S. 749, 764 [1989]).

39. *King v. Gen. Info. Servs., Inc.*, 903 F. Supp. 2d 303 (E.D. Pa. 2012).

40. David S. Tanenhaus, *Juvenile Justice in the Making* (Oxford: Oxford University Press, 2004).

41. Julian Mack, *The Juvenile Court*, 32 Annu. Rep. A.B.A. 449, 456 (1909).

42. Joel F. Handler, *The Juvenile Court and the Adversary System: Problems of Function and Form*, 1965 Wis. L. Rev. 7 (1965).

43. *In re Gault*, 387 U.S. 1, 18 (1967).

44. *Id.* at 24.

45. *Davis v. Alaska*, 415 U.S. 308 (1974).

46. *Oklahoma Publishing v. District Court*, 430 U.S. 308 (1977).

47. *Smith v. Daily Mail Publishing*, 443 U.S. 97 (1979).

48. See Jeffrey A. Butts, "Can We Do without Juvenile Justice?" in Bruce N. Waller (ed.), *You Decide! Current Debates in Criminal Justice* 321–31 (Upper Saddle River, NJ: Prentice Hall, 2009).

49. See Richard E. Redding, *Using Juvenile Adjudications for Sentence Enhancement under the Federal Sentencing Guidelines: Is It Sound Policy?*, 10 Va. J. Soc. Pol'y & L. 231 (2002).

50. Recommendation CM/Rec(2008)11 of the Council of Europe, https://wcd.coe.int/ViewDoc.jsp?id=1367113&Site=CM.

51. *Commentary to the European Rules for Juvenile Offenders Subject to Sanctions or Measures*, CM(2008)128 addendum 1, at 3.

52. *Griswold v. Connecticut*, 381 U.S. 479, 484 (1965).

53. Priscilla M. Regan, *Legislating Privacy* (Chapel Hill: University of North Carolina Press, 1995); Helen Nissenbaum, *Privacy in Context: Technology, Policy, and the Integrity of Social Life* (Stanford, CA: Stanford University Press, 2010); Erin Murphy, *The Politics of Privacy in the Criminal Justice System* 111 Mich. L. Rev. 485 (2013).

54. U.S. Department of Justice, *Freedom of Information Act Reference Guide* (January 2010), http://www.justice.gov/oip/referenceguide.htm.

55. Privacy Act of 1974, Pub. L. No. 93-579, 88 Stat. 1896 (codified at 5 U.S.C. § 552a).

56. Privacy Act of 1974, Pub. L. No. 93-579, 5 U.S.C. § 552a. See Information Practices Act of 1977, Cal. Civ. Code § 1798.

57. *Bartel v. Federal Aviation Admin.*, 725 F.2d 1403, 1407.

58. The Health Insurance Portability and Accountability Act of 1996 (HIPAA; Pub. L. 104–191, 110 Stat. 1936, enacted August 21, 1996).

59. *Id.*

60. 20 U.S.C. § 1232g, 34 CFR Part 99; Pub. L. 93–380, Title V, § 513, August 21, 1974, 88 Stat. 57.

61. *Rochin v. California*, 342 U.S. 165 (1952).

62. *Safford Unified School District #1 v. Redding*, 557 U.S. 364 (2009).

63. *Id.* at 366.

64. *Trop v. Dulles*, 356 U.S. 86, 99–100 (1958).

65. *Gregg v. Georgia*, 428 U.S. 153, 173 (1976).

66. *Brown v. Plata*, 131 S. Ct. 1910, 179 L. Ed. 2d 969 (2011).

67. *Brown v. Plata*, 131 S. Ct. 1910, 1928, 179 L. Ed. 2d 969 (2011).

68. See Federal Bureau of Investigation, *Requesting FBI Records*, http://www.fbi.gov/foia/requesting-fbi-records.

69. Jose Luis Diez Ripollez, *Derecho Penal Espanol: Parte General* (en Esquemas) (Valencia: Tirant lo Blanch, 2007); Elena Larrauri, *Entwurdigende Strafen. KritV.Sonderheft* 92 (Baden-Baden: Nomos, 2000); Santiago Mir Puig, *Derecho, Penal: Parte General* (Barcelona: Reppertor, 8th ed., 2008).

70. See the articles published in the third volume, number 1, of European Journal of Probation (2011): Martine Herzog-Evans, *Judicial Rehabilitation in France: Helping with the Desisting Process and Acknowledging Achieved Desistance*, at 4; Christine Morgenstern, *Judicial Rehabilitation in Germany: The Use of Criminal Records and the Removal of Recorded Convictions*, at 20; Miranda Boone, *Judicial Rehabilitation in the Netherlands: Balancing between Safety and Privacy*, at 63.

CHAPTER 10
Public Access to Arrestee Information

1. *Krapf v. United States*, 285 F.2d 647 (3d Cir. N.J. 1960).

2. *Kalish v. United States*, 271 F. Supp. 968 (D.P.R. 1967).

3. See, e.g., Amanda Woods, "Crime Report: A Deli Theft, Unauthorized Bank Activity and Home Burglaries," *New York Times*, http://fort-greene.thelocal.nytimes.com/tag/crime-blotter/ (retrieved September 10, 2013). The

New York Post has an NYPD Daily Blotter on its website (see, e.g., http://nypost.com/blotter/nypd-daily-blotter-4047/).

4. For an early case reasoning down this line, see *Morrow v. District of Columbia*, 417 F.2d 728, 741–42 (D.C. Cir. 1969).

5. See "Prostitution Sting Stirs Mixed Reactions," *Syosset Jericho Tribune*, June 12, 2013, http://www.antonnews.com/syossetjerichotribune/news/30242-prostitution-sting-stirs-mixed-reactions.html.

6. See generally Dan M. Kahan, *What Do Alternative Sanctions Mean*, 63 U. Chi. L. Rev. 591, at 631–32 (1996); Courtney Guyton Persons, Note, *Sex in the Sunlight: The Effectiveness, Efficiency, Constitutionality, and Advisability of Publishing Names and Pictures of Prostitutes' Patrons*, 49 Vand. L. Rev. 1525, at 1536–37 (1996).

7. See J. Douglas Allen-Taylor, "Dear Johns: For Shame," *Alternet*, January 17, 2006, http://www.alternet.org/story/30942/dear_johns%3A_for_shame.

8. David Talbot, "Johns Face Shame with TV Fame," *Boston Herald*, February 19, 1995, News Section, page 6.

9. See Edward Walsh, "'John TV' Attempts to Curb Prostitution in Kansas City Area," *Seattle Times*, August 3, 1997, http://community.seattletimes.nwsource.com/archive/?date=19970803&slug=2552909.

10. Art Hubacher, *Comments: Every Picture Tells a Story: Is Kansas City's John TV Constitutional?* 46 U. Kan. L. Rev. 551, at 552–53 (1997–1998).

11. City of Orlando, Orlando Police Department website, "RxFraud," http://www.cityoforlando.net/police/Rx/Rx.htm.

12. Maricopa County Sheriff's Office, "Mugshots," http://www.mcso.org/Mugshot/Default.aspx#.

13. National Consumer Law Center, *Broken Records: How Errors by Criminal Background Checking Companies Harm Workers and Businesses*, at 9 (April 2012).

14. *Id.* at 9–10; Editorial, "Stop Selling Them: Unreliable CHAIRS Reports Do More Harm Than Good," *Post-Standard*, April 14, 2011, http://blog.syracuse.com/opinion/2011/04/stop_selling_them_unreliable_c.html.

15. *Detroit Free Press v. DOJ*, 73 F.3d 93 (6th Cir. Mich. 1996).

16. *Id.* at 97.

17. Judge Alan E. Norris, dissenting, in *Detroit Free Press v. DOJ*, 73 F.3d 93 (6th Cir. 1996).

18. *Karantsalis v. U.S. Department of Justice*, 635 F.3d 497, 503 (11th Cir. 2011).

19. U.S. Department of Justice, United States Marshals Service Policy Notice 94-006B, Media Policy, September 20, 1997. See Gregory Nathaniel Wolfe, *Smile for the Camera, the World Is Going to See That Mug: The Dilemma of Privacy Interests in Mug Shots*, 113 Colum. L. Rev. 2227 (2013).

20. See, e.g., William Glaberson, "Faltering Courts, Mired in Delays," *New York Times*, April 13, 2013, http://www.nytimes.com/2013/04/14/nyregion/justice-denied-bronx-court-system-mired-in-delays.html?pagewanted=all&_r=0 I; Associated Press, "Judge Rules for Newspaper in Mug Shot Dispute Case," *New York Times*, April 22, 2014.

21. See Gary T. Lowenthal, *The Disclosure of Arrest Records to the Public under the Uniform Criminal History Records Act*, 28 Jurimetrics Journal 9, at 12 (1987–1988); Gary Fields and John Emschwiller, "As Arrest Records Rise,

Americans Find Consequences Can Last a Lifetime," *Wall Street Journal*, August 18, 2014.

22. Compare New York State Criminal Procedure Law sec. 160.50 (Order upon Termination of Criminal Action in Favor of the Accused) with Shawn D. Stuckey, *Collateral Effects of Arrests in Minnesota*, 5 U. St. Thomas L.J. 335, 342 (2008): "Arrest records are publicly available until individuals take the proper steps to seal their records. . . . Few individuals take the proper steps to seal their records, probably because the procedures are not well known and burdensome."

23. Legal Action Center, *The Problem of Rap Sheet Errors: An Analysis by the Legal Action Center* (2013), http://lac.org/index.php/lac/category/free_publications_library.

24. *People v. Patterson*, 78 N.Y.2d 711 (Ct. App. New York 1991).

25. *Id.*, Titone, J. (dissenting).

26. U.S. Department of Justice, Bureau of Justice Statistics, *Survey of State Criminal History Information Systems, 2010*, at 9, https://www.ncjrs.gov/pdffiles1/bjs/grants/237253.pdf.

27. *Riverside v. McLoughlin*, 500 U.S. 44 (1991).

28. *Paul v. Davis*, 424 U.S. 693 (1976).

29. *Davis v. Paul*, 505 F.2d 1180 (6th Cir. 1974) rev'd, 424 U.S. 693, 96 S. Ct. 1155, 47 L. Ed. 2d 405 (1976); *Wisconsin v. Constantineau*, 400 U.S. 433, 91 S. Ct. 507, 27 L. Ed. 2d 515 (1971).

30. *Wisconsin v. Constantineau*, 400 U.S. 433, 437, 91 S. Ct. 507, 510, 27 L. Ed. 2d 515 (1971).

31. *Paul v. Davis*, 424 U.S. 693, 702 (1976).

CHAPTER 11

Publicly Accessible Criminal Records and Punishment Theory

1. Nathaniel Hawthorne, *The Scarlet Letter* 51, 53 (1850; New York: Bantam Classic, 1986).

2. Uniform Criminal History Record Act, Drafted by the National Conference of Commissioners of Uniform State Law, Prefatory Note, at 3 (1986), http://www.uniformlaws.org/shared/docs/criminal%20history%20records/uchra_final_86.pdf.

3. See Jane Caplan and John Torpey, *Documenting Individual Identity* (Princeton, NJ: Princeton University Press, 2001).

4. See Adam Hirsch, *From Pillory to Penitentiary: The Rise of Criminal Incarceration in Early Massachusetts*, 80 Mich. L. Rev. 1179 (1982); Toni Massaro, *Shame, Culture and American Criminal Law*, 89 Mich. L. Rev. 1880 (1991); Aaron S. Book, *Shame on You: An Analysis of Modern Shame Punishments as an Alternative to Incarceration*, 40 Wm. & Mary L. Rev. 653 (1999); James Q. Whitman, *What Is Wrong with Inflicting Shame Sanctions?* 107 Yale L.J. 1055 (1998).

5. Edwin H. Sutherland, *White Collar Crime: The Uncut Version* 54 (New Haven, CT: Yale University Press, 1983).

6. Michael Davis, *Recent Work in Punishment Theory*, 4 Public Affairs Quarterly 217, 219 (1990).

7. On different versions of retribution, see, among others, Andrew von Hirsch, *Doing Justice: The Choice of Punishments* (New York: Hill and Wang, 1976); Hugo Adam Bedau, *Retribution and the Theory of Punishment*, 75 Journal of Philosophy 601 (1978); David Fogel and Joe Hudson (eds.), *Justice as Fairness* (Cincinnati, OH: Anderson, 1981); Richard S. Frase, *Punishment Purposes*, 58 Stanford L. Rev. 67, 73–74 (2005); Michael Tonry (ed.), *Retributivism Has a Past: Has It a Future?* (Oxford: Oxford University Press, 2011).

8. John Rawls, *Two Concepts of Rules*, 64 Philosophical Review 3, 4–5 (1955).

9. R.A. Duff, "Legal Punishment," in Edward N. Zalta (ed.), *The Stanford Encyclopedia of Philosophy* (Summer 2013 ed.), http://plato.stanford.edu/archives/sum2013/entries/legal-punishment/.

10. Alexandra Natapoff, *Misdemeanors*, 85 S. Cal. L. Rev. 101 (2012).

11. R.A. Duff, *Punishment, Communication, and Community* (New York: Oxford University Press, 2000); Dan Markel, *Retributive Justice and the Demands of Democratic Citizenship*, 1 Va. J. Crim. L. 1 (2012).

12. Henry M. Hart Jr., *The Aims of the Criminal Law*, 23 Law & Contemporary Problems 401, 436–37 (1958).

13. Andrew E. Taslitz, *Judging Jena's D.A.: The Prosecutor and Racial Esteem*, 44 Harv. C.R.-C.L. L. Rev. 393, 414 (2009).

14. John Braithwaite, *Crime, Shame, and Reintegration* (Cambridge: Cambridge University Press, 1989).

15. R.A. Duff, *Punishment, Communication, and Community* xvii (New York: Oxford University Press, 2000).

16. Seneca, *De Ira*, bk. I, XIX, 7.

17. See Jean Hampton, *The Moral Education Theory of Punishment*, 13 Philosophy & Public Affairs 208, 212 (1984); Stephen P. Garvey, *Can Shaming Punishments Educate?* 65 U. Chi. L. Rev. 733 (1998).

18. Johannes Andenaes, *Punishment and Deterrence* (Ann Arbor: University of Michigan Press, 1974).

19. For a thought experiment, see Dan Markel, *The Justice of Amnesty? Towards a Theory of Retributivism in Recovering States*, 49 U. Toronto L.J. 389 (1999).

20. Dan Markel, *Are Shaming Punishments Beautifully Retributive? Retributivism and the Implications for the Alternative Sanctions Debate*, 54 Vand. L. Rev. 2157, 2224 (2001).

21. Steven Klepper and Daniel Nagin, *Tax Compliance and Perceptions of the Risks of Detection and Criminal Prosecution*, 23 Law & Society Rev. 209 (1989); Steven Klepper and Daniel Nagin, *The Deterrent Effect of Perceived Certainty and Severity of Punishment Revisited*, 27 Criminology 721 (1989).

22. Daniel S. Nagin, *Criminal Deterrence Research at the Outset of the Twenty-First Century*, 23 Crime & Justice 1, 21 (1998).

23. Henry M. Hart Jr., *The Aims of the Criminal Law*, 23 Law & Contemporary Problems 401, 409 (1958).

24. Daniel S. Nagin, "Deterrence: Scaring Offenders Straight," in Francis T. Cullen and Cheryl Lero Jonson (eds.), *Correctional Theory: Context and Consequences* 69 (Los Angeles: Sage, 2012).

25. Franklin E. Zimring and Gordon Hawkins, *Deterrence; the Legal Threat in Crime Control* (Chicago: University of Chicago Press, 1973); Mark C. Stafford

and Mark Warr, *A Reconceptualization of General and Specific Deterrence*, 30 Journal of Research in Crime & Delinquency 123 (1993).

26. Alfred Blumsteim, "The Connection between Crime and Incarceration," in John P. May (ed.), *Building Violence: How America's Rush to Incarcerate Creates More Violence* 10 (Thousand Oaks, CA: Sage, 2000).

27. See Howard S. Becker, *Outsiders: Studies in the Sociology of Deviance* (New York: Free Press, 1963); Edwin M. Lemert, *Social Pathology: A Systematic Approach to the Theory of Sociopathic Behavior* (New York: McGraw-Hill, 1951); Edwin M. Lemert, *Human Deviance, Social Problems, and Social Control* (Englewood Cliffs, NJ: Prentice Hall, 1967); Edwin M. Schur, *Labeling Deviant Behavior* (New York: Harper and Row, 1971).

28. See Marijke Malsch and Marius Duker (eds.), *Incapacitation: Trends and New Perspectives* (Burlington, VT: Ashgate, 2012).

29. See, e.g., Franklin Zimring and Gordon Hawkins, *Incapacitation: Penal Confinement and the Restraint of Crime* (New York: Oxford University Press, 1995); Travis C. Pratt, *Addicted to Incarceration: Corrections Policy and the Politics of Misinformation in the United States* (Los Angeles: Sage, 2009). For a recent empirical study, see Ben Vollaard, *Preventing Crime through Selective Incapacitation*, 124 The Economic Journal, 262 (2013).

30. On vigilantism, see generally Lisa Arellano, *Vigilantes and Lynch Mobs: Narratives of Community and Nation* (Philadelphia: Temple University Press, 2012); Christopher Waldrep, *The Many Faces of Judge Lynch: Extralegal Violence and Punishment in America* (New York: Palgrave Macmillan, 2004); Richard M. Brown, *Strain of Violence: Historical Studies of American Violence and Vigilantism* (New York: Oxford University Press, 1975).

31. Wayne Logan, *Knowledge as Power: Criminal Registration and Community Notification Laws in America* 102 (Stanford, CA: Stanford Law Books, 2009).

32. See James B. Jacobs and Elena Larrauri, *Are Criminal Convictions a Public Matter? The USA and Spain*, 14 Punishment & Society 3 (2012).

33. Francis A. Allen, *The Decline of the Rehabilitative Ideal: Penal Policy and Social Purpose* (New Haven, CT: Yale University Press, 1981); Michael Tonry, *Looking Back to See the Future of Punishment in America*, 74 Social Research, No. 2, Punishment: The US Record 353, 354 (2007).

34. Michael Tonry, *The Functions of Sentencing and Sentencing Reform*, 58 Stan. L. Rev. 37, 46 (2005); Francis T. Cullen and Karen E. Gilbert, *Reaffirming Rehabilitation* (Waltham, MA: Anderson Publishing, 2nd ed., 2013); Lior Gideon and Hung-En Sung, *Rethinking Corrections: Rehabilitation, Reentry, and Reintegration* (Thousand Oaks, CA: Sage, 2010); Russ Immarigeon et al., "Ex-Offender Reintegration: Theory and Practice," in Shadd Maruna and Russ Immarigeon (eds.), *After Crime and Punishment: Pathways to Offender Reintegration* (Devon, UK: Willan, 2004). Polls consistently show that Americans support rehabilitation and reintegration. Milton Heumann et al., *Beyond the Sentence: Public Perceptions of Collateral Consequences for Felony Offenders*, 41 Criminal Law Bulletin 24 (2005).

35. See, e.g., Richard Freeman, *Employment Dimensions of Reentry: Understanding the Nexus between Prisoner Reentry and Work* (2003), http://www.urban.org/UploadedPDF/410857_freeman.pdf.

36. Harry J. Holzer et al., "The Effect of an Applicant's Criminal History on Employer Hiring Decisions and Screening Practices: Evidence from Los Angeles," in David Weiman et al., *Barriers to Reentry? The Labor Market for Released Prisoners in Post-Industrial America* 122–23 (New York: Russell Sage Foundation, 2007).

37. Aidan R. Gough, *The Expungement of Adjudication Records of Juvenile and Adult Offenders: A Problem of Status*, 1966 Wash. U. L. Q. 147, 190 (1966).

CHAPTER 12
Criminal Justice Consequences of a Criminal Record

1. 337 U.S. 241, 247–50 (1949).

2. Bernard E. Harcourt, *Against Prediction: Profiling, Policing, and Punishing in an Actuarial Age* 91 (Chicago: University of Chicago Press, 2007).

3. David Sudnow, *Normal Crimes: Sociological Features of the Penal Code in a Public Defender Office*, 12 Social Problems 255 (1965).

4. Ronald A. Farrell and Victoria Lynn Swigert, *Prior Offense Record as a Self-Fulfilling Prophecy*, 12 Law & Society Rev. 437 (1978).

5. See Michelle Alexander, *The New Jim Crow: Mass Incarceration in the Age of Colorblindness* (New York: New Press, 2010); Michelle Natividad Rodriguez and Maurice Emsellem, National Employment Law Project, *65 Million Need Not Apply* (2011).

6. See, e.g., Harold E. Pepinsky, *Better Living through Police Discretion*, 47 Law and Contemporary Problems 249 (1984); Weldon T. Johnson et al., *Arrest Probabilities for Marijuana Users as Indicators of Selective Law Enforcement*, 83 American Journal of Sociology, 681 (1977); Akiva M. Liberman, David S. Kirk, and Kideuk Kim, *Labeling Effects of First Juvenile Arrests: Secondary Deviance and Secondary Sanctioning*, 52 Criminology 345 (2014).

7. See Marc L. Miller and Ronald F. Wright, *Criminal Procedures: Prosecution and Adjudication* 97–104 (New York: Wolters Kluwer, 4th ed., 2011).

8. See Jonathan Simon, *Reversal of Fortune: The Resurgence of Individual Risk Assessment in Criminal Justice*, 1 Annual Review of Social Science 397 (2005); Jennifer L. Skeem and John Monahan, *Current Directions in Violence Risk Assessment*, 20(1) Current Directions in Psychological Science 38, 39 (2011). See also Marie VanNostrand and Christopher T. Lowenkamp, *Assessing Pretrial Risk without a Defendant Interview* (November 2013), http://www.arnoldfoundation.org/sites/default/files/pdf/LJAF_Report_no-interview_FNL.pdf; Massimo Calabresi, "Exclusive: Attorney General Eric Holder to Oppose Data Drive in Sanctioning," *Time*, July 31, 2014.

9. Thomas H. Cohen and Brian A. Reaves, *Pretrial Release of Felony Defendants in State Courts* 3 (Bureau of Justice Statistics Special Report, November 2007), http://www.bjs.gov/content/pub/pdf/prfdsc.pdf.

10. Richard. S. Frase, *Is Guided Discretion Sufficient? Overview of the State Sentencing Guidelines*, 44 Saint Louis U. L.J. 425, 440 (2000). By the same author, see also *The Decision to File Federal Criminal Charges: A Quantitative Study of Prosecutorial Discretion* 47 U. Chi. L. Rev. 246 (1980); Robert L.

Misner, *Recasting Prosecutorial Discretion*, 86J. Crim. L. & Criminology 717 (1996).

11. Marc L. Miller and Ronald F. Wright, *Criminal Procedures: Prosecution and Adjudication* 143 (New York: Wolters Kluwer, 4th ed., 2011); see also Bennett L. Gershman, *Prosecutorial Decisionmaking and Discretion in the Charging Function*, 62 Hastings L.J. 1259 (2011).

12. 18 U.S. sec. 1962(c) (emphasis added).

13. 245 U.S. 467 (1918).

14. Julia T. Rickert, *Denying Defendants the Benefit of a Reasonable Doubt: Federal Rule of Evidence 609 and Past Sex Crime Convictions*, 100 J. Crim. L. & Criminology 213 (2010).

15. See Violent Crime Control and Law Enforcement Act of 1994, Pub. L. No. 103-322, §320935(a), 108 Stat. 1796, 2135–37, FRE 413.

16. The relevant text reads as follows: "(a) In a criminal case in which the defendant is accused of an offense of sexual assault, evidence of the defendant's commission of another offense or offenses of sexual assault is admissible, and may be considered for its bearing on any matter to which it is relevant." FRE 413.

17. Many academic commentators have criticized these rules as reflecting irrational prejudice against sex offenders. The critics point out that sex offenders, as a class, have lower recidivism rates than other categories of offenders. See Julia T. Rickert, *Denying Defendants the Benefit of a Reasonable Doubt: Federal Rule of Evidence 609 and Past Sex Crime Convictions*, 100J. Crim. L. & Criminology 213 (2010); David P. Leonard, *The Federal Rules of Evidence and the Political Process*, 22 Fordham Urb. L.J. 305, 341 (1995); Louis M. Natali Jr. and R. Stephen Stigall, *"Are You Going to Arraign His Whole Life?": How Sexual Propensity Evidence Violates the Due Process Clause*, 28 Loy. U. Chi. L.J. 1, 3–4 (1996); Erik D. Ojala, *Propensity Evidence under Rule 413: The Need for Balance*, 77 Wash. U. L.Q. 947, 949 (1999).

18. See A. Bonneville de Marsangy, *De la Récidive ou des moyens les plus efficaces pour constater, rechercher et réprimer les rechutes dans toute infraction à la loi pénale* (Paris: Cotillon, 1844); Simon A. Cole, *Suspect Identities: A History of Fingerprinting and Criminal Identification* 15 (Cambridge, MA: Harvard University Press, 2001).

19. See Andre Normandeau, *Pioneers in Criminology: Arnould Bonneville De Marsangy (1802–1894)*, 60J. Crim. L. & Criminology 28, 30–31 (1969).

20. Franklin E. Zimring and Gordon Hawkins, *Deterrence: The Legal Threat in Crime Control* (Chicago: University of Chicago Press, 1973.)

21. Wayne A. Logan, *Knowledge as Power: Criminal Registration and Community Notification Laws in America* 5 (August 25, 2009), Stanford University Press, FSU College of Law, Public Law Research Paper No. 387, http://ssrn.com/abstract=1461490 or http://dx.doi.org/10.2139/ssrn.1461490.

22. Julian V. Roberts, *The Role of Criminal Record in the Sentencing Process*, 22 Crime & Justice 303, 304 (1997).

23. See Julian V. Roberts and Andrew von Hirsch (eds.), *Previous Convictions at Sentencing: Theoretical and Applied Perspectives* (Oxford: Hart, 2010); Sarah French Russell, *Rethinking Recidivist Enhancements: The Role of Prior*

Drug Convictions in Federal Sentencing, 43 UC Davis L. Rev. 1135 (2010); Julian V. Roberts and Orhun H. Yalincak, *Revisiting Prior Record Enhancement Provisions in State Sentencing Guidelines*, 26 Federal Sentencing Reporter 3 (2014).

24. Julian V. Roberts, *Public Opinion, Criminal Record, and the Sentencing Process*, 39 American Behavioral Scientist, 488–99, at 493 (February 1996).

25. *Id.*

26. Andrew von Hirsch and Committee for the Study of Incarceration, *Doing Justice: The Choice of Punishments* 46 (New York: Hill and Wang, 1976).

27. *Moore* v. *Missouri*, 159 U.S. 673, 677 (1895).

28. *Id.* (citations omitted).

29. In his opinion explaining denial of *certiori* in *Riggs v. California*, No. 98-5021 (decided January 19, 1999).

30. NY Penal Law sec. 70.06 1(a)(i).

31. *Rummel v. Estelle*, 445 U.S. 263 (1980).

32. *Solem v. Helm*, 463 U.S. 277 (1983).

33. The Violent Crime Control and Law Enforcement Act of 1994, H.R. 3355, Pub. L. 103–322, 18 U.S.C. § 3559(e).

34. *Ewing v. California*, 538 U.S. 11 (2003); *Lockyer v. Andrade*, 538 U.S. 63 (2003).

35. See, e.g., Alfred Blumstein and Jacqueline Cohen, "Characterizing Criminal Careers," *Science*, August 28, 1987, p. 985; Richard E. Redding, *Using Juvenile Adjudications for Sentence Enhancements under the Federal Sentencing Guidelines: Is It Sound Policy?*, 10 Va. J. Soc. Pol'y & L. 231 (2002); Joseph L. Goldstein-Breyer, *Calling Strikes before He Stepped to the Plate: Why Juvenile Adjudications Should Not Be Used to Enhance Subsequent Adult Sentences*, 15 Berkeley J. Crim. L. 65 (2010).

36. Richard E. Redding, *Using Juvenile Adjudications for Sentencing Enhancement under the Federal Sentencing Guidelines: Is It Sound Policy?*, 10 Va. J. Soc. Pol'y & L. 231, 231–32 (2002).

37. *Shepard v. U.S.*, 544 U.S. 13, 16 (2005); see also *Leocal v. Ashcroft*, 543 U.S. 1 (2004).

38. *Shepard v. U.S.*, 544 U.S. 13, 17 (2005).

39. *Id.* at 26.

40. See, generally, Alex Glashausser, *The Treatment of Foreign Country Convictions as Predicates for Sentence Enhancement under Recidivist Statutes*, 44 Duke L.J. 134, 136–37 (1994).

41. James B. Jacobs and Dimitra Blitsa, *Sharing Criminal Records: The United States, the European Union and Interpol Compared*, 30 Loy. L.A. Int'l & Comp. L. Rev. 125 (2008).

42. *U.S. v. Korno*, 986 F.2d 166 (7th Cir. 1993).

43. Arthur Bowker, "Prior Criminal History Investigations," *FBI Law Enforcement Bulletin* (1995).

44. See John Runda et al., *The Practice of Parole Boards* (Lexington, KY: Association of Paroling Authorities, 1994).

45. Josh Wall, *The Policy of the Massachusetts Parole Board* (Promulgated December 2006, Updated March 2012), at 7–8, http://www.mass.gov/eopss/docs/pb/paroledecision.pdf. For a critical view of overreliability on risk assessment

in the parole decision-making process, see W. David Ball, *Normative Elements of Parole Risk*, 22 Stan. L. & Pol'y Rev. 410 (2011).

CHAPTER 13
Second-Class Citizens by Law

1. Webster Hubbell, "The Mark of Cain," *San Francisco Chronicle*, June 10, 2001, at D1.

2. Roger Clegg, "Perps and Politics: Why Felons Can't Vote," *National Review Online*, October 18, 2004, http://www.nationalreview.com/articles/212573/perps-and-politics/roger-clegg.

3. Jeremy Travis, "Invisible Punishment: An Instrument of Social Exclusion," in Marc Mauer and Meda Chesnet-Lind (eds.), *Invisible Punishment: The Collateral Consequences of Mass Imprisonment* (New York: New Press, 2002).

4. Mirjan R. Damaška, *Adverse Legal Consequences of Conviction and Their Removal: A Comparative Study (Part 1)*, 59 Journal of Criminal Law, Criminology, & Police Science 347, 350–51 (1968).

5. See Harry D. Saunders, *Civil Death—A New Look at an Ancient Doctrine*, 11 Wm. & Mary L. Rev. 988 (1970).

6. Comment, *Beyond the Ken of the Courts: A Critique of Judicial Refusal to Review the Complaints of Convicts*, 72 Yale L.J. 506 (1962–1963).

7. *Wolff v. McDonnell*, 418 U.S. 539, 555–56 (1974).

8. See Nora V. Demleitner, *Preventing Internal Exile: The Need for Restrictions on Collateral Sentencing Consequences*, 11 Stan. L. & Pol'y Rev. 153 (1999); Mirjan R. Damaška, *Adverse Legal Consequences of Conviction and Their Removal: A Comparative Study (Part 1)*, 59 Journal of Criminal Law, Criminology, & Police Science 347, 350–51 (1968); Jeremy Travis, "Invisible Punishment: An Instrument of Social Exclusion," in Marc Mauer and Meda Chesney-Lind (eds.), *Invisible Punishment: The Collateral Consequences of Mass Imprisonment* (New York: New Press, 2002).

9. See Gabriel J. Chin, *The New Civil Death: Rethinking Punishment in the Era of Mass Conviction*, 160 U. Pa. L. Rev. 1789 (2012); Rebecca McLennan, "The Convict's Two Lives: Civil and Natural Death in the American Prison," in David Gardland et al. (eds.), *America's Death Penalty: Between Past and Present* (New York: New York University Press, 2011); Margaret Colgate Love et al., *Collateral Consequences of Criminal Convictions: Law, Policy and Practice* (Washington, DC: Thomson Reuters, 2013).

10. Gabriel J. Chin, *The New Civil Death: Rethinking Punishment in the Era of Mass Conviction*, 160 U. Pa. L. Rev. 1789 (2012).

11. *Padilla v. Kentucky*, 559 U.S. 356 (2010).

12. National Conference of Commissioners on Uniform State Laws, Uniform Collateral Consequences of Conviction Act (2010), http://www.uniformlaws.org/shared/docs/collateral_consequences/uccca_final_10.pdf; Connecticut, Minnesota, New Mexico, New York, and Vermont have enacted the Uniform Collateral Consequences of Conviction Act. See Uniform Law Commission, Legislative Fact Sheet—Collateral Consequences of Conviction

Act, http://www.uniformlaws.org/LegislativeFactSheet.aspx?title=Collateral%20Consequences%20of%20Conviction%20Act. The ABA has endorsed it. See American Bar Association, Resolution Approving the Uniform Collateral Consequences of Conviction Act, http://www.uniformlaws.org/Shared/Docs/ABA%20Approval%205-11-2010.pdf.

13. See National Inventory of the Collateral Consequences of Conviction, http://www.abacollateralconsequences.org/; Margaret Colgate Love et al., *Collateral Consequences of Criminal Convictions: Law, Policy and Practice* (Washington, DC: Thomson Reuters, 2013).

14. Margaret Colgate Love, *Twelfth Annual Symposium on Contemporary Urban Challenges: Starting over with a Clean Slate: In Praise of a Forgotten Section of the Model Penal Code*, 30 Fordham Urb. L.J. 1705, 1708 (2003).

15. *Id.* at 1714.

16. Walter M. Grant et al., *The Collateral Consequences of a Criminal Conviction*, 23 Vand. L. Rev. 929 (1970).

17. American Bar Association, Collateral Sanctions and Discretionary Disqualifications of Convicted Persons, http://www.americanbar.org/publications/criminal_justice_section_archive/crimjust_standards_collateral_blk.htm; Anthony C. Thompson, *Releasing Prisoners, Redeeming Communities: Reentry, Race, and Politics* (New York: New York University Press, 2008). See Michael Pinard, *Collateral Consequences of Criminal Convictions: Confronting Issues of Race and Dignity*, 85 N.Y.U. L. Rev. 457 (2010); National Employment Law Project, *65 Million "Need Not Apply": The Case for Reforming Criminal Background Checks for Employment* (March 2011), http://www.nelp.org/page/-/SCLP/2011/65_Million_Need_Not_Apply.pdf?nocdn=1.

18. Mirjan R. Damaška, *Adverse Legal Consequences of Conviction and Their Removal: A Comparative Study (Part 2)*, 59 Journal of Criminal Law, Criminology, & Police Science 542, 567 (1969).

19. The Sentencing Project, *State-Level Estimates of Felon Disenfranchisement in the United States, 2010* (July 2012), http://www.sentencingproject.org/doc/publications/fd_State_Level_Estimates_of_Felon_Disen_2010.pdf.

20. See Christopher Uggen and Jeff Manza, *Democratic Contraction? Political Consequences of Felon Disenfranchisement in the United States*, 67 American Sociological Review 777 (2002).

21. Kentucky Const. § 145, cl. 1.

22. See *Locked Out: Felon Disenfranchisement and American Democracy* (New York: Oxford University Press, 2006).

23. See Pamela Karlan, *Convictions and Doubts: Retribution, Representation and the Debate over Felon Disenfranchisement*, 56 Stan. L. Rev. 1147 (2004).

24. Hans Von Spakovsky, "Ex-Cons Should Prove They Deserve the Right to Vote," Heritage Foundation, March 15, 2013, http://www.heritage.org/research/commentary/2013/3/excons-should-prove-they-deserve-the-right-to-vote.

25. *Hirst v. United Kingdom*, European Court of Human Rights 681 §41 (2005).

26. *Richardson v. Ramirez*, 418 U.S. 24, 94 S. Ct. 2655, 41 L. Ed. 2d 551, 1974 U.S. LEXIS 84, 72 Ohio Op. 2d 232 (U.S. 1974).

27. USCS Const. Amend. 14, § 2.

28. *Richardson v. Ramirez*, 418 U.S. 24, 94 S. Ct. 2655, 41 L. Ed. 2d 551, 1974 U.S. LEXIS 84, 72 Ohio Op. 2d 232 (U.S. 1974).

29. *Richardson v. Ramirez*, 418 U.S. 24, 78–79 (U.S. 1974) (internal citations omitted).

30. Jeff Manza et al., *Public Attitudes toward Felon Disenfranchisement in the United States*, 68 Public Opinion Quarterly 275 (2004).

31. The Sentencing Project, *Expanding the Vote: State Felony Disenfranchisement Reform, 1997–2010* (October 2010), http://www.sentencingproject.org/doc/publications/publications/vr_ExpandingtheVoteFinalAddendum.pdf.

32. See, e.g., HRS § 612-4; 10 NY CLS Jud § 510; 38 Okl. St. § 28; 28 U.S.C. 1865(b)(5).

33. Brian C. Kalt, *The Exclusion of Felons from Jury Service*, 53 Am. U. L. Rev. 65 (2003–2004).

34. *Id.* at 67.

35. California, for example, strips certain misdemeanants (e.g., those convicted of assault, battery, stalking, and grossly negligent firearm discharge) of their Second Amendment rights (Cal. Penal Code § 29805). On firearms restrictions, see Margaret Colgate Love et al., *Collateral Consequences of Criminal Convictions: Law, Policy and Practice*, at 90–98 (Washington, DC: Thomson Reuters, 2013).

36. See, e.g., the following *New York Times* "Room for Debate" discussion: "Taking, and Restoring, the Rights of Felons," *New York Times*, November 14, 2011, http://www.nytimes.com/roomfordebate/2011/11/14/taking-and-restoring-the-rights-of felons?gwh=4D3831D2B64EF79121F39410AD7389C7. But see National Association of Criminal Defense Lawyers, "Collateral Damage: America's Failure to Forgive or Forget in the War on Crime, A Roadmap to Restore Rights and Status after Arrest or Conviction," 35 (May 2014).

37. *District of Columbia v. Heller*, 554 U.S. 570, 626 (2008).

38. See C. Kevin Marshall, *Why Can't Margaret Stewart Have a Gun?* 32 Harv. J.L. & Pub. Pol'y 696 (2009); Nelson Lund, *Two Faces of Judicial Restraint (or Are There More?) in* McDonald v. City of Chicago?, 63 Fla. L. Rev. 487 (2011).

39. Michael Luo, "Felons Finding It Easy to Regain Gun Rights," *New York Times*, November 31, 2011, at A1.

40. Brian C. Kalt, *The Exclusion of Felons from Jury Service*, 53 Am. U. L. Rev. 65 (2003–2004).

41. Immigration Act of February 5, 1917, 39 Stat. 889, sec. 19.

42. Anti-Drug Abuse Act of 1988, Pub. L. No. 100–690, 102 Stat. 4181, effective November 18, 1988. See also Stephen Legomsky, *The New Path of Immigration Law: Asymmetric Incorporation of Criminal Justice Norms*, 64 Wash. & Lee L. Rev. 469, 483 (2007); Juliet Stumpf, *Doing Time: Crimmigration Law and the Perils of Haste*, 58 UCLA L. Rev. 1705, 1734 (2011) ("The 'aggravated felony' has become an infamous misnomer, encompassing crimes that are neither severe nor felonies, and existing as a category apart from criminal law with no counterpart to any term or definition in criminal law").

43. INA § 208.13(c)(2)(D); 8 U.S.C. § 1101(a)(43).

44. Pub. L. No. 104-208 §321(a), effective September 30, 1996; 8 U.S.C. § 1101(a)(43) (defining "aggravated felony"). See Peter H. Schuck, *The Trans-*

formation of Immigration Law, 84 Colum. L. Rev. 1, 26 (1984) ("Deportation . . . serves as an important adjunct and supplement to criminal law enforcement, and it reflects judgments essentially indistinguishable from those that the criminal law routinely makes concerning the moral worth of individual conduct").

45. *Padilla v. Kentucky*, 559 U.S. 356 (U.S. 2010).

46. *Id.*

47. *Id.* at 360.

48. *Id.* at 356, 364.

49. Kevin Lapp, *Reforming the Good Moral Character Requirement for U.S. Citizenship*, 87 Ind. L.J. 1572 (2012); 8 U.S.C. § 1427(a) (naturalization requirements).

50. 8 U.S.C. § 1101 (f).

51. 8 U.S.C. § 1101 (f)(8) (a person who has been convicted of an aggravated felony at any time cannot be "regarded as . . . a person of good moral character").

52. 8 U.S.C. § 1101 (f)(7).

53. Andrea Steinacker, *The Prisoner's Campaign: Felony Disenfranchisement Laws and the Right to Hold Public Office*, 2003 B.Y.U. L. Rev. 801 (2003).

54. Ala. Code 36-2-1.

55. N.Y. Civ. RTS. § 79 (2011).

56. Cal. Elec. Code § 201.

57. See U.S. Department of Justice, Bureau of Justice Assistance, *Program Brief, Denial of Federal Benefits Program and Clearinghouse*, July 2002; § 5301 of P.L. 100-690, 102 Stat. 4310 (1988); 21 U.S.C.S. § 862.

58. 21 U.S.C. § 862(d)(1)(A).

59. United States Government Accountability Office, Report to Congressional Requesters, *Drug Offenders: Various Factors May Limit the Impacts of Federal Laws That Provide for Denial of Selected Benefits* at 16 (September 2005).

60. Personal Responsibility and Work Opportunity Reconciliation Act of 1996, P.L. 104-193, 104th Congress, 110 Stat. 2105.

61. Legal Action Center, "Opting Out of Federal Ban on Food Stamps and TANF," http://www.lac.org/toolkits/TANF/TANF.htm#summary (accessed February 3, 2014).

62. H.R.2642, Agriculture Act of 2014, 113th Cong. (2013–2014), s. 4008, approved by the House of Representatives on January 29, 2014, and the Senate on February 4, 2014.

63. 42 U.S.C. § 13661(b).

64. 42 U.S.C. § 13663.

65. 42 U.S.C. § 1437n.

66. Corinne A. Carey, *No Second Chance: People with Criminal Records Denied Access to Public Housing*, 36 U. Tol. L. Rev. 545, 566 (2005).

67. Katy Reckdahl, "Funeral Expenses Add to Burdens of Murder Victims' Families," *Times-Picayune*, May 21, 2012, http://www.nola.com/crime/index.ssf/2012/05/funeral_expenses_add_to_burden.html.

68. Louisiana Commission on Law Enforcement and Administration of Criminal Justice website, "Crime Victims Reparations," http://www.lcle.la.gov/programs/cvr.asp#moreinfo.

69. *Id.*; Katy Reckdahl, "Funeral Expenses Add to Burdens of Murder Victims' Families," *Times-Picayune*, May 21, 2012, http://www.nola.com/crime/index.ssf/2012/05/funeral_expenses_add_to_burden.html.

70. Louisiana Commission on Law Enforcement and Administration of Criminal Justice website, "Crime Victims Reparations," http://www.lcle.la.gov/programs/cvr.asp#moreinfo; Katy Reckdahl, "Funeral Expenses Add to Burdens of Murder Victims' Families," *Times-Picayune*, May 21, 2012, http://www.nola.com/crime/index.ssf/2012/05/funeral_expenses_add_to_burden.html.

71. See Kelley R. Brandstetter, *Law and Literature Symposium: "Some Sort of Chronicler I Am": Narration and the Poetry of Lawrence Joseph: Comment: Repealing the Drug-Free Student Loan Provision: Would Putting Dope Back into the College Classroom Help Keep Dope off the Street and out of the Prison System?*, 77 U. Cin. L. Rev. 1127.

72. Higher Education Amendments of 1998, Pub. L. No. 105-244, § 483(f)(1).

73. See Kylie Beth Crawford, *Comment: Collateral Sanctions in Higher Education: A Constitutional Challenge to the Drug-Free Student Loan Provision of the Higher Education Act of 1998*, 36 U. Tol. L. Rev. 755, 757 (2005); Mark Souder, "Actions Have Consequences," *USA Today*, June 13, 2000, at 16A.

74. Cathryn A. Chappell, *Post-Secondary Correctional Education and Recidivism: A Meta-Analysis of Research Conducted 1990–1999*, 55 Journal of Correctional Education 148 (2004); David B. Wilson et al., *A Meta-Analysis of Corrections-Based Education, Vocation, and Work Programs for Adult Offenders*, 37 Journal of Research in Crime & Delinquency 347 (2000).

75. Deficit Reduction Act of 2005, 109 Pub. L. 171, 120 Stat. 4, 178; 20 U.S.C.S. § 1091.

76. Margaret Colgate Love et al., *Collateral Consequences of Criminal Convictions: Law, Policy and Practice*, at 74 (Washington, DC: Thomson Reuters, 2013).

77. 5 C.F.R. 919.605; 5 C.F.R. 919.800; 48 C.F.R. 9.406-2; 48 C.F.R. 9.407-2. See American Bar Association Commission on Effective Criminal Sanctions and the Public Defender Service for the District of Columbia, *Internal Exile: Collateral Consequences of Conviction in Federal Laws and Regulations*, at 34–35 (2009).

78. 48 CFR 252.203-7001.

79. NYC Administrative Code 6-116.2. See James B. Jacobs and Frank Anechiarico, *Blacklisting Public Contractors as an Anti-Corruption and Racketeering Strategy*, 11 Crim. Just. Ethics 64 (1992); Frank Anechiarico and James B. Jacobs, *Purging Corruption from Public Contracting: The "Solutions" Are Now Part of the Problem*, 40 N.Y.L. Sch. L. Rev. 143 (1995).

80. Rules of the City of New York, Title 9, §2-08 (a)(1).

81. Ronald Goldstock and James B. Jacobs, *Monitors and IPSIGS: Emergence of a New Criminal Justice Role*, 43 Crim. L. Bulletin 217 (2007).

82. U.S. Department of Justice, Bureau of Justice Statistics, *State Court Organization 2004*, at 260–63. (These states are Alabama, Arkansas, Indiana, Iowa, Nevada, Ohio, and South Carolina.)

83. *Id.*

84. R.I. Gen. Laws § 28-32-5.

85. N.J. Stat. § 2C:51-2; Margaret Colgate Love et al., *Collateral Consequences of Criminal Convictions: Law, Policy and Practice*, at 50 (Washington, DC: Thomson Reuters, 2013).

86. Margaret Colgate Love et al., *Collateral Consequences of Criminal Convictions: Law, Policy and Practice*, at 51–52 (Washington, DC: Thomson Reuters, 2013).

87. See H. R. 2083, 113th Congress, "To Amend the Elementary and Secondary Education Act of 1965 to Require Criminal Background Checks for School Employees," http://docs.house.gov/billsthisweek/20131021/BILLShr2083-SUS.pdf.

88. Texas Department of Public Safety, Licensing and Registration Service—Private Security Administrative Rules, http://www.txdps.state.tx.us/rsd/psb/docs/adminrules.pdf.

89. Three Bureau of Justice Statistics studies found that recidivism rates were above 60 percent. See Allen J. Beck and Bernard E. Shipley, *Recidivism of Prisoners Released in 1983* (Bureau of Justice Statistics, Special Report NCJ 116261, April 1989); Patrick A. Langan and David J. Levin, *Recidivism of Prisoners Released in 1994* (Bureau of Justice Statistics, Special Report NCJ 193427, June 2002); Matthew R. Durose, Alexia D. Cooper, and Howard N. Snyder, Bureau of Justice Statistics, "Recidivism of Prisoners Released in 30 States in 2005: Patterns from 2005 to 2010" (2014).

90. Waterfront Commission Compact, N.J. Stat. Ann. § 32:23-1 et seq.; N.Y. Unconsol. Law § 9801 et seq.; Waterfront Commission Compact, ch. 407, 67 Stat. 541 (1953).

91. N.Y. Unconsol. Law § 9829.

92. *Id.*

93. See N.Y. Unconsol. Law §§ 9814, 9841.

94. *Id.*

95. *Id.*

96. N.Y. Unconsol. Law § 9820.

97. For a discussion, see James B. Jacobs, *Mobsters, Unions, and Feds: The Mafia and the American Labor Movement* (New York: New York University Press, 2006).

98. Labor Management Relations (Taft-Hartley) Act of 1947, 29 U.S.C. § 504(a)(2006).

99. 29 USCS § 504. See United States Department of Labor, Office of Labor-Management Standards, Prohibition against Certain Persons Holding Union Office or Employment (updated March 5, 2013), http://www.dol.gov/olms/regs/compliance/504unionoffhold.htm.

100. Nev. Gaming Comm., Regulation 5 (Operating of Gaming Establishments) §5.014, http://gaming.nv.gov/modules/showdocument.aspx?documentid=256; Nev. Rev. Stat. Ann. § 463.170.

101. Nev. Gaming Comm. § 5.104.

102. Michael Boucai, *"Balancing Your Strengths against Your Felonies": Considerations for Military Recruitment of Ex-Offenders*, 61 U. Miami L. Rev. 997. See also Lizette Alvarez, "Army and Marine Corps Grant More Felony

Waivers," *New York Times*, April 22, 2008, http://www.nytimes.com/2008/04/22/washington/22waiver.html?_r=0.

103. The Supreme Court of Kentucky denied a law school graduate's request to write the Kentucky bar exam because he is a registered sex offender. The court cited his lack of the "requisite character and fitness" to be a member of the Kentucky bar. The court stated: "Indeed, our certification could significantly mislead the public into believing that we vouch for [Hamilton-Smith's] good character. . . . Consequently, a client's subsequent discovery of the registry listing could then justifiably lead him to question the value of this court's certification of the good character of those who are permitted to take the bar examination." See Jim Vassallo, "Registered Sex Offender Denied Opportunity to Take Bar Exam," *J.D. Journal*, January 7, 2014, http://www.jdjournal.com/2014/01/07/registered-sex-offender-denied-opportunity-to-take-bar-exam/?utm_source=MCNA&utm_medium=Email&utm_campaign=t_17740–dt_20140109-cid_34270-Did_5100191-ad_JDJ~MCNA#.

104. N.Y. CLS Jud. § 90; 22 N.Y.C.R.R. 1022.34.

105. New York State Unified Court System, *Application for Admission to Practice as an Attorney and Counselor-at-Law in the State of New York, Application for Admission Questionnaire*, Question F, available at http://www.nybarexam.org/Admission/AdmissionMultiDeptPacket.htm.

106. See Anthony J. Graniere and Hilary McHugh, *Note: Are You In or Are You Out? The Effect of a Prior Criminal Conviction on Bar Admission and a Proposed National Uniform Standard*, 26 Hofstra Lab. & Emp. L.J. 223 (2008); George L. Blum, *Criminal Record as Affecting Applicant's Moral Character for Purposes of Admission to the Bar*, 3 A.L.R. 6th 49 (updated 2013). "Every person who has been or shall hereafter be convicted of a felony, in a court of this or any state or a court of the United States, manslaughter or a violation of the Internal Revenue Code excepted, shall be incapable of obtaining a license to practice law." Miss. R. Admis. St. B. Rule VIII, sec. 6.

107. "Any person being an attorney and counselor-at-law who shall be convicted of a felony as defined in paragraph e of this subdivision, shall upon such conviction, cease to be an attorney and counselor-at-law, or to be competent to practice law as such." N.Y. Jud. Law § 90(4)(a).

108. N.Y. Jud. Law § 90(4)(f).

109. See State of New Jersey Department of Banking and Insurance, *Notice to Persons Seeking a New Jersey Real Estate License*, http://www.state.nj.us/dobi/division_rec/licensing/reclicqual.htm; see also N.J.S.A. 45:15-9.

110. 42 U.S.C.A. § 13041 (West).

111. Ala. Code § 15-20A-13.

112. *Doe v. Miller*, 405 F.3d 700 (8th Cir. 2005).

113. *Doe v. Miller*, 298 F. Supp. 2d 844, 851 (S.D. Iowa 2004) rev'd, 405 F.3d 700 (8th Cir. 2005).

114. See, e.g., Cal. Penal Code §3004; Ga. Code Ann. §42-1-14(e); Catherine L. Carpenter and Amy E. Beverlin, *The Evolution of Unconstitutionality in Sex Offender Registration Laws*, 63 Hastings L.J. 1071 (2012).

115. Margaret Colgate Love et al., *Collateral Consequences of Criminal Convictions: Law, Policy and Practice*, at 112 (Washington, DC: Thomson Reuters, 2013). See Corey Rayburn Yung, *Sex Offender Exceptionalism and Preventive Detention*, 101 J. Crim. L. & Criminology 969, 1003 (2011).

116. See, e.g., American Bar Association, *American Bar Association Standards for Criminal Justice*, 3rd ed., Collateral Sanctions and Discretionary Disqualifications of Convicted Persons, Standard 19-2.2 (2004); Margaret Colgate Love, *Paying Their Debt to Society: Forgiveness, Redemption, and the Uniform Collateral Consequences of Conviction Act*, 54 Howard L.J. 753 (2010–2011); Alfred Blumstein and Kiminori Nakamura, "Paying a Price, Long after the Crime," *New York Times*, January 9, 2012, http://www.nytimes.com/2012/01/10/opinion/paying-a-price-long-after-the-crime.html; Anthony Thompson, *Releasing Prisoners, Redeeming Communities: Reentry, Race, and Politics* (New York: New York University Press, 2008); National Association of Criminal Defense Lawyers, "Collateral Damage: America's Failure to Forgive or Forget in the War on Crime, a Roadmap to Restore Rights and Status after Arrest or Conviction" (May 2014).

117. Nora V. Demleitner, *Preventing Internal Exile: The Need for Restrictions on Collateral Sentencing Consequences*, 11 Stan. L. & Pol'y Rev. 153, 154 (1999).

118. American Bar Association, American Bar Association Standards for Criminal Justice, 3rd ed., Collateral Sanctions and Discretionary Disqualifications of Convicted Persons, at 9–10 (2004).

119. National Employment Law Project, *Major U.S. Cities and Counties Adopt Hiring Policies* to *Remove Unfair Barriers to Employment of People with Criminal Records, Updated July 22, 2008; National Employment Law Project, Major U.S. Cities and Counties Adopt Fair Hiring Policies to Remove Unfair Barriers to Employment of People with Criminal Records*, July 2014.

120. W. Kessler, personal communication, April 3, 2007.

121. National Employment Law Project, *Statewide Ban the Box, Reducing Unfair Barriers to Employment of People with Criminal Records* (May 2014).

122. *Id.*

123. American Bar Association, Commission on Effective Criminal Sanctions, *Report to the House of Delegates* [on Employment and Licensure of Persons with a Criminal Record] (February 2007), http://meetings.abanet.org/webupload/commupload/CR209800/newsletterpubs/Report.III.PDF.121306.pdf.

124. See Michael Pinard, *Collateral Consequences of Criminal Convictions: Confronting Issues of Race and Dignity*, 85 N.Y.U. L. Rev. 457 (2010); Michael Pinard and Anthony C. Thompson, *Offender Reentry and the Collateral Consequences of Criminal Convictions: An Introduction*, 30 N.Y.U. Rev. L. & Soc. Change 585 (2005–2006).

125. For a discussion of "public administration" employment bars in Spain, see James B. Jacobs and Elena Larrauri, *Are Criminal Convictions a Public Matter? The USA and Spain*, 14 Punishment & Society 1 (2012); see also Elena Larrauri and James B. Jacobs, "A Spanish Window on European Law and Policy on Employment Discrimination Based on Criminal Record," in Tom Daems et al. (eds.), *European Penology?* 293 (Oxford: Hart Publishing, 2013).

CHAPTER 14
Employment Discrimination Based on a Criminal Record

1. *Barsky v. Bd. of Regents of Univ. of N.Y.*, 111 N.E.2d 222, 226 (N.Y. 1953).

2. Quoted in testimony of Amy L. Solomon (who cochairs the staff working group of the Attorney General's Reentry Council) before the Equal Employment Opportunity Commission on July 26, 2011.

3. Devah Pager, *The Mark of a Criminal Record*, 108 American Journal of Sociology 937, 961 (2003).

4. See, in general, Charles A. Sullivan and Lauren Kavanaugh, *Employment Discrimination: Law and Practice* (New York: Aspen Publishers, 4th ed., 2013).

5. Society for Human Resource Management, *Background Checking: Conducting Criminal Background Checks*, slide 3 (January 22, 2010), http://www.slideshare.net/shrm/background-check-criminal?from=share_email.

6. 10-257 Labor and Employment Law § 257.07 Matthew Bender & Co., Inc. 2011 (available via LexisNexis) (arguing that employers have a legitimate interest in defending themselves against claims of negligent hiring).

7. See, e.g., *Ponticas v. K.M.S. Investments*, 331 N.W.2d 907, 913 (Minn. 1983) ("The scope of the investigation is directly related to the severity of risk third parties are subjected to by an incompetent employee"); *Welsh Mfg*, 474 A.2d at 441 ("when an employee is being hired for a sensitive occupation, mere lack of negative evidence may not be sufficient to discharge the obligation of reasonable care"); see also *Wabash Ry. Co. v. McDaniels*, 107 U.S. 454, 459–60 (1883) ("But according to the best-considered adjudications, and upon the clearest grounds of necessity and good faith, ordinary care, in the selection and retention of servants and agents, implies that degree of diligence and precaution which the exigencies of the particular service reasonably require").

8. See, e.g., *TGM Ashley Lakes, Inc. v. Jennings*, 264 Ga. App. 456, 459, 590 S.E.2d 807, 813 (2003) (holding over whether the employer needed to inquire into criminal history to be a jury issue once employer already knew employee was "in trouble with the law").

9. See Katherine A. Peebles, *Negligent Hiring and the Information Age: How State Legislatures Can Save Employers from Inevitable Liability*, 53 Wm. & Mary L. Rev. 1397 (2012).

10. Richard D. Schwartz and Jerome Skolnick, *Two Studies of Legal Stigma*, 10 Soc. Problems 133 (1962).

11. *Id.* at 136.

12. Devah Pager, *The Mark of a Criminal Record*, 108 American Journal of Sociology 937 (2003).

13. See Harry J. Holzer, *What Employers Want: Job Prospects for Less-Educated Workers* (New York: Russell Sage Foundation, 1996); Harry J. Holzer et al., "The Effect of an Applicant's Criminal History on Employer Hiring Decisions and Screening Practices: Evidence from Los Angeles," in David Weiman et al. (eds.), *Barriers to Reentry? The Labor Market for Released Prisoners in Post-Industrial America* 117–50 (New York: Russell Sage Foundation, 2007); Amy L. Solomon et

al., *From Prison to Work: The Employment Dimensions of Prisoner Reentry. A Report of the Reentry Roundtable* (Washington, DC: Urban Institute, Justice Policy Center, 2004).

14. Employers Group Research Services, *Employment of Ex-Offenders: A Survey of Employers' Policies and Practices*, San Francisco, SF Works, April 12, 2002. See also Legal Action Center, *After Prison: Roadblocks to Reentry: A Report on State Legal Barriers Facing People with Criminal Records* 10 (New York, 2004).

15. Harry J. Holzer et al., "The Effect of an Applicant's Criminal History on Employer Hiring Decisions and Screening Practices: Evidence from Los Angeles," in David Weiman et al. (eds.), *Barriers to Reentry? The Labor Market for Released Prisoners in Post-Industrial America* 117–50 (New York: Russell Sage Foundation, 2007).

16. Devah Pager and Lincoln Quillian, *Walking the Talk? What Employers Say versus What They Do*, 70 American Sociological Review 355 (2005).

17. 42 U.S.C. §2000e-2(k)1(A)(i).

18. Haw. Rev. Stat. § 378-2.5 (2008); Wis. Stat. §§ 111.325–111.335 (2003); 18 Pa. Cons. Stat. Ann. § 9125 (West 2000); N.Y. Correct. Law. §§ 750–55 (McKinney 2003) (amended in 2007).

19. The Hawaii statute states that "an employer may inquire about and consider an individual's criminal conviction record concerning hiring, termination, or the terms, conditions, or privileges of employment; provided that the conviction record bears a *rational relationship to the duties and responsibilities of the position*." Haw. Rev. Stat. § 378-2.5 (2008) (emphasis added). On "direct relationship" in New York courts, see Jocelyn Simonson, *Rethinking "Rational Discrimination" against Ex-Offenders*, 13 Geo. J. Poverty L. & Pol'y 283, 293 (2006).

20. Marvin E. Wolfgang et al., *Delinquency in a Birth Cohort* (Chicago: University of Chicago Press, 1972); Marvin Wolfgang et al., *From Boy to Man, From Delinquency to Crime* (Chicago: University of Chicago Press, 1987).

21. 401 U.S. 424 (1971). In *Griggs*, the court found invalid the requirement that power plant workers who wished to be promoted either have a high school diploma or pass a standardized intelligence test.

22. 42 U.S.C. §2000e-2(k)1(A)(i).

23. For a comprehensive critique of the disparate impact doctrine, see Amy Wax, *Disparate Impact Realism*, 53 William & Mary L. Rev. 621 (2011).

24. See Michael Connett, Comment, *Employer Discrimination against Individuals with a Criminal Record: The Unfulfilled Role of State Fair Employment Agencies*, 83 Temple L. Rev. 1007 (2011).

25. Department of Justice, *Crime in the United States 2012*, http://www2.fbi.gov/ucr/cius2009/data/table_43.html.

26. The Sentencing Project, *Reducing Racial Disparity in the Criminal Justice System* 22, http://www.sentencingproject.org/doc/publications/rd_reducing racialdisparity.pdf.

27. 422 U.S. 405; see Linda Lye, *Title VII's Tangled Tale: The Erosion and Confusion of Disparate Impact and the Business Necessity Defense*, 19 Berkeley J. Emp. & Lab. L. 315, 324 (1998); Nicole J. DeSario, Note, *Reconceptualizing*

Meritocracy: The Decline of Disparate Impact Discrimination Law, 38 Harv. C.R.-C.L. L. Rev. 479, 493–94 (2003) (*Beazer* undermines disparate impact doctrine); Jocelyn Simonson, *Rethinking "Rational Discrimination" against Ex-Offenders*, 13 Geo. J. Poverty L. & Pol'y 283, 293 (2006) (*Beazer* significantly undermined disparate impact doctrine).

28. 440 U.S. 568, 587 n. 31 (1979).

29. 490 U.S. 642, 659–60 (1989).

30. Pub. L. 102-166, § 105, 105 Stat. 1074, 42 U.S.C. § 2000e-2(k).

31. 2002 U.S. Dist. Lexis 1698, 2002 WL 171729 (S.D. Ind.) (2002) (not reported in F. Supp.).

32. 723 F. Supp. 734, 736 (S.D. Fla. 1989) (a case decided after *Ward Coves* but before the Civil Rights Act of 1991).

33. *Id.* at 736.

34. *EEOC v. Carolina Freight*, 723 F. Supp. 734, 753 (S.D. Fla. 1989) (emphasis added).

35. 523 F.2d 1290 (8th Cir. 1975).

36. See *Carter v. Gallagher*, 452 F.2d 315, 326 (8th Cir. 1971). The precedential value was limited, however, because the parties agreed that a felony or misdemeanor conviction should not trigger such an absolute bar.

37. 523 F. 2d. 1290, 1297 (8th Cir. 1975).

38. *Green v. Missouri Pacific Railroad Co.*, 549 F.2d 1158, 1160 (8th Cir. 1977).

39. See U.S. Equal Opportunity Commission, *EEOC Enforcement Guidance*, http://www.eeoc.gov/laws/guidance/arrest_conviction.cfm.

40. *EEOC v. Freeman*, No. 09-CV-2573 (D. Md. August 9, 2013).

41. As the Supreme Court said in *Schware v. Board of Bar Examiners*, 353 U.S. 232, 241 (1957), "The mere fact that a man has been arrested has very little, if any, probative value in showing that he engaged in any misconduct" (examining the "good moral character" of a bar applicant).

42. Fix Gun Checks Act of 2011, S. 436, 112th Congress (2011–12).

43. See *Bell v. Wolfish*, 441 U.S. 520 (1979).

44. U.S. Equal Employment Opportunity Commission, *Policy Guidance on the Consideration of Arrest Records in Employment Decisions under Title VII of the Civil Rights Act of 1964*, as amended, 42 U.S.C. § 2000e et. seq. (1982), http://www.eeoc.gov/laws/guidance/arrest_conviction.cfm.

45. CPL 160.50.

46. *Watts v. United States*, 519 U.S. 148, 152 (1997) (internal quotations omitted).

47. See National Employment Law Project, *Ban the Box: Major U.S. Cities and Counties Adopt Fair Hiring Policies to Remove Unfair Barriers to Employment of People with Criminal Records*, updated July 2014, http://www.nelp.org/page/-/sclp/cityandcountyhiringinitiatives.pdf?nocdn=1.

48. Bureau of Justice Statistics, *Recidivism of Prisoners Released in 1994* (June 2002), available at http://bjs.ojp.usdoj.gov/index.cfm?ty=pbdetail&iid=1134; Matthew R. Durose, Alexia D. Cooper, and Howard N. Snyder, Bureau of Justice Statistics, "Recidivism of Prisoners Released in 30 States in 2005: Patterns from 2005 to 2010" (2014).

49. President George W. Bush, *2004 State of the Union Address* (January 20, 2004), http://www.washingtonpost.cm/wp-srv/politics/transcripts/bushtext_012004.html.

50. H.R. 1593 (110th Congress). On the Second Chance Act, see David A. Green, *Penal Optimism and Second Chances: The Legacies of American Protestantism and the Prospects for Penal Reform,* 15 Punishment & Society 123 (2013); Jessica S. Henry, *A Second Look at the Second Chance Act* 45 Criminal Law Bulletin 416 (2009).

51. Shawn D. Bushway, *Labor Market Effects of Permitting Employer Access to Criminal History Records,* 20 Journal of Contemporary Criminal Justice 276 (2004). See also Shawn D. Bushway, "Labor Markets and Crime," in Joan Petersilia and James Q. Wilson (eds.), *Crime and Public Policy* 183–209 (New York: Oxford University Press, 2011).

INDEX